# Catalonia

Art · Landscape · Architecture

*Barcelona: view up the Passeig de Colom to the Columbus Column and the Montjuïc*

© 2000 Könemann Verlagsgesellschaft mbH
Bonner Straße 126, D-50968 Cologne

Publishing and Art Director: Peter Feierabend
Design and Layout: Agentur Roman, Bold & Black
Editing: Ulrike Weber-Karge, Thomas Paffen
Maps: Studio für Landkartentechnik, Detlef Maiwald
Picture Research: Mitra Nadjafi, Achim Heinze
Production: Oliver Benecke
Reproduction: typografik, Cologne

Original Title: *Katalonien. Kunst, Landschaft, Architektur*

© 2001 for the English edition
Könemann Verlagsgesellschaft mbH

Translation and Editing from German: Translate A Book, Oxford, UK
Typesetting: Organ Graphic, Abingdon, UK
Project Coordination: Kristin Zeier
Production: Oliver Benecke
Printing and Binding: Stige, Industrie Grafiche Editoriali S.p.A., San Mauro, Turin
Printed in Italy

ISBN 3-8290-2703-6

10 9 8 7 6 4 3 2 1

Barbara Borngässer

# Catalonia

## Art · Landscape · Architecture

Editor: Rolf Toman

Photographs by: Günter Beer and Achim Bednorz

KÖNEMANN

# Contents

# Catalonia: A Land of Opposites

One glance at the map shows that Catalonia is a land of dramatic contrasts (illus. opposite). Sea and mountains, *mar i muntanya*, have determined both its appearance and its centuries-old culture. The terrain is framed by the contrasting landscapes of the Pyrenees in the north and the delta of the river Ebro in the south, each majestic in its own way. Moving inland from the coast of the Mediterranean, there is the same varied picture: wide stretches of sandy beach, picturesque bays, and characterful harbor towns – once the haunts of merchants and pirates, now of tourists – are often little more than a stone's throw away from the rugged and inaccessible rocks of the *serres*, which still provide shelter for monasteries and castles.

Nature's changing moods seem to have brilliantly suffused the creativity of its people; how else can one explain why Catalonia has produced such

gifted artists as Antoni Gaudí, Salvador Dalí and Joan Miró. For Catalonia lives on its contrasts, and has thus gained for itself a seemingly inexhaustible cultural potential. Barcelona, the vibrant capital, revels in bringing together these contradictions: anarchic yet disciplined, traditional yet avant-garde, resolutely Catalan yet engagingly cosmopolitan – all these features combine to earn it the title "City of Marvels."

Contrasts also characterize the relationship of Catalonia with the rest of Spain, in particular with the region of Castile, an ancient kingdom in central and north central Spain, the dominance of which Catalonians have long considered a burden.

An advertising slogan of the 1970s reinforced the conviction of many Spaniards that it is not Spain, but "Catalonia" that is different. With a sense of wonder, at times tinged with irritation, outsiders observe the curious customs of the *Països Catalans* (the Catalonian heartlands, comprising the regions of Valencia, the Balearics and Andorra). These are areas where the evening meal is taken at nine o'clock, where business meetings may infringe on the siesta, and where the way of life is far more akin to that in, say, France or Germany than Castile or Andalusia. There are other surprising differences. In Catalonia there is no bullfighting or flamenco for visitors to experience; the Catalans do, however, enjoy forming human pyramids, and they are happy to encourage complete strangers to join with them in the *Sardana*, the Catalan circle dance to the strains of wind ensembles. All of this remains a mystery to many Spaniards (illus. pp. 6–7, 136, 159).

St. Jordi, St. George, the knight whose slaying of the dragon is still treasured as a parable for Catalan autonomy, has inspired a wealth of creative works in Catalonia (illus. left). His influence was probably also felt back in the ninth century, when the Catalan counties were first united. This period also saw the birth of the Catalan national coat of arms, the colors of which, according to legend, originated from a wound of Count Guifréel Pelós (Wilfred the Hairy). The legendary story tells how, after the count was wounded fighting the Saracens, Louis the Pious visited him on his sick bed; on seeing that the count's shield lacked a coat of arms, the emperor dipped his finger in his blood and ran it across the gold ground (illus. p. 10, bottom). These became the *quattre barres* which run across the gold ground of the Catalan flag – and are even used as cake decorations on feast days.

The *Català* language is believed to have originated a short time later, a language that would survive numerous repressions during its thousand-year history, most recently under the Franco dictatorship. Likened to "barking" with a greater or lesser degree of affection by Castilian speakers, the Catalan language is one of the most significant Romance languages. Ramon Llull (1232–1316) (illus. p. 10, top), the great Catalan author and philosopher, is credited with the unification of the language, and is the first person recorded writing in it, while at about this time it also featured in chronicles and trading laws. Celebrated in patriotic odes in the 19th century, 100 years later *Català* was used as a medium for resistance against the Franco regime: to the sound of the "*Nova Cançó*," the "new song," it expressed to the world the rage at the repression of Catalan identity (see panel box, p. 112).

Only a few months after Franco's death in 1975 the Catalan language, for decades humiliated and silenced, rose again as a living language. Today, Catalan is once again omnipresent (not always to the delight of tourists), and numerous scientific and literary publications appreciate and use this concise and eloquent form of expression.

The succinctness and precision of expression (in *Català* almost all words are shorter than in other Romance languages) is summed up by the proverbial Catalan word *seny* (pronounced señ): the flair for the right action at the right time.

*Festa de la Mercè in Barcelona: castells, human pyramids, are raised up in front of the town hall*

ABOVE: *St. Jordi (St. George), the patron saint of Catalonia, a sculpture on the Casa Amatller in Barcelona*

OPPOSITE: *Geographical map of the Catalan heartland*

This conceals a solid pragmatism, which has repeatedly determined the country's fate, from the efforts of the Catalan Aragonese kings in building a trading empire that stretched from the western Mediterranean to Greece and Asia Minor (see panel box, p. 191), to the efforts of Catalonia in the post-World War II years in asserting itself as an independent nation – not through violence but through the vibrancy of its culture. A reflection of *seny* was seen in the organization of the 1992 Olympic Games: a dynamically reborn country presented itself to the world, proving that it had broken free from the constraints of the Franco era.

The opposite side of this pragmatism is *rauxa* (pronounced rowsha), a kind of creative and capricious exuberance, most clearly evident to foreigners in the works of Gaudí and Dalí. The art created around the turn of the 19th century – Modernisme in Catalonia, the style we know as Art Nouveau – is rich in examples of marvelously overflowing fantasy, in which a highly stylized view of life is presented as an enchanting work of art.

In Barcelona, but also in the numerous summer resorts favored by the artistic community, this era is still very much alive. However, a closer examination of the work of Gaudí, and his lesser-known but often equally gifted contemporaries, reveals how this fantasy was combined with a good deal of sensible practicality. Mention must also be made here of Josep Maria Jujol and Cèsar Martinell, creators of extraordinary, unique industrial architecture (see panel boxes, pp. 349, 361).

Salvador Dalí is the classic example of the combination of *seny* and *rauxa* (see pp. 86–91, 100–107). No one can deny the *enfant terrible* from Figueres his incredible and simultaneous powers of imagination, dextrous craftsmanship, and outstanding talent for staging and self-promotion. Dalí's works – but even more so his "residences" created together with his adored partner Gala – are, for all their eccentricity, very Catalan. Time and again, in his work tradition alternates with the avant-garde, always exuberantly and unforgettably combined.

ABOVE:
*Atlas by the Mallorcan Jews Abraham and Jafuda Cresques, 1375*
*Detail showing pearl-divers in the Chinese sea*

ABOVE:
*Sunset near Tossa de Mar*

OPPOSITE:
*Coastal landscape near Tossa de Mar*

Neither Gaudí nor Dalí, nor Picasso – who spent his youth in Barcelona – ever renounced their connections with the past. In Gaudí's case, he "soaked up" the Teutonic clarity from Gothic architecture, and even surpassed it by dispensing with external support systems; Dalí – apart from gathering around him mirrors and mustaches – also produced still lifes in the style of the Dutch Masters of the 17th century. Picasso ultimately bequeathed one of his masterpieces to the city of Barcelona, the interpretation of Velazquez' famous *Las Meninas* (1656), a painting on which he had worked throughout the year 1957 (illus. p. 169).

Any conflicts arising from the theme of nationalism versus cosmopolitanism, appear to have passed, at least since the 1992 Olympic Games, a significant landmark. Catalan pride, admittedly pronounced, has never prevented Catalans from maintaining contact with other nations, and learning from them. In one example, at the turn of the 19th century, Barcelona was a stronghold of the Wagnerian cult. Intellectuals learned German in order to be able to understand the works of the philosopher and writer Nietzsche, himself an admirer of Wagner's music and theories.

Today, the exchange with other cultures is still high on the agenda, but always with the expectation that the other party will exhibit a certain empathy and respect for the nuances of Catalan culture. A few words of *català* are often all it takes to open a number of doors.

Unfortunately the country itself has made a number of irreversible mistakes, which it now readily recognizes and deeply regrets. Its magnificent coastline was surrendered to an insatiable flow of mass tourism. Hundreds of miles of unique landscape have been sacrificed to speculative development, where the consequences include monotonous concrete complexes, the destruction of traditional infrastructures, and the loss of numerous natural resources.

Attempts now to regenerate the self-inflicted barren tracts are only drops in the ocean, but they do indicate the concern and the desire to take action. However, those travelers who take the time can still find some oases even in the most exploited tourist areas, and can gain insights into the incomparable beauty of the landscape and the subtlety of the Catalan culture (illus. above, and opposite).

To present the history of Catalonia in the context of its natural surroundings, against the appropriate backgrounds and through the medium of its works of art, this brief examination does not include separate chapters on geographic, historical, and cultural aspects – approaches that are used in the introductions to chapters, and arranged according to special points of interest, and in the panel boxes on specific places and artists.

The geographical framework in this book may not please everyone in terms of its national or linguistic boundaries. It is neither restricted to the current provincial borders nor confined to the area covered by the distribution of the Catalan language. This would have meant leaving out Andorra and that part of Catalonia which has been French since 1659, both

of which contain outstanding medieval testimony to the former Catalan-Aragonese empire. It would also have meant including such disparate and outlying regions as the País Valencià, the Balearics, and even a small part of the island of Sardinia, let alone colonies abroad, in which clear traces of Catalan culture can still be seen. Both approaches were impractical.

The author has used Catalan orthography (usage and spelling) for place-names (even if not historically correct) in the part of Catalonia on Spanish soil that has had constitutional autonomy since 1979; but for the communes in present-day France and the artists from that region, the usual French spellings have been adopted followed by their Catalan equivalent. This has been done solely to help the reader's orientation.

# The Pyrenees

A Barrier or Gateway?

"Nature here is beautiful and majestic. The mountains surround me, reaching up to the heavens, so peaceful, so impassive, so joyful! They do not play the slightest part in our daily lives or partisan struggles; they are close to insulting us with their hideous insensitivity – but perhaps that is only their rigid outer face."

The ambivalent feeling of inaccessibility and distance, which Heinrich Heine expressed during his journey through the Pyrenees still awaits the traveler to the Iberian peninsula. Long before we come to the present-day national border between France and Spain, a mountain wall rises up as high as 3404 m (11,168 ft.), uncompromisingly cutting off central Europe from its south-western part. From the Bay of Biscay in the west to the Gulf of Lyons in the east, the mountain range extends 450 km (280 miles), presenting a sheer face toward France but rolling off toward Spain in a series of gentle foothills. The forested granite ridges, which retain their mantle of snow until well into the spring, lay down a clearly defined barrier against crossing from either direction.

It is hard to imagine that the area was under the ocean in the Mesozoic era. Today's mountain range with its summits soaring up from the middle of the massif – Aneto, 3404 m (11,168 ft.), Posets, 3375 m (11,073 ft.), and Monte Perdido, 3355 m (11,007 ft. – was formed some 40 million years ago, when the European continent and the Iberian peninsula collided. The consequences of the tectonic drift led to the formation of glaciers, caves, and limestone caves,

which still form the wild, unique character of the Pyrenees (illus. pp. 16–17). A striking feature is that the valleys formed in the ice ages and subsequent thaws do not help communications through the mountains as they do in, say, the Alps. They generally run along the direction of the main range, and thus cannot be used as transport routes. Even today, travelers have only a few steep, winding passes to choose from; the motorways and railways use the lower coastal stretches of the range near Irún and Port Bou.

This hindrance to man is a boon to wildlife. In these in-accessible regions numerous rare animal species survive, including a wide variety of birds of prey, reptiles, and butterflies, and an abundance of plant life including narcissi, irises, gentians, and alpine roses. At certain times of the year the mountain pastures become carpets of flowers. Certain endemic plants are particularly rare, having found their way to the Pyrenees from South America. Mammals include chamois and marmots, which live in substantial numbers among the rocks; brown bears and mountain goats are also found, although rare because of hunting. Apart from smuggling and free trade zones, forestry and animal husbandry represent the main income of the Pyrenees, although in recent years the water economy has made a substantial contribution. People have been experiencing the health-giving effects of the numerous springs since the 18th century, while skiing, cycling, and canoeing attract ever more tourists to this wild, romantic landscape.

*Fishing in a mountain stream*

## Crossroads of World History

Despite or perhaps because of the natural border they represent, the Pyrenees have always been at the center of world and cultural history. In brief, the findings of traces of the Tautavel people represent the oldest inhabitants of our continent, and the foothills of the mountains contain an unusual wealth of prehistoric places of worship and rock paintings.

Around 1000 B.C. the Celts came to the region, bringing with them the knowledge of metal-working. The Mediterranean coastal regions were settled from the 7th century B.C. by Greeks, Phoenicians, and Carthaginians in peaceful co-existence with the Iberian tribes.

The mountains were in the limelight of world history in the year 218 B.C., when the Carthaginian general Hannibal, having set his sights on Rome, crossed the Pyrenees and later the Alps with 60,000 men and a herd of elephants. This was the start of the Second Punic war, which with alternating fortunes lasted for some 17 years until the Roman general Scipio finally defeated Hannibal in North Africa. The consequences of this victory also set the course for the Iberian peninsula, as Roman rule led to the thorough Romanization of the whole culture. Latin in its vernacular form supplanted the archaic languages which are now only preserved in a few place-names, although with one exception.

Basque, spoken in the western Pyrenean regions, stood fast against all outside influences, and is still alive today. Romanization was followed between the 3rd and 5th centuries by the advent of Christianity, resulting in the foundation of a number of bishoprics and the construction of numerous churches.

In the 8th and 9th centuries, the Pyrenees once again took center stage in world history, becoming the buffer between Christianity and Islam. The Arabs penetrated the European mainland in 711, when they landed at Gibraltar at the request of the Visigoths seeking help with hostilities over the throne. However, they did not restrict themselves to these conflicts for long, but rather by the end of two decades had conquered practically the whole of the peninsula and Aquitaine.

The advance of Islam was not halted until 732 with the victory by Charles Martel at the battle of Tours and Poitiers. During the following decades his successors succeeded in winning back the territory as far as Girona and Barcelona, incorporating them into the Frankish empire. The *Song of Roland* paints a heroic picture of this campaign, telling of the deeds of the man reputed to be the nephew of Charlemagne in the battle for Roncesvalles. In the year 801 Charlemagne founded what was known as the Spanish Mark, which formed the starting point for the subsequent *Reconquista*. The complete reconquest of the whole of Catalonia as far as the River Ebro took until 1149.

In the years following the *Reconquista* the independent counties (*comtats*) of the Pyrenees were combined to form the Christian kingdoms of Navarra in the west and Aragón in the east. The latter was joined through marriage to the House of Barcelona in 1137, and thanks to its expansion policies with ambitions out across the Mediterranean

enjoyed a meteoric rise. This flowering of the Catalan-Aragonese empire and the significance of maritime trade will be dealt with in more detail later.

However, the character of the Pyrenees and their culture was shaped by quite different influences. For centuries the Christian West was confronted by the sword of Islam, united above all by enormous religious zeal which bound princes and clergy alike.

The pilgrimage to the shrine of St. James kindled a veritable exodus to Santiago de Compostela, and anyone undertaking the journey to Galicia from abroad first had to make the arduous, often life-threatening, crossing of the Pyrenees. As the spiritual welfare of this stream of people was just as important in the Middle Ages as their practical needs, a wealth of monasteries, churches, and hospices sprang up along the pilgrim routes.

The main routes of the pilgrimage to Santiago led through the Navarran part of the Pyrenees, and are not therefore part of the scope of this book, but the area under Aragonese-Catalan rule also gave rise to an extremely rich vein of both culture and architecture, which will be examined below.

The excesses of medieval religious zeal, including the terrible campaign against the Cathars who had entrenched themselves in inaccessible fortified cliff strongholds in what is now the French part of Catalonia, will be dealt with in the final part of this book.

There is a reason for this chapter division, which is rooted in a further role – fatal for Catalonia – of the Pyrenees in world history.

In 1659 the Treaty of the Pyrenees, the culmination of centuries of conflict between France and Spain over the southern French territories, tore the Catalonian cultural region apart, leading to the decline of the Spanish Habsburg dynasty.

Fortunately, the Pyrenees were spared any further blows of fate, apart, perhaps, from the development of Andorra and Llívia as tax havens and the consequent streams of traffic bearing eager consumers. But in the age of the EU this, too, should soon become history.

Having made the above remarks, let us now return to a consideration of cultural history and a visit to a city which is rightfully regarded as the cradle of medieval Catalonia: La Seu d'Urgell.

*The Catalan principality before the Treaty of the Pyrenees of 1659*

### The City of Bishops:
### La Seu d'Urgell

The word Seu, bishopric or see, has earned its place in the name of this proud city at the confluence of the Segre and Valita rivers. It was the church leaders who brought it to a position of power and prestige, and extended its lands far into Catalan territory. A little of this glory survives to this day, as the Bishop of Urgell still rules as Co-Prince, together with the President of France, over the mountain principality of Andorra, a worldly mandate the like of which is only enjoyed by the Pope over the Vatican.

Before the Christians ruled over these strategic valleys, others had valued the place for its strategic location at a crossing point of the Pyrenees. Iberians, Basques, and Indo-Germanic tribes settled here long before the troops of Hannibal and Caesar crossed the region. As evidenced by Strabo and Pliny, a Roman settlement, Orgellia, had existed on the site of Seu d'Urgell since 195 B.C.

Sources are silent on the Christianization of the region, but it is known there was a bishop here by 527, who set up his seat in the neighboring hamlet of Castellciutat. In 793, the Arabs under Abd-el-Malik destroyed the town including its Visigothic cathedral. With the help of Louis the Pious, a new building was raised and consecrated by 839, this time in *Vicus Urgelli*. A document preserved in the cathedral archives gives us a unique description of the splendid ceremony. This parchment, extending to c. $^1/_2$ sq m (18 sq. in.), and written in a combination of Latin and later Català, contains precise geographical details of the extent of the cathedral lands and its parishes.

In the subsequent centuries the bishops expanded their power, especially as the counts of Urgell returned to the fertile plains. Thus the town grew around the clerical institutions, the cathedral, the Bishop's palace, and the houses of the canons. The arcades of the Carrer Mayor and the Carrer Canonges, as well as being the setting for lively business activity, today as in years gone by, give an atmospheric impression of the past.

The impressive cathedral as it stands today is the fourth the diocese has seen, and the third in *Vicus Urgelli* itself, its current location (illus. pp. 24, 25). The Carolingian building soon became too small, so that by the beginning of the 11th century Bishop Ermengol had a new building erected, although he did not live to see it consecrated in 1040. However, some 60 years later, Bishop Odo was seeking funds for a new building, as the old cathedral was almost in ruins. The foundations for this were laid between 1116 and 1122. Work was not fully under way until 1175 when the Italian architect Raimundus Lambardus was appointed. In 1182 the roof vaults were completed, and the cupola and belfry finished. Clearly Raimundus, or Ramon, brought with him knowledge of high Italian architecture, as many details, for example the form of the façade with its gabled frontage and three generously proportioned portals, or the division of

Opposite:
La Seu d'Urgell *Cathedral*,
*begun between 1116 and 1122*
*View of the eastern part,*
*built after 1175*

the apse with its magnificent dwarf gallery, recall Italian precedents. However, the overall form with its aisled, unusually broad nave (illus. below) and the stocky projection of the transept – which finished in two solid towers – reflects far more the Catalan tradition, recalling perhaps the monastery of St-Michel-de-Cuxa in what is now the French part of the Pyrenees. The cruciform design of the columns, which support the barrel vaulting in the central aisle and the cross-vaulting in the side aisles, is found elsewhere in Catalonia, for example in St. Viçenç de Cardona. Thus, La Seu d'Urgell introduces an innovative combination of external and vernacular influences. Dominating the decoration of the interior is a Romanesque statue of the Virgin Mary, which is positioned in the center of the five apses.

The cloisters also conceal some surprises (illus. pp. 26–27). There are no biblical or historical images portrayed on the 51 capitals of the three original preserved wings. Rather, animals, plants, and some rather earthy human figures are evidence of stylistic influences of the sculpture of Cuixà, as is the decoration of the façade. The south of the transept is flanked by the early Romanesque chapel of St. Miquel (originally St. Pere i St. Andreu), the only part of the whole structure belonging to the third cathedral of Urgell.

Unfortunately the plain but impressive structure has lost all its altars and frescoes; the most beautiful of these are today preserved in the National Museum of Catalan Art (Museu Nacional d'Art de Catalunya; MNAC), which is located in Barcelona.

Access is gained through the cloisters to the diocesan museum, which contains treasures to match those in any of Catalonia's great collections. Its rooms, which once housed an additional chapel and the deanery, were converted into a museum in 1957.

Only a few of the works on display can be described here. Outstanding among the 26 examples of Romanesque frescoes is the *Adoration of the Magi* from València d'Àneu; the Apostles from Isavarre; and the Crucifixion from Estaon, although fragmentary, are also outstanding works. Six Romanesque Madonnas give an insight into the development of this image so typical of the Middle Ages.

The museum's 12th-century enameled cross bears unique testimony to the goldsmith's craft, while the Beatus manuscript, illuminated toward the end of the 10th century, is a masterpiece of manuscript illustration, showing a total of 79 exuberantly imaginative miniatures of the Apocalypse. The finest example of Gothic panel painting is the Pere Serras retable, while some valuable church artifacts represent shining examples of Renaissance and Baroque art.

The remaining monuments of the town cannot compete with these treasures, but is closely rivaled by the pleasure of enjoying the gastronomic wealth of the town – either under the arcades of the old town or in part of the monastery of St. Domènec (now a Parador).

La Seu d'Urgell
*Cathedral*
*View of the nave, built after 1175*

La Seu d'Urgell
*Cathedral*
*Cloister, early 13th century*

*The country with 65 summits over 2000-m (6,500-ft,) – the mountains of Andorra*

*Andorra la Vella
Sculpture garden at the
Casa de la Vall*

## A Dwarf among Giants – the Free State of Andorra

Only 10 km (6 miles) divide La Seu d'Urgell from the Andorran border. The distance to Andorra la Vella, the expanding capital of the principality is twice as far. This busy mini-state in the heart of the Pyrenees can pride itself on being the place where Catalan has been an official language for longest and without periods of suppression. Of course the national anthem is also in Català. It sings the praises of Charlemagne, paying homage to him as father of the principality.

In fact the free state of Andorra owes its existence to a pact signed and sealed in 1278 between the Counts of Folx and the bishops of Urgell. The opposing parties were both unyielding in their claims to the country with its 65 over 2000-m (6,500-ft.) high peaks, and undertook mutually to recognize one another's rights.

To this day the Republic is under the auspices of the President of France and the Bishop of Urgell. Both parties appoint representatives who reach agreement with the *Consell General de les Valls*, the "Council of the valleys," which has met since 1580 in the peaceful, attractive Casa de la Vall behind a façade of irregular natural stone (illus. opposite bottom).

The interior of the Andorran parliament is as home-like as the outside walls, housing in addition to the reception hall and a chapel, a kitchen, and six bedrooms to offer the delegates respite after long and tedious debates. In the main chamber is the revered "cupboard of the seven keys," the name of which refers back to the time when it could only be opened in the presence of every parish representative of Andorra. The sculpture of the *Dancing Pair* which stands before the façade of the Casa de la Vall is by the Andorran sculptor Josep Viladomat, to whom a small museum is dedicated in the neighboring Escaldes.

This aside, Andorra is anything but romantic, at least at first sight. A bustling atmosphere pervades the free-trade zone, with some hideous buildings and speculative development incalculably scarring the once picturesque mountain valley. Andorra la Vella – above all the Avinguda Meritxell – looks like a giant supermarket appended to the slopes. The languages intermingle as freely as the currencies: (still) the French franc and the peseta. Recently ski resorts and spa developments try to maintain the dwindling flow of tourists. Anyone wishing to discover the original face of Andorra must explore beyond the main streets, preferably in an all-terrain vehicle.

However, the majority of cultural treasures are to be found in easily accessible places grouped along the course of the Gran Valira and its tributaries. There are a number of pretty little Romanesque churches with impressive belfries.

Our short tour begins with St. Miquel d'Engolasters, which stands proud a short distance from the commercial activity on the edge of Andorra la Vella/Escaldes. The frescoes which once adorned its apse are now on display in the MNAC in Barcelona, and have been replaced by replicas.

The shrine to the Virgin Mary at Meritxell near Canillo was dealt a tragic blow by fate in 1972 when it was burnt down on the feast day itself, the venerable statue of the Madonna itself even going up in flames.

A little later Ricardo Bofill established a new, highly original focus for pilgrimage with an unusual granite monument which stands on the side of the road to Prats. This is the "seven-armed cross," although it has been missing one arm for some time now. A weathered Madonna figure graces the front, while the back depicts the Crucifixion. Like many Andorran churches, St. Joan de Caselles has a late medieval vestibule.

Not so typical, however, is the stucco figure of Christ crucified, against a fresco showing the scene at Golgotha. Although it has been reconstructed from numerous fragments, the Romanesque work of art has lost none of its ability to amaze. It is one of the rare surviving examples of its kind.

The center of Pal in the mountains to the north-west of the principality's capital still retains a fair degree of its original character with its stone façades, although the snow cannon machines, which ensure favorable winter sports conditions, are alarmingly close. The parish church, St. Climent, is flanked by an elegant belfry with double openings and a *porto* (vestibule). The round, four-story tower of St. Coloma, back in the valley along the main route to Spain, is a particularly fine example of its kind. The remains of a castle of Roger III of Foix still tower above the village.

The best way of appreciating Andorra in all its glory is to take to the mountains on foot, perhaps as far as the mountain lakes of Juclar or to Port de Cabús, where the strenuous climb will be well rewarded. It is still possible to trace the tracks of smugglers along the numerous paths once used for the illicit transport of tobacco produced in Andorra to France.

Andorra la Vella
*Casa de la Vall, 1580*

*The Vall d'Aran*
*with the church of Escunhau*

## Romanesque Routes:
## From Seu d'Urgell to the Val d'Aran and the Vall de Boí

There is almost too much for the reader to choose from on a tour. For lovers of Romanesque art, a trip to the Alt-Urgell (High Urgell) area alone is extremely rewarding, with well over a hundred Romanesque parish churches – all well worth a visit and many of them positively idyllic (illus. left). Many can be reached by car, albeit via numerous hairpin bends and roads covered in snow in the winter months; getting to others involves walking, plus plenty of stamina and physical condition. Whatever way, bookshops and tourist offices stock numerous leaflets and maps, some free of charge, on the *Vías Romanicas*.

The reasons for the extraordinary number of existing Romanesque churches are, of course, historically rooted. Unlike most of the other regions of the Iberian peninsula, Catalonia did not have to fight against the Moors from the year 785 onward. With the consolidation of power, the sovereignty over Provence, and ultimately the unification of Catalonia and Aragon in 1137, the kingdom flourished early, which is most evident in the interior. Factors affecting the whole of Europe, such as the introduction of the Roman liturgy in the late 11th century – which led indirectly to new styles of sacred buildings mainly due to the increased need for space at the altar – and the lively exchange of artists and scientists throughout Europe, gave rise to an extraordinary building boom in the borderlands of the Pyrenees.

When the interests of the kingdom were turned toward the Mediterranean in the 13th century, the numerous remote mountain parishes fell into a deep fairytale sleep from which they were first rudely awakened in the 20th century. This was a mixed blessing. The removal of numerous frescoes in the 1930s, and their transfer to the MNAC in Barcelona, saved these unique images from the possible ravages of the Civil War, but nevertheless destroyed the integrity of hundreds of works of art which had hitherto survived for a thousand years. Thus the visitor must be prepared to see the majority of these idyllic and largely architecturally well-preserved churches without their decoration or, at best, with replicas of their original paintings.

The region to the west of Seu d'Urgell, encompassing the valleys of the Noguera Pallaresa and Aran rivers and the Vall de Boí, is without doubt the most spectacular in the whole of Catalonia in terms of the number of churches and its natural beauty. On leaving Seu d'Urgell the long, winding road first leads to Sort, where an increasing number of modern skiing hotels sit among the historic buildings.

But there is a choice of two routes from here. The road south leads to Gerri de la Sal, famous for two things: its saltworks and the immense Benedictine Abbey, first dedicated in 1149, and rebuilt several times since. A few miles further on, the Noguera Pallaresa narrows and forces its picturesque way through the rocks of the Congost de Collegats (illus. pp. 32–33). The beauty of the landscape and the thundering torrents attract

canoeists from all over the world to test their skills in the wild white waters of the river (illus. p. 32). Some believe that Antoní Gaudí was inspired by the limestone formations of the gorge.

Pobla del Segur is the next place reached with its modernist urban palace, Can Maurí. Beyond Tremp, which once again has a past stretching back more than a millennium, is the reservoir of Camarasa and the basin around Lleida.

Followers of the Romanesque trail now have a detour to make to the picturesque Abella de la Conca, and on to Covet where they will find two beautiful parish churches. St. Maria de Covet is particularly fine with its ambitious portal whose Tolosa sculptures depict scenes from the Old and New Testaments.

To the north from Sort we continue to follow the Noguera Pallaresa in the direction of Vielha, off to the left passing Espot, the starting point for tours in the National Park of Aigües Tortes. We come to St. Maria d'Aneu, the 11th-century Benedictine monastery and church, the wonderful frescoes of which, with seraphim and scenes of purgatory, can be seen in the MNAC in Barcelona. More delightful parish churches from the 12th and 13th centuries await us at Salardú, Arties, and Escunhau.

Vielha, "the old," has changed its face more drastically in the last few decades than in the two previous millennia since the settlement of the region. This is due to the tunnel which was constructed in 1948 connecting the little valley at the upper reaches of the Garonne, once only accessible from France during the summer months, with the Spanish

*View from the Port de la Bonaigua Pass*

BELOW AND BOTTOM:
Racing the white water
near Gerri de la Sal

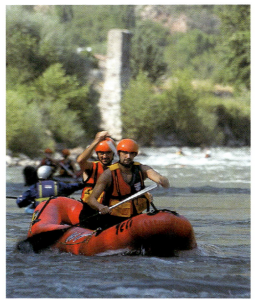

32      The Pyrenees

RIGHT:
Vielha
St. Miquel
*Wooden bust of the Crist*
*de Mijaran,*
*12th century*

BELOW:
*View down the Vall de Boí*

hinterland. This is the only area of Spain to the north of the main ridge of the Pyrenees. It has preserved its own unique characteristics over the centuries of isolation, including the Aranesic language, actually a dialect of Occitan. The climate is also different here from that to the southern side of the mountains, as the valley faces toward Aquitaine and therefore the Atlantic.

Popular, especially with the French, as a winter and summer sports center, it boasts a wonderful wooden carving, *Crist de Mijaran* (Christ of the central Aran valley, illus. left). This 12th-century sculpture, partly still colored, was probably once part of a Descent from the Cross similar to that which once could be seen in Erill-la-Vall.

The special link of the Vall d'Aran with France is particularly evident in its cuisine with its numerous French specialties. On the other hand, the folk dances are uniquely Aranese, the embodiment of ancient tradition.

The 5-km (3-mile) tunnel from Vielha takes us to the once inaccessible valley of the Noguera Ribagorçana. Shortly before Pont de Suert, where a visually striking new church was erected in 1955 (architects Torroja and

Rodríguez Mijares), the road branches off to the Vall de Boí, today equally famous for its Romanesque churches as for its ski and spa resorts (illus. opposite bottom).

Despite the proximity of the busy tourist areas, it is possible to gain an amazingly unspoiled picture of the old cultural landscape of Catalonia. Not even the tiniest of hamlets is without one or more Romanesque parish churches built in the delightful golden stone of the region in the 11th and 12th centuries. Usually single-naved, a few having aisles, their semicircular apses are usually divided by painstakingly carved pilasters and screens. The porches are also richly decorated with their capitals and tympanum, but above all the archivolts - the moldings or decoration above an arch – appear particularly resplendent to the viewer.

They are recognized from afar by their characteristic elegant, usually several-story, belfries, with one, two, or three neatly arranged and finely sculpted single, twin, or triple openings.

These village churches are a magnificent sight against a backdrop of dramatic mountain scenery, surrounded in spring and summer by meadow flowers, in autumn and winter often with a mantle of snow. Their greatest treasures, however, were their frescoes, which unfortunately can only be seen today in replica. But even though a little imagination is needed to piece together the whole, it is clear that an incredible gathering of sacred art is to be found in these remote Pyrenean valleys, unequaled in their number and quality.

The introduction to the Vall de Boí is provided by the parish church of Coll with its façade worked in two colors of stone and its fine chessboard frieze on the portal. St. Maria de Cardet, just a few miles farther on, stands in a picturesque location above a reservoir (illus. right). In Barruera, the principal settlement of the Vall de Boí, is the single-naved church of St. Feliú with pretty tiered roofs. A small detour from here leads to Durro and the Eglésia de la Nativitat de la Mare de Déu, celebrating the birthplace of the Mother of God, which in addition to its resonant name boasts the biggest belfry in the whole area as well as a side vestibule.

Back in Barruera the road climbs to Erill-la-Vall. The parish church there, St. Eulàlia, once possessed a famed group of carvings of the Descent from the Cross, whose five incredibly lifelike figures from the 12th century are unfortunately now dispersed and divided between the diocesan museum in Vic and the MNAC in Barcelona.

It is just a stone's throw from here to Boí. This ancient village, which gave the whole valley its name, lies at the feet of the church of St. Joan. While the formerly aisled main structure has undergone numerous changes, the top story of its high church tower survives practically unchanged. The walls of this church, too, were once resplendent with wonderful frescoes including a lively depiction of the stoning of St. Stephen.

These works, among the earliest examples of Catalan mural art, were only discovered recently. They were taken to Barcelona for restoration; when they will eventually return home is not known.

A steep ascent now climbs to the village of Taüll (pronounced Ta-ull) at a height of 1500 m (4,921 ft.) and also the high point of the tour. This village with its neat, gray-brown houses, steeply sloping, home-like slate roofs and old-fashioned cobbled streets is geared up for tourists, but has lost none of its appealing rustic charm.

Despite the historic significance of the location of this Pyrenean valley it remains a mystery as to how this remote village comes to possess two significant churches with frescoes unequalled in all the world. Both were dedicated within a day of each other – December 10 and 11, 1123 – and both were apparently built under the patronage of the Lords of Erill. St. Climent, the "older" by 24 hours,

*Vall de Boí*
*Sta. Maria de Cardet,*
*12th century*

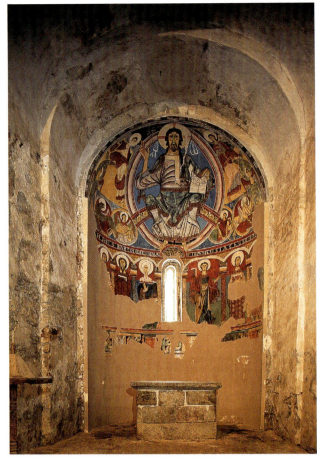

perhaps enjoys the more idyllic surroundings (illus. opposite left). The beautifully preserved aisled interior is linked to three apses of various sizes, which are subtly divided by columns, triple arcades, and tiled friezes. The six-story belfry stands against the south flank, one of the finest examples of its type. In the interior of St. Climent mighty columns support the timber-clad nave and aisles (illus. opposite bottom).

After just three bays without a transept, these lead to an outstanding of Romanesque painting (illus. opposite top). Although we would have to go to the capital Barcelona to study the originals, we can still experience the same awe and fascination before the beautifully executed replicas that the worshipers of the 12th and subsequent centuries must have felt in front of these majestic frescoes.

In brilliant shades of turquoise, red and ocher (the colors are authentic), framed by a mandorla, the image of Christ Pantocrator dominates the curved surface of the apse, around him the four Apostles, Matthew with the angel, Mark with the lion, Luke with the bull, and John with the eagle.

Beneath, on the wall of the apse, Mary and the Apostles are shown against a red background. Painted columns and arcades suggest an architectural unity. This series of images is a frequent feature of late Classical and Byzantine works, but nowhere else is it seen employed with such visual power.

The monumentality of the Pantocrator, fixing his parishioners with wide, gentle eyes and grand gesture, yet without intimidation, declaring "Ego sum lux mundi" – "I am the light of the world" – and symbols denoting the "beginning and the end," is unsurpassed among its contemporary art.

There is only one fresco cycle to compare with this explosion of creativity and skill. It adorns the apse of St. Maria de Taüll, the other parish church in the center of the village, younger by a single day (illus. below).

Architecturally similar, the building is not as well-preserved as St. Climent, and to see the original art we must once again turn to the MNAC in Barcelona. Yet a faithful replica can also be seen here, which gives an excellent idea of the visual effect of the frescoes (illus. left). With similar spatial arrangement and coloring, and with equally accom-plished lines, the Mother of God is depicted with her Son on a magnificent throne, framed by a mandorla. This time they are flanked by the Three Kings, Caspar, Melchior, and Balthazar.

We do not know either the artist or the completion date of these unique frescoes; the consecration date of 1123 only gives a vague indication. The creator is generally referred as the "Mestre de Taüll." He is believed to have had Italian training, and also to have worked elsewhere (possibly in Maderuelo and Berlanga), but this does not clarify the identity of the artist nor the reason for this incredible ensemble in the Vall de Boí.

One reason why it is so difficult to place these works in an art historical context is of course due to the isolation of the valley. From the end of the Romanesque era until just a few decades ago, it underwent few far-reaching changes, and thus preserves works which in other places would long ago have been replaced with more modern offerings or destroyed.

These remarks in no way detract from the significance of the frescoes, but rather try to give an idea of why it has not yet been possible to solve the mystery of the Vall de Boí in terms of the history of its art.

OPPOSITE, LEFT:
Taüll
St. Climent, begun 1123
View from the south-east

OPPOSITE, TOP AND BOTTOM:
Taüll
St. Climent
View of the interior with replica of the apse fresco
(Original in MNAC, Barcelona)

LEFT:
Taüll
St. Maria, begun 1123
View of the interior with replica of the apse fresco
(Original in MNAC, Barcelona)

BELOW:
Taüll
St. Maria
Exterior view

RIGHT:
"Els Encantats," the enchanted
rocks in the Aigüestortes National
Park

BELOW:
Landscape of the Cadí-Moixeró
nature reserve

## "Twisted Waters," Limestone Rocks: The National Park of Aigüestortes and Cadí-Moixeró

A chance to relax after taking in the culture is offered by the Caldes de Boí, the baths fed by a 25°C (77°F) spring which probably date back to Roman times, or a trip to the Parc Nacional d'Aigüestortes i Estany de St. Maurici. The national park – known as "twisted waters and lake of St. Maurice" – connects the Boí valley via high-altitude trails to Espot in the eastern part of the region. Part of the route can be undertaken by a four-wheel drive vehicle, but not the whole crossing.

This region of the central Pyrenees is characterized by water, a result of the glacier formations during the Ice Age. There are more than 50 lakes, and numerous waterfalls, marshes, and bogs, not to mention the meandering rivers, which give the region its name, among the granite and slate formations which came into being more than 200 million years ago.

The margin areas are home to a wide variety of flora and fauna, which is best discovered on foot. Numerous guided or individual walks can be undertaken against the backdrop of the 3000 m (9,800 ft.) peaks, the most impressive of which aptly bears the name "Els Encantats," "the enchanted" (illus. opposite above). These lead to the spellbinding peace of the darkly shimmering lakes, the coniferous and birch forests, and the treeless meadowlands. With a little luck, walkers will be rewarded with sightings of chamois, capercaillies, golden and mountain eagles, not forgetting the Pyrenean voles and the marmots.

Following the broad Segre valley from Seu d'Urgell you will hardly be aware that you are at 1100 m (3,600 ft.) above sea level. The mountains of Andorra tower up to the north, while the majestic ranges of the Serra del Cadí and Serra del Moixeró are to the south. Their limestone rocks reach up to a height of 2648 m (8,688 ft) at the Puig de la Canal Baridana, although the Pedraforca has a far more characteristic profile: the forked summit of its name visible from far and wide (illus. above). The views of the mountains are incredibly beautiful, particularly in the evenings when their flanks are bathed in shades of red light. The precipitous north face is a veritable eldorado for Catalan climbers.

The area of Cadí-Moixeró, given conservation status in 1932, and declared a nature reserve in 1983, is also open to walkers and nature-lovers (illus. opposite bottom). Characteristic villages and hamlets, where the land is husbanded using the traditional methods, are scattered across its 41,342 ha (102,157 acres). Without doubt the most beautiful of these is Josa de Cadí, where picturesque gray-brown stone houses, overlooked by the church, are huddled among the rocks. Information on walking tours and accommodation can be obtained in Bagà, worth a visit for its ruined castle alone. Venturing farther into the park one is rewarded by the abundant flora and fauna. The habitats of some rare species have been preserved in the rocky heights and expansive forests, including chamois, eagles, capercaillies, and black woodpeckers, along with numerous types of salamanders and lizards. Gentians, rhododendrons, and broom cover slopes and meadows with a blanket of bright colors.

*The "forked peak" of the Pedraforca in the Cadí-Moixeró nature reserve*

## Forgotten Bone of Contention: The Spanish Part of the Cerdanya

Now we return to the high Segre valley which forms the Spanish part of the landscape of the Cerdanya (illus. above). Far more than a place to pass through, it is bordered by pretty villages like Montella and Bellver, which lives up to its name meaning "beautiful view." Nearby are numerous caves where cave paintings have been found.

If you do not turn off beyond Bellver to take the tunnel from Cadí toward Berga, after a short distance you come to Puigcerdà and the French border. Here the valley widens out again, giving the feel of a green plain rather than a high mountain region. In recent decades the town has become a significant winter sports resort popular with the French and Spaniards alike.

Little can now be sensed of the area's far-reaching and turbulent past, although in the last century Puigcerdà suffered badly in the Civil War. The name translates as the "Hill of Cerdanya." It was the capital of the whole region from the time of Alfonso I, and received its charter in 1178. In 1344 it withstood the dramatic conflict between Peter III of Catalonia and Jaume III of Mallorca, which resulted in the end of the Mallorcan kingdom. As everywhere in this fiercely disputed gateway region to the Iberian peninsula, one siege followed the next. The town experienced a brief respite around the turn of the 19th century, when *modernista* artists and writers held their *Jocs Florals* competitions here (see panel box opposite).

TOP:
*The Segre valley*

ABOVE:
*Pobla de Lilles and the* modernista *gardens of the Font de la Magnèsia*

OPPOSITE TOP:
*Stone bridge in Pobla de Lillet*

We stay in the Spanish part of the Cerdanya and follow national route N 152 to the winter sports area of La Molina. From here two narrow, twisting minor roads lead off to Castellar de N'Hug and Pobla de Lillet, both enchanting villages with varied attractions including sausages, railways, gardens, and industrial architecture. Both stations are reached by similarly narrow lanes from Guardiola de Berguedà on the edge of the Cadí-Moixeró national park.

Castellar de N'Hug is an undiscovered treasure for those wishing to sample local produce, while for architecture and gardens a visit to Pobla de Lillet is on the agenda. The Font de la Magnèsia in Pobla de Lillet is a little-known garden in the *modernista* style (illus. opposite, bottom). Although the newly restored gardens are not quite as striking or extensive, in many aspects they are still reminiscent of Gaudí's Parc Güell in Barcelona, and are well worth a visit.

Not far from Pobla de Lillet, at Clot del Moro, the ruins of the Asland cement works loom like a ghost town. They were constructed in 1901 by Rafael Guastavino, one of the most significant industrial architects of the turn of the century. Since 1975, they have been abandoned to fall into dilapidation.

The factory-owner's villa, once an embodiment of fine living of the period, has suffered similar neglect. The railways have been better looked after, however; the Museu del Transport opens its gates to visitors on weekends, and possesses some rarities.

**The *Jocs Florals* poetry contests**

*Blinded by love for a tongue*
*I have not mastered,*
*I embark on a pilgrimage*
*through the cemetery of times past.*

*This verse by the Mallorcan poet Marià Aguilo accompanied intellectuals and aesthetes of the mid-19th century in their search for the Catalan identity they had lost during the centuries of Castilian predominance. Their aim was the renaixença, the rebirth of Catalan culture, and the Jocs Florals, the "floral games," were the means by which to proclaim their patriotic demands to the public. The tradition referred back to a contest between poets, which was celebrated with greatest ceremony toward the end of the Middle Ages at the Catalan-Aragonese court. The poet in third place received a silver violet, the second a golden rose, while the victor was awarded a real rose, which bloomed for as long as his poem lived. The contests were revived in 1859. They inspired romantic authors to return to writing and reciting poetry in català. Protagonists*

The poet and priest Jacint Verdaguer (1845–1902)

*included Joan Maragall and Jacint Verdaguer (illus. above), who was awarded the Flor Natural for his epic poem L'Atlàntida. Although displaying perhaps excessive bombast and pathos, the Jocs Florals helped pave the way for the revival of Catalan self-awareness.*

## On the Way to Ripoll:
## The "Bible in Stone"

The Marolla pass leads directly to Ripoll. An alternative route leads via the main link of La Molina through Ribes del Freser and could include a detour into the idyllic Val de Nùria. It is best to leave the car at Ribes, for this is the starting of the "Cremallera," a rack railway dating back to 1931, and a beautiful route up to the 2000 m (6,500 ft.) high upper reaches of the valley. The breathtaking ascent begins beyond Queralbs with its pretty Romanesque church of St. Jaume, the train climbing more than 1000 m (3,250 ft.) as it winds its way through gorges and tunnels. Amazing views finally open out over the Puigmal at 2913 m (9,557 ft.), the Serra de Torreneules, the Serra de Finestrelles, and the single peaks ranging between 2700 and 2800 m (8,850 and 9,186 ft.). They are the habitat of chamois, polecats, and golden eagles, while the slopes and alpine meadows are carpeted with numerous species of gentian, cyclamen, and rhododendron. The journey ends in the pilgrimage town of Núria, which has also become a mecca for winter sports. Numerous legends have grown up around the once remote town. St. Gil is said to have spent several years in a cave here c. 700, and buried a miraculous image which is supposed to have appeared to the Dalmatian pilgrim Amadeo in a vision. In 1072 Amadeo set out to look for the Madonna but could not find it. It is now therefore a later work which is worshiped, although this 12th-century wooden figure has become established as the patron saint of the shepherds of the Pyrenees. The shrine itself has been rebuilt on numerous occasions, the present one dating back to the 19th century, the cloister being as recent as 1918. The only older parts remaining are the Ermita de St. Gil (1615) and the core of the sanctuary of 1639.

The Benedictine monastery of Ripoll was among the most powerful of its time (illus. right). It was founded c. 879, when Count Guifré el Pelós (Wilfred the Hairy) led the resettlement of the area which had recently been won back from Arab control. The first church was dedicated in 888, but was replaced soon after in 935 by a new building, which in turn gave way to a structure consecrated in 977. In the meantime an urban settlement had grown up around the monastery, with armorers and smiths prominent. The monastery itself grew into an intellectual center for Christian Catalonia, which is why the establishment was rebuilt and then extended on several occasions during the 10th century. In the year 1032 the rededication of the

Ripoll
*Benedictine Abbey of St. Maria de Ripoll*
*(church rededicated 1032)*
*View from the east*

final new building took place, now with five stories and seven chapels adjoining the transept.

The driving force behind this spectacular extension was Abbot Oliba Cabreta – simultaneously Abbot of Cuixà and Bishop of Vic. He had traveled to Italy where it is believed he studied Early Christian architecture and brought back his memories of the Basilica of St. Peter to Catalonia. The monastery does have far more in common with the Early Christian St. Peter's than with the surrounding regional architecture. This led to a decisive architectural shift in Catalonia, opening it up to international influences.

Architecturally speaking, only a shadow of the former monastery church remains; the abbey was devastated by an earthquake in 1428 and then in 1835 by the popular storm of secularization. Between 1886 and 1893, with the newly awakened national consciousness, it was rebuilt in historical style by the architect Elies Rogent.

Nevertheless, the magnificent portal survives relatively unscathed, and is protected today by a vestibule, although it is visibly weathered.

In spite of this the skill of the stonemasons who contributed to this spectacular work around the middle of the 12th century is unmistakable (illus. opposite and right). The 11.6 × 7.65 m (38 × 25 ft.) façade of the monastery church of Ripoll has been justifiably called "the Bible in stone;" in fact, in all of Europe there is hardly a series of portal carvings to equal its richness and scope. The entire west front of the church is covered with sculptures – they are perfectly thematically arranged – six stone cordons dividing it into six levels.

Daniel's visions precede monsters and allusions to human frailty. Above, framed by arcades, are scenes of the glorification of David, the forefather of Christ. The next two levels show Old Testament stories from the transport of the Ark of the Covenant to the story of the manna from heaven. The top two rows are dedicated to the New Testament and its creators, the four Evangelists – an exception being the areas to the left and right, showing scenes from the apocalypse.

The portal itself testifies to the triumph of the gospels, dominated by Christ Pantocrator. The walls and archivolts are decorated with the signs of the zodiac and images of the months, embodying daily life; these are constantly intertwined with typological portrayals of the promise of salvation. The Apostles Peter and Paul, the only fully sculpted figures, incorporate through their lives and works the dawn of a new age foretold by the Son of God.

Such a complex iconological program as we have here in Ripoll has little historical context, and cannot be explained by any precedents of design or content. The structuring and selection of subject matter appears to refer to contemporary manuscripts, which would certainly have been copied in great number in the scriptorium of the abbey. The reason for designing such an ambitious program may reflect the momentous events experienced by Catalonia in the 12th century as part of the final release from Moorish rule. Thus, the portal could be interpreted as a "triumphal arch of the history of salvation."

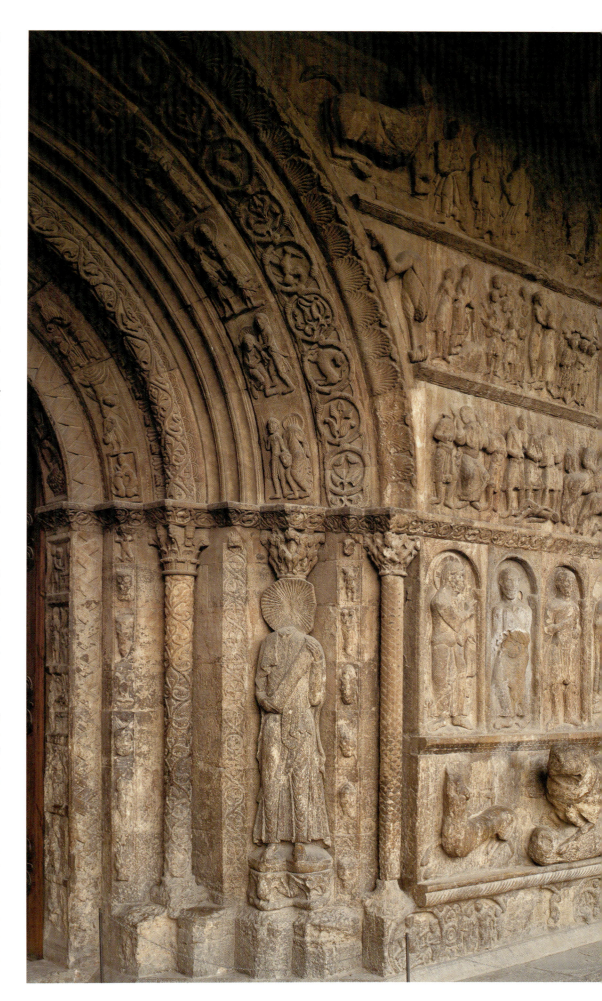

Rome, Biblioteca
Vaticana
Farfa Bible
(Bibl. lat. 5729), f. 95
Scenes from the stories of
David, Solomon and
Elias, 11th century
From the scriptorium of
St. Maria de Ripoll

Although four centuries have taken their toll, the cloister, begun c. 1170, has a remarkably unified, self-contained feel (illus. above). The oldest wing, flanking the church, has double columns with beautiful foliated capitals intertwined with numerous figures. The ceilings are adorned with fine decorative motifs. The remaining sides, built c. 1400, harmonize strikingly with their Romanesque predecessors, also having twin columns with stiff-leaf capitals and abacus plates, although the arcades are in the Classical style. The upper story, completed at the beginning of the 16th century, also conforms to its medieval precedents.

Unfortunately many of the valuable manuscripts produced in the scriptorium of Ripoll were lost as a result of the events referred to above, or are now preserved in other collections. This includes the famous Farfa Bible from the 11th century, which was among the sources of inspiration for the Catalan capital carvings, and is today kept in the Vatican library (illus. opposite).

For those with an interest in the skillful output of the monastery at Ripoll, a visit to the town's museum is highly recommended. The museum also has some magnificent examples of the Catalan metal-working craft, called the *farga catalana*.

Ripoll
*Benedictine Abbey of St. Maria de Ripoll*
*View of the cloister, begun 1170*

## St. Joan de les Abadesses and the *Santissim Misteri*

Just a few miles from Ripoll is found another major monument of medieval Catalonia: St. Joan de les Abadesses (illus. below). This is another Benedictine monastery, as in Ripoll, and the history of its beginnings shows some parallels to its neighboring abbey.

It, too, can be traced back to Guifré el Pelós, who founded it as a convent with his daughter Emma as Abbess. In 1017 the community was dissolved because of a scandal, news of which even reached the Pope. After a brief inter-regnum, Augustinian monks took it over as a monastery, and founded a new church, dedicated in 1150. Their building is another one that does not derive from the regional building tradition. Its original design is now discernible only with difficulty due to the far-reaching changes that have been made over the centuries.

Today a compact, single-aisled main building opens into a transept extending to similar width, a layout reflecting a Greek cross. Even rarer is the original plan of the east parts; the transept arm contains two deep apses, between which the spacious choir opens out with ambulatory and three further radial apses. This ambitious structure was damaged in the earthquake of 1428, which claimed more than 40 lives. Reconstructions from the 15th to the 20th centuries have sought to retain the original style to an extent.

For some years now, the greatest treasure of St. Joan de les Abadesses has returned to its rightful place; this is the *Santissim Misteri*, one of the most impressive sculpture

*Benedictine Abbey of St. Joan de les Abadesses, dedicated 1150 Exterior view*

groups of the Transitional period between Romanesque and Gothic (illus. below).

Seven extremely lifelike figures – Christ, the Virgin Mary, John the Baptist, Joseph of Arimathea, Nicodemus, and the two Jews – are carved from wood, depicting with dramatic gestures the scene of the "Most Holy of Mysteries," the deposition of Christ from the cross on the mountain of Golgotha.

Most striking is the pathos in the disposition of the Son of God, who even in death loses none of his majestic radiance. His arms form a diagonal which weld together the disparate groups of people united in grief.

The sculpture group, which is presumed to have been made by a certain Brother Dulcetus in the middle of the 13th century, is considered to represent one of the peaks of Catalan sculpture. This piece is also believed to be one of the most important examples of monumental "Descent from the Cross" groups.

The "Verge Blanca" retable, the "white Virgin," seems to have been created a hundred years later, c. 1343. The charming Mother of God in the center of the altarpiece is surrounded by 18 alabaster reliefs representing the prophets and scenes from the early life of the Redeemer. The material for these finely chiseled sculptures came from the nearby limestone quarry of Beuda.

The asymmetrical St. Michael's cloister adjoins the church to the left; this was begun in 1445, and still incorporates some parts of its Romanesque predecessor. The principal treasures of the museum include some valuable embroideries.

*Benedictine Abbey of St. Joan de les Abadesses*
*Santissim Misteri (Descent from the Cross), mid-12th century*

## Romantic and Romanesque around Camprodon

A few miles to the north of St. Joan de les Abadesses lies the delightful mountain village of Camprodon, which has developed into a popular holiday resort. More than a hundred years earlier tourists became aware of the place, but its advantages were discovered by the Benedictines who founded the abbey of St. Peter here. We do not know if these advantages included the famous local ham and sausages (illus. below).

The Romanesque monastery church with the five apses that we see today was first dedicated in 1169; the parish church of St. Maria is also worth a visit. However, the main attraction of Camprodon is the substantial stone bridge which spans the Ritort in a grand arch (illus. below). Its history goes back to the start of the 12th century, although the present structure is believed to date from the 14th century.

Beyond Camprodon a narrow, winding lane leads to Rocabruna and Beget; this is a detour of some 25 km (c. 15.5 miles). The road winds through a wonderful mountain landscape, which – depending on the season – appears either to be majestically rugged or attractively gentle. Then there are the red-brown walls and the ruins of the castle of Rocabruna, which blend beautifully with the green of the meadows and fields.

Beget, sited at the head of the valley, is built on a rock, with the waters of the Trüll roaring through the picturesque village center (illuss. opposite). The characteristic stone houses huddle together to the right and left of winding alleys, their frontages adorned with beautifully carved wooden balconies.

The parish church of St. Christòfol, which is itself an excellent example of Romanesque architecture, awaits the visitor with a unique work of art: the life-size wooden statue of *Crist en Majestat*.

There are few images of the Son of God which radiate such dignity and sublimity. Clothed in a long tunic, Christ is shown on the cross in still, impassive pride. His arms are spread out wide, as if in a gesture of embrace rather than in martyrdom. The statue, which was carved and painted in the second half of the 12th century, does not express any sign of suffering, but appears to hover before the arms of the cross.

BELOW:
*Ham and sausages in Camprodon*

BOTTOM:
Camprodon
*Medieval stone bridge,*
*12th–14th centuries*

Beget
*Views of the village*

## Artists and Craters: Olot and the Volcanic Landscape of the Garrotxa Region

We now leave the pretty conservation village of Beget, and continue the route southward to other delights: the volcanic landscape of the Garrotxa region and the artists' town of Olot. An alternative route leads via Molló with its beautiful church tower and on to France and the Catalan areas across the border.

The wild beauty of the Garrotxa has always attracted admirers. Around the middle of the 19th century the visitors were painters enchanted by the rich greens of the meadows, the deep blue of the rivers and the sky, and the ever-changing tones of the volcanic lava rocks (illus. above). It is the contrasts more than anything which are the main attraction of the Garrotxa. Firstly, there are the harsh volcanic craters which were formed around 350,000 years ago and which even today are not considered extinct, although the last activity, in El Croscat, was as far back as 17,000 years ago. Thirty cones between 10 to 160 m (30 to 525 ft.) in height – with diameters of between 300 and 1500 m (985 and 4,900 ft.) – are preserved. Their clinker and lapilli are testimony to constant magma eruptions and lava flows. They stopped up numerous river courses through the mountains, forming dams, and making lakes and sedimentation.

The rivers in turn created fertile plains and marshes which form the other, mellower, side of the national park (illus. below). Just as the colors of the landscape vary, the flora and fauna also change at every step.

Large areas are covered with durmast and sessile oak forests, while alders have colonized the marshy ground. Saxifrage and other plants have taken hold on the lava and scree slopes. Rare types of marten and genets roam the undergrowth, although wolves were eradicated from the region in the last century. However, eagles, goshawks and wrynecks still circle overhead, and all kinds of adders and lizards enjoy the habitat on the ground.

One of the most pleasing walks in the Garrotxa region is the climb to the edge of the crater of the St. Margarida volcano. The nature reserve – which comprises 121 sq km (c. 47 sq. miles) – came under official protection in 1985, following a vehement popular protest against the adverse effects of the mining of volcanic clinker on the landscape.

Our experience of the Garrotxa today is not really any different from how the artists of the 19th century saw the region. Joaquim Vayreda (1843–94) was the first Catalan painter who, following in the footsteps of the French "Barbizon School," painted landscapes direct from nature. His interest in this style and the need for realistic rendition was awakened by his teacher Ramón Martí i Alsina. Yet his lyrical pictures, which sympathetically

*The wild beauty of the Garrotxa region*

BELOW:
*Marsh landscape in the Garrotxa region*

OPPOSITE:
*Joaquim Vayreda
Autumn landscape,
c. 1880
Oil on canvas,
61 × 50.5 cm
Privately owned.*

### Folk Festivals and Customs

*The church year, ecclesiastical holy days and local patron saints' days provide plenty of opportunity for festivals. Parades are nearly always led by gegants and cap-grossos. The papier-mâché giants, 5 m (16 ft.) in height, and dressed in historical costume, walk at a dignified pace, while the dwarfs with their outsized heads frolic around them. Ever since the national patron St. Jordi, or St. George, defeated the dragon, every festival has sought to re-enact his feat. Bizarre monsters accompanied by demons proceed through the streets; the fight against Evil is enacted with much noise, commotion, and explosions of fireworks. The feast of the patum in Berga on Corpus Christi Day is the most colorful of these. The ritual attacks against the Moors, particularly popular in New Catalonia, are also raucous affairs. Stories from the Bible are also brought to life. On January 6 the Three Kings sail majestically into the harbor at Barcelona; during Holy Week the Passions of Christ are acted out; and during the Christmas period real-life nativity scenes are re-enacted. No Catalan festival is complete without the Sardana, the Catalan dance during which complete strangers take each other's hands and form circles to dance to the brassy sounds of the 11-piece cobla. Once the signal from the flabiol is heard, the dancers begin their stately steps. The castells, breathtaking human pyramids, are described in their own section (see p. 159).*

capture the atmosphere of the place, extend beyond his teacher's range, breaking the hitherto unassailable rules of academic artistic teaching.

His paintings, for example the *Autumn Landscape* of 1880, are poetic representations of nature in the changing seasons and changing light (illus. p. 53). His model was almost always his homeland, the atmospheric landscape of the Garrotxa.

Vayreda's example was soon followed by other artists, so that the "Olot School" became a trademark of Catalan art, and Spanish landscape painting as a whole in the second half of the 19th century. The most prominent artists of the time met in the School of Drawing here, restoring the institution – originally founded in 1783 – to its former glory.

Olot itself is a bustling place, with a history stretching back more than a thousand years. There are few medieval traces to be seen, however, as a devastating earthquake in 1427–8 left the old town in ruins.

After its reconstruction the town on the volcanic cone flourished in the 17th and 18th centuries, thanks to the textile industry and to arts and crafts, all of which still contribute to Olot's prosperity.

Thus the main impression of the town is its villas and parks. The manufacturers and merchants had sumptuous town houses built, in the Classical, *modernista*, medieval, or even Arabic styles, depending on personal taste and the fashion of the day.

One of the most beautiful is the Casa Solà-Morales, actually an 18th-century building, but with the later additions by Lluís Domènech i Montaner of a rich façade with graffiti, sculptures (*Eusebi Arnau*), and wrought-iron balconies, crowned by a loggia. The Casa Vayreda is also of interest to visitors, and is also the reconstruction of an older town villa.

Among the museums, the most outstanding is the Museu Comarcal de la Garrotxa in the former hospice designed by the Baroque architect Ventura Rodríguez. In addition to archaeological finds and a collection of cribs, most outstanding is the more recent exhibition of the landscape paintings of the region.

A sub-section of this museum is the Museu des Volcans, housed in the neo-Palladian Torre Castanys (1854, Josep Fontseré) in Parc Nou; in it is all manner of useful information on the volcanic landscape of the Garrotxa and its flora and fauna.

The art academy is located in the former Carmelite convent, whose Renaissance cloister is one of the few examples in the region from the 16th century.

Olot is today famous for its colorful folk festivals, the *Aplec de la Sardana*, a celebration of the Catalan circle dance, and the celebrations in honor of the town's patron saint, Mare de Déu, involving a parade of giants (*els gegants*) (see panel box opposite) and dwarfs.

The surroundings of Olot have many picturesque surprises, whether the high-altitude pilgrimage churches of Mare de Déu de la Salut or Mare de Déu del Far, the conservation village of Rupit, or the Susqueda and Sau reservoirs, which are reached by leaving Olot to the south,

linking up with the tour centered on Vic. Traveling west, you either reach Dalí's town of Figueres or, via Banyoles, the cathedral city of Girona.

The N 260 first passes Castellfollit, nestling against the rocks, before reaching Besalú, perhaps the most beautiful little town in the outlying Pyrenees. In the 9th century this was the home of a powerful independent line of counts, members of which included Guifré el Pelós, who was responsible for uniting old Catalonia.

In the year 1111 the town, with its strategic location on the intersection of important trade routes, was annexed to the Comtat of Barcelona. In the ensuing period Besalú was adorned with many splendid buildings, which give it its unique character to this day.

The town's picturesque heart is entered by crossing the Fluvià over the grand, angled stone bridge, the eight impressive stone arches of which soar high above the surface of the water (illus. opposite, top). A narrow street leads to the center which has three lovely Romanesque churches, St. Maria, the surviving part of an Augustinian choral foundation, St. Vicenç with its intricate side portal, and St. Pere, a 12th-centruy building with a fine ambulatory. Its façade is graced by a window framed by finely-carved columns and archivolts with two fierce lions peering in from either side (illus. above).

The town council used to meet in the Cúria Reial on the northern edge of the arcaded Plaça Major; today its rooms and picturesque inner courtyard house a hotel and restaurant. Another pretty sight in the town is the Casa dels Arcs in the Carrer Tallaferro with its arcades and triple-panel windows.

There is also the unique *Miqwé*, the Jewish baths for ritual washing, which is preserved above the banks of the river. Back over the medieval bridge you rejoin the main road which leads, as it has done for centuries, to the plains of the Empordà.

Besalú
St. Pere
*Detail of the façade, 12th century*

Girona "La Força"

# The Walled Stronghold

Romans, Arabs, Jews, and Christians have all left their influence on Girona, although not always without scars. Its location where the Pyrenees give way to the Iberian lands means that since Classical times Girona has been the scene of hostile conflicts on no less than 34 occasions; "the City of Sieges" is just one of the nicknames attributed to this historic metropolis over the years. Believed to have been a bishopric since the 4th century, the seat of the Counts' court, and today a culturally exuberant provincial capital, Girona is considered the most "Catalan" among its peers. This does not prevent the city at the confluence of four rivers from welcoming tourists from all over the world. The atmosphere of its old town, unchanged for centuries, and the ubiquitous wealth of artistic treasures make Girona an unforgettable experience, the high point of any visit to Catalonia.

The history of Girona is one of change. The historian Pliny told of a Roman *oppidum* called Gerunda, situated by the Via Augusta and part of the Colonia Tarraconensis administrative region. The roughly triangular fortified settlement stretches from near where the cathedral stands today up to the Torre Girondella; its walls were demolished as recently as 1895. Girona experienced its

first boom period from the 3rd century A.D. with the advent of Christianity. A lively cult grew up around the site of the martyrdom of St. Felix, leading to the foundation of the first church and ultimately inspiring the Visigoth king, Reccared, to establish the cathedral. During the 67 years of Arab control over the city, Christians were allowed to continue their worship. The cathedral was turned into a mosque, however, while the bishop pragmatically moved to the martyr's church of St. Feliú. In the year 785 Charlemagne's forces took over the city, and – with the foundation of the Spanish mark in 801 – a new era began for Girona. It became an outpost of the Frankish empire, forming a kind of buffer between Christianity and Islam during the subsequent centuries. The Frankish overlords granted the foundation of an earldom here, which soon achieved considerable independence. In 878 Guifré el Pelós (Wilfred the Hairy) succeeded in uniting the *comtats* of Girona, Urgell-Cerdanya, Osona, and Barcelona, thus laying the foundations for the separation of Old Catalonia from the rest of the Frankish empire.

In the 11th, and particularly in the 12th century Girona experienced a lively boom period along with the rest of the

PREVIOUS PAGES AND ABOVE:
Girona
*View over the River Onyar to the old town*

OPPOSITE:
Girona
*Old town with the cathedral (right) and St. Feliú (left)*

## Jews in Catalonia

From the mid-12th century the Jews in Catalonia played a prominent role in commercial life, as they did throughout Spain. As philosophers, mathematicians, astronomers, and doctors they assumed important positions in the growing communities, were given important offices at court, and accumulated wealth which they were skilled at increasing. Immune from legal provisions enshrined in acts such as the Usatges de la Cort de Barcelona (Customs of the Court in Barcelona), they settled in all the major centers of the Catalan-Aragonese kingdom and founded schools, hospitals, and universities, in which they taught Talmudic law, Biblical interpretation, and cabbalistic science. Numerous richly illustrated manuscripts in the Catalan language bear testimony to their influence and their integration into the cultural life of the land; these include the Llibre de Paraules de Savis e de Filòsofs (Book of Words of Wisdom and Philosophy), written by Jafudà Bonsenyar in 1293 by order of King Jaume II.

Girona
Monument of the Foundation of Rabbi Samuel ha-Sardi, 1314
Barcelona, Carrer Marlet 1

Jews represented around ten percent of the population in Barcelona and Girona. They usually lived in their own separate quarter, the call, with substantial autonomy. The call had a synagogue with a Miqué, the ritual washing bath, a cemetery, and a rabbi. Kosher butchers, bakers, and numerous other merchants and traders provided for the everyday needs of the community. Until the middle of the 14th century, Christians and Jews lived alongside one another in tolerance and mutual respect, but relations worsened with the outbreak of the plague –the Black Death.

The Jews were envied for their commercial success, and were made scapegoats for all the crises of the times. The church systematically fanned the flames of hatred. Those who refused to leave their homes often faced a choice between conversion or death.

In 1492 the Catholic Kings drove out all Jews who remained in their territories. In so doing, they robbed their empire of a valuable economic and spiritual contribution.

OPPOSITE:
Girona
*Cathedral*
*View of the interior,*
*begun 1321*

region. As monasteries and churches were springing up in the remotest valleys of the Pyrenees, the city spread out beyond its ancient walls and adorned itself with numerous new buildings. A new quarter grew up around the churches of St. Maria, St. Pere de Galligants, St. Feliú and St. Susanna del Mercadel, with markets, hospitals, and even thermal baths based on Arab precedents. By 1015 the foundation stone for the new Romanesque cathedral had been laid; this edifice was completed in the record time of just 21 years.

In its shadow, the *call* (see panel box p. 59) around the Carrer de la Força was where the Jewish population settled, and built their synagogues. As merchants, bankers, doctors, and philosophers, they held some of the most influential positions in the city, and enjoyed numerous privileges bestowed on them by the Counts and subsequent monarchs. A unique legal situation in Girona contributed to the Jewish quarter assuming the status of being almost a city within a city, which ultimately led to unrest between Christians and Jews. There followed successive periods of peaceful coexistence interspersed with violent outbreaks of anti-Semitism, the situation coming to a head in the late Middle Ages when the

ABOVE:
Girona
*Cathedral*
*Silver reredos, between*
*1320 and 1358*

LEFT:
Girona
*Cathedral*
*Baroque façade, begun 1680*

FOLLOWING PAGES:
Girona
*Cathedral*
*Cloister, 12th century*

Girona
*Cathedral*
*View from the south with the*
*Tower of Charlemagne*
*11th–12th centuries*

OPPOSITE:
Girona
*Cathedral treasury*
*Beatus of Liébana Commentary*
*on the Apocalypse, 975*
*"The Flood"*

Catholic Kings decreed that all Jews should be driven out of Spanish territory. However life in Girona as in other Catalonian towns and cities continued to be influenced by the exchange between the cultures.

The growth of Girona in the 11th and 12th centuries naturally led to the extension of the defensive walls, a necessity which soon became apparent. The prosperous city at the crossroads of numerous trade routes had caught the eye of many rulers; in 1285 King Philip the Bald of France dared to make an advance against the kingdom of Aragon, and besieged Girona. In a way, it was the plague that came to the rescue, and the French were ultimately forced to retreat empty-handed. This was only the first of more than 30 sieges that the city endured from then until the 19th century. A tragic climax came when Napoleon's army surrounded Girona for nine months, which cost the lives of thousands of citizens. This fate gave Girona its nickname the "City of Sieges," and its medieval heart – which had withstood so many onslaughts – was dubbed "La Força," the strong.

Despite its checkered history, since the 14th century the status of Girona has been second only to that of Barcelona among Catalan cities. Toward the mid-19th century the city was extended to the far bank of the river Onyar, and in 1895 the remains of the defenses which had withstood the assault of Napoleon were torn down. A massive, largely uncontrolled period of growth set in.

Fortunately the old town was unaffected, so that a walk among its gray-brown walls can still evoke an impressive journey into the past.

A good starting-point for a visit to historic Girona is provided by the promenade along the bank of the Riu Onyar on the new city side (illus. pp. 56–7), or in the view from one of the bridges which span the river (illus. p. 58). The ocher and red shades of the façades of the houses lining the bank are reflected in the water, and the cathedral in its full glory dominates the scene (illus. p. 59, top). The route to the cathedral involves climbing three flights of 30 steps: breathtaking both literally and due to the sight of the magnificent urban landscape. The monumental flight of steps, constructed in the 17th century, leads past Gothic and Renaissance palaces including the Pia Almoina, the welfare institution. In 1680 the new front was begun, the central section of which looks as if it is modeled on a monumental retable, as is so often the case in Spain.

If you expect the magnificent façade of the cathedral (illus. p. 61, bottom) to conceal a Baroque interior, you will be surprised. On entering, the space is austere and somber, although still one of the grandest examples of Gothic architecture from among the many Catalonia has to offer (illus. p, 60). A single 34-m (112-ft.) high and 23-m (75-ft.) wide vaulted ceiling encloses the nave, without doubt the most ambitious structure of its time. It took the architects a great deal of work to convince the cathedral chapter to undertake this venture. The actual construction work was preceded by a series of thorough and informative discussions on both technical matters and aesthetics. By 1312 the cathedral chapter had come to the decision to extend the original Romanesque building with the addition of a new choir with a light ambulatory and new polygonal chapels. Henri de Fauran was appointed to the task in 1321, succeeded by his brother Jacques, the master builder in charge of the cathedral at Narbonne. Although the eastern parts of the cathedral were largely completed in accordance with this plan by the middle of the century, only a few side chapels were built off the nave.

In 1386 and 1416 experts were commissioned to discuss the further extension as an aisled structure or alternatively the erection of a hall-type enclosure. Some doubt was expressed about the feasibility of a single vault, especially by the (competing) architects from Barcelona. However, in 1417 it was finally decided in favor of the single vault, which would be "more beautiful and more striking." It was now down to the daring of architect Guillem Bofill to undertake the daring task.

The overall design perfected the typical Barcelona style, in which the thrust of the vault is absorbed by buttresses which are built internally, and leave room between for the chapels. Externally the structural elements do not stand out; the effect is square and compact. Although the building was not entirely completed until 1604, it is nevertheless one of the finest examples of the spirit of innovation pervading Catalonian Gothic architecture.

Of the interior decorations the late-Gothic reredos above the Romanesque altar is outstanding. Measuring 2.20 × 1.80 m (7.2 × 5.9 ft.), the shrine-like "altar-piece" is a masterpiece of the Spanish gold- and silversmiths' art (illus. p. 61, top). This priceless piece was created between 1320 and 1358 by Mestre Barthomeu, Ramón Andreu, and Pedro Berneç. The innumerable figures, shaped in silver, gilded, and decorated with precious stones, describe the story of the Virgin Mary and the Son of God in lively gestures; around the edges are angels, saints, and bishops with their coats of arms. The crowning figure of Mary bears the signature "Berneç me hizo" (Berneç made me).

Above the altar-piece is a work of art which is possibly even more exciting, the silver baldachin, also once gilded and also crafted by Bartomeu and Berneç. Supported on four columns, it represents heaven with four planes on which stand rows of angels and saints. In the center is the crowning of Mary, and on the spandrels the patrons Pere and Arnau de Soler.

Behind the altar you can see what is known as the Throne of Charlemagne – actually a bishop's throne, carved from a single block, dating back to the 11th century, as evidenced by the style of its fine foliar decoration and the symbols of the evangelists. Of the numerous superb tombs in the cathedral, the alabaster monument to Bishop Berenguer de Anglesola to the left of the altar is without doubt the most beautiful. The recumbent figure of the bishop, his miter, his robes, and the figures of the prophets around the sides of the tomb are chiseled with

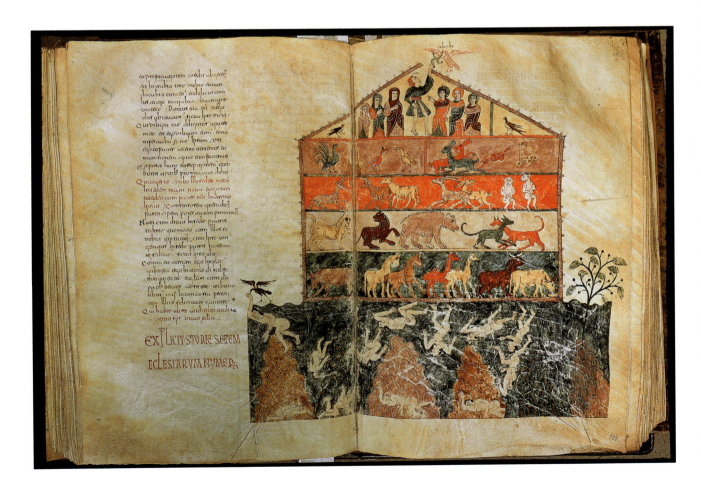

**The Spanish Commentaries on the Apocalypse**

*Spain is the proud possessor of a unique treasury of medieval book illumination, a group of 32 manuscripts with commentaries and illustrations on the Apocalypse and the Revelation of St. John. The terrifying visions contained therein have attracted the attentions of theologians and believers through the ages; one of the first to give in-depth interpretation of them was the monk Beatus of Liébana (died c. 798), who in 784 wrote a detailed, graphically illustrated Commentary on the Apocalypse. All later Beatus manuscripts, from the 9th to the 16th centuries, can be traced back to his influence. The medieval manuscripts, of which the "Apocalypse of Girona" (975) is the most important, are generally built up around the same design, with full-page miniatures showing the gruesome events of the end of the world in several layers. They are characterized by the vivid colors with which the figures and backgrounds are portrayed, and the expressive gestures used to convey the actions. The stylistic influences of Moorish art are also not to be overlooked. The "Apocalypse of Girona" comprises 284 pages with 114 colored miniatures highlighted with gold and silver; the text was written in Visigothic lettering by Senerius, the illustrations drawn by the monk Emeterius and the nun Ende. It was probably produced in the monastery of Tábara near Zamora, and came into the possession of the Cathedral of Girona in 1078.*

extraordinary skill. Pere Oller, who also worked in the *Seu* of Barcelona, was probably the creator of this work. Before turning to the further treasures of the cathedral, time should be taken to appreciate the stained glass of the choir, which includes the oldest examples of this craft in Catalonia (14th century).

The late Gothic Porta de St. Miquel now leads to the cloister and to a completely different world (illus. p. 62–3). The trapezoidal *claustrum* is one of the few remaining sections of the earlier Romanesque structure. Its magnificent decorative sculptures give an insight into the entire world view of the Middle Ages. Lively scenes similar to those found in St. Cugat del Vallés show stories from the Old and New testaments, such as the Creation and the Life of Christ. Mythic creatures with an oriental flavor, fantastical plants, and scenes from battles and everyday life all add to the overall effect. A particularly beautiful capital shows a knight drawing his bow. There is also an outstanding frieze with a lifelike depiction of the story of Jacob.

The artists behind these masterpieces were clearly inspired by the illustrations from illuminated manuscripts which gave them a wide range of patterns to follow in formulating the episodes. Some of the sources can be identified – for example the Farfa Bible – now in the Vatican library, is certainly among the influences. Despite the wide variety of the subjects and narrative structures the artists succeeded in creating a unified whole. The capitals of the double columns surrounding the four unequal sides of the cloister are to a great extent Corinthian with the characteristic acanthus leaves.

Another interesting aspect is the ingenuity of the architect in coming to terms with the uneven, steeply sloping ground. Unusually sturdy walls and stonework arch over the galleries of the Girona cloister, with the exception of the north side. The Romanesque parts also include what is known as the Torre de Carlemany, the Tower of Charlemagne, dating from the 11th–12th centuries, its six stories soaring majestically up from the south-east corner (illus. p. 64).

It is worth visiting Girona for the Cathedral Museum alone. The ecclesiastical treasures in the chapterhouse of the cathedral are resplendent with exhibits worthy of a place in any of the major collections of medieval art. These include an Arabic casket from the time of Hischam II, made c. 970, beautiful manuscripts of the early to late Middle Ages, including a Beatus of Liébana Commentary on the Apocalypse which dates from 975 (illus. and panel box p. 65), valuable book bindings, reliquaries and processional crosses.

The greatest attraction, however, is without doubt the unique *Tapís de la Creació*, (Creation Tapestry), an embroidered wool-and-linen tapestry measuring some 4.15 × 3.65 m (13.62 × 11.98 ft.), and dating from around the beginning of the 12th century (illus. left). In addition to its remarkable condition, this is considered a masterpiece both for its skillful craft and its pictorial composition. Christ appears as Pantocrator in the center of a series of cosmological images, surrounded by eight

Girona
*Cathedral Treasury*
*"Creation tapestry"*
*Wool and linen,*
*4.15 × 3.65 m*
*c. 1100*

Girona
*Museu d'Art de Girona*
*View of the exhibition galleries*

episodes from the Creation story and with the dove of the Holy Spirit above. The Creation of the fish and the birds is a particularly striking image with all manner of unusual, lovingly worked creatures. The inner circle is placed within a rectangle surrounded by a border with images representing the months and, on the badly preserved bottom edge, the story of the finding of the cross. In the central panels are personifications of the four winds in the form of winged figures blowing their horns, borne on cushions of air.

The composition of this unique work of art reflects the style of Classical floor mosaics. It is not known where the embroidery was actually made. Were Catalan patrons and artists capable of creating such a magnificent work, or does the masterpiece actually come from northern Italy?

Yet more priceless works of art can be seen in Girona's Museu d'Art, housed in the Bishop's Palace immediately adjacent to the cathedral (illus. above). This fortified building itself has a long history. Basically Romanesque, it underwent considerable extension both in the Gothic period and toward the end of the 16th century, and is now a striking complex on the Plaça dels Apostels. The modern layout of the museum, which extends over five storys around the medieval inner courtyard, contains exhibitions of Catalan art from the pre-Romanesque

period to the present. These include such important pieces as the portable altar from St. Pere de Rodes, the frescoes from Perinyà, or the altarpiece of Bernat Martorell from Púbol. The collections on the fourth story give excellent insights into the landscape painting of the 19th century and the arts and crafts of the turn of the century.

After enjoying so much art and culture, it is time for some fresh air. A passage leads to the rear of the cathedral and the picturesque Jardins de la Francesa, laid out above the remains of the canonical houses (illus. opposite top). From here you get a wonderful view over the roofs and towers of the "Força." Climbing farther, you reach the Porta St. Cristòfol, gaining access from here to the town walls. These are followed by the Passeig Arqueològic, leading over steps and bridges to the other sights of the city. The first of these are the Banys Arabs, the "Arab baths," although they do not, as their name suggests, date from the decades of Arab rule over Girona (illus. opposite bottom left and right). They were first constructed in the Romanesque period toward the end of the 12th century, when the citizens were learning to appreciate and imitate the style and comforts of the Moors. It is likely that *mudejar* craftsmen were brought in to fit out the rooms. The Roman baths also probably provided inspiration, for these

ABOVE:
Girona
*Jardins de la Francesca with cathedral chevet*

FAR LEFT AND LEFT:
Girona
*The "Arab Baths"*
*End of the 12th century*

Girona
St. Pere de Galligants
Cloister

baths followed the sequence of *apodyterium* (dressing room), *frigidarium* (cold bath), *tepidarium* (cooling-off room), and *caldarium* (hot bath). They were heated by an oven set into the floor outside. The most impressive room today is the dressing room with its pool crowned by an octagonal dome. Around the edge are eight slender columns with extremely finely worked capitals and springings.

St. Pere de Galligants is just a little farther, on the other bank of the Galligants, which owes its name to the biblical cock's crow. This former Benedictine abbey was founded c. 992, at that time outside the city walls, although the existing church dates back to 1130. It is believed, however, that older parts were incorporated into the aisled Romanesque building, as the four apses are unusually irregular and asymmetrical. A majestic belfry soars above the north of the transept, octagonal at the top and with dual openings. The façade is distinguished by a columnar

portal and a huge rose window. The monastery's greatest treasure, however, is its cloister, constructed between 1154 and 1190, and today housing the Archaeological Museum (illus. above). Here, too, the courtyard is surrounded by twin columns with ornamental and narrative capitals, and – as in the cathedral – the images remain extremely vivid. More unusually, there are no episodes from the Old Testament here.

The museum's collection brings together archaeological finds from the region, including a sarcophagus showing the seasons of the year and grave slabs and stones from the late Middle Ages, originally from the Jewish cemetery.

Close to St. Pere is the small burial chapel of St. Nicolau, erected in the 12th century on the site of an early Christian martyrium. This single-naved building with crossing-dome and trefoiled choir represents a structural type that is unusual in Catalonia.

Girona
*In the Jewish quarter, El Call*

ABOVE:
Girona
St. Feliú
*Proserpina sarcophagus, 1st half of the 3rd century*

RIGHT:
Girona
St. Feliú
*Susanna sarcophagus, 1st half of the 4th century*

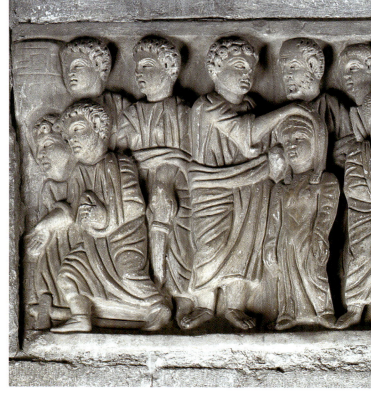

Retracing our steps back to the old town we pass the imposing church of St. Feliù, which vies with the cathedral for historical significance. As its name suggests, it was built over the tomb of the martyr St. Felix. The first sanctuary itself contained a number of outstanding Classical and Early Christian marble sarcophagi, which are now incorporated into the Romanesque-Gothic structure with its later Baroque additions.

We know that these six Christian and two pagan sarcophagi were brought to prominence in 1313, when they were incorporated into the walls of the presbytery. But we still know very little about the reasons behind and meaning of this unique reuse. The Proserpina sarcophagus (illus. pp. 72–3, top) and the Susanna sarcophagus (illus. pp. 72–3), toward the front of the chancel, are particularly fine pieces. The Baroque painting in the chapel to the side of the main altar shows the curious image of the "flying wonder" of St. Felix.

The Carrer de la Força now leads to the Jewish quarter of El Call, which retains much of its medieval character (illus. p. 71). The Centre Binatruc ça Porta on the site of the former synagogue is a museum and study center on the history of the Catalan Jews.

Although Girona's new town cannot compete with the delights of the "Força," it is worth taking a stroll across the Plaça Independencia and through the lively shopping streets. A green oasis is provided by the Parc de la Devesa in the north-west, with the biggest plane tree plantation in Catalonia. The famous trees lining La Rambla in Barcelona originate from this arboretum in Girona.

To the north of Girona, on the way to Olot is the Lake of Banyoles, which is surrounded by woods and meadows, and is a delightful place for either relaxation or water sports (illus. below).

An additional cultural detour is provided by a visit to the little Romanesque church of St. Maria de Porqueres (illus. opposite top). In addition to its pretty exterior, it also boasts some amazing columns with huge capitals at the entrance to the choir.

The town of Banyoles itself is also a good place to stop awhile. The buildings surrounding the pretty Plaça de Mercadal have some interesting porticos. The monastery of St. Esteve, which has survived numerous blows of fate during its checkered existence, still preserves some old sections and a reredos from the 15th century. An archaeological and science museum, the Museu Darder, contains interesting and richly varied collections.

Finally, do not miss Bàscara, a small village on the road to Figueres, which is transformed into a second Bethlehem in December every year when its inhabitants re-enact the scenes of the Christmas story and form living nativity scenes (illus. opposite bottom).

*The Lake of Banyoles*

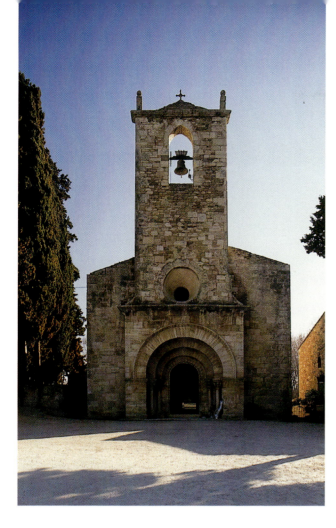

LEFT AND BELOW:
*St. Maria de Porqueres (consecrated 1182)*
*on the Lake of Banyoles*
*View (left), detail of portal carvings (below)*

BOTTOM:
*Bàscara*
*The Nativity brought to life*

# The Costa Brava

# Along the "Wild Coast"

PREVIOUS PAGES:
*The wild, romantic Cap Creus*

ABOVE:
*View of the railway terminus at
Port Bou*

Port Bou – the border – is still a tangible presence in Port Bou, although there is no longer a customs checkpoint separating Spain from France, and even the language ignores national boundaries. Some things remain the same: the cliffs still tumble into the sea, and remain equally breathtaking on either side. Travelers still experience feelings of change, new beginnings, and leave-taking despite the unification of Europe, although such feelings are also now surviving relics of history.

The former fishing port on one of the most beautiful stretches of the Costa Brava is also one of the most impressive railway junctions in the world (illus. above). The different track gauges of the French Société Nationale des Chemins de Fer (SNCF) and Spanish Red Nacional de los Ferrocarriles Españoles (RENFE) mean that before the journey can continue on to Spain the trains must be changed or – as is now possible with the newer high-speed trains – the undercarriage needs to be adjusted. The image of the place, the everyday comings and goings, are colored by rails, railway cars, and the creaking of shunting engines. The first railway cars traveled the rails back in 1878; the first cast-iron station was constructed in 1929 – just in time for the International Exhibition in Barcelona.

The idea of border also pervades the place in a more tragic sense. On September 26, 1940 the German Jewish philosopher and cultural critic Walter Benjamin (1892–1940) committed suicide in Port Bou. Fleeing from the Nazis, he had risked his life crossing the Pyrenees, hoping to travel through Spain to reach neutral Portugal. However, Spain refused him permission to pass through. Benjamin's grave in the small cemetery was neglected for a considerable time, but it is now marked by a pile of stones according to the Jewish custom.

Immediately adjacent, the Israeli artist Dani Karavan has erected a monument to the philosopher, as intense and moving as it is possible. The monument *Passages* (1990–94) blends unobtrusively into the rugged land-scape (illus. opposite). A dark shaft is formed from rust-colored metal, cutting through the rock of the hillside. Steps lead down into it until it breaks off abruptly, sealed by a glass panel. Through this the blue sea shimmers with touches of sunlight. The gloomy passage down generates feelings of oppression, except for the light at the end of the tunnel, and the sea that represents freedom, while remaining a dream. In this sublime and deeply moving way the plight and fears of the fugitive are portrayed along with his hopelessness in the face of freedom.

DANI KARAVAN
Passages, 1990–94

FOLLOWING PAGES:
*Cap Creus*

Along the "Wild Coast"     79

## The Power of the Stones:
## The Road to St. Pere de Rodes

From Port Bou the narrow regional road winds along the rugged coast offering incomparable views of the sea. Small bays with beaches and natural harbors alternate with steep cliffs, until a wider bay opens out near Port de Llançà, a haven especially for water-sports enthusiasts. The old town center, slightly inland, is dominated by an imposing belfry from the 11th century. This is not the only witness to times past.

As well as pre-Romanesque churches and abbeys, the region is rich in dolmens and menhirs that can be discovered on a circular tour: the *Ruta megalitica i preromanica*. The massive stones, artfully arranged to form tombs, have been in place for up to 3,000 years; it must have taken a huge effort to bring them to their final positions. Imaginative names such as the "Bandits' Table" or the "Abbot's Grave" show the fascination they have generated in their observers.

Turning away from the Stone Age, our route now takes us on to El Port de la Selva, the popular resort at the edge of the wild, romantic Cap Creus (illus. pp. 76–7 and left). This is the ideal starting point for excursions into the surrounding area, whether by car, by boat, or on foot. The latter is recommended, weather permitting, especially for a visit to the Benedictine monastery of St. Pere de Rodes, in a picturesque elevated position 520 m (1700 ft.) above the sea (accessible by car via Selva de Mar or more comfortably from Llançà through Vilajuïga).

A visit to this illustrious abbey – which represents a culmination of all the beginnings of Romanesque art in Catalonia, if not the whole of south-west Europe – is the high point of any visit to Catalonia. And yet even its great history is daunted by its setting; the location of St. Pere de Rodes is so beautiful that the visitor's gaze cannot help but wander away from the architecture and out across the blue sea and indented coastline that borders it. It is impossible to resist the rugged fascination of the landscape, but equally alluring are the strength and magnificence of this fortress abbey. The gray-brown solid stone walls are deeply ingrained with the highs and lows of their thousand-year history. The complex was abandoned and left to fall into ruin for many years, but has now been comprehensively restored to renewed glory.

The monastery of St. Pere de Rodas (illus. pp. 82–5) is a key work of medieval architecture and sculpture, although no amount of research has yet been able to solve all the mysteries of its creation. Its foundation was apparently strategically motivated. A monastery stood on this spot as far back as the 8th century, thus possibly while the Arabs were still in occupation. The building we see was probably begun in the 9th century; the church was dedicated in 1022 and has close connections, not only due to its age, with St-Michel-de-Cuxa in the south of France. At 37 m (120 ft.), it is unusually long for its period. The three aisles of the lofty, barrel-vaulted nave are divided by cruciform columns on plinths which are strikingly high. The nave opens out into a broad transept with apses off to the sides. In the eastern part of the crossing a staircase leads down

*Benedictine monastery of St. Pere de Rodes; begun 9th century, dedicated 1022*

OPPOSITE:
*Benedictine monastery of St. Pere de Rodes*
*Columns in the nave*

to the circular crypt. Above this the chevet opens out with a two-story ambulatory without chapels. How this form came to Rodes is unknown, but we know it did not reach the rest of the region until much later. Equally puzzling is the design of the multiple columns which line the nave arcade (illus. opposite).

These columns are topped by magnificent capitals, decorated partially with trellis patterns and partially with acanthus leaves, motifs which may trace their origins back to the Caliphate art of Córdoba. If this is the case, it would represent extraordinary testimony to the artistic interchange between conquerors and conquered. In the walls

of the apse fragments can be seen of the *opus spiccatum*, masonry that is laid in a herringbone pattern.

More is known, and with greater precision, of the sculpture of the main portal, although unfortunately this can only be seen in replica here, for the originals grace the castle at Peralada and the Marés museum in Barcelona. The expressive capitals depicting lively figures with penetrating eyes are believed to be works by the "Master of Cabestany" (see panel box p. 84), whose work from the late 12th century can be found in Roussillon and throughout Catalonia/Aragón (illus. p. 84 left). He probably derived his inspiration from late Classical sarcophagi

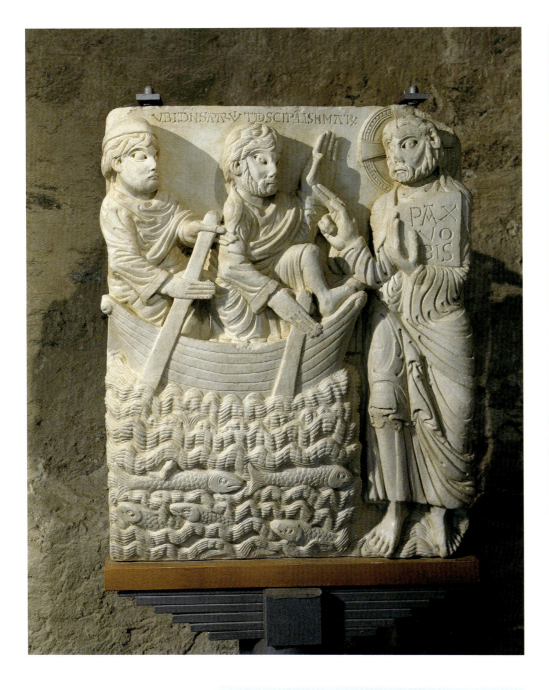

Benedictine monastery of St. Pere
de Rodes
The Master of Cabestany
Capital showing the appearance of
Christ before the Apostles Peter and
Andrew, late 12th century (cast;
original in the Museu Frederic
Marès in Barcelona)

RIGHT AND OPPOSITE:
Benedictine monastery of St. Pere
de Rodes
Main building, dedicated 1022.

**The Master of Cabestany**
The small town of Cabestany in the Rousillon region gave its
name to an outstanding sculptor, the "Master of Cabestany."
He is one of the few artists of the 12th century whose works can
be traced across different regions. In addition to the capitals to
be seen here at St. Pere de Rodes and the famous tympanum in
Cabestany (illus. p. 413, top), numerous works of excellent
quality have been attributed to him from northern Italy to
Navarra. Characteristic features of his work include flat faces
with protruding eyes and fingers, which are long in comparison
with the proportions of the body, dramatically emphasizing the
figures' gestures. The garments have classic fold motifs. Both
the composition and the technique, which involve making deep
undercuts with a stone drill, are strongly influenced by the late
Roman sarcophagus sculpture, which the Master would have
been able to study in Roussillon and Catalonia.

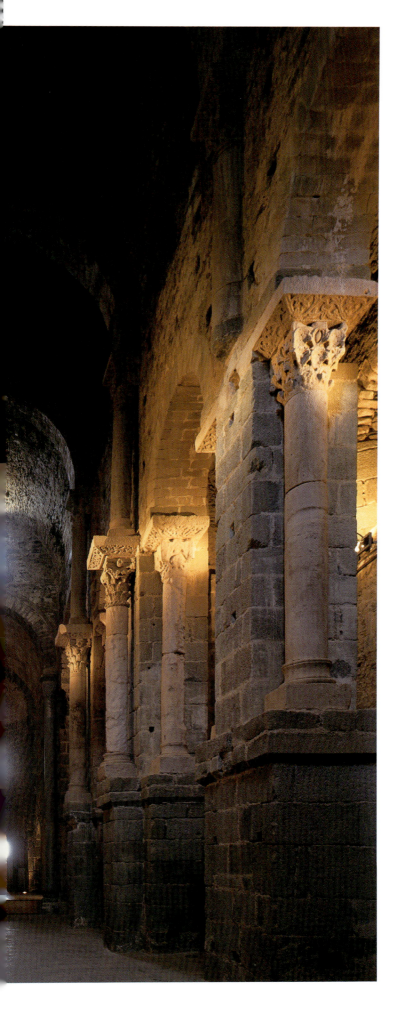

and their stone carvings. The cloister has little in the way of original sculpture, but it is nevertheless worth seeing for its cells, cellars, and the Abbot's palace. The Romanesque belfry stands proud with its elegant dual-panel windows in the upper story. This also dates from the 12th century, but has a relic from an earlier age incorporated into one of its capitals: a relief showing an old man and a siren. The former riches of the Benedictine abbey – now scattered among numerous museums all over the world – also include a famous four-volume Bible that is housed in the Bibliothèque Nationale in Paris, probably illuminated in the scriptorium of St. Pere de Rodes.

The wonderful view over the sea off Port de la Selva and across the peninsula of the Cap de Creus can be enjoyed at closer quarters by venturing out on the half-hour climb to the Castle of St. Salvador. From here the view extends over the Pyrenees to Mont Canigou in Roussillon, over the plains of the Empordà to the Gulf of Roses.

*Benedictine monastery of St. Pere de Rodes*
*Agnus Dei, cast of the façade sculpture*

## The Kingdom of Dalí and Gala

Returning from the seclusion of the mountains, we are faced with a new range of impressions. Following the winding road to Cadaqués we come across the surreal world of Salvador Dalí (see panel box left). His world is as secluded as the mountains that surround it, for the picturesque coastal village really opens up only to the sea. The few inland connections which lead here were only established in the 20th century.

The inhabitants once made their living from fishing and smuggling; in 1543 they themselves fell victim to pirates who laid waste to the port under the leadership of Cheireddin Barbarossa. Now the main source of income is from tourism, the varied night life, and numerous festivals, not to mention the all-pervading influence of Dalí that draws visitors from the four corners of the world.

Yet the natural sense of isolation can still be felt; gray-brown shale slopes surround the village overlooked by its little Baroque church, and where the houses huddle closely together across narrow alleys (illus. below). The silvery green of the olive trees and the opuntia contrast beautifully with the cheerful colors of the gardens at the edge of the village.

From the late 19th century the unique location of Cadaqués began to attract artists and thinkers. The Pitxot family of painters and musicians are said to have first "discovered" the place. They were followed by the protagonists of the modernistic movement, including Picasso, Ramon Casas, and Miquel Utrillo, along with the composers Isaac Granados and Isaac Albèniz and the guitarist Andréas Segovia. Dalí, whose family had property in Cadaqués, came to live in Port Lligat, approximately two kilometers (1.24 miles) to the north, at the end of the 1920s. Along with him, the elite of surrealism appeared on the scene, among them Paul Éluard with his wife Gala, (see panel box p. 87) who soon became the lifelong companion of the Catalan artist, André Breton, René Magritte, Federico García Lorca and Luis Buñuel. In the 1930s they were joined by Man Ray and Marcel Duchamps; they all stayed frequently and for extended periods in Cadaqués and Port Lligat.

Before turning to the Casa-Museu Salvador Dalí in Port Lligat, time should be taken to appreciate the treasures of Cadaqués itself, which are all too often overlooked. The pretty little church of Sta. Maria, rebuilt after the pirate attack, possesses an outstanding Baroque reredos, something so rarely found in Catalonia. Jacint Moretó and Pau Costa designed and made the lavishly gilded altarpiece, which portrays scenes from the life of Mary in a grand architectural frame. The Museu Perrot-Moore, housed in a former hotel, is dedicated to the graphic arts. It brings together major works by leading European artists

*The fishing port and artists' haven of Cadaqués*

### Dalí and Gala

Dalí's time in Paris in the late 1920s set the course for the development of his artistic and private life. Influenced by Sigmund Freud's psychoanalysis, he devoted himself to surrealist painting, and was soon introduced by his Catalan compatriot Joan Miró to the circle of Surrealists around André Breton. Here he got to know Gala (real name Elena Diakonova), then the wife of the French poet Paul Éluard. The radiance of this enchanting Russian with the magical look held

"thanks to an uncontrollable force and an unfathomable love, which surpass the most ambitious methods of psychoanalysis." In 1930 Dalí and Gala settled in Port Lligat, despite resistance from Dalí's family, and led a simple, secluded life, described by Dalí in his book My Secret Life. During this period he produced many of his works in which he developed his "dual perception" theory. In 1939 he portrayed Gala with two legs of lamb balanced on her shoulders, one of numerous

atomic bomb over Hiroshima generated in Dalí a deep crisis which led him to a new mysticism. With the help of this he intended to get to the bottom of "the hidden laws of things."
This change also affected his view of Gala: in 1949 he painted his beloved as "Leda atòmica," in 1950 as the "Madonna of Port Lligat."
A series of other "deifications" followed, up to the mutual apotheosis of the couple on the ceiling of the Palau del Vent (Palace of the Wind) in the Museum at Figueres (illus. p. 103).

the whole group in sway; from 1929 she became Dalí's lifelong lover and muse, a little later, he confessed his attraction with a Faustian laugh: "I love Gala more than my mother, more than my father, more than Picasso, more even than money." And: "The symptoms of my hysteria disappeared one after the other as if by magic and I was once again master of my smile, my laugh and my gestures." Throughout his life Dalí claimed that he had been "healed" by Gala,

paintings which dealt surrealistically with the "lust of the flesh." In the variations on Jean-François Millet's "Angelus" of 1859 (1935) Gala is once more seen interwoven into the artist's sexual obsessions.
After an eight-year exile in the USA, during which time he produced numerous pencil sketches and the captivating Galarina (1944/45), the couple returned to Port Lligat. The events of the Second World War did not pass unnoticed. Above all, the explosion of the

In 1958 Gala and Dalí married in secret in the Santuari dels Àngels near Púbol. In Púbol itself Dalí bought a late medieval castle which he presented to his wife in a solemn ceremony. Gala accepted the gift under one condition: Dalí could only visit her there if he had received a written invitation. This he must have done, for the pair lived together in Púbol until Gala's death in 1982. After this, Dalí did not leave the house until August 1984, when a fire burned down a part of the building.

Port Lligat
*The former fishermen's cottages, which Dalí and Gala transformed into their home from the 1930s onward*

OPPOSITE:
Port Lligat
*An egg on the roof of the Casa Dalí*

from the 15th century to the present day, including pieces by Dürer, Cranach, Rubens, Goya, Klee, and Chagall. A special section provides information on the unique aspects of graphic design and its different techniques.

A narrow road and an even more beautiful footpath across the craggy rocks lead to the picturesque harbor of Port Lligat, where Dalí and Gala, whose real name was Elena Diakanova, created their surrealistic universe (illus. left). From the beginning of the 1930s the eccentric pair bought up fishermen's cottages on the shore, and rebuilt them with inexhaustible fantasy. Almost completely cut off from the outside world, it was an embodiment of his passion and art, a life "in the light of eternity" (illus. pp. 90–91). Over the years the cottages, often no more than a few square meters each, were transformed into a luxurious complex of living and working space. With the help of the architect Emili Puignau the cubic dwellings, now painted white, "grew" up the slope, forming terraces and an internal courtyard. The final element, the swimming-pool, completed the picture in 1971.

All the rooms – furnished with an eye firmly on practicalities – combine to weave a spell formed from a love of art, nature, and the Mediterranean light. This light streams in through the large windows, their frames like picture-frames, to illuminate the whole house, and mirrors (some decorated in imitation of the paintings of the Dutch Masters) carry it to the farthest corners. Dalí lived through these mirrors; "the dandy should live and sleep in front of his mirror," as Baudelaire once said. Another recurring motif is his mustache; Dalí "collected" these male adornments, mainly in the form of photographs of famous people. He even favored the Mona Lisa herself with this characteristic attribute.

The rooms themselves, arranged on various levels and linked by short flights of steps, are practical in their interior design, although displaying all the surrealistic fantasy of their creators. Visitors are confronted by a lamp standard in the form of a white bear, while three swans, their necks craned, adorn the bookshelves in the library (illus. p. 90, top). The heart of the house is, of course, Dalí's huge studio, where he spent most of his time. Brushes, paint pots, and easel still evoke the presence of the great artist. Here, too, the emphasis is on the practical, as evidenced by the complex mechanism which Dalí used to hoist oversized canvases up and down. Through the intimate *Sala oval* access is ultimately gained to the couple's generously proportioned bedroom, dominated on the right by a monumental white fireplace (illus. p. 91, bottom right). A huge tiled border gives it a magical aura. The upper part of the complex comprises the peaceful inner courtyard and the idyllic gardens – fully screened from outside, and only overlooked by Dalí's dovecote with its oversized egg. Pop Art rules, springing numerous surprises. We stumble across a Michelin man, while, immediately adjacent is the swimming-pool, inspired by the Court of the Lions and Gardens of the Generalife in the Alhambra (p. 91, top right). They lived in this dream world until the death of Gala in June 1982 and Dalí's move back to Púbol.

ABOVE:
Port Lligat
Casa Dalí, library

RIGHT:
Port Lligat
Casa Dalí, summer dining-room
with winged rhinoceros

LEFT, MIDDLE:
Port Lligat
Casa Dalí, stairs to the studio

OPPOSITE TOP RIGHT:
Port Lligat
Casa Dalí, courtyard with
swimming pool

OPPOSITE BOTTOM RIGHT:
Port Lligat
Casa Dalí, bedroom

## Embattled Greek Towns:
## Roses and Empúries

A picturesque 5-km (3-mile) stretch of coast road leads on to Cap Creus, known to the Greeks in ancient times as Kap Aphrodision. The lighthouse is the starting-point for a footpath laid out in recent times to enjoy the wonderful views over the nearby coves.

Roses, on the other side of the Cape, also has a name of Greek origin. Colonists from the island of Rhodes were the first to settle here in 776 B.C., founding Rhoda, the oldest Catalan town (illus. above). The region around the 18-km (11-mile) wide bay – the Gulf of Roses – was at that time still permeated by lagoons and lakes. In recent times considerable finds of coins and ceramics have led to a full appreciation of the significance of this colony. Some of these treasures are in the archaeological museum in Girona; a museum is also under construction in Roses.

In the Middle Ages and the early modern period Roses was of primarily strategic importance. As defense against the Turks, Charles V had a massive citadel built in 1543, which was further extended under Philip II. The pentagonal fortification contained not only the military installations such as the arsenal, powder store, and barracks, but also the whole of the ancient and medieval settlement, including the hospital and the Romanesque monastery of St. Maria.

After withstanding the continual ebb and flow of history, the ramparts were finally blown up by the French in 1814. Fortunately, part of the Renaissance gate of the Porta del Mar was preserved. The Castell de la Trinitat was built just one year after the citadel to guard the harbor.

The Roses of today still makes its living from the sea; the afternoon landing of the catch draws buyers and spectators to the quayside from throughout the region.

Of course tourism also makes a huge contribution, and the long sandy beaches of the gulf are among the finest of the Costa Brava. Once a year the resort is transformed into a wild mayhem, when the carnival, one of the most magnificent in Catalonia, reigns supreme.

In terms of age, Roses rivals the historical Empúries, which once dominated the Gulf of Roses. Its historical name Emporion (meaning trading place) was an apt description, for the town was founded just after 600 B.C. in a strategic location on the former estuary of the Fluvià and at the intersection of several trade routes. The new Greek colony replaced a slightly older Phocacian settlement, an "offshoot" of Massilia (Marseille), which had been established on an islet (now landlocked) just

off the mainland. In the Middle Ages this *palaiapolis* was incorporated in the present-day St. Martí d'Empúries, a picturesque village with castle and late Gothic church. The *neapolis*, located on the "mainland" slightly to the south, developed into one of the most important ports of the western Mediterranean (now in the area covered by the present-day L'Escala administrative region).

Emporion achieved its greatest moment of fame when the Romans used the harbor as the starting point for their offensive against Carthage.

To give a brief resumé of this campaign, in the 6th century B.C. a bitter struggle arose between the Phoenicians, Greeks, and Carthaginians along the Iberian coast. After the decisive defeat of the Romans by the Carthaginians in the 1st Punic War (264–41 B.C.), when the Romans lost Sicily and Sardinia, the North Africans turned to what is now Spain and quickly penetrated as far as Castile. In the year 227 B.C. they founded Cartago Nova, today Cartagena, from where they controlled the profitable mineral workings and trade in ores. The appearance on the scene of the Romans, who were also interested in the treasures offered by the Iberian peninsula, quickly led to conflicts which escalated after the murder of Hasdrubal in 221 B.C. His son Hannibal

broke the Ebro treaty concluded with the Romans, and crossed the border into Roman territories, ultimately reaching Italy itself. Against this background, Gnaeus Scipio opened up a second front against the Carthaginians in 218 B.C. when he landed his troops at Emporion, and transformed the town into a Roman fortress. After the final victory in 201 B.C. the Iberian peninsula was taken by the Romans' who colonized it, more or less peacefully, over the next two centuries.

The inhabitants of Emporion initially put up a resistance, which the Roman commander Cato countered in 195 B.C. by establishing a 20-ha (50-acre) planned town. Now called Emporiae, it was substantially extended during the ensuing period to form a naval base. Finally, Caesar settled war veterans there in 45 B.C. Its golden age lasted until Caesar's time; thereafter the ancient town was abandoned, and fell prey to the plundering of Germanic and later Visigothic hosts.

In the 17th century, when the present-day regional administration center of L'Escala was founded, the venerable stones of Emporion were used as building materials. In 1992, Empúries received a kind of "reparation" for the humiliations it had suffered, when the Olympic flame was received within its walls.

*The Gulf of Roses at night*

ABOVE:
Empúries
Excavations (L'Escala district)

RIGHT:
Empúries
The walls of the Greek town with
statue of the god Asklepios, end of
the 4th century B.C.

OPPOSITE TOP:
Empúries
View across the excavation site

OPPOSITE BOTTOM:
Empúries
Portrait bust of a Roman lady,
3rd quarter of the 1st century
(replica; original in the Museu
Arqueològic de Barcelona)

The former size and beauty of the place can still be sensed despite the ruins. You do not have to be an archaeologist or historian to be entranced by the excavations which have been carried out here since 1907 (illus. opposite above, and pp. 96–97).

The incomparable location on the shore of the turquoise-blue sea, the picturesque walls between which pines and cypresses grow, the elegant floor mosaics and individual freestanding sculptures awaken romantic feelings. It is not easy to orient oneself among the streets and wall foundations, although the main axes of the original Roman plan can still be clearly discerned.

First, however, one crosses the Greek town which was enclosed by a Cyclopean wall. Immediately behind its single gate is a small square flanked by various temples. The Asklepios temple, reached by a flight of steps, was dedicated to the god of medicine; this is where the outstanding 3rd-century B.C. marble statue with the snake was found, the original of which is now housed in the Archaeological Museum in Barcelona. It is possible that the spouse of Asklepios, Hygieia, was also worshiped in the adjacent building. The cisterns that supplied the whole town with water are located – logically – close by.

There was another temple to take care of the health and well-being of the community – the huge temple to Zeus – a reconstruction of which can be marveled at in the Museu Monogràfic. Here, in a former monastery on the archaeological site, significant finds and models are on display, all of which help to bring the ancient Emporion/Emporiae to life for the visitor.

Outstanding pieces on display include the Greek mosaic showing the sacrifice of Iphigenia, which was clearly made in Athens or Antioch, and in situ there is an extremely lifelike bust of a Roman lady (illus. right), although it is a replica we see here.

Close to the museum is the agora, the broad main square of the Greek town. Around the edge was where the citizens used to stroll in the stoa or, several centuries later, worship in the Early Christian cella memoriae.

There is a clear break between the *neapolis* and the Roman colony. The classic aspects which differentiate Greek and Roman town planning can be seen from afar. While the Greeks built their towns in line with the contours of the land, and often established their settlements around the foot of an acropolis where the temples stood, the Romans preferred level sites where they laid their towns out in a characteristic grid pattern.

This was the case in Emporiae, where, as already suggested, a checkerboard system is easily discernible. Porticos and business premises surrounded the forum which stretched between the principal axes of the Roman town: the *cardo* and the *decumanus*. So far only a third of the colony has been excavated, the part where the temples and tavernas stood, where there was also an amphitheater and gymnasium for the physical exercise of the citizens. Their finer tastes are demonstrated by two luxurious villas, Casa 1 and Casa 2, each with atrium, peristylum, and wonderful ornamental mosaic floors (illus. left and below).

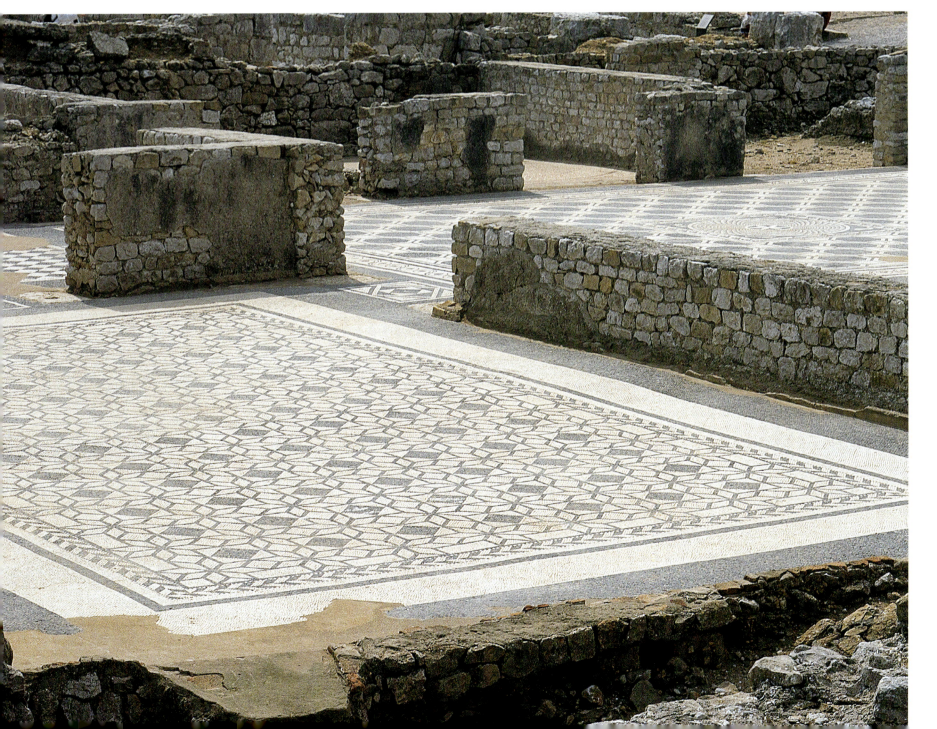

OPPOSITE:
Empúries
Mosaic floors from Roman villas
of the 1st–2nd centuries (Casa 1
top, Casa 2 bottom)

LEFT:
Empúries
View of the Roman town

At Castelló d'Empúries, c. 4 km (2.5 miles) from the sea, we are once again presented with some fine architecture dating from the Middle Ages.

The parish church of St. Maria – dubbed the "Cathedral of the Empordà" on account of its size – was begun in the early 14th century, and completed at the beginning of the 15th century by Antoni Antigó; it incorporates the belfry of an even earlier structure. The beautifully ornate portal, although with traces of 19th-century interference, leads to the vast interior, comparable in its dimensions to the church in Barcelona (illus. below). Another impressive feature is the flamboyant alabaster reredos of the high altar, carved by Vicens Borrás in 1485 with scenes from the life of Christ. There is also a central statue of Mary.

If you enjoy solitude and unspoiled nature, a visit to the nearby marshland of Aiguamolls is highly recommended (illus. opposite). These marshy lowlands, rich in animal and plant life, were designated a nature reserve in 1983, after large stretches of similar habitats along the coast were drained, and invaded by civilization. The protective measures have at least ensured that two areas to the north

and south of the Muga river have been preserved for the future. Since then, the area has been recolonized by flamingos and bee-eaters, otters, salamanders, and turtles.

The nature reserve is particularly popular with migratory birds of all kinds, which swarm here in spring and autumn, while waiting for the cold *Tramuntana* wind to abate. Then there are the salt-loving plants, such as rushes and broom, which are equally at home, as are reeds, mace, and other aquatic plants.

The Fluvià – the river which to a large extent forms the backbone of the Empordà plain – now leads either to the wonderful beach at St. Pere Pescador or, inland, to St. Miquel de Fluvià. This is where the Benedictine monks from the abbey at Cuixà settled. Nothing remains of their monastery but the church, yet this fortified building is still significant, above all for its original 11th-century capital sculptures. The aisled and galleried church, known to have been consecrated in 1066, has an extremely complicated history; this is reflected in the impressive belfry which features both Romanesque and Gothic elements.

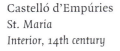

Castelló d'Empúries
*St. Maria*
*Interior, 14th century*

*Impressions of the nature reserve of Aiguamolls*

## Figueres, the Home of Genius!

The pretty capital of the Alt Empordà is famous for the fact that it bred two extraordinary characters in a short period of time. One was the eccentric artist Salvador Dalí. The other, known principally to Catalan schoolchildren and maritime engineers, Narcís Monturiol of Figueres (1819–85), who crossed the harbor of Barcelona in a wooden underwater vessel in 1859, thus developing the first Spanish submarine. His monument graces the lower end of La Rambla in the heart of the town (illus. below).

Perhaps it is the evocative atmosphere of the avenue lined with plane trees and houses from the turn of the 19th century, for the tingling feeling of an evening stroll here and an aperitif makes the imagination soar.

The earlier history of Figueres creates a similar picture to that of the majority of the region's towns. Archaeological finds have revealed Iberian origins and a Roman settlement called Juncaria. There is evidence of a Visigothic settlement known as Ficaris, to which the present-day name can probably be traced.

The town began to flourish in the Middle Ages, after it received its charter from King Jaume I in 1267, and was recognized as a Villa Reial. Soon thereafter Figueres was burnt to the ground by Hugo IV of Empùries, for whom the royal presence on the edge of his territory was an annoying thorn in his side.

Above all the town owes its growth and subsequent centuries of peaceful success to the Jews who, as was generally the case, settled together in the call. The extension of the fortress of St. Ferran between 1753 and 1766 brought military personnel and construction workers in great numbers and gave fresh impulse to Figueres. The mighty star-shaped castle, designed by Juan Martín Cermeño to the very latest specifications of the day, is the biggest fortress in Europe with an area of 32 ha (79 acres). More than 8,000 people and 500 horses could shelter in safety here for two years.

However, the castle was not fully effective in its function of providing defense against French attacks. On several occasions, most quickly during the Napoleonic campaign of 1808, it was overrun by enemy troops.

Tragic circumstances were also linked with the castle in the 20th century; in 1939 this was where the last Republican parliament met, thus elevating Figueres for one day to the seat of government of free Spain. Thereafter, the complex was used as a prison for many years. Consideration is being given to transforming it into a cultural center.

Figueres became known worldwide thanks to Dalí. One could say that the town is still a part of him. Salvador Dalí i Domènech was born in 1904 in Figueres, the son of a notary. He studied at the Madrid Academia de San Fernando from 1921 to 1926, where he came into contact with the movements of Post-Cubism and Futurism and with the Pittura Metafisica of the Italians Gino Servini and Giorgio Morandi. A deeper influence, came from his long friendship with the poet Federico García Lorca and the film director Luis Buñuel. After completing his studies, he went to Paris where – together with Juan González, Pablo Picasso, and Joan Miró – he met not only provincial figures, but also representatives of the international avant-garde. The charismatic André Breton awakened surrealistic instincts, which soon became the driving force of his life. At the end of the 1920s he created the works that made him famous: striking, beautifully executed, and meticulously painted pictures which appeared to transform the familiar into nightmare, and mercilessly presented passions as obsessions.

Salvador Dalí worked through his break with André Breton, the exclusion from the surrealist group, and ultimately the Spanish Civil War, in particular with the help of his interest in Sigmund Freud and his interpretation of dreams.

Although he refused to declare opposition to Franco's forces, Dalí and his wife Gala, left Europe and spent the years of the Civil War in the United States. In 1942 Dalí published his autobiography My Secret Life.

In 1948 the couple returned to Catalonia, and settled in Port Lligat. The works of the following years were thoroughly influenced by his conversion to Catholicism. Religious content and motifs from Renaissance painting, with which Dalí had become fascinated in the 1930s, now permeated the artist's dream worlds. Manifestos on subjects such as "nuclear mysticism" and "atomic art" reflect the nature of his thinking in the 1950s. Dalí and Gala retreated ever more into their own universe, yet not without ensuring their share of publicity. In 1974, on his

Figueres
*Monument to the submarine
inventor Narcís Monturiol*

OPPOSITE:
Figueres
*Teatre-Museu Dalí
Glass dome, based on designs by
Emilio Pérez Piñero, 1970*

70th birthday, the Dalí museum in Figueres opened its doors; after Gala's death in 1982 it became a second home to him. Dalí himself died on January 23, 1989 in the town where he was born.

Dalí's museum – the most frequently visited collection in Spain after the Prado in Madrid – is called the Teatre-Museu Dalí. The name does not refer entirely to the lifelike nature of the works of art on display there; rather to the building, built in the Historicist style by Josep Roca Bros in 1850, which was originally a theater. Burnt down in the Civil War, it was rebuilt for Dalí with the intention of using it as a museum. Little of the classical form remains; Dalí himself redesigned the building as a gigantic surrealistic installation. "Where, if not in my home town, could the most extravagant and most concrete aspects of my creation endure?" Thus the museum is a completely personal legacy of Dalí, which along with works from all the periods in his life, also includes appropriate works acquired by Dalí and Gala themselves from other artists they knew or admired.

These include the spellbindingly lifelike plaster group *La Cobla* by F. Anglès, representing the musicians of a *Sardana* orchestra, along with engravings by Piranesis, paintings by El Greco, Damià Forunys, and the Dutch "fine artist" Gerard Dou (1613–75), whom the Catalan artist admired beyond measure for his painting technique.

Dalí's hand, guided by an exuberant imagination, can be sensed everywhere. He himself called this creation process "Dalinization." From afar the huge eggs delicately poised atop the Galatea tower testify to the artist's sense of irony; the red façades of the adjacent walls are decorated with thousands of delicate cabbages (illus. left). The motif is taken from the Renaissance façade of the Casa de las Conchas in Salamanca, although here, instead of vegetables, the image is one of scallops suggesting the pilgrimage of the building's owner to Santiago. Dalí spent the last years of his life behind these walls; today it also houses the library associated with the museum. The stage area of the former theater has also been "Dalinized," crowned with a glass dome in 1970 by Emilio Pérez Piñero. Dalí found his last resting-place in this "Temple of Surrealism" (illus. previous page).

There is only room here to describe some of the more outstanding of the artist's innumerable paintings, which never fail to surprise. Upon visiting the museum, a deeper insight into the world of Dalí must be experienced. In order to weigh up the enormous breadth of his creativity, firstly two paintings from a similar period are compared: the *Soft self-portrait with grilled bacon* (1941, in the *Sala de les Peixateries*) and *Basket of bread* (1945, in what is called the Treasury), after the style of Baroque still-life painting, and executed with the finest brush-strokes. The first one, a surrealistic painting, reveals a disturbing insight into the psychological world of Dalí, while the second testifies to an apparently realistic world view.

Playing with perception in all its facets is one of Dalí's leitmotivs, found again in the grotesque ceiling painting in the Hall of the Palace of the Wind, where the soles of the feet of two foreshortened figures can be made out (1973, illus. right). The artist's immortalization of himself with his muse in a daring ascension scene is not without a touch of self-irony.

The museum's star has to be *Mae West*, whose features form a living-room layout (illus. below). The idea for this humorous installation arose in 1934–5, when Dalí retouched a portrait photograph of the actress in gouache, and developed this into the idea of a three-dimensional version of the work.

By 1936, no less than five "lip sofas" with bright red satin upholstery had come into being, although it was not until the early 1970s that Dalí found in the Barcelona architect and designer Òscar Tusquets a willing collaborator for the complete implementation of his ideas. Tusquets depicted the full lips of Mae West in the red *Saliva sofa* and constructed the "face room," while Dalí

formed the eyes from two pointillist pictures of Paris. The shining nose and the outsized wig framing the whole are also Dalí's inventions. Finally, it is left to the viewer to piece together the familiar two-dimensional image from this spatial set-piece.

We move on to the vast domed hall where Dalí rests under a simple gravestone. Death is also present in the pictures, for on the wall of the former stage area is a huge canvas backdrop showing the tragic *Metamorphosis of Narcissus*, a theme which also preoccupied Dalí in his literary work (illus. following page).

The moment at which the youth loses his human form is depicted mercilessly and with crystal clarity; a hole in his breast further emphasizes the resultant emptiness and lifelessness of death. The canvas (now a replica) was used in 1941 as a stage set for a ballet at the Metropolitan Opera in New York.

A glass wall divides the hall from the auditorium of the former theater. This is where the *Rain Cadillac* is on display, now considered to be another major work of Surrealism, but which once traveled the highways of the USA (illus. p. 105). The version shown here – with the Ernst Fuchs statue – is the fourth one; the first version, *El taxi plujós*, was exhibited at the International Surrealism Exhibition in Paris in 1938.

Of course the other works by Dalí in the smaller rooms and corridors are all worth attention. As well as the technical skills of the master and his inexhaustible imaginative fantasy, another aspect is the ironic commentary which many of these works give on artistic trends of past times.

The fact that Dalí was deeply rooted in Christian art can be felt everywhere. An incredible human closeness pervades the numerous, endlessly varying portraits which Dalí captured on canvas of his unique partner Gala.

OPPOSITE:
Figueres
*Teatre-Museu Dalí*
*Torre Galatea, 1983*

LEFT:
*Teatre-Museu Dalí*
*Mae West installation, 1974, in collaboration with Òscar Tusquets*

ABOVE:
Figueres
*Teatre-Museu Dalí*
*Hall of the Palace of the Wind, ceiling painting showing the Apotheosis of Dalí and Gala, 1973*

OPPOSITE:
Figueres
*Teatre-Museu Dalí*
*Stage set showing the*
*Metamorphosis of Narcissus*
*(original 1941)*

Figueres
*Teatre-Museu Dalí*
*El Cadillac plujós (Rain Cadillac)*
*installation with Ernst Fuchs*
*statue (after original version*
*of 1938)*

ABOVE:
Púbol castle
*Renovation of the late medieval castle 1970–71*

RIGHT:
Púbol castle
*Gardens with "Elephant"*

In Figueres there are some – albeit few – Dalí-free zones: for example the centrally located late Gothic church of St. Pere immediately adjacent to the museum or the Museu de l'Empordà on La Rambla with archaeological finds and contemporary art of the region. There is also the toy museum with puppet theaters, movies, and automata, for diversion of a different kind.

Those wishing to follow Dalí's trail farther, and who have already been to Port Lligat, could turn toward Púbol, a few kilometers to the south near La Pera. Dalí acquired the late medieval castle here, to give as a gift to his wife Gala in 1970 (illus. above). They fitted out the rooms of the property together in their own unique and surrealistic way, and stayed here frequently.

When Gala became seriously ill in 1982, Dalí had the "crypt" of the house converted to a tomb. On June 10 of that year Gala was buried in Púbol. Dalí lived here for two more years, until in August 1984 part of the castle went up in flames, and he was forced to return to Figueres.

As in Port Lligat, an animal watches over the entrance to the house; in this case, a stuffed white horse which Dalí had "presented" to his Muse in 1970; this spectacle took place on the fifth floor of the Ritz Hotel in Barcelona, where the couple were living at the time.

Knightly imagery is found elsewhere, for the imposing reception room on the first floor is Dalí's version of a medieval armory (illus. opposite bottom). The artist would receive journalists seated on a golden throne

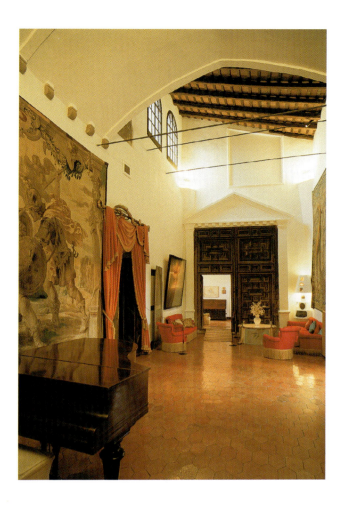

surrounded by blue drapery. On the ceiling is a bright painting which he created at the request of Gala, showing cosmic scenes and birds. It extends the room upward, as well as giving the visitor the impression of looking into a battlemented castle courtyard.

A painting on wood, showing Gala in the form of an angel, frames the door that leads to the couple's private quarters: the piano room (illus. left), the library, the bedroom, and the living-room.

All the rooms in the castle are decorated in delicate tones with the utmost flair. Dalí's works, including atmospheric surrealistic landscapes such as El camí de Púbol, adorn the walls.

On the second floor of the building is Gala's collection of *haute-couture* fashion, the "Gales de Gala." As well as her own designs, there is a wonderful display of creations from the most expensive fashion houses of the world, which the stylish Gala wore for her appearances in public.

However, it is not the interiors of Púbol which leave the most lasting impression, but the romantic gardens with their fairy-tale sculptures. Among the trees, one suddenly comes across four elephants tottering on stilt-like legs, made from Portland cement, and which can squirt water from their trunks (illus. opposite bottom).

Together with the *trompe-l'œil* patterns of the fountain decoration, they are reminiscent of the park of Bomarzo – the "Monster Park" – the enigmatic and exotic Mannerist sculpture gardens that can be seen north of Rome.

LEFT:
*Púbol castle*
*Piano room*

BELOW:
*Púbol castle*
*Throne room*

Peralada
*Castle, begun 13th century, rebuilt late 16th to late 19th centuries*
*Gardens, designed from 1877 by François Duviller*

## Around Figueres

On the edge of Figueres, between the arterial roads to La Jonquera and Port Bou, is the former Augustinian abbey of Vilabertran, around which a small hamlet has grown up.

The plain yet impressive aisled church with its three apses originates mainly from the 11th century, although the façade, the elegant belfry, and the intimate cloister with sparing architectural decoration, were all added in the 12th century.

The remains of the stately abbot's palace, built by Antoni Girgós between 1410 and 1424 in the Late Gothic style, suggest more worldly considerations. The outstanding piece among the church's decorative treasures is a golden processional cross, the Creu de Vilabertrán. It should also be mentioned that the abbey was the scene of a royal wedding in 1295, when the Aragonese King Jaume II married Blanca of Anjou.

Gambling, sampling fine wines and spirits, or culture: it is not easy to choose from the things when visiting Peralada, 6 km (c. 4 miles) to the north of Figueres. Its walls reflect the proud history of the place, known as Tolon in Classical times and also given the name *pagus* (meaning village) at the turn of the first millennium.

For a long time this was the residence of viscounts, firstly the Comtes d'Empúries and then the Vescomtes de Rocabertí, who were responsible for the medieval castle (illus. above). Contrary to its appearance, only a little of the original structure is preserved, for this picturesque castle was substantially altered, for the first time c. 1600 and then by French architects in the 19th century. The parks and the lake – which decoratively reflects the castle with its solid round towers – were designed by François Duvilliers in 1877.

Today the walls of the castle house the most popular casino in Catalonia, and in summer also hosts a music festival which draws musicians and audiences from all over the world.

The grand collections of the lords of the castle – which include significant examples of Baroque painting and Romanesque capitals from St. Pere de Rodes – are on display in the adjacent convents of Mare del Déu del Carme and St. Domènec (illus. opposite, bottom). The library of the Rocabertís, to which the present owner, Miquel Mateu, has added a few more priceless treasures, contains more than 50,000 volumes, including around 200 incunabula (illus. opposite, top and right).

There is also the elegant cloister in the Carme convent from the 14th century, and a collection of vintner's equipment and wine glasses.

In the town itself, palatial medieval and Baroque town houses recall the glories of its past. Peralada was home to the Catalan chronicler Ramon Muntaner (1265–1336), who recorded the Catalan forays into Asia Minor. He gave us the detailed description of the acts of Roger de Flors and the portrait of an age when Catalonia could be considered lord over part of the Aegean Sea.

ABOVE, AND OPPOSITE:
*The strange rock formations of the Illes Medes*

## A World under Water: The Illes Medes

The limestone rocks of the Serra de Montgrí comprise the boundary between the mountainous Alt Empordà and the region known as the Baix Empodà, formed from the Gulf of Roses and the flood plain of the Ter river.

As if to confirm the solidity of this natural boundary, the fort of Montgrí is perched on the ridge. It has been sweepingly restored, and is well worth the 45-minute climb to appreciate its sturdy ramparts and the wonderful views to be enjoyed from here over the coast – and on clear days as far as Canigou.

At the feet of the castle is the former residence of Torroella de Montgrí, within whose walls King John I often stayed; the Palau Reial is now a parador. Its heyday in the late Middle Ages is recalled by the beautiful church of St. Genis, an atmospheric setting for the concerts that take place here every summer as part of an international music festival.

The former fishing port of L'Estartit today makes its living from holidaymakers, who are captivated by the combination of sandy beaches and rocky coves. This is the starting point for excursions into the underwater world of the Illes Medes and for enchanting boat trips along the rugged coast.

The Illes Medes, less than 1 km ($^1/_2$ mile) off the mainland, are, geologically speaking, an extension of the Montagrí range into the sea. The seven outcrops, of which two are islands, have been designated nature reserves since 1990, and visiting is limited. They are a paradise for divers and nature-lovers, for the sheer limestone rocks have formed numerous clefts and caves which provide habitats for unique fauna and also some rare plant species. The strict control of visitors means a rich variety of herring gulls, shags, hoopoes, and cormorants, and certain mammal species accidentally introduced to the bare islands by humans.

However, the underwater world is even more colorful, with corals in numerous vivid colors forming miniature forests that are home to up to 600 different animal species. The algae, which have colonized those parts of the rocks to which the light penetrates, are also resplendent in a variety of shimmering shades. The grass-like *Posidonia oceanica*, which has colonized the sandy sea bed close to the coast, attracts a vast array of marine

wildlife, the smaller varieties providing prey for the carnivores. The deeper waters are home to cat sharks, angler fish, and various rare varieties of ray. There is a variety of the underwater caves, ideal hideouts for all kinds of shellfish, predatory fish, and perch.

Rigorous measures undertaken by the local government have enabled the conservation or survival of this biotope and its ecosystem. The uniqueness of nature was not always foremost; in earlier times it was the strategic location of the Medes islands which attracted attention, and from them pirates launched coastal raids. King Martí I established a monastery for the Knights of the Holy Sepulcher, which was burnt down by the Genoese in 1442 before falling into the sea during a landslide in 1552. In 1794 the French took possession of the islands, and subsequently the English who used them as a prison.

The lighthouse, with its small adjacent keeper's quarters, stands atop the Meda Gran. It was built in 1886 during the reign of Isabel II. A groundkeeper lived here until 1930, and was responsible for maintaining the signal alight. In 1932 the automatic lighthouse was built; from that time the islands have been uninhabited.

### Lluís Llach and the "Nova Cançó"

*Begun as a renewal of the Catalan folk song, the "Nova Cançó" (New Song) movement was transformed in the 1960s into a mouthpiece for the protest against the Franco regime. Groups such as "Els setze jutges" (The sixteen judges), the singers Raimon, Joan Manuel Serrat, and Pi de la Serra entered the public arena with songs in their forbidden mother tongue. In 1963, Raimon's Diguem no (Let us say no) broke the silence which had oppressed the Catalan people for decades. A little later Lluís Llach, born in Verges in 1948, wrote the song which became the "resistance hymn" of Catalonia: L'estaca (The Stake, 1968). It includes the lines:*

*"Siset, do you not see the stake to which we are all bound?*
*If we cannot release ourselves, we will never be free!*
*If we all pull together it will fall,*
*It cannot hold much longer,*
*It is already rotten."*

*The song about the hen which refused to lay (La gallineta, 1971), reflected a stance against the dictator. Neither arrests nor bans on public appearances could prevent the success of songs such as these. Through international appearances,*

The singer Lluís Llach in 1976

*the performers of the "Nova Cançó" made a significant contribution to publicizing the Catalan cause abroad. After Franco's death the subject-matter of Catalan songs changed, but their quality and popularity was undiminished. A younger generation of singer-songwriters has ensured that Catalan lyrics continue to be popular. They still fill stadiums and concert halls both in Catalonia and beyond.*

## 2,500 years of Living Culture: The Inland Region of the Baix Empordà

Now we move inland where a wealth of contrasting sights await in the area around La Bisbal: the bishop's town. La Bisbal itself is a mercurial little town, its daily life unfolding beneath the Voltes – the arcades – which has been famed for c. 500 years for its ceramics. Its past history as the seat of the bishops of Girona can be seen from the bishop's palace, begun in the Romanesque period and subsequently extended on numerous occasions. The town has a second treasure: the "Cobla Principa" – this is the most famous *Sardana* orchestra in all of Catalonia.

Verges, a few miles to the north of La Bisbal, draws hordes of visitors, especially on Maundy Thursday, the eve of Good Friday, when its narrow medieval streets are the scene of a grotesque dance of death. Skeletons with evilly grinning skulls form a bewildering parade behind the Easter procession (illus. above). Verges was the birthplace of two significant personalities who fought for Catalonia with all their heart and soul. They were Francesc Cambó, the founder of the Lliga Regionalista, and the singer Lluis Llach, who wrote the most beautiful songs for the anti-Franco "Nova Cançó" movement (see panel box, left).

However, the Catalan singing tradition was unheard of when the Iberians founded what is now known as Poblat Ibèric near Ullastret in the 6th century B.C. As shown by inscriptions in their language, the Iberian tribes who settled here were concerned for the defense of their town, and constructed an imposing wall of cut stone, fortified with both round and square towers. These walls and

towers guarded the settlement, of which the foundations and shaft-like cisterns of the houses can still be seen (illus. below).

The archaeological finds – many of them quite surprising – are on display in a museum that is housed in the chapel near the former acropolis.

There are also two temples nearby that were dedicated to heathen deities. The excavations that have been systematically undertaken since 1947 are far from complete, so there is still every chance of making new discoveries about the Iberian culture.

However, it is known that the inhabitants, who had a highly developed everyday culture, were in constant contact with the neighboring Greeks. It is thought that they probably remained in their settlement here until the 2nd century B.C.

Peratallada, a town which owes its name to a quarry, is only a few miles to the south of Ullastret. Despite extensive building activity in the 18th and 19th centuries, it is still one of the most picturesque medieval corners of Catalonia, and thus welcomes numerous visitors.

The former inhabitants built three defensive rings on the bare rock; these encircle the Romanesque castle, the palace of the local aristocratic Cruïlles family, and indeed the whole village with its narrow streets and alleys.

The parish church of St. Esteve stands outside these walls; the church is an unusual double-naved Romanesque building with two apses. It contains the tomb and coat-of-arms of the feudal lord Gilabert de Cruïlles who died in 1348.

The route to Pals – a pleasure in itself – passes the pre-Romanesque church of St. Julià de Boada, only of real interest to architectural specialists. Pals itself has numerous outstanding medieval monuments, which helps make it one of the most delightful places in the coastal region (illus. above).

Pals is majestically dominated by the *Torre de les Hores* (Tower of Hours) – all that remains of the castle which once guarded the plain around the estuary of the Daro river. The parish church of St. Pere interestingly conceals behind its Romanesque façade a thoroughly impressive late Gothic interior. In addition to the numerous historical sights, the museum of underwater archaeology is also well worth a visit.

OPPOSITE TOP:
*Dance of death on the eve of Good Friday in Verges*

ABOVE:
Pals
*View of the town with the "Tower of Hours"*

BELOW:
*The "Iberian village" near Ullastret with cisterns, 6th century B.C.*

## Pirate Hideouts and Merchants' Villas:
## The Coast between Pals and St. Feliu Guixols

A detour into the nearby marshlands that gave Pals its name (Latin *palus*: marsh) will be well rewarded. Rice paddies and sedge meads offer habitats for the numerous bird species that are attracted here.

A castle also dominates the village of Begur which – just a few miles from the sea – is one of the focal points of the central Costa Brava. This was clearly also the case in the Middle Ages, as Begur appears to have been visited with alarming frequency by pirates and corsairs. At least this is what the observer is led to surmise from the numerous remaining watchtowers of the castle ruins. This was clearly no longer a problem in the 19th century, when the merchants who had made their fortunes in South America – the Indianos – built their villas in the "Colonial" style (illus. right and below).

There are several small holiday resorts in the vicinity of Begur (Sa Riera, Sa Tuna, Fornells, and Aiguablava), which have largely been spared the ravages of mass tourism. Time may not have stood still here, but nevertheless the beauty of the coast in this area is relatively unspoiled. Where the sharply eroded cliffs of the Gavarres range fall steeply into the crystal-clear sea, a number of idyllic coves have formed, which only allow limited space for development. The green of the pine forests forms a delightful contrast to the soft "apricot" color of the stone and the irresistible turquoise blue of the water.

A fine description of this landscape was given by the writer Josep Pla (1897–1981; see panel opposite), who came from Palafrugell, the region's commercial center. The house where he was born stands on the Carrer del

TOP:
Begur
*Villa of an "Indiano"*

RIGHT:
Begur
*Gallery of an "Indiano" villa*

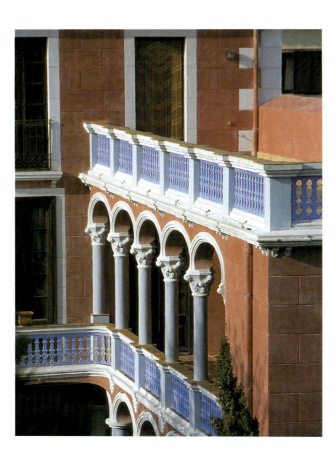

Progrés (now called Carrer Nou); he spent the majority of his life in Llofriu to the north-west of the town (illus. opposite, top right).

Palafrugell itself is a town of trade and industry, which devoted itself to the production of corks for wines and spirits around the turn of the 19th century. The raw material was cultivated in the surrounding cork oak woods and, after processing, found its way into the necks of the bottles in almost all Catalonia's wine cellars.

A small museum, the Museu del Suro, explains all the facets of the harvesting and processing of this valuable raw material. In line with the town's history, Palafrugell's most interesting buildings also date from the turn of the century, when factory owners and merchants settled here.

In more recent times Palafrugell has relied on tourism, with visitors flocking to the former fishing villages of Tamariu, Llafranc, and Aigua Xel-lida. The main attractions include the "Cantada d'Havaneres" festival, held annually in July in Calella de Palafrugell; this is a celebration of sea shanties sung in the traditional Cuban Habanera style.

Two excursions, to the rocky promontories of Cap St. Sebastiá and Cap Roig, enable us to enjoy scenes of incomparable natural beauty. The small chapel of St. Sebastiá gave its name to the lighthouse and the rocks which drop a sheer 150 m (490 ft.) into the sea, with Cap

### Josep Pla

Josep Pla i Casadevall is considered the greatest Catalan writer of poetic prose of the 20th century. His life's work consists of 46 novels and travel diaries, predominantly in the Catalan language.

He was born in Palafrugell in 1897, the son of a farmer, and worked from 1918 as a correspondent for well-known periodicals in Catalonia, from 1919 traveling to France, Germany, the Soviet Union, and America. In 1925 he published his first literary travelogue, **Coses Vistes**. Further journals, stories, and biographies followed almost annually, demonstrating his gift for subtle observation. His authentic descriptions of countries and people often formed the background for novels. Known to have a quick temper, Pla's impressions and perceptions, above all relating to nature, nevertheless are particularly subtle and delightful to read.

After a substantial period spent abroad, Pla finally settled in Palafrugell in 1939. In the ensuing years he published works in Castilian, such as the 1941 **Guia de la Costa Brava**, which to this day is still a fascinating travel essay on the region. From 1947 he returned to his mother tongue, and enjoyed his greatest success with works such as **Cadaqués** (1947),

*Josep Pla in his house in Palafrugell*

**Un senyor de Barcelona** and **El carrer estret** (both 1951).

Although Pla never openly opposed the Franco regime, his works relating to Catalonia contributed considerably to the country's self-discovery. In 1966 the Edicions Destino began publication of his collected works.

Pla died on April 23, 1981 in Llofriu.

**ABOVE LEFT:**
*Cap Roig*
*Botanical gardens with*
*Mediterranean plants*

**LEFT:**
*Cap Roig*
*Botanical gardens*
*Flower beds in front of the*
*neo-Gothic castle*

The Cova d'en Daina near
Romanyà
Megalithic dolmen

Roig, the "red cape" offering similarly beautiful views. At its tip, there is a fascinating castle to visit.

In 1927 the Tsarist colonel Nicolas Weovowsky and his wife Dorothy Webster built a neo-Gothic castle standing in unique botanical gardens (illus. previous page, top left and bottom), which offer amazing views over the cliffs. A spirit of romance is awakened by the wonderful combination of the architecture and untamed nature.

The nearby Palamós was declared a "royal port" in 1279 by order of Pere el Gran. Toward the end of the 15th century, it was elevated to the status of residence of the noble Requesens family, but suffered devastating onslaughts from Turkish pirates, the most destructive being in 1543 under the leadership of Barba-roja. Like Palafrugell and Begur it flourished at the turn of the 19th century due to two things: the cork industry and the return of the Indianos.

The medieval town center is dominated by the late Gothic parish church of St. Maria del Mar; there are also wonderful views to be seen over the nearby bay from the Plaça Murada. From Palamos you can explore the extensive beaches, popular with tourists, of Platja d'Aro and S'Agaro.

Or you can return inland where you will find the pretty, traditional villages of Calonge and Romanyà de la Selva. A little outside Romanyà stands the most impressive Stone Age monument in Catalonia; it is the Cova d'en Daina (illus. above). This megalithic dolmen with galleried tomb is believed to be almost 3,000 years old; thus, the oldest testimony of cultural history on Catalan soil.

Leaving the Serra de les Gavarre and returning to the coast, we come – as did the Benedictines in the 10th century – to St. Feliu de Guixols. Here, the Order dedicated a mighty monastery to St. Felix, who is believed to have been drowned in the Mediterranean nearby. Little remains of the medieval complex which once rivaled St. Pere de Rodes. The gates date from the Baroque period; they are predated by the two towers known as Fum and Corn and by the 14th-century parish church.

The unique and historically significant Porta Ferra, with its stilted arches, probably dates from the pre-Romanesque period (illus. opposite). Despite – or perhaps because of – the fate of its patron saint, St. Feliu de Guixols has developed into a lively resort with numerous tourist attractions on offer.

An essential contribution is provided by the picturesque Nou Casino de la Constància, which was built in the neo-Arabic style.

St. Feliu de Guixols
*General view (above) and detail
(bottom), 11th/12th century*

Tossa de Mar

## Treasures among the High-rise hotels

An enchantingly beautiful coast road with breathtaking views over the steep cliffs and blue sea now leads to Tossa de Mar. Fortunately nature itself has prevented this stretch of coastline from being concreted over.

Tossa has a delightful old town, completely ringed around by walls with sturdy round towers (illus. above). Its picturesque alleys and steep steps have attracted artists from the beginning of the 20th century – inspired by the medieval atmosphere. Their work can be admired in the Museu Municipal, housed in the former governor's palace; among them are some works by Marc Chagall.

On the western edge of the town, in Ametllers, Adolf Schulten excavated the Roman villa of Tossa (2nd–4th centuries), from which some mosaics and the inscription "Salvo Vitale Felix Turissa" are preserved. The pretty promenade, lined with modern sculptures, stretches off to the north.

Lloret de Mar opens up to the sea across an imposing palm-lined avenue and a broad sandy beach (illus. opposite bottom). The town also contains a number of neo-classical and Historicist buildings.

A classic example of the imagination of modern architects is the sacrament chapel of the parish church of

St. Romà, where Bonaventura Conill decorated the roofs of the cupola and towers with brilliantly colored ceramic tiles (illus. opposite top).

However, without doubt the main attraction is the bronze sculpture of the Dona Marina; if you touch her foot while looking out to sea your wish will be granted.

The wishes of garden-lovers will be fulfilled in any case by visiting the nearby Parc de St. Clotilde (illus. p. 120). The steep slopes of the coastal cliff were tamed in the 1920s to form a Mediterranean Garden of Eden by the Marquis de Roviralta, the architect Domingo Carles, and his wife Maria Llimona.

Terraces, steps, and paths are framed by the emerald green of the cypresses, pines, and conifers, while statues line the way to cascades and fountains adorned with sirens and seashells.

On the way to Blanes we pass the pilgrims' chapel of St. Cristina, which is the destination of a pilgrimage on July 24 each year involving a procession carrying the saint's skull, "Sa Relíquia." A pilgrimage of a more worldly kind, although equally uplifting, is in the form of a boat trip along the magnificent coast.

Blanes, which tourism has made into the biggest town on the Costa Brava, originated from the Roman military

Above:
Lloret de Mar
St. Romà
*Cupola with Modernist tile
decoration*

Left:
*The beach of Lloret de Mar*

base of Blanda. The oldest building now, however, is the castle of St. Joan from the 11th century. The old town is crowned by the late Gothic church of St. Maria.

Plant lovers should not miss the botanical gardens of Mar i Mitra, laid out in 1921 by the German merchant Karl Faust, working together with the Catalan botanist Pius Font i Quer (illus. p. 122). A former vineyard, the grounds are now home to thousands of different plants from all the corners of the globe, with the additional romantic touches of a circular temple and plaques with quotes from Goethe. These trimmings aside, the views across the elysian landscape are simply breathtaking. Shortly beyond Blanes, near the mouth of the Tordera river, the landscape changes. The rocky coast softens, running into the long sandy beaches of the Maresme, part of the Costa Daurada.

In Malgrat de Mar we now join the busy N 11 coast road, which leads to the tourist centers of Pineda de Mar, Calella, Canet de Mar, and Arenys de Mar. These places have retained one or two architectural jewels, such as the castle of St. Florentina near Canet de Mar. This castle, dating from the 14th century, was extended and rebuilt at the beginning of the 20th century by Lluís Domènech i Montaner, and has the effect of a fairytale castle (illus. p. 123, right). The town itself still preserves a surprising

number of Modernist buildings, increasingly over-shadowed by apartment blocks. Although the proportion of Catalans in the population is hardly able to match that of British and German visitors, nevertheless there is a great effort to keep local culture alive, with Calella holding a *Sardana* competition every June, and Canet considered the stronghold of the "Nova Cançó."

Only the industrial town of Mataró now separates us from Barcelona. The first railway on the Iberian peninsula leads from here to Barcelona. If you want to avoid the traffic jams of the coast road or the motorway, it is worth making a detour through the nearby mountain country which awaits with some spectacular scenery and some architectural gems.

From Blanes you pass through Tordera to Hostalric, defended by its huge town walls and eight cylindrical towers. These have been constantly asked to prove their strength over the years, as the strategically-important town has been the scene of numerous conflicts.

We then come to St. Celoni, the starting point for walking in the Montseny and Montnegre nature reserves. The parish church at St. Celoni has a unique Baroque

façade which is covered with inscriptions (1762). From here it is possible to visit the Renaissance palace of El Castellnou in Llinars del Vallès, and complete the tour in good style at Argentona. The earliest reference to this town was in 878, although it was at the beginning of the 20th century that the wealthy inhabitants of Barcelona came here in search of relaxation, and built their fine villas. These include two houses by Josep Puig i Cadafalch, "Can Cabanyes" and "El Cros." The Museu del Càntir is also worth a visit; it includes a display of more than 1,400 wine pitchers.

# Barcelona

City of Marvels

The Catalan metropolis has been called "The City of Marvels" by significant writers in recent times. In 1989 the Spanish author Eduardo Mendoza gave this title to his historical novel based on the International Exhibition of 1888; in 1992 the Australian Robert Hughes touched on the sobriquet in his fascinating cultural history, *Barcelona*. What linked both authors – each starting from a very different premise – is a sense of wonder at a city which formulated its dreams and made them come true, a city in which tradition and the avant-garde, commerce, and creativity unite to form a harmonious whole.

The pleasure of contrast applies particularly to life in Barcelona. Strolling through the narrow alleys of the *Barri Gòtic*, the "Gothic Quarter," one finds that its venerable walls now house stylish galleries side by side with gaudy fashion boutiques and tempting delicatessens, not to mention the numerous restaurants and bars, some with classic interiors, some exuberantly extravagant – all providing sustenance not only for the eyes. At every step one encounters modern art and contemporary design blending exquisitely with the historical surroundings.

In the *Eixample* – the 19th-century grid-plan new town where clients and architects once vied to build the most magnificent and original façades – it is now the shop windows with their sumptuous Art Nouveau surrounds that compete to offer the most luxurious and striking displays. The beach at Barcelona, where Don Quixote fell ignominiously from his horse, is lined by a colorful promenade offering a wide variety of pleasures. It can safely be said that the people of Barcelona work hard, but play all the harder. There is good reason for this. Barcelona – neglected and left to degenerate under the decades of Franco's dictatorship – has, since his death, risen like a phoenix from the ashes.

Wonders of this kind are not new to Barcelona, as the city has fully experienced all the highs and lows of history. The proud residence of the Catalan-Aragonese kings was "demoted" to the status of secondary residence after the unification of Castile and Aragon. Its fleet, which once crossed the whole of the Mediterranean, was considered second class from the 16th century, as the caravels that sailed to the New World left from Seville. In the confusion of the War of the Spanish Succession, Barcelona, often on the losing (Habsburg) side, suffered the presence of the Bourbon stronghold until the 19th century.

PP. 124–5:
*Detail of the façade of the Casa Batlló, built 1904–07 by Antoni Gaudí*

LEFT:
*View from the Collserola Massif across the Eixample, the extension to the city built in the 19th century*

The tables turned with the advent of industrialization, as the self-assured Barcelona bourgeoisie formulated the *Renaixença*, the "rebirth," of Catalan culture. With his *Oda a la Pàtria* (Ode to the Fatherland), the writer Bonaventura Aribau set off an avalanche which first swept through cultural circles, and later involved the whole population. The awareness of their status as a strong trading power was reawakened, for citizens had drawn up their own code of laws as far back as the 11th century.

As Barcelona succeeded in the mid-19th century in freeing itself from its city walls and thus from the hated oppression from Madrid, an incredible creativity was unleashed, which made a decisive mark on the appearance of the city. Ildefons Cerdà designed the *Eixample*, the extension of the city, on progressive, egalitarian principles (illus. pp. 126–7, 200–01, 203). Lluís Domènech i Montaner and Josep Puig i Cadafalch, both architects and politicians, searched for a modern architecture for the Catalan nation – and Gaudí found it (illus. opposite and right). The International Exhibition of 1888 turned out to be the manifesto of Modernisme, the Catalan Art Nouveau. Literature, theater, and textiles captured the attention of almost every citizen as, indeed, they do today. Attitudes were cosmopolitan. Barcelona was the most important Wagnerian city after Bayreuth, while Picasso and his artist friends brought a touch of Parisian chic to the city beside the Mediterranean.

The loss of the Spanish colonies in 1898 and the associated socio-economic consequences led to a wave of strikes and anarchy. These culminated in 1909 in the *Setmana Tràgica*, the "tragic week," when around 80 churches, monasteries, and ecclesiastical establishments went up in flames (illus. p. 130). The clergy had sided with the military and thus against the proletariat.

The establishment of the *Mancomunitat*, the unification of the four Catalan provincial authorities from 1913 further strengthened feelings of regional separatism. This was primarily manifested in the development of the education system.

Once again the idea arose of emphasizing the cosmopolitan character of Barcelona in an international exhibition. The dictator Miguel Primo de Riveras (1923–30) changed the plans, however, so that it was a conservative affair with a thoroughly Spanish feel which opened on the Montjuïc in 1929.

The dictator was only able to bring the waves of anarchy to a superficial halt. Progressive forces drew ever tighter together to implement the self-determination of the region after the fall of Primo de Riveras. In 1931 Francesc

Opposite and right:
*Antoni Gaudí:*
*Tower pinnacles (opposite) and tower detail (right) on the*
*Sagrada Família, unfinished (foundation stone laid 1882,*
*definitive project 1906)*

Macià proclaimed the autonomous region of Catalonia from the balcony of the Generalitat (illus. p. 131, top).

The advent of the Second Republic unleashed a variety of disparate forces, which came to the forefront in the artistic and literary avant-garde and in social Utopias. One group of young architects set themselves the objective of creating a "functional" town in the style of Le Corbusier.

Social reforms and avant-garde tendencies came to an abrupt end, however, with the outbreak of the Civil War in 1936. Barcelona became a center of the resistance against Franco. The forces which had joined together to form the Popular Front alliance, the anarchists, the socialists, and the Communists, resisted the Fascist troops until the beginning of 1939, but on January 26 Barcelona fell (illus. p. 131, bottom).

With the proclamation of the "New Spanish State" all special rights the region had enjoyed were lifted. Everything Catalan, including the use of the Catalan language, was considered to be separatism, and was cruelly punished. The Franco regime believed that Catalonia was a conquered enemy region, whose resistance must be broken at all cost. More than 10,000 people lost their lives as a result.

Franco's death in 1975 was like the end of a long, grim night. Hardly had the news broken when the streets were filled with people, the forbidden Catalan flag was raised everywhere, and the *Cava*, the wonderful Catalan spirit, sold out. Things quickly returned to how they had been; the media published in Catalan, and preparations were begun for free elections and the drawing up of a

statute for autonomy. The high point of this activity was the demonstration on December 11, 1977, when several million people demonstrated peacefully for the amnesty of political prisoners and the autonomy of Catalonia (illus. p. 207).

The Barcelona of today seems light years away from these events; an avant-garde urban building program, the courage of the planners, and the pragmatic openness of the citizens – the famed Catalan *seny* – have helped the wounds to heal. The communal efforts were crowned by the location and successful staging of the Olympic Games here in 1992.

The courage to dream has once more awakened powerful creative forces, which will ensure that the "marvels" of Barcelona can become reality.

ABOVE:
*View of the skyscrapers in the Olympic Village, to the left the Hotel Arts by SOM, to the right the Edifici MAPFRE by Iñigo Ortiz/Enrique León, 1992*

OPPOSITE:
*Frank Gehry
Peix (Fish), 1992
Installation, seen from the Hotel de les Arts in the Olympic Village*

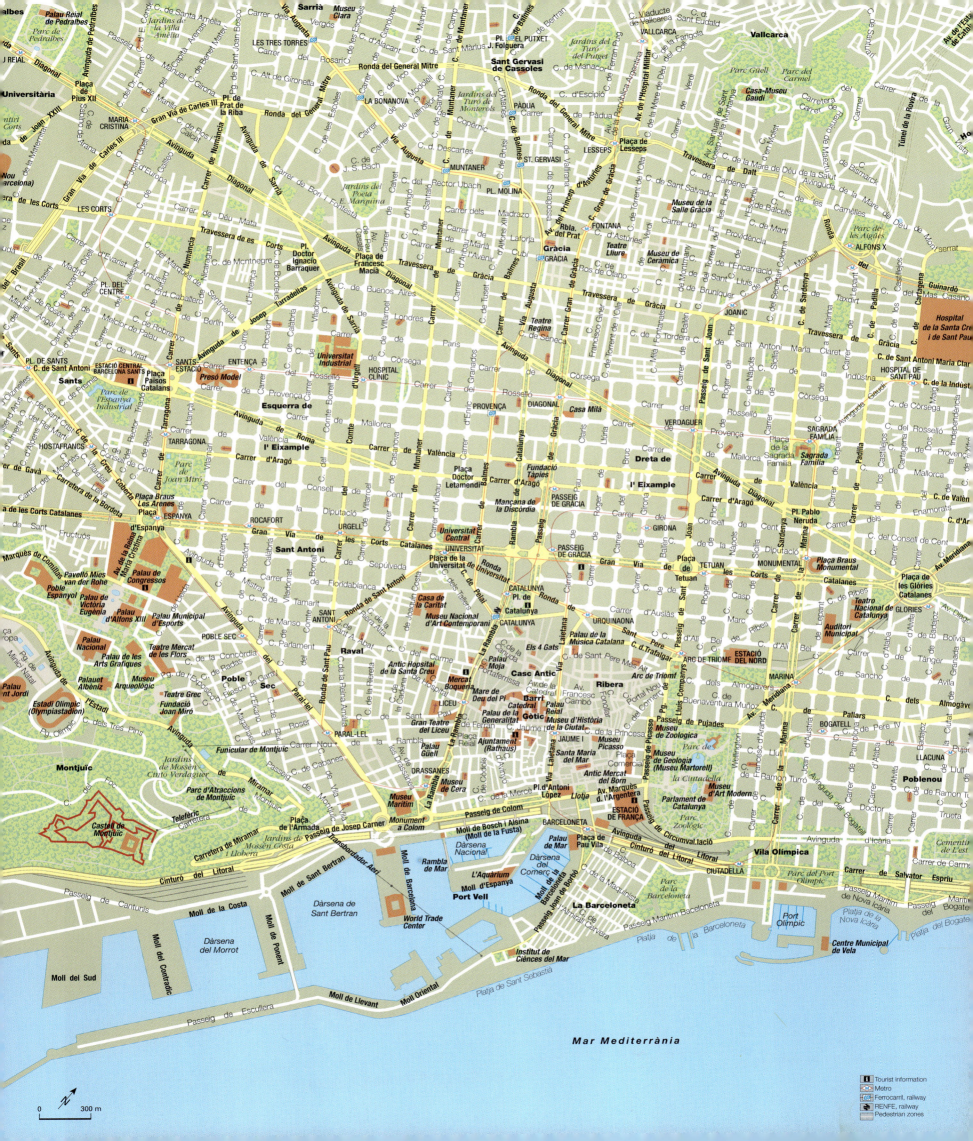

# A History Lesson in *Barri Gòtic*

The "Gothic Quarter," or *Barri Gòtic*, to the east of La Rambla – main thoroughfare – in the medieval heart of the city of Barcelona, is somewhat confusingly named. For, anyone who strolls between the protective walls to discover the tremendous royal palaces, to admire the cathedral – dominating everything – and to see its equally impressive rival, the parish church of St. Maria del Mar, can easily imagine themselves to be in a gigantic and living open-air museum. Narrow alleys wind like ravines through the historic residential area, only intruded on by impressive "palaces" of the community and aristocracy in the few wider streets and squares.

One is confronted by the evidence of more than 2,000 years of history, yet this scene – probably unique – is anything but museum-like: its vitality is most apparent everywhere, for it has been given a new lease of life.

Young life pulsates in this picturesque quarter because new occupants have moved within the venerable walls. Now, famous galleries and leading cultural activities, elegant businesses and hip junk shops, and traditional and ultra-cool bars all benefit from the charm of the historical buildings vibrantly to combine tasteful antiquity with experimental modernity. This has given the Gothic Quarter its original atmosphere, and visitors come from all over the world to experience such timeless appeal.

This lively quarter seemed doomed until a little over 25 years ago. In the late 19th century the up-and-coming bourgeoisie of Barcelona found the old town too cramped and unhealthy; at that time the town hall was moved to the new district of Ildefons Cerdà, with its reassuringly regular layout. The result was the insidious downfall of the historical center, which eventually became populated by those who were the weakest in society and by fringe groups. Around the early 1960s it was clear that steps were needed against the widespread drugs-related crime that by then dominated the Gothic Quarter.

After 1975 the Gothic Quarter rose like a phoenix from the ashes. For, immediately following the death of Franco, the mayor Narcís Serra and architect Oriol Bohígas set in action a comprehensive town renewal program aimed at rehabilitation, helped by careful intervention. The revival of the center to what is the marvel of Barcelona today was due to this initiative (illus. pp. 138–9).

As far as the Gothic Quarter is concerned, the revival is completed, but work continues at the time of the Millennium in Raval in the western part of La Rambla. Complete restructuring here includes the building of a museum of contemporary art and center for contemporary culture, and the extension of the university. Inevitably, hand in hand with such improvements, parts of the old Barcelona have been lost forever.

Barcelona derives its name from two sources: the Carthaginians and the military leader Hamilkar Barkas. No one really knows from exactly when the original settlement dates; however, it is certain that the Romans conquered the Iberian coast during the 2nd Punic War, and founded the first settlement in the region between the mouths of the rivers Llobregat and Besòs. This colony bore the proud name *Favencia Julia Augusta Paterna Barcino*, forming part of the province of Hispania Citerior, with its

OPPOSITE:
*Young and old together dance the Sardana – Barcelona's enchanting circle dance – in front of the cathedral.*

BELOW:
*Installation* Barcelona *next to the Porta Nova*

capital Tarraco, present-day Tarragona. Around 15 B.C., the soldiers established a *castrum* on the modest heights of Mount Taber; the forum of this extended to the site of the present-day Plaça de St. Jaume, and the main alignment corresponds with today's streets Carrer Ferran and Llibreteria (*cardo*), and also Carrer Bisbe Irurita and Ciutat (*decumanus*).

It has been established that the construction was probably somewhat later. The encircling walls, built of massive blocks of stone – and still defining the outline of the town – were added c. A.D. 263 (illus. p. 140, bottom). Until the 13th century, this 1270-m (c. 1,400-yd.) long, 9-m (c. 30-ft.) high, and 3.56-m (c. 11.5-ft.) wide fortified ring defended the town.

Later, when construction of a second ring began, dwellings were built within the Roman walls. These are

ABOVE AND OPPOSITE:
*The Plaça Reial is the meeting place of the old town once more following re-modelling in the "Espais Urbans" (city space) program of 1985*

impressive on the Porta Nova with their massive towers that can be seen from both the Plaça Berenguer el Gran and along the Carrer Sotstinent Navarro.

Further evidence of Roman times is found in the extensive basement of the Museu d'Historia de la Ciutat, where visitors can stroll through the excavations (illus. p. 141, top). Four columns with Corinthian capitals, possibly dedicated to Caesar Augustus, are displayed in the building of the Centre Excursionista in the Carrer Paradis.

In the early Middle Ages, the town went through turbulent times. After the incursion of the Alans, the year 415 saw the arrival of the Visigoths who governed the territory for three centuries, and sometimes lived in Barcelona. In 718–19, the Moors took possession of Catalonia, after having initially been summonded to resolve a dispute over the throne.

The Franks under Ludwig the Pious conquered Barcelona for Christendom once again in 801. He founded the Frankish Marches as a bulwark against the "might of Islam," and created a number of earldoms that came under the control of Barcelona.

The desire for independence from the Carolingian empire first surfaced under Borrell II (950–92). Disappointed by the lack of support against the incursion of the Almansors, Borrell refused in 985 to grant the feudal lords greater allegiance.

When Ramon Berenguer IV freed Petronella, the female Aragonese successor to the throne, in 1137, the rapid rise of the Catalans was assured. The earldom of Catalonia was then united with the crown of Aragon and Barcelona rose in importance to become a place of royal residence.

The succeeding kings, especially Jaume I el Conqueridor (Jacob the Conqueror, 1213–76), Pere II el Gran (Peter the Great, 1276–85), and Pere II el Cerimoniós (Peter the Ceremonious, 1336–87), succeeded in bringing almost the entire coastal areas of the western Mediterranean and also parts of Greece and Asia Minor under Catalan-Aragonese control. Trade expanded and science and the arts also flourished.

Barcelona, capital of the realm, blossomed significantly. Building on a large scale quickly created a unified town plan and a density of fine buildings unequaled at the time. Most of these monuments were erected within about a hundred years, between the late 13th and late 14th centuries. It is, therefore, valid to speak of the "Gothic Quarter," although other eras have also left significant impressions.

In the late Middle Ages the most pressing matter was the construction of a new wall to enclose the suburb and parishes of St. Pere and St. Maria. These had expanded to the area north of La Rambla. The Visigoth royal palace was of course also enlarged and modernized, and the Romanesque cathedral acquired Gothic form. Both parish churches of St. Maria del Mar and St. Maria del Pi were erected with the greatest of architectural aspirations, ensuring that late Catalan Gothic was world class.

In addition, so many churches, cloisters, and hospitals came into being that Peter the Ceremonious banned the building of new churches and monasteries.

Because community institutions, the regional parliament, and the Casa de la Ciutat (town hall) were all decisive influences on the great trading city, these institutions moved to buildings of appropriate stature located on the Plaça de St. Jaume.

With the construction of the *Drassanes* or shipyard one of the most impressive utilitarian buildings of the entire Mediterranean region came into being in Barcelona around the end of the 14th century (illus. opposite bottom). This is now the Maritime Museum. The *Llotja* or exchange and the Consol de Mar (consulate of the sea) housed the administration of the Catalan-Aragonese trading league. Both the nobility and leading citizens built their grand houses in the nearby quarter of Barri St. Maria, the most impressive example of which can still be seen from the street today in the Carrer de Montcada.

Toward the end of the 15th century, two events brought an end to Barcelona's prosperity. The first was the marriage of Ferran II to Isabel of Castile, which resulted in the Catalan capital being downgraded to a secondary royal residence.

The second occurrence – the discovery of the Americas – was of far more enduring influence on Barcelona and the country. Now, a more modern port, one facing the Atlantic, was required for trade with the New World. The meteoric rise of Seville was the result.

The Gothic Quarter of Barcelona, on the other hand, was condemned to slumber for the coming epochs. Firstly, in the 18th and then the 19th centuries, definitive plans were made to modernize the lanquishing old town, or to create a new city center on the Pla del Palau, the main trading center of Barcelona.

More effective urban structural renewal did occur in Barcelona with the opening of the Plaça Reial, which is located close to La Rambla. This area became the heart of the old town quarters following much renewed redevelopment in 1985.

ABOVE:
*View of Mirador del Rei Martí from the Plaça del Rei with the Casa Clariana Padellàs: today's Museu d'Historia de la Ciutat*

RIGHT:
*The medieval city walls of Barcelona with the monument to Count Berenguer el Gran*

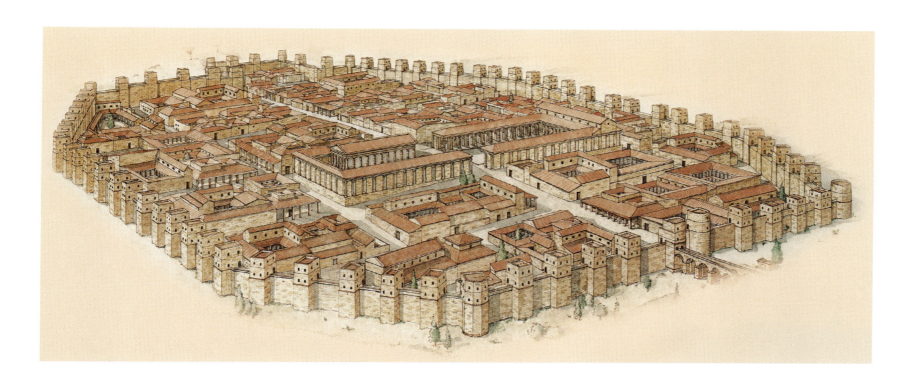

## The Ensemble of the Plaça del Rei and the Palau Reial Major

At least 2,000 years of history have etched the scene at the Plaça del Rei in the northern quarter within the Roman walls (illus. opposite). Long before the Aragonese royal palace was erected on the massive walls, this site was an early Christian cemetery.

Later, the Visigoths built their residence here, where a 5th-century, three-winged building is being excavated close to the Carrer des Comtes. The oldest written sources, from the time of Count Ramon Borrel (992–1018), were by a *palati custos* or palace guard.

The Palau Reial Major – a major attraction today – dates mainly from the 13th and 14th centuries: the golden age of the Aragonese realm. The "modern" Gothic buildings were incorporated into many parts of the older walls, including the powerful frontage that dominates the Plaça del Rei, although its defiant monumental style hardly compares with the pontifical palace in Avignon. The massive arcades and walls act as a foil to the impressive dome of Salo del Tinell.

The banqueting hall, with its flying buttresses that have a span of 33.5 m (c. 110 ft.), is one of the greatest examples of bold construction from the Middle Ages. A flight of steps connects with the frontage of the Tinell building, thus forming an elegant quadrant that links the corner of the banqueting hall and the palace chapel, leading upward to the main gateway. In 1492 this spot was the scene of an attempted assassination of the last Aragon king, Ferran II.

The Gothic palace chapel of St. Àgata, on the right-hand side of the square, rises from the foundations of the Roman city wall (illus. above). The north-east flank forms the backdrop for the Plaça Berenguer el Gran.

The left-hand corner of the Plaça del Rei protrudes into the so-called Mirador del Rio, an observation tower with five galleries set one above the other. This provides a magnificent view of the entire Gothic Quarter.

The 16th-century Palau del Lloctínent that served as Governor's residence following the union of Aragon with Castile is spread out at the base of this tower. This older section of the Palau Reial now houses the royal archives of the Catalan kingdom. The living-quarters wing of the palace was extensively expanded, and today houses part of the Museu d'Historia de la Ciutat and the Museu Marés; the latter comprises an extensive collection of sacred sculpture, and the Museu Sentimental where Frederic Marés created his charming collection of everyday objects.

Following the union of Aragon with Castile, the palace was the home of the Inquisition and from 1542 home of the Reial Audiènca or royal court of justice. Since 1931 the eastern end of the Plaça del Rei has formed the Casa Clariani-Padellàs, which now houses the Museu d'Historia de la Ciutat. This is where one enters the Palau Reial Major. The late Gothic palace, with its picturesque courtyard, once stood on Carrer dels Mercadors. When the Via Laitena was opened up, the palace was moved, stone by stone, to its present position.

In the Middle Ages, trading activity was played out in front of these important historical façades. The Plaça del Rei acted as a market for livestock fodder and a corn market, with the cries of the traders resounding from the surrounding walls. The importance of the square and palace – of all Barcelona – was diminished following the union of the Castilian and Aragonese crowns. The square anticipated new life for the first time in the 1930s after restoration of the palace and an addition to the ensemble of buildings, which was the Casa Clariana-Padellàs.

Finally the project "*Espais Urbans*" – following the death of Franco and giving the entire city a rejuvenated image – came to terms with the fossilized Plaça del Rei. A sculpture in iron by Chilladas harmonizes with the historical surroundings, while providing a touch of the avant-garde. Today the square is an impressive setting for concerts and theatrical performances as well as being a popular place to meet and have a drink.

## The Saló del Tinell and the Palace Chapel of St. Àgata

Pere III, the Ceremonious, commissioned the Catalan court architect, Guillem Carbonell, to build a throne room and banqueting hall: the Saló del Tinell (illus. opposite bottom). For this, he selected the area of land between the Plaça del Rei and the Verger palace gardens. The name is probably derived from the *tines* or vats that were placed on the wall during lavish banquets.

The Tinell acted as backdrop for court banquets, important receptions, and funerals. At a funeral the knight was mounted on a catafalque as a sign of honor. Afterwards, to express their sadness and consternation, the knights fell from their saddles. History was also made by the *Corts*, the council of state or parliament, which sat in the Saló del Tinell between 1372 and 1377.

One important historical event held here was the reception given by the Catholic king for Christopher Columbus when he returned from his voyage to the Americas.

The throne room and banqueting hall is 17 × 33.5 m (c. 56 × 110 ft.), and marks a high-point of Catalan secular architecture. The size, grandiose breadth, and vision are exceptional, although good examples can be seen in the dormitories and refectories of Catalan cloisters.

The banqueting area is not subdivided; instead the space is spanned by six broad vaulted arches borne on buttresses also supporting the wooden roof trusses. External buttresses and structural arches support and brace the construction. Parts of the previous Romanesque structure were incorporated into the front elevation of the newer building. The old double panel window can still be seen in the masonry between the triple panel windows of the basement and the rose windows of the arcade.

During the restoration in 1936, an exciting discovery was made on the north wall, where a 5 × 15 m (c. 16.5 × 50 ft.) fresco was uncovered that chronicles the conquest of Majorca (illus. opposite top). In it Jaume I and Bishop Berenguer el Palou lead a long column of knights who can be easily identified from their different coats of arms. The most important Catalan families of the Queralts, Montcadas, Allemanys, and many others are proudly recorded in the fresco for posterity.

Jaume II and his successor Alfons the Benign had a palace chapel built on the foundations of the Roman city wall, where formerly a Maria oratory stood (illus. right). For this late Gothic building the commission was probably given to the court architect, Bertran de Riquer, who produced plans, and completed the polygonal apse in 1306 with his colleagues Jaume del Rei and Pere Oliva.

The Tinell is captivating in its simplicity and through the clarity of its interior, while the fortress-like exterior flanks the Plaça del Rei, and imposes itself on the viewer as impressively as the city walls, for as far as the Plaça Berenguer el Gran.

Like the Ste. Chapelle in Paris, this chapel acts as a place of safekeeping for state relics. It was first consecrated to St. Àgata (St. Agatha) in 1601, who is safeguarded there in stonework from the man who cut off her breast. In the

confusion of the 18th and 19th centuries, the chapel was secularized, and later opened to the public. The head of the academy of architecture, Elies Rogent, took on the task of saving the neglected building in 1856, restoring it in keeping with the period.

One of the most outstanding objects is the altarpiece by Jaume Huguet, who was the most important Catalan painter of his time. It was painted in 1465 for the Condestable of Portugal – who was chosen as Pere IV for the Catalan-Aragonese throne – replacing an earlier work by Ferrer Bassa. In keeping with royal wishes, the altar painting depicts the adoration of the king as well as scenes from the life of Mary, who Huguet arranges in the courtly manner, influenced by Flemish style.

*Palau Reial Major*
*Interior of the palace chapel of St. Àgata, begun in the early 14th century*

## The Palau del Lloctinent
### (today's Arxiu de la Corona d'Aragó)

With the marriage of the Catholic king in 1469, the Aragonese realm lost its independence. Until then Barcelona had still been home to a regent or governor. Parts of the older wings of the royal palaces to the south of the Plaça del Rei were established as their domicile, known as the Palau del Lloctinent.

Its frontages are plain, but exceptionally well proportioned, with few late Gothic or Classical adornments. The grand courtyard is evidence of the Renaissance in Barcelona. The fine three-section staircase has an extremely unusual wooden roof in the tradition of Moorish woodcarving of *artesonado* with impressed Renaissance motifs.

RIGHT:
*Palau del Lloctinent (governor's palace)*
*Built between 1549 and 1557 by Guillem Carbonell,*
*it today houses Arxiu de la Corona d'Aragó:*
*Artesonado roof covering the staircase*

BELOW:
*Palau del Lloctinent*
*View of staircase and courtyard*

## The Cathedral, La Seu

For centuries men and women have gone to mass or to confession, or have lit a candle to his or her saint in one of the cathedral chapels, and probably have thoughtfully taken the time to admire the superb Gothic interior.

Many traditions are kept alive at the cathedral, such as the keeping of geese and the "dancing egg" in the cloisters, and also the veneration of the "Christ of Lepanto," who defeated the Turks. The most colorful hustle and bustle regularly unfolds in front of the cathedral's powerful façade. On Sundays and special days the *cobla* is played here, with young and old dancing the unusual and enchanting *Sardana* folk dance together to the curious sound of wind instruments (panel p. 159).

The foundation stone was laid on May 1, 1298, the cathedral replacing two older buildings. The first Visigoth building had been so severely damaged during Moorish invasions in the 8th and 10th centuries that Bishop Guislabert decided in 1046 to have a new Romanesque church built. This was dedicated to the Holy Cross and St. Eulàlia. Few traces remain of these buildings (only capitals and sculpture) because of the needs of the expanding Catalan-Aragonese empire.

Under the leadership of the Majorcan architect Jaume Fabre, one of the most imposing Catalan Gothic interiors came into being, and has endured (illus. p. 151). Above a floor area of 79 × 25 m (c. 260 × 82 ft.) rose the broad central nave and side aisles with chapels that lead to a processional chancel. Mighty composite columns bear the four-part ribbed vaults that terminate at the height of 26 m (c. 85 ft.) in huge colorful, sculptural stone bosses.

The impression of both grandiose breadth and monumentality is further enhanced by two galleries borne on deep trusses above the chapels, galleries that allow the light through. These create an illusion that the building has seven sections of nave instead of five.

In contrast to this stunning concept of space, the exterior more readily conjures up notions of a fortification than of a house of God, in common with all Catalan churches (illus. p. 150). Bare expanses and few horizontal features characterize the walls. The entrances date from different eras. The oldest is the Porta de St. Iu, sited within a remnant of the previous building with a foundation inscription. Here too one looks in vain for any richly molded adornment. Generally, the building represents the religious side of Gothic architecture.

The structural columns of the interior, between the chapels, are transposed, confining the visible structure to arches between the upper clerestory and the walls of the aisles, also characteristic of this region. The transept – apparent only from within – barely extends beyond the alignment of the nave, thereby accentuating the axis of two massive octagonal towers.

A crossing tower is missing; instead the entrance arch is crowned by a filigree turret, somewhat similar to those of Freiburg or to Münster near Ulm in Germany. Together with these *cimbori*, the pentagonal frontage forms a most impressive backdrop to the Plaça de la Seu, along with the towering central entrance.

LEFT:

*La Seu cathedral, Barcelona, begun in 1298. The front, by Josep Orial Mestres and August Font, dates from 1906–13*

TOP:
*View of the cathedral from the east*

OPPOSITE:
*Interior of the cathedral, built in the early
14th century by Jaum Fabre*

There is a ready explanation for these elements, which reveal to us the entire sample book of Gothic architecture: the western part was built between 1906–13 by Josep Oriol Mestres and August Font (illus. pp. 148–9). Prior to this the cathedral was only closed off provisionally, with the work being discontinued in the late Middle Ages. Examples for the completion of the front and towers were provided by sketches of the French master Carli from the early 15th century.

The decision to build a neo-Gothic front was not unanimously accepted, but was fashionable at the time. This historic solution was guided by the nostalgia for the Middle Ages – which was considered a golden era for Catalonia – and also by the rediscovery of the positive and aesthetic qualities of Gothic architecture.

Visiting the interior of the church is no less than a stroll through at least 700 years of the history of the cathedral. The crypt, for example, was completed in 1337. This area, with its 12-fold fan vaulting, was created, like the rest of the building, by the architect Jaume Fabre. His construction also influenced Antoni Gaudí who was stimulated to produce similar monumental works of art.

A focal point is the alabaster sarcophagus with the mortal remains of the patron saint of the cathedral and city: St. Eulàlia (illus. p. 152, bottom). She came from Sarrià, today a suburb of Barcelona, and succumbed to a cruel martyrdom as a young girl in A.D. 204 for resisting the following of Diocletian. The sarcophagus is a unique example of Italianate sculpture in Catalonia, probably having been created in Italy in 1327 in the style of the studio of Pisani.

Similar Italianate influences are found in the sculptural form of the entrance wall of the *coro*, the monumental canonical choir in the central nave. The carvings graphically reproduce in bold perspective a simplified version of the martyrdom of St. Eulàlia, and are mainly the work of Bartolomé Ardóñez in 1517 (illus. p. 152, bottom).

If one passes through the barricade – normal practice in Spain – and steps into the *coro* or choir, which is entirely hidden from the gaze of the public, a world of astonishing splendor and purity opens up. The seating in which the choristers sit or stand during their seemingly endless litanies, resting upon the misericord, is among the finest examples of this art form. Father Ça Anglada had traveled to Brussels in 1394 specially to order the best oak for this purpose. In 1399 the chairs of the upper row and particularly the gargoyle-like figures of the folding seats below, graphically depicting to the clergy who saw them the virtues and the vices, were carved from this oak.

When Charles V summoned the mighty to a sitting of the Order of the Golden Fleece in Barcelona in 1519, the choir of the cathedral was rearranged as a kind of conference hall. The painter Juan de Borgoña was commissioned to paint the names and coats of arms of the knights and also the insignia of Maximilian and Charles V on the backs of the seats.

Among the more significant items of furnishing is the reclining figure of Bishop Olegario (also known as Father Ça Anglada), of which countless painted altarpieces of the

14th and 15th centuries are found in museums (including the work of Bernard Martorell and Lluis Borrassa), and also the famous Pietà of Cordoban artist Bartolomé Bermejo. The latter shows the influence of elements from the Low Countries on Spanish art in the late 15th century. There is great reverence for the "Christ of Lepanto" in the chapel of the Sacrament on the right of the entrance; He decorated the figurehead of the galley of Juan of Austria who defeated the Turks during the sea battle of Lepanto.

Through the right-hand doorway to the transept are the cloisters, the most atmospheric corner of the entire Gothic Quarter with their palms, magnolias, and orange trees (illus. opposite bottom). In a centuries-old tradition, snow-white geese watch over cathedral and city.

A late Gothic fountain close to the Porta de la Pieta catches the eye. Its artistically sculpted stone boss by Antoni or Joan Chaperós depicts St. George slaying the dragon; the patron saint of Catalonia is portrayed as a courtly knight. At the feast of Corpus Christi the fountain is a place of special interest. It is decorated with broom or gorse and cherries, while a blown-out egg is allowed to "dance" on the jet of water, known as "l'ou com balla."

The cloisters are unusual in architectural terms, being enclosed on three sides by chapels. The fourth – western – side extended in the 17th century, is taken up by the Lepanto chapel and the chapter house, where the cathedral museum is now housed. The cloisters were started by Bernat Roquer, and completed by Andreu Escuder on September 26, 1448, when the final vault was finished at "three hours after the midday meal."

A series of structures are grouped around La Seu, which were directly or indirectly dependent on the cathedral. These include the bishop's palace of course, close to the Porta Nova. For almost 600 years buildings were constructed around the courtyard formed by them.

The canons too resided in appropriate comfort in houses behind the line of the cathedral in Carrer de la Pietat. Previously they had lived in simple communal accommodation at the side of the cathedral frontage.

The Pia Almoina building with its characteristic pointed gable was erected for their benefit c. 1450. This organization, founded by 1009, dedicated itself to feeding the poor. Today, this space, together with the neighboring wing built one hundred years later, is occupied by the Diocesan museum. The house of the archdeacon Lluís Deplà in Carrer St. Llúcia belongs in the broadest sense to the cathedral city at the end of the Middle Ages. Late Gothic is freely interspersed with Renaissance decorative forms.

The courtyard with its Gothic wells is particularly atmospheric. Famous guests have been welcomed within its walls, such as Francisco de Borja, the Catalan regent and subsequent Jesuit general. Today the courtyard houses the city archives building. An attractive detail added during the era of Modernisme is a stone letterbox with carved tortoises and swallows representing the deligent work carried out in the lawyer's chambers.

OPPOSITE:
*Carving of the martyrdom of St. Eulàlia on the choir stalls by Bartolomé Ordoñez in 1517 (top); alabaster sarcophagus in the crypt with scenes depicting the legend of the saint, probably created in 1327 in the style of the studio of Pisani in Italy (bottom)*

TOP AND ABOVE:
*The cathedral
View of the arches of the choir (top); view of the cloisters, with the pond of the white geese (above)*

## The Other Churches of the Gothic Quarter

The Gothic Quarter has other important late Gothic churches in addition to the cathedral and royal palaces. The parish church of St. Maria del Mar – almost as popular as La Seu – soars upward in the Barri de la Ribera, the trading quarter on the sea-front. In the golden age of the Aragonese realm, this was the meeting place for fishermen and seafarers, merchants, and bold conquerors. Their history is closely linked to the expansion of the kingdom and the prosperity of Barcelona. Alfons III, the Benign, laid the foundation stone in 1329 after Maria had proven helpful in the conquest of Sardinia.

The construction was completed in the unusually short period of 54 years because every guild of the quarter as well as the carriers and casual laborers worked for nothing. Their selfless work is recalled in various designs on capitals, in the carvings on the altar steps, and on the bronze tableaux at the main entrance. The period of the building is well documented – as so often the case in Catalonia. Architects Ramon Despuig and Berenguer de Montagut signed the contract on March 2, 1329, and were succeeded by Guillem Merge, although he died shortly before the consecration in 1384.

St. Maria del Mar is probably the most impressive of all Catalan Gothic buildings, even though it is externally of such succinct simplicity. The bare brick walls are only divided by two ledges, and supporting columns emerge from the solid mass only in the upper part of the structure. The rather sober façade is complemented by the proud side towers, sculptural entrance, and rose window (although altered countless times). Behind it one of the most splendid interiors of the entire Mediterranean is hidden (illus. above, and opposite). Outstanding proportions and subtle use of light give the space an almost heavenly sublimity. Plainness is an asset; simple octagonal columns, which are reduced to a minimum, carry the arches allowing the architecture to speak for itself.

The simple ground plan follows both Catalan and western tradition: a tripartite nave without accentuated transept, side aisles with chapels situated between the supporting columns are built around the choir; it is similar to the cathedral of Manresa, also conceived by Berenguer de Montagut. The exceptional width of the span of the four central nave sections is 14 m (c. 46 ft.), only surpassed by the cathedral of Girona. The side aisles reach an exceptional height compared with French buildings, almost making a grand hall of the church.

The aesthetic high point is the internal ring of pillars of the apse which allows the sunlight to shine through as though from a celestial source. Unfortunately, as a consequence of wars of succession and the Spanish Civil War, virtually the entire interior was destroyed; almost

every window except for the southern side has been reconstructed or originates from the 19th century.

Only slightly less important is the parish church of St. Mari del Pi, which follows the same pattern as Maria del Mar. The idyllically situated church, positioned between two old town squares, gets its name from the huge pine tree that adorns its front.

The exterior here is also massive and fortification-like, although relieved by fine detailing of the entrance and tracery of the window (illus. opposite). The horizontal is delineated by copings and ledges. At the sides there are structural pillars – the customary Catalan feature, the skeletal appearance of which has been borrowed by central European Gothic – that only appear in the upper clerestory as powerful tongues, but they disappear into the walls of the perimeter of the chapels.

It appears that a start was made in 1322 on a more spacious interior with a breadth of 16 m (c. 52 ft.). There is almost no sculpture, with the only adornment being the glass of the windows, of which only a few are original. However, the 18th-century *Adoration of the King* by Antoni Vildomat is well worth contemplating. The modern copies of the other panes, especially in the rose window of the front which was a victim of the Spanish Civil War, recreate the original festive yet solemn occasion.

The Plaça del Pi and the neighboring Plaça St. Josp Oriol with their cafés are always popular places to meet, to see, and be seen, and to enjoy a drink or *Xoxolata amb nata* (chocolate with cream). A small art market is held here at the weekends.

The single nave church of St. Just, on the square of that name, deserves consideration above all else for its interior decoration. This church is also one that dates from the 14th century.

Other churches are hidden away in the middle of the Gothic Quarter but remote from the hustle and bustle, such as the late Gothic convent of St. Felip Neri. The tranquil atmosphere of this spiritual place invites one to linger here. But on further study another side of history reveals itself: bullet holes in the front of the church are painful reminders of the Spanish Civil War that raged with exceptional brutality in Barcelona.

A visit to the shoe museum (Museu del Calçat Antic) is a happier affair where historical examples are displayed alongside footwear of famous Catalans. The palatial building in which the museum is housed is the guild hall from 1565 of the shoemakers' guild that was originally sited elsewhere but moved here in connection with the construction of the Via Laietana.

St. Anna, in the immediate vicinity of the Plaça de Catalunya, is another oasis from the lively character that predominates in the Gothic Quarter. This cruciform Romanesque church was vaulted in the 15th century, and extended with a late Gothic cloister. In 1493, the Catholic king held court within its walls.

St. Pere de les Puelles can also look back at a long history, with the legend based on Ludwig dem Frommen. The former Benedictine cloister has undergone great misfortune, so that little remains of its former structure.

OPPOSITE:
*Front of St. Maria del Pi, started in 1322*

ABOVE AND BELOW:
*The Plaça del Pi
The square is surrounded by traditional businesses and convivial bars and cafés, which are popular meeting places to*
drink or sip Xoxolata amb nata *(chocolate with cream). At weekends it becomes an outdoor art gallery where pictures are offered for sale.*

*Plaça St. Jaume*
*The square becomes an open-air theater on special days.*
*The castells or human towers are famous.*

## Ajuntament and Generalitat

Since the time of the Romans, the Plaça de St. Jaume has been the center of city life in Barcelona. The *forum* extended as far as here, at the junction of *cardo* and *decumanus*, which formed the main axis of the Roman encampment. In its place the *Diputacío* (regional parliament) and *Ajuntament* (city council) were built, creating the focal point of the community of Barcelona.

The present generous layout of the square dates from the 19th century; when two churches and their cemeteries closed, it enabled the present spatial ensemble to be created. On special days and also occasionally during political rallies the square becomes an open-air theater. The *castells* or human towers and the dance of the *gegants* or giants are famous (illus. left, and opposite). This spectacle is only surpassed by the fire-breathing dragons and devils that appear on the festival of Mercé (the merciful Mother of God) and Carnival.

Catalan history has been made here twice in recent times: firstly with the declaration of the Republic of Catalonia in 1931 from the balcony of the Generalitat by Francesc Macià, which was abruptly ended by the Spanish Civil War. Many more years of repression later, Catalonia once more gained a degree of autonomy on September 29, 1977 when the President, Josep Taradellas, concluded with the words "*Ja sóc aqui*," (so here I am) to the jubilant crowd.

The history of the Generalitat stretches back to the 15th century when the Catalan parliament first acquired a home on the Carrer St. Honorat (illus. p. 160, top). In 1425 it was decided to erect an appropriate building that was not completed until the 17th century.

A visit to the Generalitat (free, but you must book first) is like a journey through Catalan history. The oldest parts include the Gothic façade on the Carrer del Bisbe with its plaque of St. George by Pere Johan (illus. p. 160, bottom), but particularly the charming courtyard with its delicate pointed arch arcades and the adjoining St. George's chapel, both the work of Marc Safont, completed in 1434 (illus. pp. 162–3).

The front of the chapel is a masterpiece of flamboyant masonry. The tracery forms of the façade are spun like a web, leaving the walls almost overlooked. The Pati del Taronges – 16th-century orangery – adjoins the Gothic courtyard. It is raised on stilts above the ground, and serves as an airy meeting-room.

Toward the end of the 16th and start of the 17th centuries the Generalitat acquired a new façade (not including the picturesque bridges over the Carrer del Bisbe, for these date from as late as 1928). Pere Blay was inspired by the Palazzo Farnese, and so created one of the few Romanesque impressions in Barcelona.

Of the sumptuous rooms established at this time, the Saló de St. Jordi is the most important (illus. p. 163, top). Its tripartite chamber was originally conceived as a chapel, but it was and is used above all as a reception and ceremonial hall. Large-format historical pictures from 1928 depict the Catalan past. *The Quatre Cròniques* by Antoni Tapies on the walls of the new intimate council chamber are smaller, more artistic, and more significant. The large

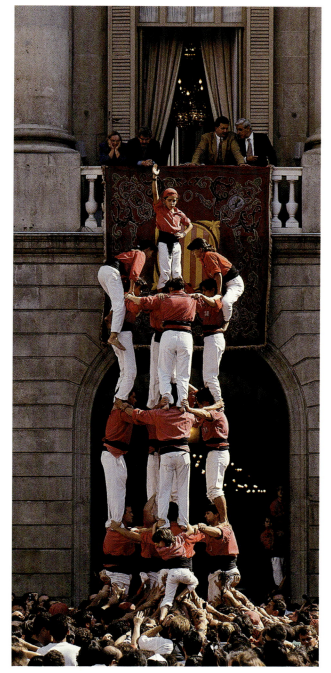

**Sardana and Castells**
*Scarcely a special day passes in Catalonia without the Sardana or the creation of human towers known as castells. The Sardana, a Catalan folk dance, is danced by young and old to the sounds of the cobla, an 11-piece wind band. The fabiol starts the dance, tenora, tible, trombó, and fiscorn pick it up, supported by the contrabaix and tambori. At the same time men and women form a circle in which they put down their bags, join hands, and start by making passing steps in a rhythm of long and short paces. The hands are lowered for the short steps and raised with the long ones. The practice of this communal dance – typically Catalan – was banned for a time under Franco. It is said that the human towers hark back to the myth of the revolt of the Titans; in any event, the castells are a remarkable art. Men form columns up to nine people high in a matter of moments. The form of these structures is laid down. A pillar consists of just one column, but a torre consists of two, and true castells require more pillars. The base of the pinya or cone is made of supporting men, while the tip or pom de dalt is formed of two layers of boys or girls on whom a person known as the anxeneta climbs to the top. It is only when this person has raised four fingers of the right hand to represent the Catalan flag, and the second "floor" has been supported, that the castell is deemed to have been erected.*

murals recall the four chronicles of the Middle Ages which bring to life the dramatic sweep of history during the Catalan-Aragonese realm (illus. p. 163, bottom).

The Ajuntament or town hall of Barcelona has a similar lively past (illus. p. 164, top). Its origins take one back to the 13th century, when the city established a council of a hundred men who, as well as being respected citizens, ranged from merchants and artists to craftsmen. Initially they met in monasteries or private premises, but in 1372 they acquired the house of Simó Oller on the Plaça St. Jaume, and had this extended by Pere Llobert to form a large council chamber: the Saló de Cent.

In the 16th century, the Trentenari or council of 30 evolved, for which a new chamber was erected. The town hall first acquired its present frontage in the 19th century when the small church of St. Jacob was demolished so the square could be rearranged, and the neo-classical façade constructed by Josep Mas i Vila. Before this the main entrance was on the Carrer de la Ciutat, where the Gothic frontage with its filigree windows and powerful horizontal molding can still be admired (architects: Arnau Bargués and Francesc Marenya; sculptors Jordi de Déu, Jordi John, and others). Here, the elements of palatial Catalan architecture attained their own grandeur. Entrance to the city's clerical department is through an elegantly walled and rounded doorway that has been connected to the main building by black marble steps since 1926.

Like the north-eastern frontage, the Pati Gòtic, with its fine pointed arch arcades, came into being after 1400 (illus. p. 164, bottom). It extends diagonally behind the present main frontage, and contains the entrance to the

ABOVE:
*Palau de la Generalitat
Frontage to the Plaça St. Jaume,
built by Pere Blay in 1597*

RIGHT:
*Palau de la Generalitat
Frontage to the Carrer del Bisbe
Plaque of St. George, early 15th
century, by Pere Johan*

OPPOSITE:
*Palau de la Generalitat
Courtyard completed in 1434
by Marc Safont*

Saló de Cent, where the Council of One Hundred sat (illus. p. 165, top). This wider and more rectangular space was spanned by arches, in the Catalan manner, on which wooden roof trusses rest. Originally there were only three trusses; the lower ones both originate from the 19th century. Nothing remains of their Gothic decoration because the room was decorated in the Baroque style in the 1th century, and was further renovated in 1914.

Of all the rooms, the Saló de les Cròniques deserves consideration, for its pictures celebrate the Catalan nation (illus. p. 165, bottom). Large paintings framed in black marble and gilt depict the history of Catalonia, which reached its zenith with the military expedition by Roger de Flors to Asia Minor in 1303–24.

Josep Maria Sert, who also painted the cathedral of Vic, completed the dramatic cycle of paintings in 1928, paintings that are now being recognized in intellectual circles as classical culture of the Mediterranean.

Animated by the writing of Eugeni d'Ors, Barcelona has been described as the "Athens of the western Mediterranean." The more or less contemporary painter Xavier Nogues celebrates the "spirit of the city" and other Catalan virtues in Alcadia.

There is art too, as with the Generalitat, in the town hall. Francesc Gali created frescoes of Don Quixote, Tàpies decorated the bar, Josep Maria Subirachs – who enlivens the mind with his works of the Sagrada family – made the aluminum reliefs of the annex to the Ajuntament on the Plaça de St. Miquel.

162    Barcelona

Opposite:
Palau de la Generalitat
Exterior of the chapel

Left:
Palau de la Generalitat
Salo de St. Jordi, 16th–18th
centuries, with murals from 1928

Below:
Palau de la Generalitat
New council chamber with
mural Quatre Cròniques by
Antoni Tàpies

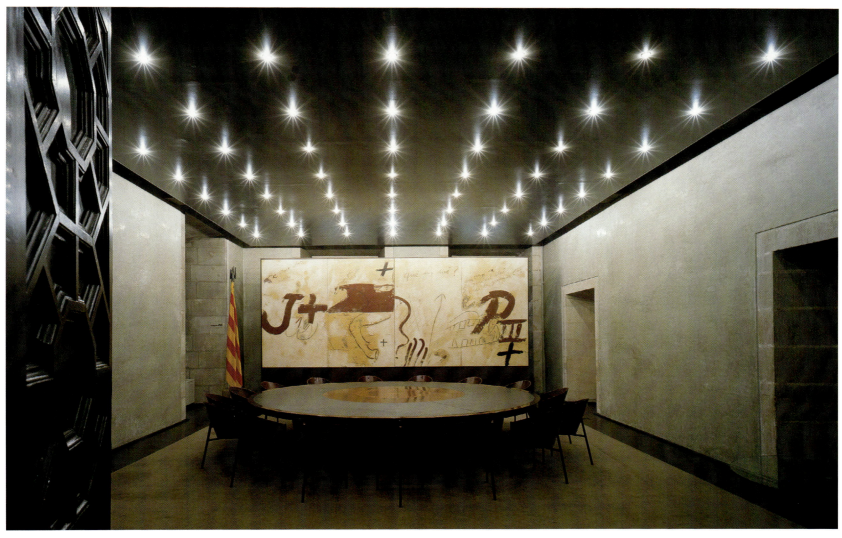

RIGHT:
Ajuntament (town hall)
Exterior dating from 1847
by Josep Mas i Vila

BELOW:
Ajuntament
Pati gòtic (Gothic courtyard)
of 1400

LEFT:
*Ajuntament*
*Saló de Cent (chamber of the*
*Council of One Hundred) started*
*in 1372 by Pere Llobert*

BELOW:
*Ajuntament*
*Saló de les Cròniques with cycle*
*of frescoes by Josep Maria Sert*
*in 1928*

## Carrer Montcada

The Carrer Montcada – an unusually broad, dead straight street for its time – in the eastern part of the Gothic Quarter, was the most favored address of the Catalan patricians (illus. left, and below). The most influential families of Barcelona settled here in the 14th century, including the Dalmases, the Marquesos de Lló, the Marquesos de St. Coloma, and the Aquilar family. In their noble palatial villas, most of which are grouped around an open courtyard and staircase or *pati*, today mainly museums and galleries are found.

Their diverse collections offer a welcome supplement to the grandiose architecture of the Middle Ages and the early neo-style architecture. Intervention in the 19th century, when many of these villas were turned into homes for rent, was reversed in 1947, so that this unique collection can now continue in its original glory.

The Carrer Montcada was constructed before the 12th century, and at that time was outside the city walls. When the Catalan-Aragonese realm expanded in the Middle Ages – and with it its trading power – the eastern side of the city became more important, and was enclosed by a wall in the 14th century. As a link between the harbor and the trading quarter, the Carrer Montcada attracted both nobility and

merchants, and in the course of the next three centuries it developed into the fine residential street that we see today. Between the Placeta de Montcada and the Placeta d'En Marcus, which were widened to make turning points for the many professions, the well-to-do families built their town villas. Defensive from the outside, the interiors were, in contrast, both intimate and furnished to provide a refined and comfortable life for their inhabitants. Despite the astonishingly reclusive character of the street fronts – stemming from different periods – they were frequently altered, and extensively rebuilt according to whatever style was fashionable at the time.

The Casa dels Marquesos de Llió dates in part from the 14th century with its triple panel window. (It is currently a textile museum.) The Palau Cervelló that houses the Galerie Maeght is an example of extremely fine masonry with its round doorway with keystones and a wooden gallery from the turn of the 15th and 16th centuries (but with windows that were altered later).

An imposing Baroque frontage decorates the Palau Dalmases, which is Gothic at heart (and is home to the cultural association, *Omnium Cultural*). Its courtyard is the finest example of the otherwise not particularly prevalent Renaissance architecture in Barcelona. The stone balustrade is especially fine; images of vine leaves and birds, and Neptune with a fluttering cloak gliding over the waves and capturing Europa's bull are playfully incorporated (illus. bottom left).

Two palaces that are also mainly late Gothic are the Palau Berenguer d'Aguilar (illus. below right) and the Pala de Castellet. Since 1963 the latter palace has safeguarded a precious treasure: the extensive collection of early works by Pablo Picasso.

As so often in Barcelona, and certainly in the Carrer Montcada, tradition and the avant-garde go hand in hand in a stimulating relationship. Both palaces were developed around and above an open courtyard with, as usual, stairs to an upper corner leading to the *planta noble* or main part of the building. These structures were acquired by the city and ten years later the Picasso Museum was opened. The initiative came from a graphic arts foundation through Jaum Sabartés, a close friend of the artist, who suggested the city take possession. Picasso himself donated his *Las Meninas* series, and in 1970 added the entire collection of his early work still in his hands.

The Andalusian-born Picasso had close ties with Barcelona (see panel box p. 168). His father taught at the *Llojta*, the art academy to which he himself applied for

OPPOSITE:
*Carrer Montcada*

LEFT:
*Palau Dalmases*
*View of the 15th–16th century courtyard*

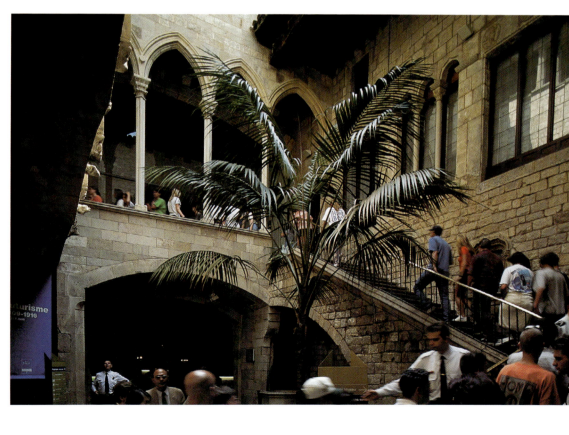

ABOVE:
*Palau Berenguer d'Aguilar*
*View of the 15th-century courtyard*

### Picasso in Barcelona

Pablo Ruiz Picasso, painter, graphic artist, and sculptor was born in Málaga in 1881. In 1891 his family moved to Coruña, where he began to draw regularly. In 1895 the Picasso family settled in Barcelona in the Carrer de la Mercé. The 14-year-old Picasso started his art education at the art academy that was then held in rooms at the Llotja or Exchange. Picasso studied in Paris in 1897, where he gained a first prize for the symbolic oil painting Cìencia i Carìtat (now in the Museu Picasso in Barcelona). In 1899 he shared a studio in Barcelona with his friends Carles Casagemas and Josep Cardona. The artists' hang out, "Els 4 Gats," had opened two years earlier in the Carrer Montsío; like the "Chat Noir" in Paris it attracted the avant-garde with stimulating conversation and cabaret. Picasso was quickly accepted within the circle of modernist artists that the "all-round good egg" Pere Romeu collected around himself. These included the painters Santiago Rusiñol, Ramon Casa, Miquel Utrillo, and the clearly younger Isidre Nonell, and also the composers Isaac Albéniz and Enric Granados. In "Els 4 Gats" one encountered tertulias or group discussions, puppet and shadow theater, original performances, lectures, and exhibitions. The ideas of the idealistic group were disseminated through their own publication. Picasso's work had been introduced to "Els 4 Gats" by 1899. Soon after this he produced a menu card for the place that had become his second home. In 1900, Picasso first traveled with Casagemas to Paris where he joined the circle of Post-Impressionist artists. In 1904, when he finally settled in the city on the Seine, he shuttled between both metropolises. Toward the end of 1901 he entered his so-called Blue Period, during which time he painted unsmiling human faces in clear and simple forms using blue tones. Between 1904 and 1906 his palette brightened during his Pink Period. With Demoiselles d'Avignon in 1907 Picasso endorsed Cubism, and opened the way to the abstract forms of art of the 20th century. It is possible that the artist incorporated recollections of Barcelona in this mold-breaking work, with the Carrer Avingó being home to a number of establishments that might have prompted his portrayals of women. Picasso, whose further artistic development occurred outside Catalonia, remained close to Barcelona throughout his life, although he only returned there once in 1917 in the company of the Ballets Russes of Sergei Diaghilev. Picasso died in Mougins in 1973.

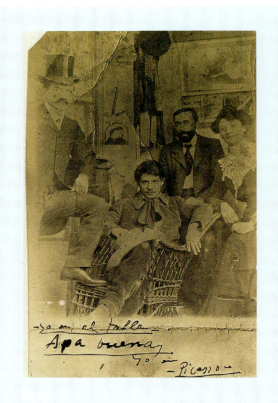

Picasso in his studio with friends

admission in 1895. He stayed in the Catalan metropolis until 1904, and lived through an important period in its history: the World Exhibition of 1888 with its increasing sense of national identity and the culture of Modernisme, which like Jugendstil, Art Nouveau, and Secession furthered a new philosophy imbued with art. The social changes after 1898 (the loss of the overseas colonies) and the waves of strikes and anarchism of the following years were an equally strong influence on the art of the time.

Picasso's artistic development did not result from his training at the academy, but was influenced more by his contacts with his Catalan artist friends Pere Romeu, Ramon Casas, and Santiago Rusiñol, for he was regularly in their company. The famous *tertulias*, the conversations in "Els 4 Gats," focused on the latest developments, and set the cultural scene for the coming century.

Picasso first traveled to Paris in 1900 where he became part of the colony of Catalan artists. In the years that followed he shuttled between the French capital and Barcelona, fascinated on the one hand by the metropolis on the Seine, but on the other hand drawn to home.

The collection of the Picasso Museum in Barcelona has a different perspective from other institutions. Alongside the extensive display of graphic works and ceramics, the focus is Picasso's early work from Coruña, Málaga, Barcelona, and Madrid, and also from his first encounters with the Catalan avant-garde.

Among his principal works from these years prior to 1900 are *Primera Comunió* (First Communion, 1896, illus.

opposite top left) and *Ciència i Caritat* (Science and Compassion, 1897); these moralistic and symbolic subjects so early on displayed his extraordinary talent as a painter. He developed the somber and melancholic style of the "Blue Period" after 1901 with works such as *Desamparts* (roughly translated as The Hopeless, 1903, illus. opposite top right) and *Dona del floc* (Woman with Curls, 1903). Following his final move to the Seine, his palette brightened, and his style became more linear and less three-dimensional. His elegant portrait of Senyora Canals – who had already sat for Degas – originates from this period. Soon afterward he shook the established art world with his *Demoiselles d'Avignon*.

Picasso returned for the first time to Barcelona in 1917, and in that year he produced *Harlequin*, which created a huge gulf between him and the Classical school. One of the gems of the exhibition is undoubtedly the *Meninas* series, created 40 years later over a few months in Cannes in 1957 (illus. below).

Picasso produced in total 54 studies and more larger canvases, all inspired by the famous portrayal by Diego Velazquez of the family of Philip IV. With single-minded assuredness Picasso captured the distinctive character of the figures in only a few lines, at the same time demonstrating reverence in his own distinctive way for the greatest Spanish Baroque painter.

The graphical series of *Tauromachie* and most of his ceramic works, which his widow Jacqueline passed on to the museum in 1982, stem from about the same period.

RIGHT:
The "Els 4 Gats" bar, built
1895–96 by Josep Puig i
Cadafalch

OPPOSITE, LEFT:
Ramon Casas
Ramon Casas and Rere
Romeu on a tandem, 1897
Oil on canvas, 191 × 215 cm

OPPOSITE, BELOW:
"Els 4 Gats"
Interior view

## Els 4 Gats

The bar "Els 4 Gats" (The 4 Cats) was the most popular meeting place for artists in Barcelona at the turn of the 19th century. The name of the bar is a play on the Catalan expression for a colorful group thrown together, and it is also an echo of the name of the famous "Chat Noir" bar of Montmartre in Paris. A lively circle of painters, sculptors, and writers met one another in the "medieval" ambiance of this bar, with the intention of paying homage to the "juice of the barley."

"Els 4 Gats" was much more than a bar: Pere Romeu and his friends Miquel Utrillo, Ramon Casas, and Santiago Rusiñol arranged lectures, concerts, shadow plays, and puppet theater here, and discussions in *tertulias* (lively conversations between regulars in their local tavern) about art and business. The first issue of their publication, "Els 4 Gats," appeared in 1899, and in February 1900 Picasso exhibited his work here for the first time.

"Els 4 Gats" has carefully preserved its modernist flair, although many of the drawings and paintings on the walls have been replaced by reproductions. This is also true of the large painting of Ramon Casas in which he is shown with Pere Romeu on a tandem (illus. right) and also in a car, and equally so of Picasso's menu card for the restaurant, which he quickly sketched using only a few deft lines.

PREVIOUS PAGES:
*Palau de la Música Catalana,*
*built 1905–1908 by Lluis Comènech i Montaner.*
*Concert Hall*

## Palau de la Música Catalana

A feast for the senses, an ecstasy of color – the Palau de la Música Catalana is without doubt the most spectacular building of Catalan Jugendstil (illus. pp. 172–3, above, and opposite). The building erected between 1905–08 clearly demonstrates the splendor and multifaceted culture of Modernisme, showing allegiance with its extensive sculpture to the great Catalans of history. Contemporaries regarded it as a "temple of Catalan art": a palace to mark their renaissance (*Renaixença*). Although present-day observers may well find the indulgent decoration overdone, it nevertheless provides an interplay of architecture and decoration, of sensory stimuli and symbolism that probably comprises the most perfect synthesis of the arts of its time.

It is no accident that one of the most notable uses emanating from the building was that of a musical association, the Orféo Catalá, which took on the task of preserving Catalan songs, and making them better known. Music played an important part in Barcelona at the turn of the century; but the rediscovery of national work coincided with an almost feverish Wagnerian cult that resulted in a decline in the performance program.

The luxurious decor of the Palau de la Música is so overpowering that it is easy to overlook the architecture, which was itself both of the highest order and innovative. Lluis Domènech i Montaner (see panel box p. 227) who, along with Antoni Gaudí and Josep Puigi Cadafalch, was a protagonist of modernist architecture, constructed the palace on a steel frame, a technique that had been used experimentally in the construction of the World Exhibition of 1888. The new method of construction was used, not to save money or time, but to provide greater freedom in the placement of the ground plan and arrangement of the elevations. The external walls are therefore not load-bearing, anticipating the suspended façades of modern architecture. The concert hall itself could be extensively glazed in a novel manner, and comes across as a "greenhouse in a brick case" (David Mackay).

The contrast between the red bricks and the colorful ceramic mosaics dominates the exterior of the Palau de la Música. The walls are extensively broken up by windows, galleries, and balconies, while a web of pillars, arches, and balustrades creates a variety of visual associations, reminding one of Venetian palazzi, Tudor buildings, or Moorish examples. The remaining surfaces, colonnaded

ABOVE AND LEFT:
*Palau de la Música Catalana*
*detail of the exterior*

OPPOSITE:
*Palau de la Música Catalana*
*Stage with musical allegories by*
*Eusebi Arnau and a bust of*
*Beethoven, created by Lluis*
*Domènech i Montaner and Pau*
*Gargallo in 1905–08*

porticoes, and arches are covered with floral mosaics, constantly bringing new patterns into play. Even the capitals display luxuriant bouquets of flowers.

Between all the eclectic architectural motifs, space is still found for an equally multilayered collection of sculpture: in front of the balcony are busts of Palestrina, Bach, Beethoven, and Wagner.

A prominent corner of the palace is reserved for an allegory of Catalan songs: a nymph personifying folk songs (*Cancó Popular*) is encircled by representations of the Catalan people. The mosaic on the upper part of the main frontage illustrates the song *La Balanguera* by Amadeu Vives. In front of the backdrop of Montserrat – the "fate" of the Catalans – spins the "future" of the country; at the same time the muse looks up to the members of the *Orféo Català*. The sculptures were created by Miquel Blay, the mosaics were designed by Lluis Bru.

Attending a concert is, of course, the best way to appreciate the marvels of the interior of the Palau de la Música (illus. pp. 172–3). In an interplay of all the arts, the overwhelming spell of the unique space becomes apparent.

In addition to the mosaics and tiled decoration, the panes of the glass are also painted. The "greenhouse" can be considered a shrine to sound, light, and color. Here too the most modern techniques of the time were used to create a stunning atmosphere. The central high window is a masterpiece: it hangs down like a colossal droplet. Thousands of painted pieces of glass mosaics form an "inside-out cupola" through which the sunlight penetrates the temple of the arts. The circle is lit by hundreds of electric light bulbs incorporated in the blossoming capitals of the columns.

It must be said that the symbolic splendor of the audience space is surpassed – only just – by the sculptural adornment of the proscenium as well as the decoration of the stage (illus. right).

The fundamental ideals of the Orféo are symbolized here in scenes rich in meaning and significance: to the left, the bust of Anselm Clavés embodies "*Flors de Maig*" (May blossom), and the maiden beneath the tree in the meadow is from the Catalan folk song; to the right, Beethoven and Wagner's *Ride of the Valkyrie* encompasses an enchanting tradition of European music (by Domènech i Montaner and Pau Gargallo). The wall of the choir circle is adorned with musical allegories by Eusebi Arnau, below which torsos are depicted in mosaic as figures in relief.

Nature is the link between the sensory experiences of the Palau de la Música Catalana and the significant body of thought from which it originates. The natural world can be said to oversee the architecture through the mosaic decoration, while at the same time it provides the background for the mythological scenes. The concert hall embodies a kind of Garden of Eden, in which Catalan music takes its rightful place.

The building was restored during the 1980s, and extended through careful addition by Oscar Tusquets and Carl Diaz. The Palau de la Música Catalana can be visited by appointment.

*In the Parc de la Ciutadella*

## Parc de la Ciutadella

At the eastern edge of the Gothic Quarter, between the grid-iron street pattern of the *Eixample* and the spurs of La Barceloneta, lies the Parc de la Ciutadella, one of the oases of present-day Barcelona (illus. above). The grand and spacious landscaping hardly allows one to imagine that one of the darkest chapters in Catalan history was played out here.

The Bourbon king, Philip V, once had a citadel erected in the area of the park to hold the city – loyal to the Habsburgs – in check. The fortress existed up to the 19th century, as a symbol of subjugation by the central power of Madrid. Barcelona attained possession in 1869, and razed the walls and the citadel. The governor's palace, arsenal, and chapel of the fortifications were retained.

In 1881 the grounds were laid out as a landscape park by Josep Fontserè, the main attraction being the cascades with their extensive collection of mythological sculpture (illus. opposite top). Fontserè had a talented colleague on the project: Antoni Gaudí.

Shortly after, it became the venue for the first Spanish World Exhibition. Even though this event created considerable problems for Barcelona – described in Robert Hugh's book *Barcelona* – it helped the city rise to the status of metropolis.

Modernisme established itself as the all-embracing cultural manifestation in the buildings and exhibition of this "*Exposició Universal.*" Architecture, the graphic arts, and arts and crafts were all given an immense impulse that ensured creativity and prosperity were carried into the new century. Many buildings of the World Exhibition were pulled down when it closed and the interiors and exhibits dispersed. This was also true of the semicircular Palau de la Indústria and the Hotel Internacional that had been built in a very few weeks by Lluis Domènech i Montaner. The buildings retained imparted sufficient flair to keep the atmosphere of 1888 tangible.

To welcome visitors to the World Exhibition, on the Saló de St. Joan (today Passeig Lluis Companys), the triumphal arch of Josep Vilaseca presented a picturesque prelude (illus. opposite bottom). Throughout the buildings and structures of the exhibition, extensive use was made of bricks and ceramics – typical Catalan/Aragonese materials – in tribute to the crafts and industry of Catalonia. An avenue of statuary led from the arch to the entrance of the exhibition (where the Museu de Zoologia is today) on the right (illus. p. 178, bottom left). The building, by Domènech i Montaner, used revolutionary techniques: a visible steel frame acted as scaffolding, enabling a pair of rooms to be built on top of each other in the upper and lower parts of the structure. Double-skinned enclosing walls with maintenance access between the wall layers permitted a façade independent of the interior space.

The exterior of the former café/restaurant recalls the Exchange in Valencia dating from the late Middle Ages, the best-known secular building of its time. Brick, battlements, and ceramic decoration were among the preferred modern materials that were used here both traditionally and effectively.

Two greenhouses attached to the Museu de Zoologia form the *Hivernacle,* or winter garden, to keep plants through the winter, and the Umbracle or shade house. Both are fantastic cast-iron constructions by Josep Fontserè (illus. p. 178, top right, and below). Between them lies the neo-Pompeian Museu Martorell, a building that is dedicated to geology.

From the mounted statue of General Prim i Prats, who handed the citadel over to the city in 1869, the way continues to those citadel buildings that were retained, designed by military architect Prosper Verboom in 1716–29.

Today the Arsenal is home to the Catalan parliament, and it is also an annex of the Museu d'Art Modern (illus. p. 179, top). In the museum, Catalan art and craft ranging from neo-classical through Impressionist to classical modern is exhibited. The cultural roots of the young Pablo Picasso can be seen here.

Among the outstanding items are the paintings of Marià Fortuny and Santiago Rusiñol, the sculpture of Josep Llimona (illus. p. 179, bottom) and Juli González, as well as the Col·lecció, Josep Clará whose work encompasses both "Noucentism" and the neoclassical style of the early 20th century. The nearby zoo offers children and adults art of an entirely different kind, for its top attraction is a white gorilla named "Snowflake."

Left:
*Parc de la Ciutadella Cascades built by Josep Fontserè and Antoni Gaudí 1871–81*

Below:
*Triumphal arch for the World Exhibition of 1888 (today on Passeig Lluis Companys) built by Josep Vilaseca*

**ABOVE:**
Cafe/restaurant of the 1888 World Exhibition (today the Museu de Zoologia) built by Lluis Domènech i Montaner

**TOP RIGHT:**
Umbracle (shade house) built by Josep Fontserè in 1888

**RIGHT:**
Hivernacle (winter garden) built by Josep Fontserè in 1888

LEFT:
*Wing of the Arsenal of the former Citadel, today the Museu d'Art Modern, built by Prosper Verboom in 1716–29*

BELOW:
Josep Llimona
*Desconsol (Desolate), 1907*

## Llotja and the Pla del Palau

The late medieval commercial center of Barcelona developed around the square that is today's Pla del Palau on the eastern edge of the Gothic Quarter. The *Llotja* or Exchange and the Corn Market were erected here, as spacious late-Gothic halls like those in Valencia, Perpignan, and Palma de Mallorca which have been preserved. The exchange room of the *Llotja*, – perched upon just four slender columns – is hidden behind the neoclassical façade of the present-day building.

In subsequent centuries the *Llotja* was extended a number of times in order to incorporate the customs authorities and the Consolat de Mar. It reached today's form in the late 18th century. The staircase in particular – set apart from the Gothic interior – is well worth seeing (illus. below). In the 19th century the Exchange was used for other purposes for a time, such as the Escola de Belle Arts, where Picasso, Miró, and many other important artists took their first steps in art. The extravagant parties celebrated by the Modernists at the turn of the 19th century became legendary.

Opposite the *Llotja* the palace of the regent – from which the Pla del Palau gets its name – towered over the square, but burned down in 1875. The palace, that occupied the space of the corn and later cloth markets, acted as governor's residence from 1668, and even was where the Spanish kings stayed during periods of residence in Barcelona. The Pla del Palau was first extensively redeveloped in the early 19th century. The concept was part of a long-term plan to redirect the center of Barcelona toward the sea.

One result was the building of the neoclassical Cases d'en Xifré. Their name was derived from a merchant called Xifré who became rich through trade with America, and it

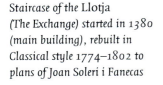

*Staircase of the Llotja (The Exchange) started in 1380 (main building), rebuilt in Classical style 1774–1802 to plans of Joan Soleri i Fanecas*

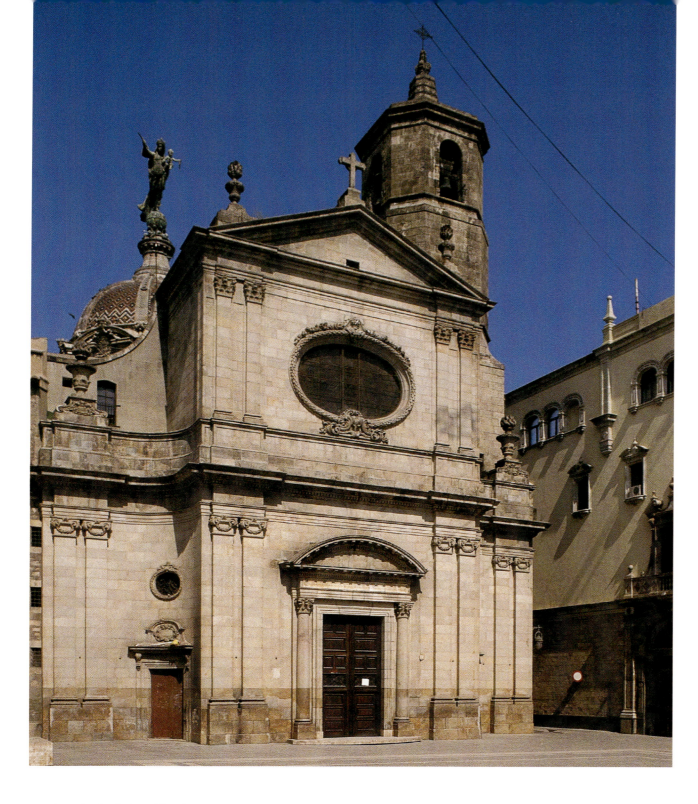

La Mercé, built 1765–75 by
Josep Mass, façade by Carles Grau

was he who had the office block and apartments built. They are an outstanding example of middle-class upward mobility. The importance of shipping and trade is apparent from the sculptural adornment of the doorways. There is also extensive allegorical decoration of the customs house opposite. Its frontages, by an Andalusian architect in 1770, give Barcelona an extremely rare touch of Rococo.

The broad street, appropriately named Carrer Ample, is also in the architectural style of the 18th and 19th centuries, and it is a place where the most important nobility have lived since the 15th and 16th centuries. To one side is the Església de la Mercé, the church of the Merciful Mother of God, the patron saint of Barcelona. This late Gothic building (constructed in 1765–75 by

Josep Mas with a façade by Carles Grau) came first in a listing by merit of the city's churches, and led by a substantial margin (illus. above). On feast and other special days – and also whenever there are exhibitions – there are crowds of both locals and visitors here.

To conclude our stroll through the renovated quarter of Barri Gòtic, we pass the temptations of the many colorful local bars walking toward the Plaça Reial.

Traversing the superb Carrer Avinyó, we pass the delightful building of the Borsí, the private Exchange that the merchants of Barcelona had built in 1883. Today it functions as school for the arts and crafts. The Carrer Avinyó has other attractions: it has been suggested that Picasso found the Demoiselles d'Avignon in a bordello here.

After the twisting alleys of the Gothic Quarter the Plaça Reial is like a mirage. Since its alteration as part of the *Espais Urbans* redevelopment program, it has become the most popular meeting place for every strata in society (illus. left and below). The Plaça Reial's layout also originates in the 19th century, when it was turned from the French Baroque Place Royales to an enclosed square framed by porticoes with unified style of development.

As usual with town redevelopment, the demolition of monasteries during secularization enabled new urban solutions. Since traffic was banned from the square in the 1980s – replaced with palms and benches surrounding the fountains and the Graces – a new vitality has been attracted to the square. The restaurants and bars clustered between numerous shops provide not particularly cheap seats in a living theater where one can enjoy the colorful bustle of activity the square has to offer.

*Place Reial, built 1848 by Francesc Daniel Molina,*
*newly laid out by Federico and Alfonso Milà*

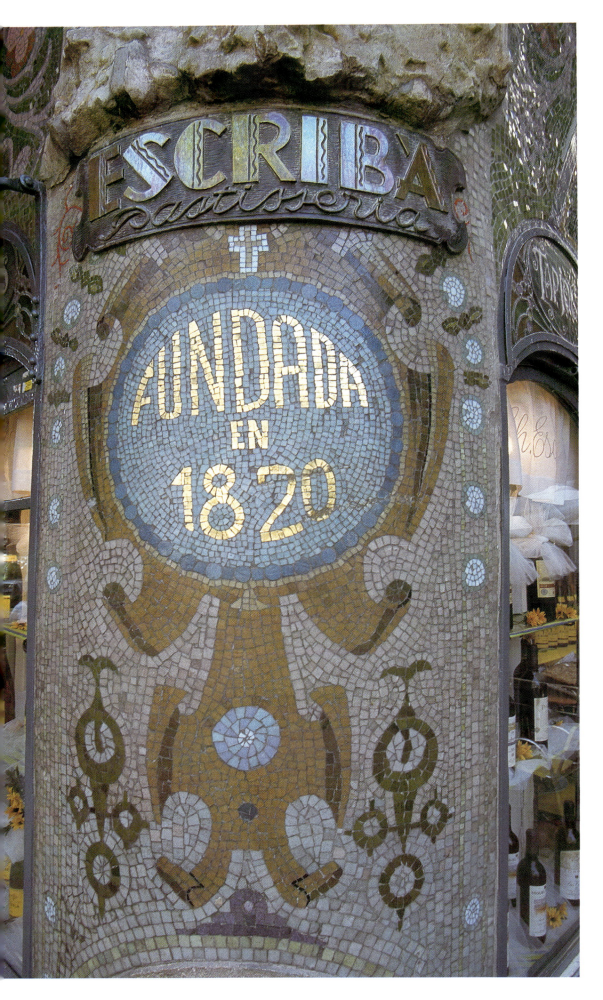

## La Rambla and Raval

La Rambla is much more than a boulevard: it is one of the widest, most dynamic stages in Europe (illus. opposite and pp. 186–7). In the course of a circular progress of 1.5 km (c. 1 mile) between Plaça de Catalunya and the sea, you will encounter an endless variety of scenes that are performed by countless actors. Street performers, dancers, and fire-eaters gather beneath the shade of the plane trees and between the cast-iron kiosks, period lanterns, and urinals, while the periphery is lined with living sculptures. Here and there dreamers discuss their theories, while others promise to foretell the future through cards. Day and night one is surrounded by people from all over the world drifting aimlessly, absorbing the sights and atmosphere – and also by voyeurs and pickpockets.

On many days La Rambla belongs, above all, to the Catalans: the most impressive occasion is on St. George's day (*Dia de St. Jordi*), April 23, when thousands of roses in honor of the saint adorn the countless Catalan bookstalls, from where the roses are generously given to passersby.

Not for nothing do people call this La Rambla. From the business-like Plaça de Catalunya to the proud Columbus column at the old harbor, the boulevard crosses no less than five zones, each of which retains a character very different from the others. They comprise the Rambla de Canaletes, the Rambla dels Estudis, the Rambla de St. Josep, the Rambla dels Caputxins, and the Rambla de St. Monica.

The Arabic word "ramla" indicates a dry river bed. The Spanish borrowed the word for the strip of sand in front of the western part of the original medieval city wall. Small squares were created in front of the gates from where traders could sell their wares. These are still clearly apparent, bearing their old names, for example Plaça de la Boqueria (meat market).

When a new outer wall enclosed the suburb of Raval in the 13th century, La Rambla became important as a north-south link between parts of the city within the walls. Monasteries and colleges of various denominations settled on the perimeter. The street was converted to a boulevard for the first time in the 18th century, when avenues of elms and poplars were planted on the strips of sand. At that time the first patrician and aristocratic families established themselves on La Rambla.

Secularization in 1835 brought a radical change here, as throughout the city. In the following years most of the cloistered orders were disbanded, and the buildings demolished or burnt down to be replaced by either homes for the citizens, new places of business, or new squares. The present-day avenue of plane trees was planted in 1859.

The boulevard quickly acquired its historic "street furniture" thanks to the new material of cast iron, and the promenade became a place where the citizens of Barcelona enjoyed strolling along under the trees.

Let us explore the different sections of La Rambla, each of which has preserved its own character. Close to the

Plaça de Catalunya is La Rambla de Canaletes, probably the most original part of La Rambla. The name comes from the Font de Canaletes fountain. The rows of neatly ordered chairs on which one could sit and rest for a few pesetas have been replaced by street cafés and kiosks. This is the open-air "drawing room" of the old town, where the older inhabitants of Barcelona meet to discuss events such as the victory or defeat of the Barcelona soccer team.

The connecting Rambla dels Estudis gets its name from the university buildings of the *Estudi General* (founded 1450) and a Jesuit college that was once here. Both were closed by Philip V, and turned into barracks because of Bourbon suspicion of the political activity of the students; the barracks were demolished in the 19th century.

The Baroque Betlem church of the same era has survived. The building was erected by Pater Tort and Dídac de Lacarse to plans of Josep Juli, based on counter-Reformation models. The superb diamond quartering of the façade is in contrast to the "medieval" supporting pillars of the clerestory. The Palau Moja (No. 118) opposite is 18th century, while the premises of the Reial Acadèmia Ciències – with its standard time clock and *Teatre Poliorama* – is 19th century. Close by at No. 109 one can see the premises of the mighty tobacco concern, Compañía General de Tabacos de Filipinas.

There are fewer argumentative students today in La Rambla dels Estudis than there are chirping or screeching birds. For, since the turn of the 19th century, bird traders have established a market here. At night the stands (unfortunately replaced with new ones) are simply closed up, complete with the cages and their occupants inside.

Central in La Rambla are Rambla de St. Josep and Rambla dels Caputxins, both named after former cloisters. It is more appropriately called Rambla del Flors, since, in close proximity to the bird traders, this is where the flower-sellers offer their wares from stands brimming over with vivid color, exotic shapes, and wonderful scent.

The boundary between the sections is marked by a mosaic pavement by Joan Miró – a popular meeting place. Then, countless street cafés invite one to linger – however, such a unique setting is somewhat expensive. Between the Carrer del la Portaferissa and the Carrer de la Boqueria, La Rambla is flanked by some of the most important institutions of Barcelona life.

The first is the Mercat de la Boqueria, also named Mercat de St. Josep, sited on the foundations of a former Carmelite cloister. Everything that Mediterranean and Iberian cooking has to offer can be found here, housed in the sumptuous glory of a cast-iron market of 1835. The items on display alone are a feast for the eyes: the

Along its 1.5-km (c. 1-mile) course from the commercial Plaça de Catalunya to the Columbus column in the old port, the boulevard crosses five zones: each retains its own distinctive character. The neat rows of chairs on which could sit for a few pesetas have now been replaced by street cafés and kiosks. The nearby Rambla del Estudis is named after the Estudi General university buildings and the Jesuit college once established here. Today it is populated by bird sellers with their cheeping or screeching "wares." La Rambla de St. Josep and Rambla dels

Caputxins are midway along the length, named after former cloistered sanctuaries. The description Rambla dels Flors is more appropriate, since this is the territory of the flower-sellers with their colorful overflowing stalls.

The boundary between the two areas is marked by a pavement mosaic by Joan Miró, which is the most popular meeting place on the boulevard. Countless street cafés tempt one to linger off La Rambla de St Mònica: but one has to pay the price for their unique position.

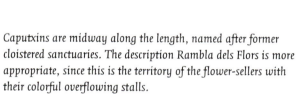

overwhelming smells and colors of the fruit, the quality of the meat, but above all the seafood and fish with their silvery bodies entwined like ribbons. Between the rows of stalls with cheese and olives, you reach the edge of the market where there are small stalls that allow you to sample the food or enjoy a snack. It is well worth a visit.

Not far away, somewhat set back, is the Palau de la Virreine of the power-hungry Minister of Philip V, Manuel Amat i Junyent, started by Josep Ausich in 1772. After its completion in 1778, the statesman was to live in the largest private palace in Barcelona for only four years. Junyent died in 1782, but his widow continued to reside in the lavish building as Regentess. Today it is used for avant-garde and design exhibitions, and also accommodates art-book businesses and cultural associations.

Opposite to it, at an angle, where the Carrer de la Boqueria broadens to a small square, make a point of looking up to see where Bruno Quadras, owner of a parasol, umbrella, and fan factory, had a most original advertisement created for his products (illus. left, top).

The complex of the Teatre del Liceu extends behind the junction with Carrer St. Pau. The famous Barcelona opera house caught fire in 1994, but as early as the autumn of 1999 the completely new opera house was reopened. The first building had been completed in 1847 by Miquel Garriga i Roca; this caught fire a number of times in the following 14 years, and in 1861 almost burnt down. As a result, the interior was renewed in even more pompous and old-fashioned style. After Italian opera, the work of Wagner was praised above all. In 1914, the first authorized performance of *Parsifal* outside Bayreuth was given here.

An institution almost as important as the Liceu is the Opera Café opposite, of which the original charm of the 1920s has been entirely retained. The traditional Oriente and Quatre Nacions hotels have also preserved an air of bygone days. In the Oriente hotel, the former cloisters of a Franciscan monastery have been turned into a unique lounge for guests and visitors.

Farthest removed from its cloistered origins is La Rambla de St Mònica, the bottom section of the boulevard. For a long time the future of this area was a burning issue, and not just because of its fire-eaters. Slowly but surely, efforts were made to rehabilitate this corner of La Rambla, especially the neighboring western quarter, through improvements to the infrastructure.

The Teatre Principal was restored and became a rehearsal stage for the Liceu; the Convent of St Mònica was redesigned in minimalistic style by Helio Piñón and Albert Viaplana, and in recent years has housed many significant exhibitions.

The Catalan ministry of culture occupies the Classical Palau March de Reus (No. 8). The Museu de Cera (Passatge de la Banca 7) to the left of La Rambla is well worth a detour to see the extremely lively display of wax figures.

Before the stroll along La Rambla comes to an end, one passes a further Classical building of great significance in the defence of the city: the cannon foundry to the side of Plaça del Portal de la Pau.

One of the most famous landmarks in Barcelona is the approximately 70-m (c. 230-ft.) high Columbus Monument that towers up from the Port Vell at the end of La Rambla. The iron column, erected by Gaietà Buigas Monravà, acted as visible "high-point" of the World Exhibition of 1888 (illus. above). Oddly, the larger-than-life-size statue looks east – not west to the New World. Perhaps this was a belated act of revenge by the Catalans who saw their economic supremacy lost through the Atlantic trade. Those who do not take the elevator to the viewing platform can study the powerful lions and reliefs on the plinth that illustrates Catalan conquests.

OPPOSITE TOP:
*Dragon and fan of the parasol works of Bruno Quadras, 1890*

OPPOSITE BOTTOM:
*Pavement mosaic of Joan Miró in the middle of La Rambla*

TOP:
*View of the Columbus column and La Rambla from a cable car*

## The *Drassanes* (shipyard)

The *Drassanes* or shipyard, constructed in the immediate vicinity of Port Vell, is extensive and impressive evidence of the glorious seafaring past (illus. above and left). Today it accommodates the Maritime Museum which depicts the naval power of the Catalan-Aragonese realm in a lively and interesting way.

The *Drassanes* shipyard is a unique industrial monument. The origin of the shipyard lies in the late 13th century when King Pere el Gran had it constructed as an open colonnaded courtyard with military defenses. In the 14th century the main building was extended with eight parallel roofed sheds in which about 30 galleons could be worked on at the same time. Cleverly, the place in front of the *Drassanes* could be partially flooded so that a ship could be slipped into the harbor basin. In the 16th century the Generalitat took over the *Drassanes*, but they were claimed in 1663 by the Spanish crown. In the 18th century the two central parts were brought together and raised up in order to construct the larger ships then being built. The massive sheds are all spanned by transverse arches which carry brickwork roof trusses.

Today the museum is part of the most popular visitor destination in Barcelona. Nowhere is the magnificent history of Catalan-Aragonese naval power displayed so vividly as here. At its heart is the galleon of Juan de Austria, half brother of Philip II, who defeated the Turks in the naval battle of Lepanto in 1571.

Its recreation recalls the glorious times of conquest of the sea (illus. opposite). The first steam-powered submarine – developed by the Catalan Narcis Monturiol of Figueres – can also be admired in the impressive sheds. In addition, there are fishing boats, charts, tools, and figureheads, all colorful images encompassing both the joy and the suffering of Christian seafaring.

TOP:
Drassanes (shipyard),
14th–18th centuries; today the
Maritime Museum

ABOVE:
Drassanes
View of the sheds

OPPOSITE:
Reconstruction of the 16th-
century galleon of Juan de
Austria

## The Catalan-Aragonese Mediterranean Empire

The rise of the Catalan-Aragonese empire through naval and trading power began in the early 13th century when King Jaume I, The Conqueror, recaptured Majorca (1229), Eivissa (Ibiza, 1235), and Valencia (1238) from the Moors. His son, Pere II, succeeded in extending the boundary of the empire to Sicily. Alfons II finally took Minorca in 1287, Jaume II added Sardinia (1324), and in 1343 Pere IV annexed the kingdom of Majorca that then stretched to southern France. A spectacular event allowed the Catalan-Aragonese realm to rule almost the entire Mediterranean for a short time. Between 1303 and 1324 a 4,000-strong army – the almogàvers – led by Admiral Roger de Flor, reached Constantinople to fight in the service of the Byzantine emperor against the Ottomans. Roger de Flor, son of a German falconer to the court of Friedrich II, married the emperor's niece, and led a successful campaign to Asia Minor, but was murdered by the emperor's son. The Catalans, supported by supplies, practiced "venjança catalana" (Catalan vengeance), which resulted in bringing the northern Aegean under Catalan rule in 1390. Athens acquired Barcelona's city constitution. In the 15th century, Alfons el Magnànim removed his seat of government to Naples, which remained Catalan-Aragonese until the War of Spanish Succession (1701–1713).

## Raval: St. Pau del Camp and the Hospital de la Sta. Creu

The Raval – the only westerly suburb of La Rambla – has experienced rapid change. Until recently the historic quarter, which was enclosed by the city walls in the 14th century, was not a place for a peaceful stroll. The appalling housing conditions in the narrow, dirty, and neglected old town left its mark: criminality and drug problems were openly visible. But strangely, there was a plus side: the lively sub-culture that developed here contributed to Barcelona's reputation as a city "where it's at."

The planning measures developed soon after the death of Franco began to bear fruit. The aim – with well-directed cultural facilities and rehabilitation of the housing – was to improve the quality of life in the Raval. As a consequence, the northern Barri de L'Hospital and the area known as Barri Xinès in the south are now well established points on any visitor's itinerary.

The varied history has also given rise to various cultural monuments. The oldest is probably the Romanesque cloister of St. Pau del Camp: the Benedictine monastery of St. Paul "of the fields." The building, founded in the time of the Visigoths and rebuilt in 1117 after the invasion of the Moors, is somewhat out of place in its gray surroundings, although for the visitor this helps to heighten the contemplative atmosphere emanating from both the venerable walls of the monastery and the superb medieval sculpture. The capitals of the 13th-century cloister were made particularly imaginatively. However, the barrel-vaulted interior itself is rather plain, and the transept is covered by an octagonal tower.

The picturesque Mercat de St. Antoni at the edge of the Raval on the Ronda de St. Pau is decorated with an entirely different form of "transept" and "tower." The cast-iron market building is laid out in the form of a cross, externally clad with tiles. The market was erected by Antoni Rovira i Trias between 1872 and 1882 (illus. below). Beneath the dome, the loud cries of traders advertise the gleaming, silvery fish.

Together with the Boqueria in La Rambla and the Mercat del Born at the other end of the old town – converted for cultural activities – this is the most visited market of Barcelona.

Those interested in the architecture of the 1930s can see an outstanding example in the Carrer Torres Amat, close to the center of the Plaça de Goya. The tuberculosis clinic – recently restored by the GATCPAC architectural association (with the involvement of Josep Lluís Sert) – is an impressive example of the quality of buildings of the Second Republic.

The "L"-shaped steel-framed building with strip windows, and composed of delicate colors is the most important example of Spanish Rationalism.

Close to St. Pau is the imposing complex of the Hospital de la Sta. Creu. Originally an ancient pilgrim hospital, this Holy Cross hospital of 1401 was founded by King Martí I, and supported by people of high rank. Even Pope Benedict XII donated 10,000 gold florins for its

*In Mercat de St. Antoni*

construction. Under the leadership of Guillem Abiell, the building quickly grew into one of the most important hospitals of its age. This house for the sick comprises four large wings with cross-vaulted groins at ground level and flying buttresses supporting the upper structure and wooden roof (illus. right). It was still occupied in the second quarter of the 20th century. Antoni Gaudí died here – virtually unknown – on June 7, 1926, following an accident. Today the late Middle Age Gothic space is home to the Biblioteca de Catalunya. The Gothic arcaded courtyard is part of the main building, with capitals of threatening dragons and other legendary animals.

Between the 16th and 18th centuries the complex more or less doubled in size, partially through rebuilding and also by absorbing neighboring buildings. The monumental staircase, which is flanked by statues of Compassion and the saintly Rochus of the plague, was constructed in 1585.

In 1629 a group of aristocratic women made it possible for the Baroque Casa de Convalescència – a luxurious convalescent home adorned with decorative tiles – to be built. Today it is home to the Institut d'Estudis Catalans. Opposite it, behind the fine Classical façade of the Coli·legi de Cirurgia, is the anatomical theater.

The entirely successful building of 1761, which was built to plans by the court architect Ventura Rodriguez, is well worth seeing, and especially its revolving marble dissection table surrounded by the elevated circles of the auditorium (illus. below).

LEFT:
*Hospital de la St. Creu*
*View of one of the four wings,*
*started 1401, today the Biblioteca*
*de Catalunya*

BELOW:
*Anatomical theater of Coli·legi de*
*Cirurgia, built by Ventura*
*Rodríguez in 1761*

## The Town Villa of Count Güell

The last place one would expect to find a magnificent town villa is in the middle of the somewhat oppressive darkness of the Carrer Nou de la Rambla. Surprisingly, the surroundings were little better at the end of the 19th century, when the rich textile manufacturer Eusebi Güell decided to build a villa here. In addition, the small and awkwardly situated piece of land made great demands on the architect.

Not surprisingly, Güell's choice was the young architect Antoni Gaudí, whose geniality and skill in dealing with other projects had already impressed him. A year after the Finca Güell of 1885, the count entrusted Gaudí with this important commission, and gave him complete creative freedom and a lavish budget.

Given the nature of the site, Gaudí encased the façade on Carrer Nou with coarse stone dressing. The upper part of the building in particular is opened up with tracery window frames in the form of a corbel, recalling something of Venetian palazzi. Dominating features are the parabolic gateways which are closed off by artistic grilles with a wrought-iron version of the Catalan arms between them (illus. left bottom).

When the count lived there the interior of the Palau Güell was reached by coach through the gateway. An explosion of splendor and imaginative style awaited the visitor. After handing over his horse to be taken to the stables in the basement, the visitor stepped with amazement into the mystical domed hall that rises through all the floors, and is shrouded in darkness (illus. p. 165). Reminiscent of a medieval inner courtyard, the domed hall is the centerpiece of the residence.

Güell – in common with many of his Catalan contemporaries who were simultaneously both religious and avant-garde – received his guests here for parties and concerts, and for religious services that were accompanied by organ music.

A high-point in every sense, the dome was engineered so that light penetrates slightly through minute apertures, creating a star-filled firmament. The living space is more intimate but hardly less grand, divided on three floors grouped around the central hall. Gaudí pulled out all the stops here, for he artistically and imaginatively combined both innovation and an arts-and-crafts form.

The architecture of the second floor is mold-breaking with its dual-scale approach to the space and to the oriole windows that open onto the street. Iron elements, such as pillars and lintels, are incorporated in the whole both functionally and decoratively.

Medieval, Mudéjar art, and Jugendstil are equal sources of inspiration in the style of the interior. Artesonado canopies, arched galleries, decorative window glass, and wall coverings, but above all the carvings and intarsia work together with extravagant furniture testify to Gaudí's virtually inexhaustible creative imagination.

Recently the roof terrace of Eusebi Güell's Palau Güell has been opened up again, with its amusing ventilation shafts and biomorphic decoration that anticipates the roof landscape of Casa Milà (illus. left top).

## Avant-garde in the Old Town: CCC and MACBA

Leaving the Hospital de la St. Creu heading in a northerly direction, and following the Carrer dels Angels, one penetrates farther into this historic yet entirely newly conceived quarter of the city.

The sparkling white Museu d'Art Contemporani de Barcelona (MACBA), opened in 1995, is built in the unmistakable style of Richard Meier, and in the Raval it shines like a "UFO" (illus. above). This structure flanks the Plaça dels Angels, along with the cloister of the same name, having been converted by Lluis Clotet, Carles Diaz, and Ignacio Paricio into the present-day conference and cultural center.

New university buildings of quality have recently been built behind the MACBA, a place where the complex of the medieval Casa de la Caritat orphanage is also situated. The Centre de Cultura Contemporània (CCC), which is dedicated to exhibiting and organizing both urban development and avant-garde culture within an urban context, is currently housed in this four-winged early 19th-century building.

Further structures, such as the late Gothic Edifici Manning, with its atmospheric courtyard and the recently restored premises in what was a former cloistered order, together form the extensive cultural and economic quarter of Raval. This mix of aesthetic and university establishments leads the way in a long-term re-evaluation of the redevelopment area.

The intervention in the old town is bearing fruit: the Raval is developing at an astounding speed – certainly too fast for many of its older inhabitants. The modern architecture acts as a catalyst in this process of change. The outstanding buildings by both Catalan and famous international architects – regarded as out of place until a few years ago – have proven to be an "intense and powerful beam of light" in this urban setting. Squares and passages, galleries, and cafés help ease the still densely packed housing of the quarter.

Richard Meier's museum is currently the most visited building in Barcelona. The block, dazzling white – like all his work – flanks the northern side of the Plaça dels Angels. Its plinth is barely noticeable above the level of the square. The ground plan of the four-story building with 13,000 sq. m (c. 43,000 sq. ft.) of usable space comprises different cubic elements combined as if in a collage, and slightly resembling a mirrored "L."

The cross-framing of the main front and staircase is the east–west backbone to which the box-like general exhibition area, the rounded reception and special exhibition space, and the rectangular eight-floor administration building – linked respectively by a passageway and bridge – are attached. The eastern end of the main frontage springs from a vibrant annex, which includes space for shows to be held in studios.

To the north of the complex, where the transition is made to the courtyard of the CCC, an exciting square has

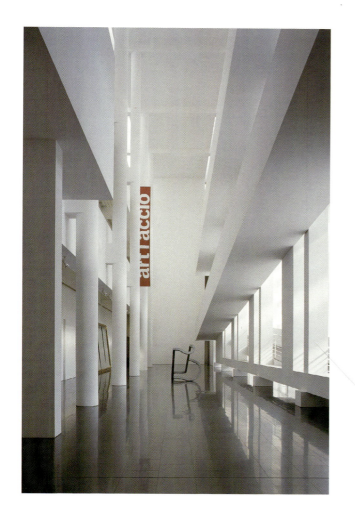

been formed by the rotunda and the elegant and reserved administration wing that is used as an open-air art gallery. Unexpectedly, a winding passage leads from there: this is the architect's reminder and echo of the tortuous streets of the quarter in which the structure is placed.

The southern frontage, which serves as both entrance and showpiece of the Plaça dels Angels, contrasts with this almost intimate area. The monumentality of the massive white blocks is bound together by three collage-like elements: the screening formed in front of the entrance, the horizontally arranged façade of green glass, and the sculptural annex at the eastern end. Behind this broadly supported front, the access ramp space – so typical of Meier's style – that connects the building both metaphorically and in reality is hidden (illus. p. 197, top left and right).

The ramp opposite leads the visitor to an *arcanum*, in which contemporary art is exhibited against white walls. In addition to various international exhibitions, the work exhibited is by Catalan artists from 1940 to today, such as the Dau al Set group, Antoni Tapies, Joan Brossa, Francesc Torres, and Perejaume (illus. p. 197, bottom left).

While the internationally renowned Meier made his mark on the Raval with his white cube, Catalan architects followed a different approach in designing the neighboring buildings.

The CCC is an outstanding example of avant-garde architecture in historic surroundings. Helio Piñón and Albert Viaplana, both from Barcelona, designed an independent connecting section for the ruined fourth wing of the Casa de la Caritat, dominated by a cantilevered glass wall (illus. left).

In contrast to the existing material, the architects intentionally opted for modernity. The horizontally arranged glistening green façade takes its window line from that of the surrounding wings, so that the 19th-century design is now crowned impressively with an outstanding Attica-like finish.

The entrance to the Center for Contemporary Culture conceals surprises: one moves into the foyer by means of a ramp opposite the glass wall that – in a way is similar to the new entrance to the Louvre – is set below the patio level. The 730 sq. m (c. 2,400 sq. ft.) space that opens out onto two floors envokes a certain forlornness, a kind of metaphysical emptiness. These feelings are slightly mitigated, fortunately, by the soft green of the travertine glass, the perfect concrete surfaces, as well as by the minimalist pale green fixtures and fittings that have been selected specially for the building.

The exit is equally rewarding, as one moves upward on the escalator alongside the glass façade to the areas for instruction, exhibitions, seminars, and administration in the upper floors (illus. right). The exhibition space has been usefully split between the three other wings of this four-winged building.

The Center for Contemporary Culture, which has a firm place in Barcelona's cultural scene thanks to its manifold activities, also has an auditorium, four large halls, a cafeteria, and a book-shop.

OPPOSITE:

*Exterior of Centre de Cultura Contemporània, built by Helio Piñón and Albert Viaplana in 1994*

ABOVE:

*Centre de Cultura Contemporània
Foyer*

# Eixample: Synthesis of Art

*Eixample*, or *Ensache* in Castilian, is the name given by the Spanish to the late 19th century town expansion that was intended to put an end to the housing demands and the appalling living conditions in the historical center. Barcelona was not the only place to establish an extensive new town with regular wide streets and spacious squares. Modern homes for rent, gardens, and social institutions aimed to give the inhabitants a healthy and happy life.

Barcelona's *Eixample* was a European-wide example of this town-planning utopia. For the urban grid-iron that extended from the sea to the mountains, encircling the Gothic Quarter and the Raval, is probably the biggest and most powerfully unified example of its kind, a unique testimony to middle-class homes, and a show-piece of modern Catalan architecture (illus. right).

The town plan is best understood from the air. Over an expanse of 4.5 × 3 km (c. 3 × 2 miles) all the streets run either parallel to the sea or are at right-angles to it. Three diagonals cut across this chessboard pattern, linking the center with the perimeter: Avinguada del Diagonal, the Paral-lel, and the Meridiana. The old town is incorporated within these axes; the crucial point between *Barri Gòtic* and the *Eixample* forms the Plaça de Catalunya. The thoroughfares form regular blocks or *mançanes* of 133.33 × 133.33 m (c. 440 × 440 ft.), now entirely built over, contrary to the original intentions.

The width of the street varies but is never less than 20 m (c. 66 ft.). An unusual feature is the "flattening" or rounding off of the corners – the *xamfrá* – at intersections which form a square, and make it easier for buses to turn.

The creator of this grid-iron pattern was the engineer Ildefons Cerdà (1815–76), commissioned by the Spanish crown to present a plan for the expansion of Barcelona (illus. p. 203). At the time of the siege by the Bourbons in 1714, the town was still constricted by its medieval walls, preventing any expansion. This became catastrophic when the population shot up during the economic growth of the 19th century. The population density in the dilapidated old town was higher than in any other European city, and the sanitary conditions were unhealthy. Epidemics struck families at regular intervals. Much too late, in 1851, the

*The western part of the Eixample seen from the air*

Decorative tiles in houses in the
Eixample

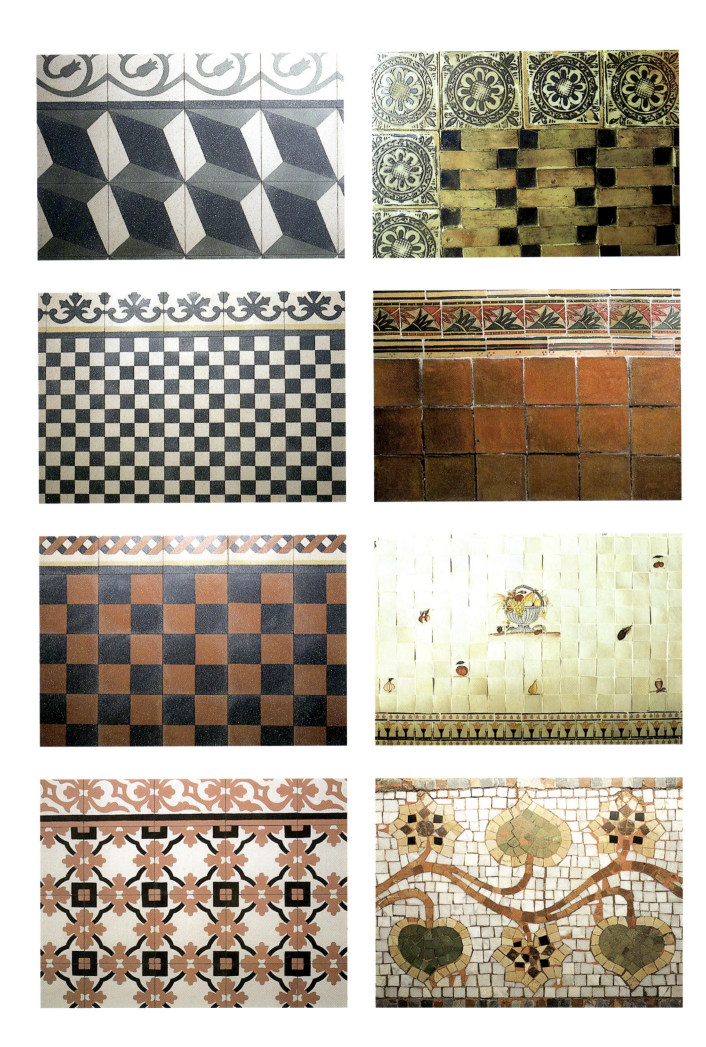

central government in Madrid finally permitted expansion outside the fortifications.

Now Cerdà's town expansion plans offered all the citizens of Barcelona similar decent living conditions and the requirements needed to create a modern metropolis. But his forward-looking concept was not accepted without conditions. The decision caused long-term political friction between Barcelona and Madrid, for construction could only begin on a directive from the central government. The expanded new town of Barcelona, with homes for about 175,000 people, was created eventually over five decades, roughly between 1860 and 1910.

Those who were able to, escaped from the confinement of the *Barri Gòtic*. Houses and plots of land in *Eixample* quickly became desirable homes or investments. The most well-to-do families had appropriate and original homes built on the main thoroughfares of Diagonal, Gran Via, and Passeig de Grácia. Most of them had made their money in the textile trade or through trade with the Catalan colony in Cuba.

The quarter formed between Carrer Aribau, Passeig St. Joan, the Rondes, and the Diagonal were developed with homes for the rich, and quickly gained the name Quadrat d'Or or "Golden Quarter." It comprises an exceptional

architectural collection of some 150 luxurious homes and offices dating from 1890 to 1910.

The utopian social proposals of Cerdà fell by the wayside in view of the building boom. According to his plans, each block was only to be built with houses on two sides, leaving space between for refreshing green landscaping and sufficient markets, schools, and hospitals to meet the people's needs. However, the tremendous growth of Barcelona caused by out-of-control speculation quickly put an end to Cerdà's ideals. The building stock by the 20th century had easily increased more than fourfold beyond what had been planned.

Nevertheless Barcelona developed a unified urban appearance. Thanks to rigid application of the planning rules, apart from some contrary individualism, few buildings exceeded the prescribed dimensions. Corner buildings are emphasized architecturally, recalling the "cross-roads" of Cerdà's plans. On the other hand, the façades mirror the range in imagination and animation of 20th-century architecture. Great importance was given to the "street furniture" with vegetal mosaics on the street paving, wrought-iron street lanterns, and sleek stone benches. They make the *Eixample* a collective and unified work of art.

*Expansion plan for Barcelona designed by Ildefons Cerdà in 1859*
*Museu d'Historia de la Ciutat*

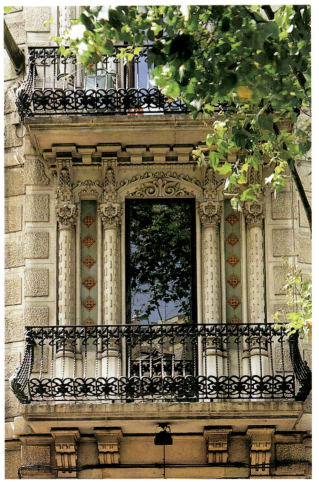

OPPOSITE, LEFT:
View of two buildings of the Mançana de la Discòrdia
Casa Amatlló of Josep Puig i Cadafalch (left)
Casa Batlló of Antoni Gaudí (right)

OPPOSITE TOP AND RIGHT, BOTTOM:
Window of a private house in Eixample

ABOVE:
Gable of the Casa Papallona built by Josep Graner i Prat in 1912

RIGHT:
House with turret on the Passeig de Gràcia

## The Main Thoroughfares and Intersections

Before we look at some of the specific buildings of the *Eixample*, let us look at the main arteries through which life pulses every day. The heart of the city beats from the commercial Plaça de Catalunya that is the crucial point between the old town and the *Eixample* and between the past and the present (illus. left, and below).

By 1977, the year in which about one and a half million people peacefully celebrated the end of the Franco dictatorship and the first free elections on *Diada* – the Catalan national day of September 11 – the Plaça de Catalunya had become an institution (illus. opposite).

People come here for special occasions in the city, to demonstrate, for a drink in the Café Zurich, or to stroll through the Corte Inglés department store, the roof terrace of which offers a unique view.

The Plaça de Catalunya had an earlier important role in Barcelona life. Before the Cerdà town expansion, it served as a promenade area at the edge of the city. The square first acquired its present form with banks and businesses in 1927. Unfortunately the Hotel Colón – rich in tradition, acting as headquarters of the Catalan Socialist Party (PSUC) during the Civil War and as a center of resistance against Franco – was later demolished.

A star-shaped pavement mosaic marks the center of the trapezoid layout. Fountains and planting create an oasis of peace from the everyday hubbub. Sculpture by Pau Gargallo and Josep Clarà invokes an idyll that is almost palpable amid the commotion.

Those who shun daylight can find variety in the extensive Metro complex. Fortune-tellers, musicians, and peddlers set themselves up in the long passageway. The acoustics of the entrance are so good that rock concerts are held here from time to time.

ABOVE AND LEFT, BOTTOM:
*Plaça de Catalunya – boundary between the old town and the Eixample*

OPPOSITE:
*La Diada – the Catalan national day on September 11, 1977*

The Passeig de Gràcia leads from the Plaça de Catalunya to the former suburb of Gràcia – a popular and trendy living area – and cuts through the *Eixample* from southeast to northwest. It is lined with elegant homes and offices, some extremely luxurious, including three outstanding buildings:"Mançana de la Discòrdia (illus. opposite, left, and p. 212) and the Casa Milà (illus. pp. 222–3).

The boulevard is crossed at right-angles by the equally wide and lively Gran Via de la Corts Catalanes. This extends from Plaça de les Glòries Catalanes to the foot of Montjuïc. It passes the central university building – the first monumental structure erected in the *Eixample* in 1863–72 by Elies Rogent.

Today Barcelona looks across the Plaça de les Glòries Catalanes where a new cultural center has been established with the Teatre Nacional of Ricardo Bofill (illus. p. 208, top) and the Auditori Municipal of Rafael Moneo. The aim, achieved at the start of the 20th century – based on the ideas of the 1859 Cerdà plan – saw the expansion of the city toward the east, and the creation of a more broadly based urban center.

The Plaça de les Glòries is also the starting point of the Avinguda Diagonal which cuts across the grid-iron, and is also the crossing point of the Meridiana, which extends into the eastern suburbs.

The Diagonal runs through the city dead straight for 10 km (c. 6 miles), and finally becomes the main road to Madrid. It has a varied history. Like the other residential and business streets of the *Eixample*, large expanses of workers' houses were intended to be built at the perimeter during the Second Republic. The Spanish Civil War prevented this from being accomplished. Instead the renamed "Avenida de Generalísimo Franco" served the dictator as a troop deployment area, and as route to his residence in Pedralbes. In 1952 it acted as backdrop for the celebration of the "Eucharistic Congress" – a megalo-maniac demonstration of unity between the authoritarian State and the Church. The statues on the Diagonal were accordingly changed. Construction of the new university began in the western part in 1955. Later many business centers have sprung up along its length, and spacious sporting facilities were added for the Olympic Games.

The thoroughfare of Paral-lel is aptly named. It runs parallel to the Diagonal from the port to the western suburbs. Near Raval it is flanked by establishments that have given it the nickname of "Barcelona's Montmartre."

At the intersection of the Paral-lel with the Granvia, the Plaça d'Espanya opens out; its colonnades are reminiscent of St. Peter's Square, and the characteristic twin towers of Ramon Raventós provide a brilliant prelude to the exhibition, sport, and cultural site of Montjuïc (illus. pp. 236–55). Here at the western edge of the *Eixample* one is confronted by a town-planning project of considerable architectural audacity, carried out after the death of Franco. This is the most imaginative – but somewhat dilapidated – Parc de l'Espanya Industrial, with its light towers and ponds occupying a former industrial site. A metal dragon guards the terrain, and also acts as a water slide (illus. p. 210, top).

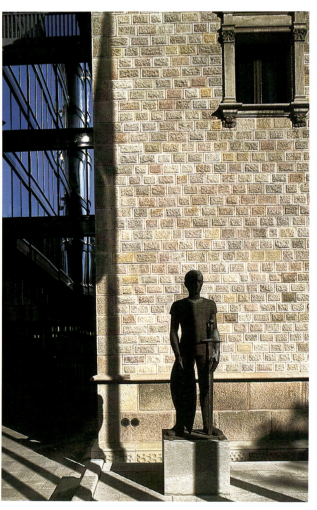

OPPOSITE, TOP:
*Teatre Nacional on the Plaça de les Glòries, built by Ricardo Bofill in 1997*

OPPOSITE, BELOW AND ABOVE AND RIGHT:
*Impressions of the Avinguda Diagonal*

The Plaça dels Països Catalans, better known as the square of the Sants rail station, is close by; with its consistently minimalist design, it featured on the front pages of architectural magazines in the 1980s. The architects Helio Piñón and Albert Viaplana opposed the trend toward the trivializing of urban wasteland, and so created a deliberately sober and abstract ambiance that drew on the theme of urban wasteland, rather than drawing a veil over it (illus. p. 210, bottom).

The main elements are the delicate metal sail above 15-m (c. 50-ft.) high steel supports and the wave-form pergola that give the space dynamism. Simple cones, tubes, benches, and water columns provide graphical accents to the structure.

The third project of this era, another that renewed Barcelona's claim to be a city of avant-garde architecture, is the Parc Joan Miró. The famous sculptor created *Dona i Ocell (Woman and Bird* 1984, illus. p. 211) for it in the final years of his life. This park, which incorporates the site of a former slaughterhouse, is also designed to strict architectural principles.

Anyone who passes through the *Eixample* with open eyes can still discover quite a few traces of the forward-looking "Espais Urbans" town-planning program. In many places well-chosen architectural intervention has created a better local environment, and has brought about a kind of "self-healing" process in neglected quarters. Occasionally, as in the case of Sants, the citizens vigorously oppose uncompromising planning that is driven solely by aesthetic considerations.

OPPOSITE, TOP:
Parc de l'Espanya, built in
1984–5 by Lluis Peña Ganchegui,
Francesc Ruis, and Andrés Nagel
(dragon sculpture)

OPPOSITE, BOTTOM:
Plaça dels Països Catalans (Estació
Sants), built by Helio Piñon and
Albert Viaplana in 1983

RIGHT:
Joan Miró
Dona i Ocell sculpture, 1984

BARCELONA. 86 - *Paseo de Gracia - Construcciones modernas.*
*(Manzana entre las calles Consejo de Ciento y Aragón.)*

## Imagination and Inquiring Minds: building the *Eixample*

It would take weeks to visit all the sites worth seeing in the *Eixample* because of the sheer numbers of Modernist citizen's "palaces." Romanesque, Gothic, and Arabesque houses are interspersed with traditional blocks or avant-garde experiments, according to the preference and funds of the commissioning client. To give some idea of the considerable choice of important buildings, it is believed that there are at least 150 outstanding buildings in the Quadrat d'Or area alone, in the heart of the *Eixample*. It makes sense therefore to either restrict oneself on foot to the Passeig de Gràcia, or to visit specifically the work of Gaudí and his contemporaries – best done by taxi.

With all due respect to Gaudí and his brilliant creative work, one must remember that he was just one of a handful of exceptional creative architects who together created the Barcelona of the 20th century. Lluis Domènech i Montaner and his pupil Josep Puig i Cadafalch rightfully deserve an important place in architectural history; they propagated Modernisme longer than Gaudí, forming the taste of their contemporaries. Both were, as Oriol Bohigas is today, simultaneously architect, art historian, and politician. Both placed a reawakening of a "national" Catalan culture at the core of their work, although nothing would have been achieved without a profound knowledge of European history.

Antoni Gaudí (1852–1926) (see panel box p. 232) held a rather special position among the intellectual, open-minded architects of the turn of the century in Barcelona. Deemed an artist, he refused throughout his life to speak any language other than Catalan, and by his later life was somewhat bigoted and a loner. Systematic research into the past interested him as little as architectural theory or the classification of his art in an historical context. Regardless, he created work, perhaps for this reason, far ahead of its time, so that today it still has the power to move and arouse us.

Gaudí was an empiricist, who therefore found practice an astonishing discovery. The only teacher he accepted was Nature. It guided him in his mold-breaking and stunningly artistic solutions.

The "Mançana de la Discòrdia" in Passeig de Gràcia is a brilliant prelude to any stroll through turn-of-the-century Barcelona (illus. above). The name is a play on words in Catalan, suggesting that the building is a bone of contention. It certainly irritated its contemporaries. People felt that the only explanation for the differences exhibited by the three buildings next to each other was that the temperaments of the three architects had been indulged. In fact the Casa Lleó Morer (No. 35), Casa Amatller (No. 41), and Casa Batlló (No. 43) were built or altered in their different forms by three protagonists of Modernisme.

Lluis Domènech i Montaner erected the house on the corner of Carrer Conell de Cent in 1902–06 for the businessman Francesc Morera in the form of a Venetian palace (illus. opposite). The façades are broken by neo-Gothic strip windows, and the corner is crowned in the form of a tempietto. Simultaneously, the present day was also glorified. Sculptor Eusebi Arnau created richly symbolical adornments – unfortunately lost from the lower floor in 1943 by alterations for commercial use. The decorative figures of maidens on the balcony, though,

## Modernisme and Noucentism

Modernisme, or in Castilian Modernismo, is the name given to the cultural movement in Spain during the final decade of the 19th century and the first one of the 20th. Other related modernizing movements existed, such as the British Arts and Crafts, French and Belgian Art Nouveau, Viennese Secession, and German Jugendstil, but Modernisme for the Catalans included a national component. Catalans had sought specific Catalan forms of expression in literature since the middle of the 19th century, and united in 1880 against all existing forms of art in favor of Catalan and European forms of expression. The domestic lifestyle exemplified by Eixample testifies to this. The breeding ground for this movement, which encompassed all strata of society, was manifested in the tremendous economic upswing of Catalan industry and the development of the middle class. It received an impulse from the World Exhibition in Barcelona in 1888. Its exponents achieved a style that became generally accepted; it borrowed from nature, and had a preference for clean lines and a trend toward use of modern materials (steel and glass) in anticipation of the 20th century.

Protagonists of modern architecture were Lluis Domènech i Montaner, Josep Puig i Cadafalch, and Antoni Gaudí who worked as architects and designers. Shining stars among the graphic arts of painting and printmaking were Santiago Rusiñol, Ramon Casa, and Isidre Nonell, a circle of friends that soon included Picasso. Arts and crafts, sculpture, literature, theater, and music contributed to a bright array of all the arts. Noucentism was to a certain extent a Classical backlash against the "excesses" of the turn of the century, making itself known through Eugeni d'Ors' novel La Ben Plantada of 1912, in which a clear indigenous conception of Man was developed in the 20th century, rooted in Mediterranean culture. The nude woman of Aristide Maillol or the frescoes and paintings of Joaquim Torres Garcia, Josep Maria Sert, and Joaquim Sunyer impressively embodied these ideals.

With architecture, on the other hand, a forbidding neoclassicism took hold that culminated in the pomposity of the World Exhibition buildings being erected in 1929 in Montjuïc. Noucentism ended with the architectural Rationalism of the Second Republic. Classical monumentality was more or less the imprint of the time of Franco.

ABOVE, RIGHT, AND
OPPOSITE:
*Casa Lleó Morera
Interior view
Eusebi Arnau. Alfons Juyol, and
Gaspar Homar were among those
who worked on the interior design*

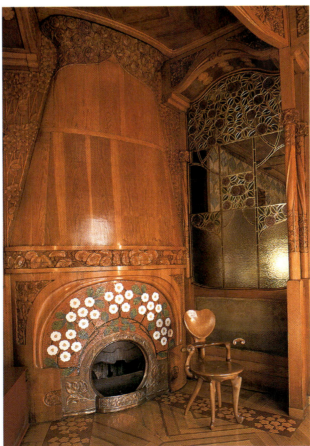

have been preserved. They are relevant to the present day, for they hold a gramophone and a camera in their hands.

The interior too – now the Patronat de Turisme – exudes the spirit of the age. One imagines a world of idylls amid the blossoming economic metropolis. Through an entrance decorated with luxuriant floral motifs, one reaches the main floor with its splendid furniture, sculpture, painted glass, and mosaics. Today these are copies of the originals that are in the Museu d'Art Modern (illus. above, left, and opposite). The main theme of the pictorial representations is the glorification of country life. A mosaic decorating the chimney-breast suggests a picnic where fashionably dressed women with well-filled hampers eat under the shade of a pergola. The cool bright colors are typical of the time. The sculptural execution of the heads on the other hand is original, although we have already encountered it in the Palau de la Musica Catalana (illus. p. 175).

The Casa Amatller, which Josep Puig i Cadafalch altered for the chocolate-maker Antoni Amarller in 1898–1900, gives a rather northern impression (illus. p. 216). Undoubtedly the stepped gables of northern German or Dutch houses were in his mind when he created the striking design of the house. On the other hand, the decoration of the doorway and framing of the windows is reminiscent of late medieval Castilian art of the Isabella style. Ceramic cladding and *esgrafiats* flat stucco are

fairly typical Catalan materials. An extremely impressive scene is enacted between the asymmetric main entrances: St. George boldly pierces the throat of the terrifying dragon with his lance. The legend of St. George (St. Jordi), patron saint of Barcelona, is deeply rooted in the minds of the people of Barcelona. The knight is also the city's emblem.

The interior of the Casa Amatller (today the Amatller research institute, which can be visited by appointment) provides a unique, virtually unaltered view of the home interior at the turn of the century (illus. pp. 217–19). In confined space, one imagines a Moorish palace with a Romanesque cloister leading off it, or is reminded of a grand Renaissance room, or admires the craftmanship of Modernisme carried out by Eusebi Arnau and Gaspar Homar. New meaning is given to Spanish art through such an *in situ* collection.

The third and most recent of the "Mançana de la Discòrdia" houses was designed by Antoni Gaudí between 1904 and 1907 following a commission by Josep Batlló i Casanovas. Here too the architect had to contend with an older building, yet he created one of the most unusual front elevations of all time (illus. p. 220, and p. 221, top and left). The showpiece building projects over the pavement like a vegetal-form sculpture. The planning authorities raised objections to the "elephantine" supports, though in the end without success. The floor

which thereby cantilevers resembles white bones. On the other floors balconies "cling" to the walls like birds' nests. Their artistic balustrades were created by Gaudí's most talented pupil, Josep Maria Jujol. Even the roof of the Casa Batlló, which is reminiscent of a scaly monster, is sculptured (illus. p. 221, top). In strange contrast the asymmetric towers act as finials. A further unusual characteristic of the house is discovered in sunshine: the entire upper part of the façade is clad with *trencadís* or shards and small discs which make it glisten.

Gaudí also found new, more flexible ways of dealing with the interior. Rigidly structured rooms gave way to cell-like modules, stairs, windows, and doors, with the entire fitting-out appearing to respond to a living organism that breathes, and seems to have formed itself by natural means. The entire furnishings also fall within this biomorphic approach.

Some of the fixtures and fittings are today housed in the Casa Gaudí in Parc Güell, where a "sofa" with body-shaped, gentle curving contours formed from 2 armchairs can be admired (illus. p. 221, right). That Gaudí also regarded functionality alongside his "natural" ideas is proven by the staircase of clean lines, clad with bright blue tiles, which of course incorporates a chair-lift as a technical element.

Just three blocks farther on at the intersection of Passeig de Gràcia and Carrer Provença is another individual property, the Casa Milà that Gaudí was commissioned to build for the Milà family. Its towering eroded rock frontage has given it the name of "La Pedrera" or "The Quarry" (illus. p. 222, left).

Ridiculed at the time, the building erected between 1905 and 1911 is regarded today as a precursor of Expressionist architecture. In the daring exterior, Gaudí led the way with innovative concepts that anticipated future forms of housing.

The exterior impression is bizarre in its effect, and does not suggest well-functioning apartments within. The front has a wave-like appearance; the roof soars upward like a mountain range and finishes in an droll pinnacle. The entire building resembles an enormous sculpture inspired by nature. The unique, and wildly rampant balcony balustrades further emphasize the vegetal effect. With them, Josep Maria Jujol created one of the major examples of Catalan wrought-iron artistry (illus. p. 223, bottom left and right).

More astonishing even than the sculptural detailing of the Casa Milà, however, is its structural conception – of course, not visible. The entire complex grouped around two courtyards rests upon a steel framework and stone pillars. There are no load-bearing walls, and the façade is simply mounted on the inner frame. The limestone blocks of the cladding were each precisely worked, and then anchored in the required place.

These structural frames enabled architect and inhabitants relative freedom in the arrangement of the inner space. The floor plan and position of the walls could be considered individually, although the starting point was the most asymmetric and irregular division of

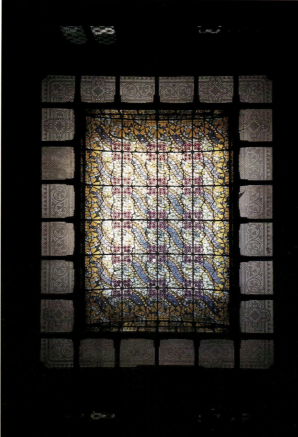

OPPOSITE:
*Casa Amatller, built by Josep Puig i Cadafalch, 1898–1900*

ABOVE:
*Casa Amatller Window*

LEFT:
*Casa Amatller Colored window*

apartments possible. But this extravagance had disadvantages too, of course: Gaudí advised a tenant who complained she could not accommodate her grand piano that she would be better off playing the violin.

On the other hand, the overall concept of the Casa Milá is extremely practical and extraordinarily modern. Gaudí incorporated an underground car park reached by a spiral ramp. Instead of an imposing staircase the building was accessed through completely decentralized entrances and exits. The courtyards served for ventilation rather than as an imposing feature.

The fantastic roof terrace was planned for the tenants' relaxation, a feature that Gaudí used 20 years later for the Palau Güell. A surrealist roof-top landscape was created with chimneys like knights in futuristic armor, and ventilation shafts rising upward like snails covered in mosaic fragments (illus. pp. 222–3, top). The surface rises and falls, suggesting a stroll through undulating country.

These changes in level also influence the arrangement of the top floors immediately beneath, which had to be amended soon after the building was completed. Here again, one can admire Gaudí's perfect use of parabolic arches. They enabled the flexibility to create arches of differing heights above a level floor.

Despite the unconventionality of his architecture Gaudí did not go against his deep religious conviction. Hence the eye-catching inscription "Ave Maria, Gratia Plena" is prominently displayed above the main floor. The ventilation shafts on the roof are surmounted by crosses – albeit in a playful style. Gaudí had intended to place a Madonna above the main entrance, but fear of vandalism in the anticlerical mood of 1909 forced the owner to ban this feature.

Lluis Domènech i Montaner (1849–1923) is the oldest of the three Modernist "stars." With his manifesto "In search of a national architecture," he formulated the theoretical basis for architecture at the turn of the century.

As leader of the *Jocs Florals*, a "medieval" contest of Catalan art, president of the respected cultural institution of Ateneu Barcelonès and head of the Lliga Regionalista, Montaner steered the cultural life of Barcelona. In common with most of his contemporaries, he placed equal emphasis on architectural design, craftsmanship and explicit decoration. His work in the old town, the symbolic Palau de la Música Catalana, and the stately

*Casa Amatller*
*Staircase*

Modernist café/-restaurant have already been described. The Casa Lleó Morera in the Passeig de Gràcia gives the viewer a glimpse of his creativity.

His later homes for citizens of the *Eixample*, such as the Casa Thomas (Carrer Mallorca 291–3; built 1895–1898) or the delicate Casa Fuster (Passeig de Gràcia 132; built 1908–11) show the variety of his eclectic and highly fashionable style. Domènech's publishing house of Montaner i Simón has recently been in the limelight.

Carrer Aragó 255, which was built in 1881–6, was chosen in 1989–1990 by the most important present-day Catalan artist Antoni Tàpies (see panel box p. 224) as the home of his foundation, and was internally redesigned by Roser Amadó and Lluis Domènech (ilus. p. 224, top). The exhibits are convincingly supported by the interior architecture, and even at times are integrated with the building. Library, lecture room, and space for changing exhibitions of contemporary art supplement the collection. The unique publishing house was very innovative before becoming a victim of the years of dictatorship. Domènach i Montaner was, after all, the

first to use steel-frame construction – normally reserved for industrial construction – to build a house. Bricks and glass, both of them traditional and inexpensive materials, replaced the stone customary until then. The turning away from the eclecticism of the 19th century was apparent in his façades. Instead of historic motifs, the steel frame dominated the external form.

During the change of ownership the widely visible sculpture of *Cloud and Chair* proclaimed the new use of the building. In the impressive setting of the interior, about 300 paintings, drawings, and sculptures of every phase of Antoni Tàpies' creativity are safely housed.

Over three floors the path of this artist, born in 1923, is set out from his early work influenced by surrealism to the mainly large-scale pieces of recent years, with canvases painted in earthy colors and symbolical formulae, often enhanced three-dimensionally with natural materials (illus. p. 225, bottom).

The play with visual perception is architecturally continued by a staircase that obeys the same logical rules (illus. p. 225, top). In addition to the collection, the

LEFT:
*Casa Batlló*
*Detail of the roof*

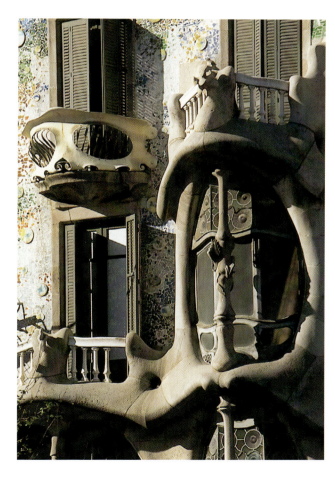

OPPOSITE, TOP, BOTTOM AND ABOVE:
*Casa Batlló, built by Antoni Gaudí 1904–07*
*Details of the façade*

RIGHT:
*Casa Batlló*
*"Sofa" made by Antoni Gaudí from two armchairs*

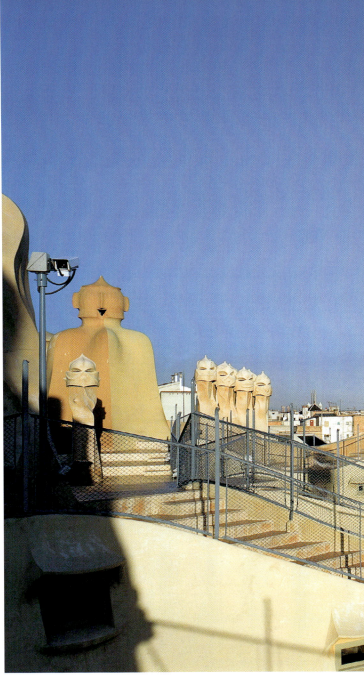

*Casa Milà, built by Antoni Gaudí,*
*1905–11*

Fundació Tàpies also encompasses a wealth of documentation about art in the 20th century and the culture of the Far East.

The most important work of Domènech i Montaner, apart from the Palau de la Música, is surely another functional building: the Hospital de la Sta. Creu i de St. Pau in the north of *Eixample* (illus. p. 226, bottom). The Hospital de St. Pau is probably the finest and most individual hospital of any age. It replaced the medieval Hospital de la Sta. Creu in the Raval that had been the most important hospital in Barcelona until it was damaged by fire.

Thanks to a bequest in the will of Banker Paul Gil i Serra, Domènech i Montaner was able to start building in 1901. The building was continued by his son in 1923, and today forms part of the university.

A tall neo-Romanesque portal forms the entrance to an extensive series of pavilions encompassing nine blocks of the *Eixample*. According to the garden-city plan, 48 individual buildings are arranged on either side of two diagonal thoroughfares. All the treatment areas and wards

are heated and ventilated. Garden areas provide relaxation for the patients.

Through a stroke of genius, Domènech i Montaner separated the patient areas from the care facilities. He placed the latter underground, and linked them by subterranean passages. Advancement of hygiene and functionality was achieved in a manner hitherto unknown.

Domènech i Montaner's pavilions are at one moment reminiscent of a medieval sacred building and another of a Moorish palace, adorned with ornamentation of the *Jugendstil* or similar movement (illus. p.227, top). No one pavilion is the same as another.

The best-known artists of Barcelona, including Eusebi Arnau and Pau Gargallo, were brought in to carry out the huge project. In keeping with the imaginative architecture, sparkling mosaics, sculptures, colorful ceramics, and glass painting create a fantastic magical world that quickly makes one forget the serious purpose of this collection of buildings. The sensuous decoration is more than adornment though. There is a full range of complex historical and cultural history in the contents for those

Fundació Tapies, formerly the
publishing house of Montaner i
Simon, built by Lluís Domènech i
Montaner 1881–6; converted
1989–90

On the roof:
Antoni Tapies
Núvol i Cadira
(Cloud and Chair)
Sculpture

## Antoni Tàpies i Puig

Antoni Tapies is the most important internationally known post-war Catalan artist.
Initially inspired by the work of Joan Miró and Paul Klee, he became a painter of magical
realism in the 1950s, but turned his attention to the use of objects and materials in the 1960s
and 1970s. Large-scale materials, rough surfaces, and everyday objects with graffiti,
calligraphy, and mystical signs have become a means to poetic meditation.
Not only was Tàpies avowedly against the Franco dictatorship, creating countless political
works, but he also incorporated Catalonia as a theme in many of his creations. As a follower
of oriental philosophy, he possessed an outstanding library now held by the Fundació Tàpies.
Antoni Tàpies, was born in Barcelona in 1923, founded the avant-garde publication Dau al
Set in 1948, and held his first one-man exhibition in the Galeries Laietanes in Barcelona in
1949. His contact with the art dealer Aimé Maeght in 1967 pointed the way to his
international career. He wrote his autobiography Memòria personal in 1977, and was
awarded the Imperial Prize in Japan in 1990.

Self-portrait by Antoni Tàpies,
1945
Ink on paper, 43 × 31 cm
Fundació Tàpies

who are interested. The façades and interiors are adorned with saint and angel, allegories of the Virtues and science, and portraits of famous Catalans. Lizards and other wildlife are mingled together with flowers of every color and sort. This is an earthly and very Catalan paradise that provides healing for both body and soul even today.

Josep Puig i Cadafalch is without doubt the favorite of the series of architects of Barcelona at the turn of the century (see panel box p. 228). Like his teacher, Domènech i Montaner, he was simultaneously an important art historian and an influential politician, standing for the resuscitation of national culture. One of Puig's greatest services to Catalonia resulted from his rediscovery and creation of public awareness of the Catalan architecture of the Middle Ages.

In addition to this strand of Catalan patriotism in his personality, though, Puig was cosmopolitan. In his travels to France, Germany, and the Netherlands, he always tried to broaden both his scientific and his artistic horizons, and thereby sought to bring Catalonia and the northern countries closer together. This synthesis of Mediterranean and central European culture was to make a decisive impression on style of his architecture.

*Fundació Tàpies*
*View of interior designed 1989–90*
*by Roser Amadó*

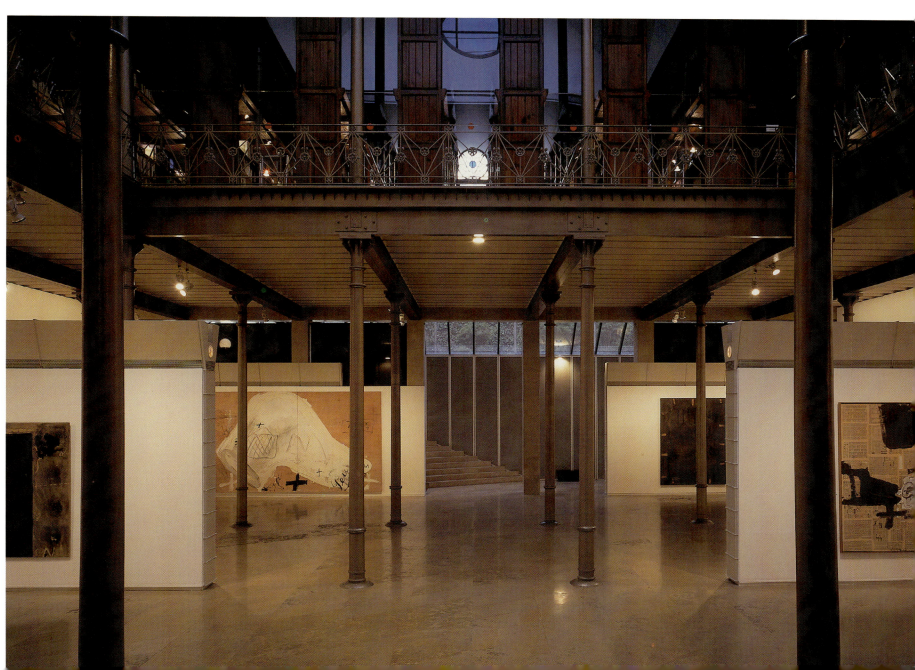

The Casa de les Punxes (actually Casa Terrades, Diagonal 416–29; built 1903–05) is immediately next to Casa Milà – in a challenging position in planning terms – on the Diagonal (illus. p. 228, top). It owes its nickname, "house of the spires," to its pseudo-medieval turreted spires – unusual in Barcelona – which appropriately accentuate the small frontage of the triangular piece of land.

Josep Puig i Cadafalch successfully combined traditional northern European architectural motifs with Catalan craftsmanship and patriotic decor, which he had used previously for "Els 4 Gats" and the Casa Amatller. Casa Macaya (Passeig de St. Joan 108; built 1898–1902) brings the debate about Spanish architectural history to a close by incorporating elements of the Isabella, late Gothic, and vernacular styles.

On the other hand the Palau del Baró de Quadra (Diagonal 373; built 1902–04) is externally northern/late Gothic, and internally Arabesque/Andalusian. Today it houses the Museu de la Música. Can Serra (Rambla de Catalunya 126; built 1903–08) also combines the different styles in a picturesque way without losing a typical Catalan appearance. It is almost superfluous to point out that these houses were also designed to the smallest detail by the architect with his client.

OPPOSITE, TOP:
Hospital de la Sta. Creu i de St.
Pau, started by Lluís Domènech i
Montaner in 1901
Entrance hall

OPPOSITE, BOTTOM:
Hospital de la Sta. Creu i de St.
Pau
Front entrance

ABOVE:
Hospital de la Sta. Creu i de St.
Pau
Pavilions within the hospital

RIGHT:
Lluís Domènech i Montaner in the
hospital entrance hall in 1912

### Lluís Domènech i Montaner

*Lluís Domènech i Montaner, the earliest and most productive of the three architectural "stars," was one of the pioneers of modern steel-frame and brick construction in Europe. With the grandiose Palau de la Música Catalan, he constructed the most comprehensive Moderniste work of art. His essay "In search of a national architecture" of 1878 formulated the theoretical basis for Catalan architecture of 1900.*

1848 Born in Barcelona
1875 Professor of the Escola
d'Arquitectura in Barcelona
1881–6 Publishing house Montaner
(today Fundació Tàpies)
1888 Creative breakthrough with the
building of the World Exhibition (Hotel
Internacional and Cafe/Restaurant)

1896–7 Institute Pere Mata, Reus
1897 Casino, Canet de Mar
1895–8 Casa Thomas, Barcelona
1900 Casa Rull, Reus
1901 Casa Navàs, Reus
1902 Casa Lamadrid, Barcelona
1902–06 Casa Lleo Morera,
Barcelona
1902–12 Gran Hotel de Ciutat de
Mallorca
1903–30 Hospital de la Sta. Creu i
de St. Pau
1905–07 Monte de Piedad building,
Santander
1905–08 Palau de la Música
Catalana
1908–11 Casa Fuster, Barcelona
1911–12 Casa Gasull, Reus
1913–14 Espluga de Francolí winery
(together with his son)
1913–16 Casa Solà, Olot
1923 Died in Barcelona

### Josep Puig i Cadafalch

Josep Puig i Cadafalch belongs with Lluís Domènech i Montaner and Antoni Gaudí among the most important Moderniste architects. As an influential politician and open-minded art historian he acted as a link between Catalan and central European architectural trends. In his homeland he also became famous for the rediscovery and restoration of Romanesque churches.

1867 born in Mataró; 1889 town architect in Mataró; 1895–6 Casa Marti ("Els 4 Gats"), Barcelona; 1896–1906 Caves Codorniu, St. Sadurní d'Anoia; 1897–1900 Casa Puig, Argentona; 1898 El Cros, Argentona; 1898–1900 Casa Amatller, Barcelona; 1901 Casa Macaya, Barcelona; 1903–05 Casa Terrades (de les Punxes), Barcelona; 1904 Casa Quadras, Barcelona; 1911 Fábrica Casarramona, Barcelona; 1917–23 President of the Mancomunitat de Catalunya; 1920–29 Designs for the World Exhibition; 1957 died in Barcelona. Most important publications: L'arquitectura romànica a Catalunya, 1900–1918; La geografia i els origens del primer art romànic, 1930

OPPOSITE, TOP:
*Casa de les Punxes (Casa Terrades),
built by Josep Puig i Cadafalch,
1903–05.*

OPPOSITE, BOTTOM:
*Josep Puig i Cadafalch in his study*

LEFT:
*Textile factory of Casarramona,
built by Josep Puig i Cadafalch,
1909–11.*

From the internal architecture, the furnishings, and the items of practical use down to the decoration – even the occupants' clothing – were all carefully harmonized with each other.

Despite his love of detail and craftsmanship, Puig did not ignore large-scale projects. Hence, he designed countless town-development projects, ranging from those that were completed at one time to those constructed in several stages. Nevertheless they testified to his extensive image of cultural history and the strength of his mission.

The Casarramona textile works, recently restored, once again showed the practical-thinking, industrial architect, who was also aware of tradition. This enormous complex at the foot of Montjuïc looks like a neo-Gothic monastery with its supporting pillars, pinnacles, and pediments, recalling the golden era of the Catalan-Aragonese realm (see above). The production departments for spinning, cotton handling, and weaving were housed under the three long "naves." The polygonal external wing incorporated the administrative offices, while the turrets provided water storage. The entire building was constructed of brick over a steel frame. The construction of this structure was up-to-date at the time, yet also managed to retain traditional Catalan elements in its appearance.

In addition to Domènech i Montaner and Puig i Cadafalch, countless other architects contributed to the imaginative yet unified countenance of the *Eixample*.

Outstanding among their work are the bay-windowed Casa Comalat on Diagonal (Salvador Valeri i Pupurull, Diagonal 442; built 1911); the butterfly-like Casa de la Papallona near the Plaça Espanya of Josep Graner i Prat, built 1912 (illus. p. 205, left).

It is well worth acquainting yourself with the amazing diversity to be found within the *Eixample*, where no two houses are alike. No one can deny that Catalan individualism promotes unique and outstanding performances from its architects.

Now to Antoni Gaudí (see panel box p. 232), whose work even today holds many scholarly and personal enigmas. Three of his creations have already been extensively described: the early Casa Güell in Raval, the Casa Vatlló, and the later Casa Milá – both on Passeig de Gràcia. Further important examples of his work, including the Parc Güell, the Finca Güell, and the Colònia Güell in Santa Coloma, take a different approach. Yet these houses give some idea of the way Gaudí's architecture was established. From the historical principles of cladding of frames, he arrived at his brilliant concepts of sculptural molded architecture.

Among the comparatively few private houses in *Eixample* is the Casa Calvet (Carrer Casp 48; built 1898–9), certainly Gaudí's most conventional building. The entire frontage constructed of stone, plays with Baroque and Rococo elements. This example of Gaudí's work is also characterized by Catalan pragmatism and a touch of irony, for the heads of three martyrs that adorn the upper part of the façade also serve as anchoring point for a hoist to lift furniture in and out. Other details refer to a great interest of the occupant: Calvet was a passionate collector of fungi. The visitor is received – in the form of a door-knocker – by a louse, which he or she must symbolically crush in order to leave evil behind before entering the house.

## The Sagrada Família

In the already very individualist society of Barcelona, it was obvious that a sacred building by Gaudí would break all the rules. The foundation stone of the Sagrada Família was laid more than a hundred years ago, and it has been the premier tourist attraction in Barcelona for almost as long (illus. right, and opposite). Planned as "temple of atonement" for the excesses of the time (including artistic excesses), it became the embodiment of that creativity bursting to get out which accompanied the turn of the century. Dreamt of as an eccentric or final Gothic cathedral, it became a curiosity, particularly after Gaudí died in 1926, taking his ideas with him to the grave.

Only the east front was more or less completed at that time. However, designs existed for the west and south façades. The work "rested" until the 1950s when the genius of Gaudí's work was rediscovered. Significantly it was the Surrealists who recognized the building's quality and its antirationalist power. (Salvador Dali urged that the structure should be covered with a glass dome.) The completion of the building, however, was not a serious debate for the people of Barcelona themselves. The costly construction is today financed by donations.

The main efforts were therefore not "whether to" or "why" but "how?" Should they stick precisely to the remaining extremely vague proposals of Gaudí and his methods of construction, or would a contemporary reworking of his ideas be acceptable? The controversy finally led to a practical solution. Gaudí's project was to be continued – with retention of his formal proposals – using present-day construction techniques.

The sculpture created by Josep Maria Subirachs took the proposed iconography for the building into account and was exposed to harsh criticism of its abstract style.

Meanwhile work continues apace to complete the nave (illus. p. 233). Gaudí's aesthetic proposals are being adhered to, but preformed concrete units are used to speed up the work and also to keep the costs within acceptable bounds.

In spite of the turning away from the ethos of turn-of-the-century craftmanship, the visitor still has a unique glimpse of the creation of an image that in future centuries will form an everyday part of the city.

Let us go back to the origins of the "Templo Expiatorio de la Sagrada Família," which gives this unusual church its full name. It was established as a sort of memorial to the national conservative brotherhood of St. Joseph, who propagated a return to the forms of society of the Middle Ages. Appropriately the first plans for the Sagrada Família were extremely conventional. A neo-Gothic design by Francesc de P. del Villar was chosen, and the foundation stone was laid on St. Joseph's day, March 19, 1882.

Yet only two years later Antoni Gaudí took over the management of the construction. At this time the crypt was already rising above the foundations, so that – as so often before – the architect had to build on the foundations of others. Gaudí himself set out an overall plan in 1885 that broadly reflected the Barcelona cathedral, of which only the choir was completed.

OPPOSITE, AND ABOVE:

*La Sagrada Família, foundation stone laid 1882 by Francesc de P. del Villar, definitive design by Antoni Gaudí in 1906; building in progress*
*View of the eastern front (opposite), view of the western front (above); sculpture by Josep Maria Subirachs, in line with Gaudí's proposals*

ABOVE:
La Sagrada Família
Detail of the west front with scenes
from the Passion of Christ created
in 1986 by Josep Maria Subirachs

RIGHT:
Antoni Gaudí during a Corpus
Christi procession

**Antoni Gaudí i Cornet**

"Nature is a great open book and we should make ourselves
read it." (Antoni Gaudí)

Antoni Gaudí, the most important architect of Catalan
Modernisme, created his works from a broad repertoire of
historical elements (including medieval and Arabesque) to
develop an expressionist and sculptural style of his own. Nature
was the source of his important innovations (stresses borne
through parabolic arches) and also in his sculptural form of
construction. Gaudí maintained a practical studio in which
Josep Maria Jujol and others worked.

1852 born Reus; 1878 completed his architectural studies in
Barcelona; 1883 started work on the Sagrada Família,
Barcelona; 1883–5 El Capricho, Camillas (Catabria) and Casa
Vicens, Barcelona; 1884–7 Finca Güell, Barcelona; 1885–1900
Palau Güell, Barcelona; 1887–93 Bishop's Palace, Astorga;
1889–94 Col·legi de les Tereses, Barcelona; 1891–3 Casa de los
Botines, León; 1898–9 Casa Calvet, Barcelona; 1898–1913
Colònia Güell, Sta. Colom de Cervelló; 1900–14 Parc Güell,
Barcelona; 1904–07 Casa Batlló, Barcelona; 1905–11 Casa
Milà, Barcelona; 1906 final design for the Sagrada Família;
1926 died following an accident with a tram in Barcelona.

The architect subsequently constantly modified his proposals without ever setting them down in firm plans. It was not until 20 years later, in 1906, that the definitive ground plan of the present building was published.

In the meantime Gaudí no longer regarded Catalan Gothic as valid on its own, but took a more general, more international concept as his model. He decided that the "Temple of the Poor" should now compete with the cathedrals of Cologne and Rheims, with similarities in the ground plan: a nave with five lateral sections and three part transept. In the height, too, of 45 m (c. 150 ft.), there is evident similarity with Cologne cathedral. The tower above the transept at 170 m (c. 560 ft.) and its 18 satellite towers would outdo all previous examples.

The outline differed from all historical examples. Gaudí found a new structural system derived from nature that made supporting columns unnecessary. The forces on the arches were directly borne by the foundations through slanting supports.

Gaudí gained this knowledge through a "chain" model, with which he assessed the loads to be borne. He calculated that the load on the arch could be correspondingly equated to the pull of a sandbag hung on a chain (illus. p. 304). Gaudí simulated the thrust acting on every element of his building with hundreds of chains of different lengths. By this means he created imaginary models for the entire construction. One result of this process was the parabolic form of the arches that for many characterize his work.

Despite the top-flight architecture that Gaudí devised for the Sagrada Família, the form was determined by the symbolic content. The Sagrada Família is a manifesto in stone for the Christian faith. Three massive façades were dedicated to the life of Christ according to Gaudí's proposals. The east front (on the right, to the north of the church) illustrated the Birth, the west the Passion, and the south front would lavishly and finally depict the Glorification of Christ before one's eyes. The slender parallel towers form part of the intellectual reasoning. The tallest central one symbolizes the Savior, the tower above the apse represents the Virgin Mary, and four others are dedicated to the Evangelists with their gospels written in stone. Three further spires soar above each of the three façades, symbolizing the 12 apostles. The tower of the eastern portal can be climbed by means of a vertiginous spiral staircase or accessed half-way up by a lift. The view of the building site from here is unforgettable.

The sculpture for the façades is no less complex than the architectural features, of which only those for the east front were completed in Gaudí's lifetime. This façade is dedicated to the Birth of Christ (illus. p. 234). The biblical scenes are spread out on the portals, in their jambs, tympana, and openwork gables as on a medieval cathedral. Only by looking more closely with a certain amount of professional knowledge can one differentiate that this was work of a craftsman at the turn of the century. Plant decoration overgrows the entire façade, and the architecture seems to comprise twisted vegetal forms. Representations of the Christian virtues of faith, hope, and charity, adorn the three portals, completing the group of figures of the early history of Christ that decorate both framing and pediments.

*La Sagrada Família*
*View of the building of the nave*
*from the towers of the east portal*

*La Sagrada Família
Details of the east front with
biblical scenes, created by Antoni
Gaudí, 1899–1930.*

In the center stands the Annunciation of the birth of the Savior, the root of Jesse giving the lineage of Christ winds around the central jamb, which also symbolizes the Old and New Testaments. A pelican represents sacrificial love.

The Assumption of the Virgin Mary appears from the highest point, only surmounted by anagrams of the names of Jesus (illus. opposite, top). A wingless angel blows a trumpet to proclaim salvation's story.

The left portal dedicated to the theme of "hope" depicts Mary's initials, the slaughter of the innocents, and the flight into Egypt in projecting Montserrat stone.

On the right the visitation and scenes of the virtue of faith from the story of Joseph are portrayed. Grapes and thorns refer to the Eucharist.

Gaudí's biblical scenes resemble a vernacular Christmas crib; as always they are enlivened by animals and plants, so that the entire portal grows upward like a kind of paradisical primeval forest. In spite of the convincing collection of sculpture, much mystery still surrounds the significance of the snails and tortoises, which carry some of the columns of the façade.

Much debate accompanied the completion in the 1980s of the west front of the Sagrada Família. The renowned, though not uncontroversial, Catalan sculptor Josep Maria Subirachs had taken on the thankless task of carrying out the "passion" portal.

While careful adaptation of the architecture obtained approval, Subirach's differences regarding Gaudí meant the artist had to face violent derision and public abuse. In reality the crude abstract style of Christ bearing the cross, the scourging, and the scenes at Golgotha set them apart from the "cuteness" of the earlier turn-of-the-century works. The "facelessness" of Christ in particular (illus. opposite, p. 232, top ) was striking. Nevertheless, Subirachs did not sufficiently distance himself clearly

Barcelona

La Sagrada Família
*Details from the west front of scenes of the Passion of Christ, completed in 1986 by Josep Maria Subirachs.*

from his predecessor, and flirted with Gaudí's motifs such as the robot-like henchmen, which are reminiscent of the chimneys of the Casa Milà. But as he weathered the storm of indignation, Subirach's work was already being categorized as historic.

At the moment everyone awaits with bated breath the next stage: the construction of the south front whose theme is recent history.

A visit to the museum of the Sagrada Família is not to be missed. Admittedly most of the models displayed are reproductions or trial efforts intended to continue Gaudi's work, yet even these give valuable insights into the genius of the architect himself. Gaudí left extremely little behind. He seldom created final plans, preferring to see his buildings evolve slowly, one step after the next to completion. Whether this method of working was beneficial for those working with him or for his client is another matter. Furthermore, the entire collection of archive material that did exist was lost in a fire in the crypt. In 1936 the building was stormed by anarchists, who regarded the Sagrada Família as a powerful symbol of a conservative, clerical ideology. Despite this, the exhibits such as progress photography and photographs of earlier projects provide an animated picture of the more than a hundred years of construction history of the Sagrada Família.

Paradoxically a portion of Gaudí's architecture has been kept in its original state, although it should have been demolished long ago: the *Escola* or school was used as the temporary premises for the building site until the church could be completed. Le Corbusier was so enthusiastic in 1928 about this remaining simple brick building with its wave-form façade and sine-curved roof, that he captured the *Escola* in a sketch.

*Eixample: Collective Work of Art*

ABOVE:
*The "Font Magica" of 1929*

OPPOSITE:
*View of Montjuïc from the Plaça d'Espanya*

# Montjuïc

The name "Montjuic" is a puzzle to this day. Was the Roman god Jupiter behind the name of the 213-m (c. 700-ft.) high *mons Jovis* on the southern outskirts of the city? Or does the name refer to a Jewish grave mound found in the Middle Ages? The only thing not in dispute is the fact that Montjuïc is Barcelona's most popular place for recreation, after the Tibidabo. The fine parks and gardens, an enchanting view of the city and the sea, the ultra-modern sporting facilities, and above all the outstanding museums that hug its slopes, all blend together cultural life and leisure time in a way unique to Barcelona.

The history of the Montjuïc was not always as carefree as today's mood would suggest. Once the site of insignificant Iberian and Roman settlements, it gained strategic importance at the end of the Middle Ages. During the 1640 rebellion of the Catalans against the central Castilian power – known as the "War of the Reaper" – the first fortifications were erected here. These were soon in the hands of the crown, and were used by the Bourbons as a

means to oppress Barcelona. During the War of the Spanish Succession, 800 soldiers were slain at Montjuïc. In the Spanish Civil War, too, the castle was the scene of tragic events: Lluis Companys, the President of the Generalitat, was executed by Francoists within its walls. Today one can enjoy the fabulous view, then look with a certain shudder at the many historic weapons displayed in the military museum that the fortifications have now become.

Montjuïc first became a garden and vineyard in the 19th century, following the lifting of fortifications of the city. The gates of the Cementiri Nou, or new cemetery, were opened in 1883. The cemetery is well worth visiting for its luxurious *Moderniste* tombs. In the following years the process began of transforming the hill into a municipal recreation area. By and by, the city authorities bought up privately owned land, and demolished the small settlement on the slope. In 1894 Josep Amargós was commissioned to design a park, but responsibility was later

Above:
*Montjuïc with the Palau
Nacional, today the Museu
Nacional d'Art de Catalunya
(MNAC), built in 1929 by Pere
Cendoya and Enric Catà*

Right:
*View of the city from the terraces of
the Palau National*

taken over by the Frenchman Jean-Claude-Nicolas Forestier. The most attractive gardens for the visitor to see are the Mossèn Costa i Llobera cacti park, Jardí Laribal, and Jardí Amargós with its viewing platforms and water features.

The city had toyed with the idea of making Montjuïc an exhibition center as early as 1913. However, the project was only realized in 1929, when Barcelona was chosen once again to organize a World Exhibition, following the earlier success in the Parc de la Ciutadella in 1888. But, this second *Exposición universal* in the Catalan metropolis was less of a product exhibition than a justification of the reactionary conservative attitude of the dictator Primo de Riveras (1923–31). For this event, the idea was – unfortunately – conjured up of the Mediterranean as the cradle of civilization with Barcelona as its capital city, and the Montjuïc as its Acropolis. With a few exceptions, such as the Weimar Republic's pavilion by Mies van der Rohe,

that was soon recognized as a landmark of modern architecture, the rest was more or less commonplace.

The central themes of the exhibition were technology, sport, and art in Spain. To represent these themes, pavilions were built in the early Renaissance Italianate style. A Greek theater, stadium and the bombastic National Palace were designed as real eye-catchers. The "Spanish Village" was intended to represent unity in the country. More successful than the grandiose buildings, however, were the "Font Magica," the romantic water and light features by engineer Carles Buigas (illus. p. 236). All this eclectic architecture can still be seen as one climbs Montjuïc – unless one decides to take the leisurely Transbordador Aeri cable car that links the port with the summit (illus. p. 257, bottom left).

More impressive is the route from Plaça d'Espanya by way of Avinguda de la Reina Maria Cristina upward to the Palau Nacional, home of the Museu Nacional d'Art de

*Palau Nacional (MNAC)*
*Oval Salon, reworked in 1992*
*by Gae Aulenti*

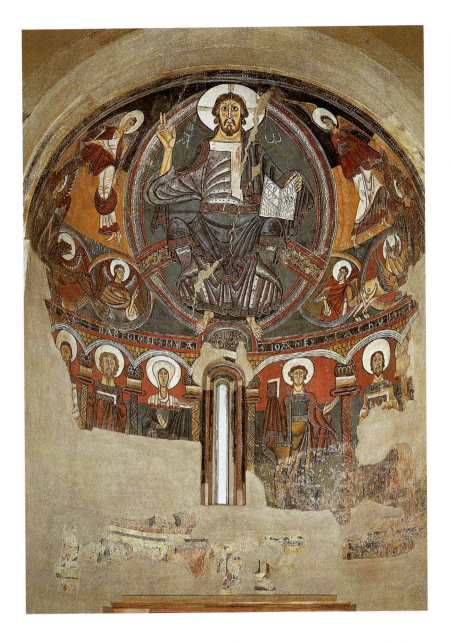

Catalunya (MNAC), (illus. p. 238, top). Just where the long flight of steps begins, visitors can take the excellent escalator, which has been in place since 1992.

The Plaça d'Espanya would be far better named "Plaça d'Italia," since it is surrounded by buildings that pass themselves off as being from that other culture-laden Mediterranean country.

A pair of buildings resembling the colonnades of St. Peter's Square enclose the southern corner of this square, and two *campanili* echoing those of the Piazzi S. Marco in Venice mark the start of the Avinguda Maria Cristina; then there are the neo-Baroque fountains of Josep Maria Jujol, reminiscent of the Bernini fountains in Rome.

The entire concept was that of Josep Puig i Cadafalch, who in his later years left Modernisme behind to pursue a Mediterranean eclecticism. The square – the entrance to Montjuïc – has recently been restored. Some buildings have new uses; the bullring of August Font at its perimeter is now an open-air theater.

The route from the Avinguda Maria Cristina passes some old and many new exhibition buildings. It is worth visiting on summer evenings when the water features are illuminated, and you can see a performance of the *fonts illuminoses* – the fountains and cascades at the foot of Montjuïc – that the engineer Carles Buigas also created originally for the World Exhibition of 1929. The "Font Màgica," or magical fountains, are appropriately named, for the spectacle is almost overwhelming (illus. p. 236). Today colored columns of water rise and fall, gyrating to the music of the Barcelona anthem sung by Montserrat Caballé and Freddy Mercury.

The technical equipment for this treat for the eyes and the ears includes 3,600 water jets, a 5,500-horsepower motor, and 3.25 million liters (860,000 gal.) of water. Everything is bathed with colored beams of light that radiate from the Palau Nacional into the evening sky.

This spectacle of lighting and technology is not accidental: the World Exhibition of 1929 was planned to promote the many benefits of the electrical industry.

Four columns once stood in front of the fountains, representing the four red stripes of the Catalan flag. Considered provocative by the dictator, Primo de Riveras,

they were removed. Behind this, alongside the pavilion of King Alfons XIII and his consort Victoria Eugenia, are the massive steps to the Palau Nacional. This building was the high point of the World Exhibition, both visually and in terms of content. The purpose of this palace of culture was to represent Spanish art. On its site rising above the edge of the city, the architects, Pedro Cendoya, Enric Cataya, and Pere Domènech i Roura, chose elements from the Monastery of El Escorial, and the cathedral of Santiago de Compostela; the monument is a synonym for the broader spiritual strength of an earlier Spain (illus. p. 238, top).

The main feature of the interior is the large oval salon. The dome is decorated in the style of the École de Beaux-Arts, and was adorned with allegorical frescoes by the Catalan painter Francesc Gali (1880–1965), though they were later removed.

The modern reworking of the interior by Gae Aulentis has been superimposed on the space (illus. p. 239). The Milanese architect, who had already caused a sensation with his work for the Parisian Gare d'Orsay, is also responsible – not without controversy – for the new design of the exhibition space.

Barcelona's objective in the restructuring of its museums was to bring together the collections of Catalan art previously spread over a number of sites. The nucleus is the unique department of Romanesque frescoes that have been displayed in the exhibition space against an acceptable architectural background since the 1930s. The outstandingly preserved large format murals of the 12th and 13th centuries come from small churches in remote parts of the Pyrenees. They were removed in the 1920s by Italian specialists, and conserved because they were in danger of being lost *in situ*.

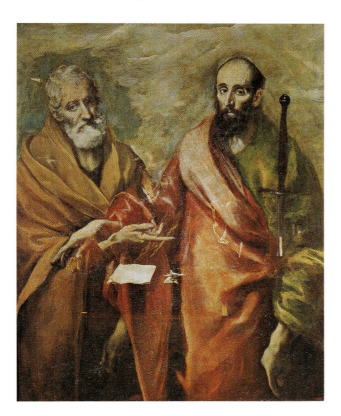

The showpieces are the cycle of frescoes from St. Climent and St. Maria de Taüll (illus. pp. 36–7, 240). The massive Christ of the *Majestas* picture and the enthroned Mother of God have lost none of their fascination since their origin c. 1123. Bible stories are represented too: the leprous Lazarus leans back resignedly; the delicate David is defiant and self-assured, as he prepares to chop off the head of the ungainly Goliath (illus. opposite). Also spectacular are the cycles from St. Quirze and St. Maria d'Aneu.

A second major feature of the MNAC is the Catalan altarpieces, regarded as world class ever since the purchase of the Plandiura collection in 1932.

In contrast with Castile, Catalonia is close to the borders with France and Italy; hence, the painting from the altar of Our Lady (1345–1405), painted for the cathedral of Tortosa by Barcelona artist Pere Serra, is in the style of the Siennese school.

But by the mid-15th century, Flemish painting was preferred over Italian. The detailed oil paintings of Van Eyck were also models for Catalan artists. The *Mare de Deu dels Consellers*, Madonna and the Counselors, completed by Valencian artist Lluís Dalmau in 1445, demonstrates this change (illus. p. 241).

OPPOSITE:
MNAC
*Frescoes from St. Maria de Taüll*
David and Goliath, c. 1123

LEFT:
MNAC
El Greco
St. Peter and St. Paul
c. 1600

ABOVE:
MNAC
Diego Velázquez
St. Paul, 1619

Esplanada, *designed in 1992 by Federico Correa, Alfonso Milà, Joan Margarit, Carles Buxadé and others*
*In the background the Olympic Stadium of 1929, erected by Pere Domènech i Roura; refashioned in 1992 by Vittorio Gregotti and Partners*

During the Baroque era, the side altars became less significant, which was reflected in the art contained in the side altars, for it does not equal that of the main altar-pieces.

Nevertheless, the Catalan national museum possesses outstanding works of other provenance from the 16th to 18th centuries. The twin images of St. Peter and St. Paul by El Greco were painted shortly before 1600 in colors derived from those of Venetian painting (illus. p. 243, bottom). An early work by Velázquez from his time in Seville depicts St. Paul (1619), (illus. p. 243, top).

The representation of the Apostles by Greeks and Andalusians are worlds apart. El Greco's Paul is ascetic, alienated from this world, and spiritual; Velázquez sees him as a man of the people, tired, and exhausted, yet responding to his duty with dignity. A third painting is the

*Martyrdom of St. Bartholomew,* depicted in unsparing realism by the Spanish artist Jusepe de Ribera in 1644, who was working in Naples.

The planned integration of the Col·lecció Francesc Cambó and the Museu d'Art de Catalunya will soon add another dimension to the study of Italian and French Baroque paintings.

The Montjuïc of the Olympic Games begins behind the temple of culture. The area is connected by the *Anell Olímpic* ring road that links all the sporting facilities.

The heart is the *Esplanada* between the Olympic stadium and the Palau de St. Jordi, which has long been a sight-seeing destination, even when there are no specific events (illus. above). People stroll across the vast terraces, follow the source of the water cascades, and enjoy the view of the city. At night in particular, when 18 m (60 ft.) high lighting columns softly but clearly illuminate them, the terraces have an atmosphere of their own. The lighting columns, just as with the water and the steps, follow the architectural style of the 1929 World Exhibition. However, an avant-garde touch is provided by the lighting "sculptures" that were created by the Japanese artist Aiko Miyawaki.

The other end of the *Esplanada* is monumentality bounded by the sports stadium of 1929 (architect Domènech Roura). In its time the stadium was a symbol of unity of the body and spirit, but it soon became a symbol of resistance against the Fascists. In protest at the awarding of the Olympic Games of 1936 to Berlin, Barcelona planned to hold its own "People's Olympiad," but it was broken up just before its opening by Franco's troops.

This historical significance was borne in mind in planning the 1992 Olympic Games: the eclectic exterior was retained and only the interior of the stadium was modernized. In an optical illusion, the lighting columns in front of the façade lessen the severity of the monumental structure.

Nearby is the avant-garde Palau de St. Jordi sports hall, which is also used as a concert hall thanks to its excellent acoustics. The creator of this building – often likened to a

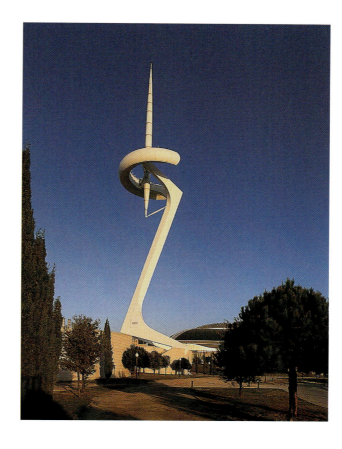

LEFT:
*Telecommunications tower, built by Santiago Calatrava in 1992*

BELOW:
*Palau de St. Jordi, modified by Arata Isozaki in 1992*

Montjuïc  245

tortoise – is the Japanese architect Arata Isozaki, whose most important work was constructed here in 1992 (illus. p. 245, bottom). High-tech and local materials (stone and ceramics) are happily combined. The 45-m (c. 148-ft.) high, extensively naturally lit building of metal-frame construction holds 17,000 spectators, and is one of the most atmospheric sporting facilities in the world. Its roof was assembled on the ground, and then carefully moved into position using computer technology.

To its right is the Bernat Picornell swimming arena, which was elegantly reworked by Moisés Gallego and Franc Fernández. Beyond it the broad open space of the *Esplanada* leads down the slope to the round Plaça d'Europa that is bordered by porticos. The idiosyncratic telecommunications needle, which was erected by Spanish architect Santiago Calatrava, towers above the buildings of the square (illus. p. 245, top).

Barcelona

Opposite is a 105-m (c. 350-ft.) high concrete monolith, which is another memorial to the Barcelona Olympic Games of 1992.

Among the sports facilities of Montjuïc, the INEFC institute for physical education is worth mentioning. The Classical style was once again adopted, by Ricardo Bofill: a Greek palaistra (fighting area) with inner courtyard and arcaded passages. Construction, though, was quite modern with the use of preformed sections.

After looking at the sports facilities, it is time to experience other aspects of the variety that the area of Montjuïc has to offer visitors.

By following the twists of the Avinguda del Marquès de Comillas downward, one reaches the *Poble Espanyol* or "Spanish Village," which was originally built by Miquel Utrillo and Xavier Nogués for the World Exhibition (illus. above and opposite).

Of course, a visit cannot replace a journey through Spain, yet the delight of Spanish food, the purchase of arts and crafts, a night in the bar of the top designer Marsical can only enhance the study of Spanish architecture, and make it a pleasingly sensuous experience.

National villages and architectural plagiarism were all part of the repertoire of any major exhibition in the 19th century, and such events were intended to be both educational and entertaining.

Today when one visits a theme park there is a tendency to forget their very different predecessors in the 19th and early 20th centuries.

The "Spanish Village" in Barcelona also had a political purpose: the dictator Primo de Riveras intended to present to the world a united Spain, the economic and political differences of which would be concealed by the presentation of an architectural idyll. Hence, the "typical"

buildings from each region were reproduced with little accuracy and to different standards.

The entrance to the "Spanish Village" is guarded by the mighty medieval town tower of Avila. Then the way leads directly to the Plaza Mayor, which is surrounded by porticos similar to those built in many Spanish towns in the 15th century. Houses from various regions line the perimeter of the square, including the town hall from Vall-de-Roures (Terol).

One climbs the Baroque steps of Compostela to a small Aragonese church. The original of this ceramic-decorated Mudéjar-style bell-tower can be found in Utebo near Zaragoza (illus. p. 246, bottom).

The Andalusian quarter is grouped around the Plaza de la Hermandad (Córdoba) with its Madonna columns. Whitewashed walls and luxuriant floral decoration are reminiscent of "the lanes of Seville" (illus. p. 247, right). Majorcan loggias, Valencian Baroque frontages, and the Romanesque palace of the Marquesos de la Floresta in Tàrrega await the visitor in the Barri Català.

To finish the walk around the complex, visit the Museu d'Arts i Industries Populars on the Plaza Mayor to see displays of folk art from every part of Spain. Inside the Torres de Ávila a bar has been installed, which is anything but traditional. The designer has turned both towers into fantasy worlds celebrating the Aragonese stars, sun, and moon (illus. p. 246, top right, p. 247, left).

The avant-garde of the 1980s and the 1920s share similarities. An early example of modern architecture can be admired at the edge of Avinguda del Marquès de Comillas: the Barcelona pavilion for the 1929 World Exhibition, designed by the ground-breaking German architect Ludwig Mies van der Rohe.

Although the original was taken down at the end of the exhibition and its materials sold, a decade after its demolition the importance of the building was recognized, and in 1986 a more or less exact copy was reconstructed on where it stood (illus. pp. 248–9 and above).

The original structure was built by the Weimar Republic, which wished to present itself to the world through modern architecture. The building was, however, like a fish out of water amid the other pompous monuments of the World Exhibition.

With just two basic building elements – supports and slab – and also with fine materials – glass, marble, and chromed steel – Mies van der Rohe created a reflective architecture, that, in spite of its obvious functionality, also possessed a high degree of poetry. The original pavilion contained only the Barcelona chair – later to become famous – a carpet, and a bronze by Georg Kolbe.

Mies van der Rohe presented his architecture to the world with the Barcelona pavilion in a radical way. The plinth was formed from uniform sheets of travertine,

LEFT:
*Fundació Miró, built by Josep
Lluís Sert in 1975*

BELOW:
*Fundació Miró
View of the terrace*

giving the effect more or less of indissolubility. Filigree cruciform supports of chromed steel bear the roof. The walls themselves have an aesthetic function only. Glass sliding-doors reach from floor to roof, allowing the boundaries between inside the structure and outside to become refreshingly blurred.

The pavilion borders two rectangular pools. Their water surfaces form a dark expanse that effectively highlights the aesthetic materials chosen for the architecture (illus. p. 250). It was built at a cost of about 550,000 Deutschmarks – almost double the budget – and the threat of bankruptcy was only avoided at the last minute by a guarantee from the German state.

The treasures of Montjuïc have not been exhausted with the Barcelona pavilion of Mies van der Rohe. Left of the axis of the Avinguda de la Reina Maria Cristina, about half-way up, one next passes the modern Museu Etnogràfic Andino-amazònic. In it is an unusual collection of objects from Central and South America, which were collected by Catalan Capuchin friars.

The Passeig de St. Madrona leads to both "early Renaissance" buildings of the Palau de l'Agricultura and to the Palau de les Arts Gràfiques that were also built for the World Exhibition.

The latter has housed the archaeological museum since 1935, and was renewed in 1986–9 by Josep Llinàs (illus. p. 254, top bottom). A fascinating view of Catalan and Balearic archaeology brought to life in this museum. The outstanding exhibit is the *Dama d'Eiviss*, (Woman from Ibiza, illus. p. 254, top left).

Nearby is the Mercat de les Flors – a playhouse for theater groups such as La Fura dels Baus (see panel box p. 255). Miquel Barceló created a most moving ceiling painting for its dome (illus. p. 255, left). The Teatre Grec, or "Grecian" theater, is also used for performances and summer concerts.

The culmination of the stroll across the Montjuïc is undoubtedly a visit to the Fundació Miró, opened in 1975. Rarely have museum architecture, landscape, exhibits, and presentation been so symbiotically fused as in this building. The gallery owner and collector Joan Prats and architect Josep Lluís Sert dedicated it to their friend Joan Miró (1893–1983) (illus. pp. 251–3).

Using the cubic architecture of the Balearics, Sert designed a complex which creates the ideal surroundings for the work of Miró, who is represented and documented across his full range here. No other place in the world allows you to come to terms with this artist's Mediterranean world in a better way than does the Fundació Miró.

His works – with their sparkling colors and droll forms – contrast effectively with the straightforward outlined and whitewashed cubes of the exhibition space and with the brilliant blue of the sky. Inside and out, the rooms and courtyards of the Fundació Miró are interwoven in a manner similar to the nearby exhibition pavilion of Mies van der Rohe.

The collection of more than 10,000 works of Joan Miró was donated to the city of Barcelona by the artist. It comprises 217 paintings, 153 sculptures, the complete graphic and textile work, and it extends from the early

BELOW:
*Fundació Miró*
*Large salon with Miró's model of*
Couple d'amoureux aux jeux
de fleurs d'amandiers, 1975

OPPOSITE:
*Fundació Miró*
Quicksilver Fountain,
*created by Alexander Calder, 1937*

*Joan Miró*
*Self Portrait*
*Mongins, Private Collection*

**Joan Miró Ferrà**
The painter and sculptor Joan Miró reached a poetic abstract
expression of his art following the cubism, fauvism, and
surrealism phases of his early years in the 1940s. Elements
such as woman, bird, moon, and sun characterize, from time
to time, his personal mythology. In frequent cooperation
with the ceramicist Josep Llorens i Artiga, he turned largely
to sculpture and arts and crafts after World War II.

Born 1893 Barcelona
1919 Traveled to Paris; contact with Picasso and the dadaists
1924 Signing of the surrealists' manifesto in Paris
1929/32 Stage designs for the Ballets Russes
1931 Exhibition of sculpture and paintings at the Galerie
Pierre in Paris
1936–9 Influenced by the Spanish Civil War; returns to
figurative and realistic painting
1939–41 In his 23 Constellations he finds his
characteristic means of expression
1947 Traveled to USA; first exhibition in New York
1956 Miró finally settles in Palma de Mallorca, where his
friend Josep Lluis Sert prepares a studio
1959 Retrospective at MOMA in New York
1974 Major exhibition at the Grand Palais in Paris
1970–80s Countless monumental sculptural works
1983 Died in Majorca

ABOVE:
Museu d'Arqueologia, 1935–89
Dama d'Eivissa
("Woman from Ibiza")

RIGHT TOP:
Museu d'Arqueologia
View of the exhibition space with
Grecian marble statue of
Aesculapius from Empùries
Late 4th century B.C.

RIGHT:
Museu d'Arqueologia
Reconstruction of the Casa del
Centenaria room of Pompeii
with faun spring

OPPOSITE TOP:
Mercat de les Flors
Ceiling Painting,
created by Miquel Barceló

OPPOSITE BOTTOM:
Staging for the theater group,
La Fura dels Baus

### Theater in Catalonia

*Silenced during the Franco dictatorship, Catalan language theater is now livelier than ever. With the benefit of hindsight, it even appears that the decades of repression have stimulated Catalan theater; since the Catalan language was forbidden, people used non-verbal forms of communication. The most blatant case of this was a performance of Joglars, which showed the execution of an innocent by the Spanish military as a pantomime; as recently as 1977, it was brought before a court martial. Catalan groups such as "La Fura dels Baus," "Els Joglars," and "Els Comedians" are now established participants in international festivals. The "Fura" in particular have caused a sensation worldwide with their shocking, aggressive, often nauseating – but arousing – scenes. Today, they mainly put on strongly visual performances using stimulating staging that is both acoustic and tactile, clearly related to street theater. The countless festivals with their colorful repertoires and presentations provide an inexhaustible source of inspiration. Noise, stench, and fiery magic accompany the performers and the public. Pantomime and improvisation remain, however, derived from the tradition of the "Commedia dell'arte." In recent times a new change of direction has seen the use of words and playwrights emerging.*

works – influenced by cubism – through the landscapes of the 1920s to the style the artist developed toward the end of his life with surrealist elements and lyrical abstractions.

Apparently naively combined, they possess an enigmatic astuteness. The ironically amusing sculptures, such as the *Caress of a Bird* (1967) or *Person* (1967), are ideally exhibited on the terrace (illus. p. 251, bottom). One of Miró's final large works was created for the new development area of La Defense in Paris, *Couple d'amoureux aux jeux de fleurs d'amandiers*, (Loving couple engaged in a game with almond blossom). The 1975 model in synthetic resin is an eye-catcher in the large salon in the basement (illus. p. 252). The same is true of the sculpture *Dona i Ocell*, 1984 (Woman and Bird, illus. p. 211), exhibited in Parc Joan Miró. Massive, and with sexually symbolism, it is decorated with yellow, red, and blue.

Associations with sun and moon – positive and negative – but also the horns of Spanish bulls come to the fore, as do all the themes that Miró occupied himself with throughout his life, and that he mystically transfigured.

Beside Miró's work the Fundació possesses a gem: the *Quicksilver fountain* by the American Alexander Calder, created for the Spanish pavilion of the 1937 Paris World Exhibition (illus. p. 253, right). With Picasso's *Guernica* and Miro's *Catalan Reaper*, it represents modern Spanish art at the outbreak of the Spanish Civil War. The pavilion that Josep Lluis Sert and Luís Lacasa designed has been reconstructed on the edge of the city of Barcelona.

# The Sea Front

RIGHT:
*La Barceloneta*

BELOW:
*On the beach at Barcelona*

OPPOSITE, TOP:
*Barcelona Head,
created by Roy Lichtenstein, 1991*

OPPOSITE, BOTTOM LEFT:
*The cable car between the harbor
and Montjuïc, built by
Josep R. Roda in 1931*

OPPOSITE, BOTTOM RIGHT:
*Moll de la Fusta, built by Manuel
de Solà Morales and others, 1987*

The sea front has changed more in recent years than any other side of Barcelona. The city – that for hundreds of years had more or less turned its back on the sea – in the 1980s discovered a treasure: the sea front. As part of the *Espais Urbans* project and the planning for the Olympic Games, Catalan architects began to give Barcelona a new orientation toward the Mediterranean, with a program for the sea-front promenades, harbor, and recreation areas.

Two key factors created the preconditions for this new orientation: the tram and rail lines, which for so long had blocked access to the sea, were moved underground, and vacated industrial sites on the sea front became available for residential and leisure use.

The results can be seen today: the new sea front is not just a tourist attraction, but also has much to offer the citizens of Barcelona, especially the restaurants and bars of the old harbor and the Port Olímpic.

That Barcelona directed itself so little toward the sea may in part be due to troubled memories of the settlement of La Barceloneta. The triangular part of the city between the old town and the sea came into being during the oppression by the Bourbons, when it was besieged in the turmoil of the War of the Spanish Succession after they had demolished the entire Barri de la Ribera quarter in order to construct their stronghold there. The inhabitants – mainly seafarers and fishing families – were offered instead the wedge-shaped tongue of land of Barceloneta. But the new homesteads created here by the forced settlers cannot have been much more comfortable than the old.

The construction began in 1753 according to the plans – modern in concept – of military architects Juan Martín Cermeño and Prósper Verboom. Broad, uniform streets and low-rise buildings were to guarantee the occupants light, air, and comfort (illus. opposite, top). These utopian plans were quickly ignored, though, due to speculation.

Three squares cut into the grid of Barcelona formed by the elongated "island": the Plaça Pompeu Fabra, Plaça de la Font, and Plaça de St. Miquel – the center of the quarter. The frontage of the church of St. Miquel del Port (1753–5), which is one of the few remaining Baroque buildings in Barcelona, rises as a backcloth to its longer side.

For a considerable time La Barceloneta was not just the boundary between the city and the sea, but it also was a kind of buffer between the middle-class Barcelona citizen and the colorful sub-cultural scene.

Special favorites were the shack restaurants – *els beranadors* – on what was formerly the only beach in Barcelona. These fell victim to excessive redevelopment. In their place today the quarter offers a palm-tree lined sandy beach with astonishingly good water quality (illus. opposite, bottom).

Even the oriental baths that August Font built in neo-Arabesque style in 1872 were demolished. A fountain recalls the gypsy Carmen Amaya, one of the few flamenco dancers to originate from Barcelona, who was born in one of the shacks on the Passeig Marítim.

A visit to Barcelona should include a trip on the Transbordador Aeri cable car that was installed for the World Exhibition of 1929. It runs from Barceloneta to Montjuïc, and gives unique views across the city and the harbor (illus. below left).

For those who prefer to keep their feet on the ground, a walk along the wooden jetty of the Moll de la Fusta is recommended (illus. p. 257, bottom right). Here – where until the beginning of the 1980s the railway and trams thundered – one now sees a broad shoreline stretching from Roy Lichtenstein's *Barcelona Head* to the Columbus Monument, thanks to the planning genius of Manuel Solà Morales (illus p. 257, top). This is both vertically and horizontally divided into zones with different functions: local and long-distance traffic run separately and mainly underground. The visual line of the embankment is accentuated by palm trees and street lights.

The promenade itself, with colorful tiled benches and low palms, lies on top of a huge car park that can be glimpsed occasionally. Restaurants and bars such as the "Gambrinus," offering huge shrimp, line one's route for a stroll. One descends from the terrace and reaches the beach and the harbor by means of red drawbridges that resemble those of Van Gogh's famous paintings of Arles.

The renovation of the Port Vell or old port is the most recent attraction of Barcelona. Here, where La Rambla ends beneath the Columbus Monument, a walk full of variety has been opened up over undulating wooden decking, drawbridges, and pontoons leading to the tongue of reclaimed land in the harbor basin.

The aquarium housing the 4.5 million liters (1.2 million gal.) of water of the Oceanari can be spotted from far off. One passes through the marine world in an 80-m (c. 260-ft.) long glass tunnel, strolling beneath sharks, sawfish, and colorful exotic creatures of the sea (illus. opposite bottom).

Close by are the countless bars and restaurants of the Maremàgnum shopping center that looks like a sinking ship from a distance (illus. above). Variety is offered for film enthusiasts with 18 cinemas and the Barcelona IMAX.

At the other end is the "semi-island" of Port Vell with the newly restored grounds of the Palau del Mar. The Museu d'Historia de Catalunya, which brings Catalan history to life even in this computer age, has recently been attracted to former warehouses (illus right, bottom).

Rebuilding of the industrial area of Poble Nou, the "Catalan Manchester," was done in readiness for the Olympics. The Olympic Village and water-sports' marina rose up here from the ruins of former factories, guaranteeing improvement in living quality for eastern Barcelona after the Olympic Games.

In memory of the utopian dream of the socialist worker's movement, the new area of the city was named "Nova Icària." Such idealism was soon forgotten, and the area planned for social housing quickly became highly desirable properties.

The master plan for this area of the city was developed by the MEMP architectural practice (Josep Martorell, Oriol Bohigas, David Mackay, and Albert Puigdomènech). Their idea reflected the 1920s: advancing the grid-pattern of Cerdà to the sea front. The basis therefore was to form *supermançanes* from many enlarged blocks with the characteristic flattening of the corners of the *Eixample*. Within these units further layout was left to the individual

LEFT:
*Maremàgum shopping center*

BELOW:
*Museu d'Historia de Catalunya*

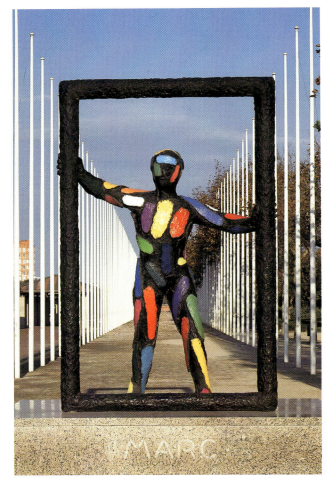

TOP:
*Open-air sculpture in the Olympic Village*

BELOW:
*Edificis Porta, built by Albert Viaplana and Helio Piñón, 1992*

architects to determine. The Passeig Carles I was built as the main thoroughfare of the Olympic Village; it now runs from the Sagrada Família to the harbor where it crosses over the thoroughfares of Avinguda d'Icària and Avinguda Litoral, which are laid out with gardens and sculpture (illus. opposite top).

The residential blocks of the Olympic Village give a comprehensive view of the diversity of contemporary architecture in Catalonia. According to the master plan of MEMP, 34 buildings were to be built using a number of different architectural solutions.

The *Edificis Porta* gateway building is especially attractive, perhaps the most attractive (illus. opposite bottom). The stepped, cantilevered blocks of Albert Viaplana and Helio Piñon are both innovative and consistent in planning terms.

The telephone exchange by Jaume Bach and Gabriel Mora is an exciting composition with an ellipsoid body, which is linked to a conical block by an asymmetric bridge. Like trees in a storm, metal branches are used as wooden planks in the pergola on the Avinguda Icària that Enric Miralles has put together.

The Olympic Village is heralded by the skyscrapers at the end of the Passeig Carles I. At 153.5 m (c. 500 ft.) they are the highest homes in the Iberian peninsula at present (illus. above).

The western one was erected by Bruce Graham of SOM (Skidmore, Owings, and Merril) and houses the "Hotel de les Arts." In common with most building by Chicago architectural practices, the structural frame is both visible and decorative on the outside of the building. The counterpart of this structure is the "Edifici MAPFRE" office block by the Spanish architects Iñigo Ortiz and Enrique León.

The Port Olímpic with its numerous bars and restaurants forms a sort of annex to the town center that is popular with both locals and visitors. Here too, spacious promenades have been created that invite strolling, cycling, or skating, surrounded by avant-garde art.

Among the architecture, two attractive buildings clearly stand out: the cubic reception building at the end of the harbor arm (MEMP), and the rounded meteorological center by the Portuguese architect Álvaro Siza.

The main attraction of the Olympic Village is the shimmering fish, *Peix*, that can be seen for miles around, designed for Barcelona by the American architect Frank O. Gehry (illus. above). It juts out above the shopping center, where fast food restaurants with elaborate interior decor have established themselves, along with many other restaurants, bars, novelty shops, and attractive boutiques.

Ambitious plans were put in train for the new millennium, and for Barcelona to host the International Cultural Forum in 2004. After this, it will become the major center, encompassing the latest communication and leisure technology.

*View of the Olympic Village with skyscrapers and the Peix (fish) sculpture created by Frank O. Geary, 1992*

# At the Foot of the Hills

Barcelona has more natural beauty than just the sea. It has hills, and the housing at the foot of the hills was – and is – by far the most attractive in the city. This happened because in the past industry was established on the coast, and the main traffic arteries developed there too. So, some people, those who were able to, chose the fresh air and refreshing presence of the nearby hills. The outlying situation had other advantages: outside the *Eixample* there were no strict planning rules, nor any restricting business requirements; at the turn of the century this gave lots of opportunity for experimentation by architects, people who, in any event, were extremely creative.

Not only the upper middle class was attracted to the north-western part of Barcelona. Back in 1326 Elisenda de Montcada, the fourth and final consort of King Jaume I, founded a convent there for the order of St. Clare. The white stone (Petras Alba) of a nearby bridge gave it – and later the entire area – the name of Pedralbes. With its noble simplicity and purity of style, the convent is one of the finest examples of Catalan Gothic (illus. right).

The single nave church with ribbed vaults was started in the year of its foundation by Ferrer Peiró and Domènec Granyer. Twenty years later it became the final resting place for Elisenda in a sarcophagus of colored alabaster.

The dormitory of the convent and also the main hall of the royal palace are now home to a small but exquisite part of the collection of Thyssen-Bornemisza. The paintings and sculptures provide a glimpse of the golden

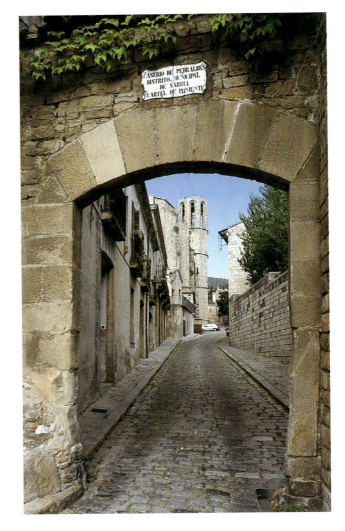

RIGHT:

*View of the convent church of St. Maria de Pedralbes, founded 1326*

BELOW:

*St. Michael's chapel in the cloisters of the convent Fresco cycle, created by Ferrer Bassa, 1343–6*

era of Italian and German painting between the late Middle Ages and the 18th century. The outstanding item is a *Madonna dell' Umiltà*, (Madonna with humility), painted by the Florentine artist Fr. Angelico c. 1430. Further attractions are the works of Lucas Cranach, Wolf Huber, and Bernhard Strigel, and also the Venetian paintings from Titian through to Guardi.

The space of the cloister has been lovingly converted into a museum, as the St. Michael chapel shelters an exceptional treasure. Behind the wooden paneling of the chapel – which was then being used as a vestry – the nuns found an outstandingly preserved cycle of Gothic frescoes (illus. left). They represent a rarity for the Iberian peninsula, since there were few artists who possessed the necessary techniques.

The frescoes of the St. Michael chapel proved to be the 1343–6 work of the Catalan artist Ferrer Bassa, who had contact with Simone Martini and the Siennese school of painting. The Passion of Christ and the life of Our Lady are represented against an exciting blue background. In spite of the Italian influence, there is an unsparing realism to most of the scenes in the Spanish tradition: a nail is pulled from the foot of Christ with enormous pliers.

Many centuries later, the upper middle classes once again favored the hilly area. In addition to their town villa in the *Eixample* most also treated themselves to a summer or country house on the outskirts of the city. The Casa Vicens (Carrer Carolines 24) that Antoni Gaudí built for the brick- and tile-maker Manuel Vicens in 1883–5 is one of them (illus. right).

In what was his first major commission, the young architect broke with all academic traditions, and created a villa with an oriental feel to it that was based on no specific example. Arabesque motifs, cantilevered coins, tongued walls, blind galleries, stepped recesses, and turrets give the property a bizarre appearance that is reinforced by the irregular roof line.

The unusual stimulating effect of the building is brought about by the colorful ceramic cladding. Light and dark tiles are interposed in checkerboard fashion, while others bear floral motifs.

Vicens could hardly have wished for a better advertisement for his products. Since the modern design of the interior of the house is not open to view, one has to make do with the palm-like form of the railings that are a masterpiece in wrought-iron work.

In 1889 Gaudí took over an extremely thankless task. Under difficult conditions, both financial and time-wise, he was to build a theological college for the nuns of the order of St. Theresa – the Col·legi de les Tereses (Carrer Ganduixer 105). Since it was made of the comparatively cheaper materials of brick and undressed stone, the building deserves even greater admiration.

Solely through the effect of the structural elements, he changed the building – at a point when it was already rising from its foundations – into a palace that belies the vows of poverty of the order. Gaudí employed Gothic

LEFT:
*Casa Vicens, built by Antoni Gaudí, 1883–5*

BELOW:
*Finca Güell, built by Antoni Gaudí, 1884–7*
*Dragon gate*

forms and Mudejar-like wall techniques, such as the principle of "false arches," in which the bricks are radially arranged with each course offset until the aperture is closed. His parabolic arches – that span the interior while offering attractive external perspectives – were the most forward looking of all the features.

Through his work on the convent, Gaudí had already associated himself with Mudejar and medieval elements; he now took on the construction of the Villa Bellesguard of 1900–02 with Catalan history clearly in mind. He created the slate building on the slopes of Tibidabo for a rich noble woman: Doña Maria Sagués. Its fortified and medieval character recalls the fact that King Marti I, the last of the Catalan-Aragonese monarchs, once had his summer resort here.

It was the buildings for Count Eusebi Güell, though, that furthered Gaudí's full talents, and gave him unusual freedom. Güell – a textile manufacturer with a social conscience – and Gaudí – the man with a mission who relished a challenge – were kindred spirits who mutually encouraged outstanding performance.

Exuberant creativity and intentional functionalism, which form the basis of Gaudí's creations, clearly surfaced in the Finca Güell (Av. de Pedralbes 7, 1884–7). Gaudí's first major commission required the design of stables, indoor riding school, and porter's lodge for the count's estate at Pedralbes.

As with all his early buildings, the architect employed elements borrowed from Moorish art to adorn the façades, turrets, and domes. The construction of the interior of the

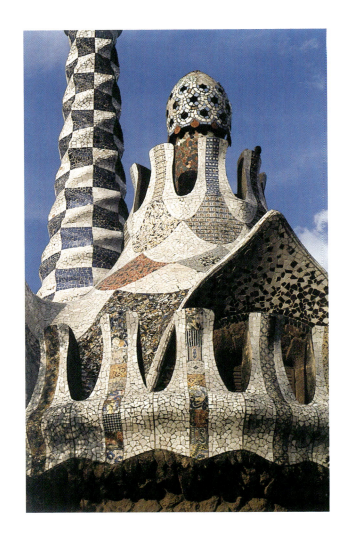

LEFT:
*Parc Güell, built by Antoni Gaudí and colleagues, 1910–14. Detail of the porter's lodge*

BELOW:
*Parc Güell
Colonnades*

OPPOSITE TOP:
*Parc Güell
Lizard*

OPPOSITE BOTTOM:
*Parc Güell
Steps up to the Room of 100 Columns*

stables is interesting: Gaudí already uses parabolic arches with brick capping, spanning a considerable width, that were to become characteristic of his technique of arching and vaulting. Today the Cátedra Gaudí has found a home for itself in Count Güell's stables. Anyone wishing to visit this research institute must first pass the iron dragon that guards the entrance gate (illus. p. 263, bottom).

Gaudí has obviously done something very special with the gate-house and porter's lodge. In Parc Güell too (Carrer Olot, 1910–14), the entrance is flanked by two magical pavilions, leading to a wonder-world of fantasy (illus. opposite, top).

It is hardly conceivable that the extensive park with all its surprising buildings was established to act as an example of housing development for affluent towns. Inspired by an English garden city, the terrain was intended to include homes, offices, workshops, restaurants, and social facilities. The 60 plots for sale were so expensive, though, that only two were sold: one to Güell and the other to a friend. Nevertheless, further building occurred in 1914. For Güell and Gaudí, who were both firm Catalan nationalists, the project was an act of faith in their social and romantic proposals.

The fascinating thing today is the perfect symbiosis of nature and architecture, and once again the union of technique and artistic imagination. The walls alone, that enclose the "settlement," act as if they had naturally

*Parc Güell*
*Bench*

sprung from the ground, and are covered with a mosaic capping in which the name "Güell" is inset. Through an artistic wrought-iron grille, the path passes the porter's lodge, built of gray-brown stone (illus. p. 264, top). The amusing roof cap, clad in ceramic fragments, forms waves, scales, and battlements. The roof is crowned by a soaring tower, and is topped with a cross and cupola in the form of a flying mushroom – visible from far off.

Gaudí liked to give his buildings symbolic adornment, yet his visual language – Christian or profane – was rarely purely decorative. Hence, the magnificent mosaic-adorned staircase that leads to the upper part of the structure conceals a technical secret. At first glance it seems to represent the client's private mythology: a colorful lizard stretches out beside the Catalan coat of arms (illus. p. 265, top), while above it waits a snake – reminding one of the dragon of the Catalan patron saint St. George or of the dragon that guards the Güell estate in Pedralbes. After closer examination the fantasy creatures turn out to be overflow outlets for a cistern beneath.

One reaches the so-called "room of one hundred columns" – which was to have been the market for the planned settlement – by means of a flight of steps that are coated in tile fragments (illus. p. 265, bottom). Although there are only 86, the somewhat Doric-looking columns create a sacred atmosphere. Gaudí had practical ideas here too: the hollow pillars direct rain water to the cistern beneath, invisibly solving the drainage of the slope.

The ceiling of the "room" was decorated by Gaudí and his famous colleague Josep Maria Jujol with a variety of fragments artistically arranged into a pattern. Some joke that it kept about 30 people constantly occupied smashing the crockery, and even more to stick it together again. In reality Gaudí relied on colleagues to collect bottles, tiles, and crockery to make the raw material for his mosaics.

From the winding paths of the park one grasps how much Gaudí's architecture is derived from, and entwined with, nature. Often it is barely possible to recognize where construction starts and natural growth ends. Hence, the "colonnades," built of slanting pieces of hewn rock, form a hollow-like passageway that also acts as the base for the promenade above. The "columns" fit into their surroundings perfectly. Their inclination and rough surfaces recall old tree trunks stooped over by the wind. But suddenly on the last pillar a woman carved in stone emerges from the darkness, carrying the full weight of the vault

last of the Barcelona trams, passes through one of the most attractive quarters of the city, In a matter of minutes the funicular achieves the height of 512 m (c. 1,700 ft.) at the top of the Tibidabo. The hill gets its peculiar name from the reference in the Bible when the devil offers Christ the world at his feet from a mountain in Jerusalem: "Tibi dabo." (I will give to you.)

The temptation today is quite different: the oldest amusement park in Spain is sited on Tibidabo (illus. below). With the purchase of a reduced entry ticket one can use the "classic" amusements of the Lunapark established in 1899. The newer technology or more spectacular rides cost extra. The biggest attraction of the park is the museum of automatons. A collection of mechanical toys, even models of the universe, can be brought to life at the press of a button. One encounters jazz ensemble orchestras, dance groups, bird cages, but above all the original Barcelona "Moños" – an eccentric old person from La Rambla whose enchanting glance still enraptures visitors.

From here the view of Barcelona is priceless – spread out at one's feet. The view can be seen from even greater heights if you are prepared to trust the 50-m (c. 165-ft) high metal "Atalaya" pendulum. Those who are happy to forego that thrill can visit the votive church of Sagrat Cor, which was established in 1902 through the vows of the priest and social educationalist Don Bosco. More turn-of-the-century buildings lie off the path of the middle station of the rack railway; they include the Pompeu Fabra observatory and a small natural science museum.

ABOVE:
Tramvia Blau, the last of the Barcelona trams

RIGHT:
Spain's oldest amusement park on Tibidabo

(illus. p. 264, bottom). Tricks of the senses of this kind are highly regarded in Mannerist garden design. For Gaudí the emulation of nature meant more than just an optical illusion. Nature was his teacher, his source of inspiration, and what led to his revolutionary static system. "Nature," as he liked to say, "is a great open book and we should make ourselves read it."

Close to the market area the Plaça opens up with a splendid terrace for viewing the city. It borders the world-famous snake-like bench that Gaudí and Jujol decorated with mosaic using broken ceramics (illus. pp. 266–7). The diversity of shapes and colors added for decoration, which soften the contours of the stones they cling to, seems never-ending. The original "furniture," that besides being beautiful is also comfortable, has influenced Catalan design to this day. However, Gaudí did not forget his love of God in this work of art. Religious inscriptions are integrated into the cheerful decor.

Some way off the main road lies a small, relatively modest house in which the architect led a secluded life for some years. The building by Francesc Berenguer, a colleague of Gaudí, was originally a show house for the colony. It now houses a museum with furniture, fixtures and fittings of the Modernist era.

For those prepared to venture farther upward, a visit to Tibidabo or the neighboring Collserola is recommended. The nostalgic trip with the Tramvia Blau (illus. left), the

In view – but detached by the lie of the land – the Torre de Collserola has functioned as the new landmark of Barcelona since 1992 (illus. right). The television tower by the British architect Sir Norman Foster is particularly noted for its unusually light appearance. This is deceptive, however, as it is the height – 265.5 m (c. 870 ft.) – that makes the tower appear so delicate. Somewhat resembling a horsetail weed, the tower possesses outstanding static characteristics, achieved through the application of high-tech elements.

The architect remained true to his principle of keeping the structure as minimal as possible, and hence achieved a great technical and aesthetic effect. The concrete mast of triangular section sits on an underground base, securely anchored to the hill by stays. There are 13 spade-shaped platforms to carry both the transmitter and maintenance equipment, which are suspended from the concrete mast.

Even at the foot of the hills, interesting areas of parkland can be enjoyed. They were designed in the 1980s and early 1990s in an avant-garde manner. Among them are the Parc de la Creuata del Coll with Chilida's "floating" steel sculpture (currently being restored) or the neighborhood surrounding the velodrome in Horta which represents a kind of visual poem by the poet Joan Brossa.

Climbing the hill one reaches the very extensive garden of the Marquès de Llupa i d'Alfarràs. The gardens have created a romantic refuge for visitors in the foothills of the Collserola Massif. The visitor's sense of direction will be put to the test by an elaborate labyrinth of cypresses (illus. below).

LEFT:
*Torre de Collserola, built by Sir Norman Foster, 1992*

BELOW:
*The elaborate cypress labyrinth in the garden of the Marquès de Llupa i d'Alfarràs in Horta*

# Barcelona's Hinterland

# Under the Influence of Montserrat

## Terrassa: St. Maria de Barbarà and St. Cugat

About 50 km (31 miles) northwest of Barcelona, the majestic spine and crevasses of Montserrat suddenly rise up from the plains of Llobregat. At a height of 1,236 m (c. 4,000 ft.) the massif imperiously dominates the hinterland of Barcelona (illus. pp. 270–71). Looking at it, it is easy to believe that its strange silhouette was created by mysterious forces, so it is no surprise that myths and legends surround its formation, many which have found their way into European literature.

Even today, when a journey by fast train is common-place, Montserrat has lost none of its fascination. In Monistrol, the visitor can take the breathtakingly steep cable-car to the rocky heights.

However, before turning to the "holy mountain of Catalonia," we stop off at Terrassa, the center of the textile industry located to the northwest of Barcelona. Here one unexpectedly encounters evidence of more than 1,500 years of history. Three picturesque sacred buildings of the late Roman, Visigoth, and Romanesque periods have been preserved in an idyllic park; this grouping forms one of the few remaining examples of churches from different eras sited together in one place.

They testify to the importance of the settlement founded by the Romans – named Egrara – and elevated to a

bishopric in the 5th century; it experienced a high-point in its history with the Hispanic Council of 615. The driving force behind its continuing prosperity even today was and remains the processing of wool. This guaranteed good fortune and royal privileges for the town, which later adopted the name of the castle of Terrassa.

The oldest monument in the church complex is the 5th-century baptistery of St. Miquel: a square building with horseshoe-shaped apse. At its center is a reconstructed deep immersion pool, which is covered by a vaulted dome (illus. opposite bottom). The rites at the time required the complete immersion of the person being baptized. The eight pillars supporting the canopy are evidently taken from the spoils of a Roman temple.

Both neighboring churches are overwhelmingly Romanesque: the old parish church of St. Pere and the former bishop's church of St. Maria. The simple, elongated buildings contain a fascinating wealth of mosaics, frescoes, and altarpieces. In front of the façade of St. Maria, part of a Roman pavement has been uncovered that in addition to its geometric patterns includes Christian motifs of fish and bread (illus. opposite top).

Among the frescoes of St. Maria's interior, the scenes on the walls of the side apse of the straight transept are special. They date from the late 12th century (illus. right). They depict the unusual subject of the murder of Thomas à Beckett in Canterbury Cathedral in 1170. Only three years later the archbishop was canonized. This fresco in Terrassa illustrates how quickly the cult surrounding this martyr spread throughout Europe.

St. Maria also has two outstanding late Gothic altarpieces: a retable of St. Peter that the Gironese artists Lluís Borrassà painted in 1441, and a retable of the saintly physicians St. Abdon and St. Sennen both of whom were highly revered in Catalonia. The confident skill evident in the alrarpieces is the work of Jaume Huguet, who signed a contract for it in 1460. In contrast to the so-called international style required of Borassà, the Flemish influence that was defining Spanish painting in the second half of the 15th century is recognizable here.

St. Pere preserves an unusual work: a kind of stone retable cut into the wall of the apse of the parish church, the purpose and date of which remain uncertain. Remnants of figurative representations and evangelical symbols are still recognizable. It is possible that this eastern part belongs to a forerunner of the Romanesque building.

Close to the three churches lie the castle and Carthusian monastery of Vallparadis in which the Museu Municipal d'Art is housed today. The turn-of-the-century buildings – which reflected an economic revival – are particularly worth seeing. Factories and factory owner's villas, such as those of Masia Freixe, the Magatzem Farnés, or Fábrica Aymerich i Amat – where there is now a science and technology museum in its boiler house – are gems of Modern architecture. As almost always, whenever functional Catalan buildings are being discussed, this should be done in conjunction with the name of Lluis Moncunill.

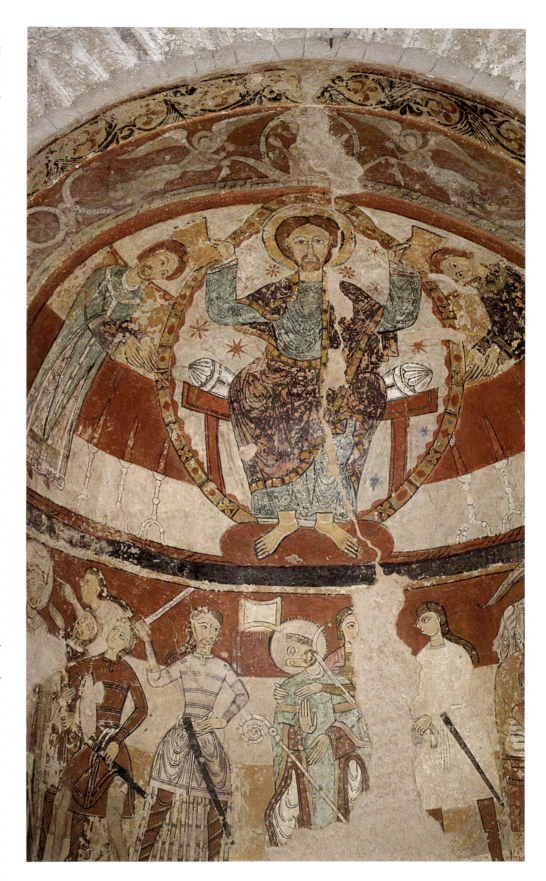

PP. 270–71:
At 1236-m (c. 4,000-ft.) high, the massif of Montserrat dominates the hinterland of Barcelona

OPPOSITE:
The 12-century St. Maria, Terrassa (above)
The vaulting above the font of St. Miquel, started in the 5th century (below)

ABOVE:
St. Maria, Terrassa
Frescoes of St. Thomas à Beckett surmounted by Christ in the Mandorla, late 12th century

For those who prefer to remain in the Middle Ages, a visit to St. Maria de Barberà and St. Cugat de Vallès is recommended. Now there is a choice. From either place you can reach the road back to Barcelona, if you take the route via Sabadell; this, however, means passing-up the delightful landscape of the road through the hills to the slopes of Tibidabo.

The simple Romanesque church of St. Maria de Barberà (illus. left) lies in close proximity to the gates of the "Catalan Manchester." So many of its contemporaries from the early 12th century occupy the three apses that connect with the high nave and the squat transept. Blind arcades and flat pilasters divide the head of the choir. Alongside the church there is a rectangular belfry.

The church's main claim to fame, though, are its painted frescoes – some of the very few still *in situ* in Catalonia (illus. left below). They were discovered in 1919 under a thick layer of plaster. Not all the parts of the decoration could be saved or reconstructed, yet what remains is astonishing enough. In the adjoining apses one can still recognize episodes from the lives and martyrdom of St. Peter and St. Paul, as well as the unusual story for Catalonia: the discovery and veneration of the Holy Cross by the Roman emperor Constantin and his mother Helena. On a triumphal arch, scenes from the Old Testament are depicted and in the main apse there are others from the New Testament.

The Pantocrator in the dome is heavily overworked. Differences in style between the paintings of the side apses and those of the main apse suggest that more than three-quarters of a century elapsed between their creation. This is apparent both from the change of the style of the figures and also in the systematized manner in which the life of Christ is represented.

In contrast to the outwardly modest parish church in Barberà, the monastery of St. Cugat des Vallès is almost strangely exquisite (illus. opposite top). A monastery was quickly erected here, where Bishop Cugat – who came from Africa – met a martyr's death, but the church fell victim to the invasion by the Moors. The present building was erected by the Benedictines after 1013, uniting Romanesque, Gothic, and Baroque elements.

Whereas the elegant belfry stems from the late 11th century, the church itself was constructed later, step-by-step from Romanesque to late Gothic. The most important part of the church interior is the altar of All Saints by Pere Serra of 1375. The cloisters dating from the late 12th through the mid-14th centuries are unique. The entire gamut of medieval life is depicted in the molding of its 144 capitals. Themes from the Old and New Testaments, such as the stories of Adam and Noah, and the life of Christ, are interspersed with paintings of the those living in cloisters and the everyday life of those working on the land (illus. opposite bottom). The greatest proportion of the painted decoration deals with imaginative mythological animals such as centaurs, winged lions, and other hybrid creatures, the meaning of which has been lost. The sculptor, Arnau Gatell, has been portrayed on one of the corner pillars.

ABOVE:
St. Maria de Barberà,
12th-century Romanesque church

RIGHT:
St. Maria de Barberà
Romanesque church
Apse decorated with 12th-century frescoes

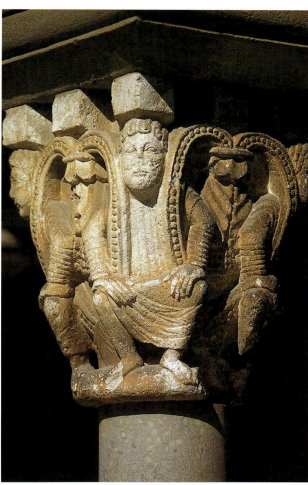

ABOVE:
St. Cugat del Vallès,
11th-to-14th century monastery

FAR LEFT AND LEFT:
St. Cugat del Vallès
Late 12th-century capital in
cloisters

ABOVE, RIGHT, AND OPPOSITE,
BOTTOM:
*Impressions of Montserrat*
The colors and moods of
Montserrat change with the time
of day and the weather. Its gray-
brown pinnacles soar into the blue
sky, but are tinged with a red glow
in the evening. When its slopes are
shrouded in clouds they can have a
threatening black sheen.

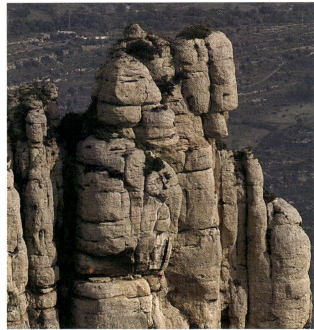

## Montserrat

Anyone who catches sight of the strange rock formations of Montserrat cannot escape its magic. Bare rock needles rise abruptly above the green of the Llobregat valley to a height of 1236 m (c. 4,000 ft.), like the fingers of the Cyclops or a sea of stone peaks (illus. opposite). The mountain was formed in the Eocene period, and for thousands of years erosion by wind and water have created precipitous ridges and worn away chunks of rock that bring primeval life to view on the surface.

The colors and moods of Montserrat – the serrated mountain – change with the time of day and the weather. Its gray-brown peaks rise up to a blue sky, but in the evening they are suffused in a red veil. The slopes have a menacingly black sheen when they are shrouded in clouds.

Creative people have been drawn to this mountain, setting down in words the legends and rumors about the magic of this special place. One of the finest examples is from the ode, *Virolai*, by the Catalan Nationalist poet, Jacint Verdaguer:

*Amb serra d'or els angelets serraren*
*eixos turons per fer-vous...*
(With golden saw the angel sawed up this hill,
in order to build you [the Mother God of Montserrat] a palace...)

Others compared the rare formations to animals or fairy-tale forms, and gave them individual names, such as "the camel," "the elephant's trunk," or "the bewitched giant." Still others suspect that Montserrat is the "Munsalvaesche" of the legend of Parsifal, and even that the Holy Grail is hidden in the mountain. Richard Wagner grasped all these ideas and used the rocks of Montserrat as inspiration for the staging of his *Parsifal*.

Today the magic of the mountain can be enjoyed in complete peace only early in the morning or late in the

*Above:*
*Montserrat's cable-car*

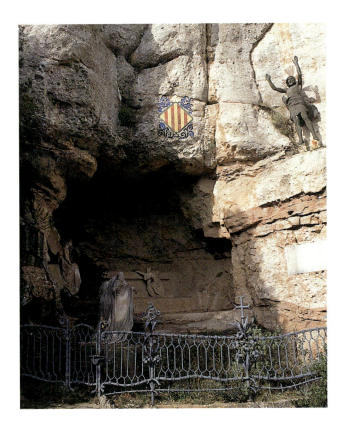

RIGHT:
*Track to St. Cova
Chapel with 20th-century
portrayals of the resurrection*

BELOW:
*La Moreneta, the 12th-century
"Black Madonna of Montserrat"*

evening. Because the monastery of Monistrol is so easy to reach, it more often resembles a busy anthill than a calm place of retreat. This atmosphere on the mountain changes abruptly, however, as soon as the last gondola leaves the cable-car station.

Anyone who wants to place themselves in proximity to the mountain and its legends should spend a night in one of the comfortable hospices. Then it is possible to go on more extensive walks and climbing trips in a nature reserve that is rich in rare species of plants and animals, or even to explore deep into rocky caves.

Referring back to the mystical atmosphere of this "sawn-up" mountain, the Catalan Montserrat is a holy mountain. Hermits sought solitude and communion with nature here from very early times. The first shrine was documented in 888, and Benedictine monks established a chapel to Our Lady in 1025 under orders from the Abbess Oliva of Ripoll.

So many believers were soon attracted here that in the 12th century a larger Romanesque abbey was erected. Later, this was extended in Gothic style, and finally in 1409 the abbey was made independent of its parent cloisters. In 1560, it was decided to build a new church, which was dedicated in 1592.

Its extraordinary rise was due to the shrine of a Romanesque Madonna: La Moreneta or the "Black Madonna of Montserrat" (illus. oposite bottom). Her image in dark-colored wood has been traced back to various strange events, but a Black Madonna is not that unusual in Christian art, for she illustrates a verse from the Old Testament, Song of Songs (1, 5): "*Nigra sum sed formosa*" or "I am black but lovely."

Legends surround the gold-framed sculpture. It was said to have been carved by the apostle St. Luke himself, and it was also claimed to have been found by shepherds in a grotto in 888 – in itself miraculous since the sculpture dates from the late 12th century.

On one occasion, when an attempt was made to carry the statue around the town, it was said to have become so heavy that it could no longer be moved. This was taken as an omen, one indicating the founding of religious cloisters on Montserrat.

However, La Moreneta (the dark maiden) is the soul of Montserrat, and from 1881 she has been the patroness of Catalonia. She can be admired in an elevated chapel in the east wing of the church. Long lines of pilgrims wait for their few seconds in her presence and the opportunity to kiss her wooden orb. The cave in which she was supposedly found – Santa Cova – is now a place revered by believers where they make their votive offerings.

The path to Santa Cova takes about half an hour downhill by steps (or by elevator). The sides are flanked by chapels containing larger-than-life representations of the joy and pain of Mary (illus. opposite top). They were created by artists of the 19th century, including Antoni Gaudí.

The monastery complex as it stands today dates mainly from the 19th and 20th centuries, because the abbey was plundered in 1811 by Napoleon's troops, and extensively destroyed.

Only a few historic parts remain including the late Gothic cloisters founded by Giulianó della Rovere (later Pope Julius II) when he was abbot (illus. p. 281, top).

The wall tomb of Prince Joan d'Arago, a grandson of Ferdinand the Catholic, has also been preserved, although it is not in its original position. The superb lifelike craftmanship suggests the involvement of an Italian artist.

Many other valuable art treasures from the high points in Montserrat's intriguing history can now only be seen in the Pinakothek. These include works by painters, such as El Greco and Caravaggio, and also valuable manuscripts.

Following the storming by the French and secularization, the monastery was severely put to the test in the early 19th century. This chapter finally ended with the appointment of Abbot Miguel Muntades in 1858.

The rebuilding of the shrine is linked to the *Renaixença* – the rebirth of Catalan intellectualism and politics. The abbey developed into a center of Catalan culture, a position not even Franco's dictatorship of could break.

After the Spanish Civil War, the intellectual elite and Catalan opposition gathered on the holy mountain. The abbey's publishers – founded in 1499 – brought out the publication *Serra d'Or* in the then banned Catalan language. Montserrat changed from a place of pilgrimage into a sanctuary for those opposed to the Franco regime. Today, these events – which took place long ago – seem extremely remote, for little trace can be found of those heroic times.

Now, streams of tourists and commercial exploitation determine the atmosphere – at least during the day. Even the singing of the *Virolai* (the Montserrat hymn) by the

*View from the east of the church and Benedictine monastery on Montserrat, rebuilt in the 19th and 20th centuries by Francesc Villar i Lozana, Josep Puig i Cadafalch, and Francesc Folguera*

boys' choir that was founded in the 12th century – the famous Escolania – is rarely able to restore the atmosphere of retreat and composure.

The demands of rebuilding of the abbey too, which were pushed forward in the late 19th and early 20th centuries, were not entirely conducive to contemplation. Admittedly important architects, such as Josep Puig i Cadafalch and Francesc Folguera, were responsible for the plans, yet they did not succeed in breathing life into these stark buildings or imparting the appropriate spirituality. Hence, even the interior of the new church – which rose from the old foundations – with its frescoes and sculpture by important artists (Josep Llimona, the Vallmitjana brothers, and Josep Maria Subirachs) is unusually bland. The façade, with Gothic-style figures of the apostles by Venanci and Agapit Vallmitjana was completed in 1900–01 by Francesc de P. Villar. The positioning of the cloisters is truly stunning, for they cling to precipitous rocks like an eagle's nest.

Inside the abbey, in addition to the Pinakothek, the museum for prehistory, the Bible museum and a museum for modern Catalan painting can be seen. The library – burnt in 1811 during the storming of the French troops – today contains 250,000 volumes, including the famous *Llibre Vermell*, or "Red Book" of the abbey's administration.

Nature lovers and those who wish to experience the unspoiled nature of Montserrat, are advised to take the special elevator to the pilgrims' chapels, which can be reached, if required, by a shorter route using the Funicular de St. Joan. There are delightful views from the footpath across the highest point of the massif to the hermitages of St. Miquel, St Joan, St. Trinitat, and St. Jeroni. When the weather is good, you can see as far as the ocean.

Those traveling by car on the return journey through the Llobregat valley can visit the abbey of St. Cecilia. This inspiring building was founded between 942 and 945, but the head of the choir, with three Romanesque apses, and their fine decorative niches are 11th century. We end our visit to the "holy mountain of Catalonia" in what is probably the oldest preserved shrine on Montserrat.

ABOVE:
Interior of the church of the monastery on Montserrat

LEFT:
Cloisters of the Benedictine monastery on Montserrat, built in 1472 by Jaume Alfons and Pere Bassets

OPPOSITE:
The Benedictine monastery on Montserrat, seen from the St. Joan mountain

## Manresa

It is said that the appearance of Manresa is of a scattering of both monasteries and factories. The main town of the Bages region is situated on the banks of the Cardoner, which shortly afterward joins the Llobregat that flows on to Barcelona. The town forms an important crossroads for access to the interior of Catalonia. Its situation on and between various hills – the *puigs* – makes it most picturesque. The view of the stone-brown Seu from the Romanesque bridge is a particularly impressive one, with the cathedral poised on its mount somewhat like the Acropolis (illus. above).

As the Roman *municipium* of "Minoresa," this place attained considerable importance during the *Reconquista*. An important fortress was established here on the boundary between the Spanish lands and the newly Islamic Castile. The Comtat de Manresa, which stretched to the foothills of the Pyrenees, was established under Guifré el Pelós (Wilfred the Hairy).

In the late Middle Ages Manresa developed into a lively market town requiring the protection of walls. The clergy and town fathers decided to build a new Gothic collegiate church in the late 13th century as a visible sign of the town's well-being, and the foundation stone was laid in 1328. It was built under the leadership of Berenguer de

Montagut, who, at the same time, was working on the St. Maria del Mar in Barcelona, a magnificent house of God that scarcely matches its sister church in the Catalan metropolis. Its completion was delayed until the 16th century. The façade, atrium, and baptistery of 1915 are neo-Gothic.

In spite of the amount of time it took to build it, the entire interior is in accordance with Berenguer's ideas on the fascinating use of space (illus. opposite bottom). A unique nave without a transept was lined with deep chapels which continue into the choir. At 18.5-m (c. 60-ft.) wide, it is perhaps the broadest in Europe after Girona.

The chapels are linked one below the other by arcades, forming a kind of side aisle – an original architectural solution that emphatically contributes to the uniformity of the space. Slim octagonal pillars support the arcades and serve the clerestory that continues in the fine ribbing of the vaulting. Exceptionally large tracery windows – for Catalonia – bathe the interior in festive light. Today, almost all the window panes are from the 19th and 20th centuries because the church was damaged by fire during the War of Spanish Succession of 1714 and again in 1936. The 18 double flying buttresses dominate the building's exterior, rising out of the chapel's roofline. The rectangular tower dates from 1592.

The splendor of the collegiate church of Manresa is plain for all to see, but does not explain how the name Seu became established in the 14th century. The term is only correct for the church of a bishop; Manresa does not have its own bishop but falls under the diocese of Vic.

The interior decoration of the Seu comprises architecture of the highest standard. The Holy Ghost retable of Pere Serra is worth particular mention, and is clearly the best work of a Catalan master (illus. right). Serra produced the unusually large altarpiece in 1394 in response to a commission by the Brotherhood of the Holy Ghost, in which the guild of tanners were also involved.

Scenes from the Creation story, the life of Mary and Christ, and also the effusion of the Holy Spirit are depicted in 15 large, and many smaller, tableaux, with the saints and prophets represented in smaller tableaux. The predella, with the astonishing realism of the depiction of the entombment of Christ, originates from another retable that Lluís Borassà created in 1411.

Opposite the main part of the retable, a new stylistic direction can be seen: the so-called court style (c. 1400). The St. Mark altarpiece of Arnau Bassa (1346) and the retable of St. Michael and St. Nicholas – created by Jaumes Cabrera in 1406 for the community of canons, clerics, and doctors – are just as interesting. Probably the most important work housed here is the statue of Mare de Déu de l'Alba (Madonna of the Red Dawn) by Pere Puig (late 14th century). It suffered from arson during the night of May 28, 1979; the present-day statue is a reproduction.

The Madonna of the Red Dawn leads us on though to another important part of the story of Manresa: the retreat of Ignatius Loyola, who is said to have prayed in front of the statue. Ignatius was a knight in the service of the

Catholic king who was wounded during the siege of Pamplona and withdrew to Catalonia. After a retreat on Montserrat, he lived in a cave below the collegiate church of Manresa for eight months in 1522, and devoted himself to spiritual practice, setting down his experience in his "Spiritual Exercises." This book was to be the basis for the vocation of Ignatius Loyola as a missionary and his foundation of the Society of Jesus (the Jesuits). In the past 250 years a complex of Baroque, neo-classical, and post-Modernisme buildings have been built around the place of inner retreat; all are decorated with the most sumptuous sculptures and mosaics.

The center of the town of Manresa and the Seu suffered considerable damage during the Spanish Civil War, so that little remains of medieval structures. The Casa de la Ciutat (1739–77) belongs to the Classical era where the "Bases de Manresa" draft of a Catalan constitution was adopted in 1892. Among the "fathers" of the constitution was the famous Modernist architect Lluís Domènech i Montaner. The outwardly Baroque palace of justice (1661–71) incorporates older architectural styles, and has itself frequently been altered.

Manresa was first able, in the 19th century, to develop its own appearance through renewal. The town did not keep to a standard Eixample as in other towns, but quickly grew

OPPOSITE TOP:
Manresa and its cathedral ("La Seu")

OPPOSITE BOTTOM:
Manresa
Cathedral, started in 1328.

ABOVE:
Manresa
Cathedral
Retable of the Holy Ghost, created by Pere Serra in 1394

extensively beyond its old walls. As already mentioned, Manresa established factories between the monasteries, which were then still in existence.

The starting point for the new quarter was the Plaça St. Domènec in the north of the historical center. A remarkable collection of historic and Modernisme buildings came into being here, such as the Casa Torrents of 1905, the Casa de Cultura, and finally the Art Deco Cal Jorba department store.

The throng of activity on the Passeig Carles III – surely the finest place for a stroll in Catalonian after La Rambla in Barcelona – is a memorable experience (illus. opposite). The lime-tree lined avenue leads past countless houses from the turn of the 19th and early 20th centuries, now housing many of the cultural organizations that make life in Manresa so full of variety.

Just a few miles northeast of the town, a little way off the main road to Vic in the village of St. Fruitós de Bages, lies the atmospheric Benedictine monastery of St. Benet – certainly worth a detour. The extensive monastery was enlarged continuously from the 10th to the 18th centuries, but the buildings are still predominantly medieval in appearance. The Romanesque church with transept, three apses, and crypt date from the 12th century but the belfry rises up from separate foundations. The most impressive feature is the idyllic cloisters with its wealth of narrative capitals adorning the twin columns (illus. above). They were completed in 1225. The stories are depicted through just a few essentials on squat trapezoid blocks. Not only biblical scenes are represented here: more frequently there are mythological themes and paintings based on everyday rural life. They have been done in a somewhat archaic, yet highly impressive, manner. Their preservation in the cloisters – like most others, it was secularized in 1835, and left to fall into ruin – is due to the family of the Modernisme painter, Ramon Casas, who most fortunately purchased the building in 1907, and then proceeded to ensure the restoration and maintenance of the former Benedictine monastery of St. Benet.

The Parc Natural de St. Llorenc del Munt extends between Manresa and Terrassa, with another Romanesque Benedictine monastery that gives its name to the mountain ridge. The picturesque monastery situated at 1095 m (c. 3,600 ft.) is one of the best examples of the Lombardic style. Today it serves as a refuge and restaurant for mountain walkers.

ABOVE:
*Capitals in the cloisters of Benedictine monastery St. Benet St. Fruitós de Bages*

OPPOSITE:
*Manresa*
*An amble along the Passeig Carles III, the finest place for a stroll in Catalonia after La Rambla in Barcelona*

RIGHT:
*St Viçenç de Cardona, 1029–40*

BELOW:
*The fortified mound of Cardona*

OPPOSITE:
*Interior views*
*Viçenç de Cardona*

## Cardona

If one follows the valley of the Cardoner, one will soon reach the impressive fortified hill of Cordona (illus. below). It was once a bastion on the border to defend the Spanish lands against the Moors, and has lost none of its grandeur. Nevertheless, the castle plays only a secondary historical role in Cardona.

In ancient times the region's wealth and strategic importance was due to deposits of salt and potash, which are still produced at the Muntanya de Sal. Salt was so valuable to everyone that it was deemed sensible to protect the mine. The 170-m (c. 560-ft.) high hill has stalactite and stalagmite galleries that are up to a kilometer (about $^1/_2$ a mile) deep. The history and culture of the rock salt is explained in a small museum at Carrer Pompeu Fabra 4.

The castle and settlement look back across a thousand years of history. Louis the Pious, and later Guifré el Pelós (Wilfred the Hairy), established early settlements, which were first fortified by Count Borrell II following the attack of Almansor. The oldest remaining parts are the cylindrical Torre de la Minyona. The castle today is a

parador hotel and originates mainly from the 11th century. The castle mound was surrounded in the 18th century with modern bastions.

More impressive and of greater significance in terms of its art history is the castle church of St. Viçenç (illus. opposite, top). Founded by Viscount Beremund, and built between 1029 and 1040, it is one of the earliest examples of Romanesque architecture in Catalonia.

The ground plan and elevations show unusual standards of uniformity and clarity. The narthex, or vestibule, follows three broad square bays in the central nave which are flanked by three smaller ones in the side aisles. The choir, central, and side apses connect with the transept that is deep, yet barely projects beyond the walls of the nave. The crypt extends beneath the choir. (Incidentally, a scene from one of Orson Welles' movies was filmed in the triple vaulted space.)

Back to the church itself, the transept is covered by a dome supported by squinches (illus. right). The other parts of the building are also systematically arched. The nave and transept are barrel vaulted; their height of just 19 m (c. 62 ft.) compared with width of about 6 m (c. 20 ft.) makes the space appear deep but not restricted. The rather low side aisle retains small-scale cross-vaulting, a technique that appears here in the castle church of St. Viçenç for the first time in Spanish architecture.

The structure of the wall is clear and systematic, and also economical yet subtle, giving the building a collective unity. The main motif is the double-stepped pattern of the pillars that continues into the strapped arches of the vaulting. The apparent relief of this feature more or less gives the impression that the wall is set back and not part of the structure. The exterior is also elegantly decorated with lesene (pilasters without base or capital) and blind niches which influence the towering structure of the building, forming a differentiated yet uniform harmonic unison of the whole.

Study of the architecture of St. Viçenç in Cardona is so important that it has been the subject of a continuing debate about the origins of Romanesque and the development of the so-called Lombardic style. The Lombardics were in reality troops of masons found throughout Europe, who guaranteed good quality craftmanship. Through them, the early Romanesque style became established everywhere. It is thought that there was definite influence of Lombardic workshops in Cardona too, an aspect not unusual in Catalonia.

More recent research however takes exception to this theory, and points instead to the regional characteristics which the building clearly exhibits. Examples of these regional elements are above all the upright proportions and strap-supported barrel vaults previously used at St. Pere de Rodes. Little remains of the interior fittings of the church, but you can still see the Renaissance tomb of Count Joan Ramón Folch and his wife Francisca Manrique de Lara. Some frescoes from St. Viçenç are exhibited today in the Museu Nacional d'Art de Catalunya in Barcelona. The remnants of a late Gothic cloister are preserved in front of the church of St. Viçenç.

## Solsona

If one follows the C1410 farther along the valley, after 15 km (c. 9 miles) one reaches the proud town of Solsona. The old town sits picturesquely raised above the Riu Negre. The name is derived from an Iberian settlement known as "Setelsona," and was later occupied by the Romans. Louis the Pious first rescued it from the Moors, but the town was re-Christianized by Count Guifré in 886.

In the period that followed the town was placed under the bishopric and lands of the Count of Urgell. In 1217 the ruling aristocrats of Torroja assumed the title Viscount of Cardona. The consequence of this was endless disputes between the diocese and the feudal lord regarding the sovereignty. At the time of the counter-reformation Pope Clemens VIII established a bishopric of Solsona in 1593 at the behest of King Philip II, and the following year it was granted its town charter.

The castle (12th century) and remains of the city wall of 1374 are a prelude to a stroll through the atmospheric old town, where narrow alleys alternate with grand houses of the aristocracy. The most important monument is clearly the cathedral, which brings together the distinctly different styles of Romanesque and Baroque. The oldest parts are the 12th-century apses, the 14th- and 15th-century cloister entrance, belfry, and nave; however, the main front was not built until the 18th century. In the chapel of the Mare de Déu del Claustre, in the straight transept, there is a statue of the Madonna that is given the

same name. Unusually fine, it is made of black stone (illus. opposite, bottom), and the Mother and Child exhibit serious, dignified expressions. The artists paid particular attention to the form of the vestments that are lined with precious edging, and which flow around the limbs in hundreds of fine folds. The work, from the 12th century, is attributed to the sculpture school of Tolsane in the style of Gilabertus.

The second main attraction of Solsona is the diocesan museum housed in the neoclassical bishop's palace. Its treasure mainly comprises a number of outstanding Romanesque frescoes that originate from the churches in the area.

This includes the enigmatic picture of a bearded man (God the Father or perhaps just a worshiper) of the 10th century, painted with childlike naivety and enclosed within an ornamental circle. Above it a bird is sketched in red and green – perhaps a phoenix that soars above the symbol of the world, in a metaphor for the Resurrection.

The Apocalyptic scenes and martyrdom of St. Quiricus and St. Julitta are about 200 years later. They are attributed to the so-called "master of Pedret," and originate like the older frescoes from the nearby church of St. Quirce de Pedret. Other – earlier – Romanesque frescoes were only discovered when these later ones were in the process of being conserved.

The paintings from St. Pere de Casseres are further treasures, dating from the 13th century. The scene of the Last Judgment is particularly impressive with astonish-ingly lively, trumpet-blowing angels. Gothic altarpieces, sculpture, and work of goldsmiths complete the exceptionally rich collection of Catalan art.

Outside the gates of Solsona lies the little hamlet of Olius and is well worth a detour. Its parish church of St. Esteve possesses a remarkable crypt, in which three slender naves are separated by unusually diverse pillars. The crypt may be even older than the single nave church above it that was dedicated in 1079. The modern graveyard near the church also holds a surprise. A grave monument of naturalistic design seem to grow organically from the rock in the manner of Antoni Gaudí. The monument was designed by Bernardí Martelli in 1916 (illus. below, left). To the northwest of Olius one can visit the remains of the Castelvell or "old castle" of Solsona. One of the Gothic rooms was subsequently turned into a shrine to Mare de Déu del Remei.

A more ambitious Baroque building for the Mare de Déu del Miracle (Mother of God of Miracles) was to have been built in the village of Riner; however, the death of the architect Josep Moretó in 1672 prevented its being completed. Fortunately the precious retable was erected in the following century. It is one of the major pieces of Baroque art in Catalonia, where there are few examples of this style (illus. below, right).

Berga is the third and final place on this tour before the route leads right into the heights of the Pyrenees. One reaches the larger community of Berguedà, either directly from Manresa through the valley of the Llobregat or from

BELOW LEFT:
Olius
*Cemetery with Modernisme memorial by Bernardí Martelli of 1916*

BELOW:
*Mare de Déu del Miracle, 17th-century (at Riner)*

Solsona via the mountainous C149. Home of the troubadour Guillem de Berguadà (d. 1196), the lively trading town at the foot of the mountains is evidence of its thousands of years of history in addition to fine houses from the turn of the century.

The main reason for visiting Berga is its festivals – celebrated with a great display of splendor. In June, at the time of the feast of Corpus Christi, the town changes into a unique theater. *La Patum*, a mythological animal, and other mythical forms bring visitors from throughout Catalonia under their spell.

Ritual battles are played out, personifying the victory of good in the form of the Archangel Michael over the evil of the world, in which the Moors are driven back by the Christians. The devil and traditional giants, *els gegants*, stride around the town. Everything goes – in typical Catalan manner – with grandiose fireworks and a great deal of noise; both heaven and hell appear to rise up.

For those who require some peace and solitude after this assault on their senses, a visit to Pedret and climb to the little pre-Romanesque church of St. Quirze is recommended (illus. above). The route leads on to an idyllic ancient stone bridge (illus. opposite, bottom) and then back up the hill over a stone road to the simple three-nave St. Quirze. The interior architecture is determined by its broad horseshoe-shaped arches that separate the nave and apses. Unfortunately the principal treasure of the village can no longer be admired *in situ*. The outstanding cycle of frescoes that decorated the walls were removed in the 1930s, and taken to the museums in Barcelona (MNAC) and Solsona. By car one reaches the C149, and then heads northeast to the church of St. Jaume de Frontanyà, which lies equally secluded in wonderful mountain scenery. The church belongs to an Augustinian order, and represents one of the finest examples of 11th-century Catalan

*Parish church of St. Llorenc de Morunys
Baroque chapel of Mare de Déu dels Colls. The sculptural adornment was created in 1773–84 by Josep Pujol*

Romanesque. As usual the ground plan is in the form of a Latin cross on which the eastern main apse connects with the transept and side apses. A 12-sided cupola is set high above the crossing, supported on the inside by squinches, or small supportive arches, that were an example for the reconstruction of the towers above the crossings at Ripoll. Massive, squat walls make the church look fortified, an impression quickly forgotten on viewing the fineness of the ornamentation. Lesene (pilasters without bases or capitals) and blind niches elegantly divide the apses.

A few miles to the west of Berga is the shrine of St. Maria de Queralt – worth visiting for the fantastic panoramic views. Situated at 1024 m (c. 3,360 ft.), it can easily be reached by car. Here, in the transition to the Serra del Cadi in the hill country landscape of Berguedà, there are unique views of the striking silhouette of the Montserrat massif. At the shrine a Madonna is revered, which dates from the transitional period between Romanesque and Gothic. The building is partly 18th century and partly early 20th century. Somewhat farther on is the little Romanesque church of St. Pere de Madrona, a favorite place of pilgrimage on the last Sunday in June.

A winding road leads on to St. Llorenç de Morunys where the parish church was once part of an important Benedictine monastery. The building itself with its extensively altered Romanesque architecture is interesting for the treasures it contains.

The Baroque chapel of the Mare de Déu dels Colls contains a magnificent retable (illus. opposite bottom). Between 1773 and 1784, when the crisis-ridden land began to recover, Josep Pujol created the marvelous sculptural work that covers the wall and dome with biblical and legendary scenes.

TOP:
*Scenery at St. Llorenc de Morunys*

BOTTOM:
*Stone bridge at Pedret*

## Vic and Its Surroundings

Vic, in the Comara Osona, is a small town with a great past, many art treasures, and even more culinary attractions (see panel box right). Vic was the main settlement of the Iberian Ausetans people who fiercely opposed the intrusion of the Romans, but were then forced to make peace with them. Following the arrival of Christianity and the creation of a diocese (in 516), the inhabitants remained here for only 200 years before the Moors seized power in 715.

The site was re-established in the late ninth century as Vicus Ausonae, from which today's name is derived. At this point a happier and more prosperous period was initiated with Vic becoming an important trading and cultural center, and acquiring much of the appearance it has today.

Wherever you go you are confronted with history, so it is not surprising that the proud town became a center of the *Renaixença*, or Catalan Renaissance of the 19th century. The town retains this awareness of tradition, which manifests itself in a variety of cultural and political activities.

It is easy for today's visitor to journey back through the history of the ancient town. A well-signposted tour around the town – the Ruta Turística – passes the most important monuments within the largely retained city walls. This starts at the arcade-lined Plaça Major or El Mercadal – the broad, historical market place (illus. above). On each side of the market are private houses and offices from different eras, such as the town hall – begun in 1388, extended in 1670 and again in 1922.

At the heart of the town hall is the large Sala de la Columna room on the main floor with a solitary column –

really a pillar – from which the building derives its name. A gallery of illustrious citizens was created here in 1890. The loggia, clock-tower, and the Sala del Consistori are all in the Baroque style.

Most of the neighboring fine houses were started in medieval times and modified in later centuries. Despite this, the Mercadal is unusually unified and one of the finest *places majors* in Catalonia.

The tour that starts from the square passes the original Gothic Església de St. Just, later used as a church for a Jesuit monastery and the Hospital de la Santa Creu, which was founded by Ramon de Terrades in 1348. Two broad Gothic rooms have survived from this era, while the façade and courtyard are Renaissance in style. A new church and the Casa de Convalescència (convalescent home) were built in the 18th century; the pharmacy added by Josep Maria Pericas in 1933 is also well worth seeing.

Back in the town center one of the highlights of the visit to Vic awaits visitors: the cathedral and the episcopal museum; the treasures of the latter were distributed for exhibition in the year 2000 to various monasteries because of major new building in the Plaça Bisbe Oliba.

When the work is completed, an exceptional and rich collection of antique and Christian art will be brought together in this place. These include Romanesque frescoes from St. Sadurni d'Osormort, St. Martí Sescorts, and Seu d'Urgell, and wood-carvings. Then there are the colorfully decorated Madonnas, as well as reliefs and the work of goldsmiths from a similar era.

The Catalan Gothic altarpiece in the cathedral represents the work of several of the finest Catalan masters: Ferrer Bassa, whose style resembles that of the

**Catalan Cooking**

*Catalan cooking is a refined blend of heavy and fine, of seafood and game, and of Spanish, Arab, and French recipes. They are not afraid to serve chicken breast with garlic and chocolate sauce, or to combine rabbit with mussels, snails seared with ham, or lobster garnished with chicken. Ducks cannot expect a long life in Catalonia. There is also a simple traditional style of local cooking, of course, that always contains crisp fresh ingredients. One exception is simply the popular pickled stockfish, bacallà, that is prepared in countless ways.*

*The meal usually starts with pa amb tomàquet, toasted bread with tomato mousse and garlic followed by salad, amanides, sausage or fish morsels and vol-au-vents.*

*The main course, mainly seafood, fish, poultry, or game, is often served with tasty sauces, such as samfaina, which is made with peppers, eggplants, and zucchini, or, in the region of Tarragona, a romesco piquant almond-paprika/capsium cream sauce. In the area around Valencia, one finds paella or its noodle equivalent, fideua. Maó, the main town of Minorca, is renowned for the preparation of a delicate mayonnaise, naturally created from allioli (aïoli). The meal ends with creme catalana, made from eggs, milk, and vanilla with a caramelized crust. With this the outstanding still or sparkling wine of Penedès or Priorat is served.*

Siennese painters, Pere Serra, master painter of Cardona, and Lluis Borrassà. The famous retable of Guimera from the hand of Ramón Mur (illus. right) dates from the 15th century. The other works that overlook it by Bernat Martorell, Jaume Huguet, and Juan Gascó were already in existence during the Renaissance. In addition the manuscript illustrations and textile arts are worth the visitor's attention, as indeed is the collection of Egyptian art that a French soldier donated to the diocese.

Like the town hall of Vic, the cathedral displays a lively mixture of styles. It was dedicated in 1038 by the famous Abbot Oliba of Ripoll: a tripartite crypt with capitals – possibly from an earlier date – and an impressive belfry, remain from this era. The cloisters were started in 1318, and gained their fine figurative and vegetal molding c. 1400. When the cathedral was rebuilt in Classical style to the design of Josep Moretó, between 1781 and 1803, the cloisters were taken down and rebuilt in the smaller form that can be seen today. The interior of the cathedral possesses undiminished power and impact that imparts an experience of sacred art that could hardly be more impressive.

It is not the showy architecture, though, but the outstanding frescoes by Josep Maria Sert that take the breath away (illus. p. 294). In a delicate interplay, the large murals are almost restricted to monochrome gray and brown tones in contrast to the gold and black of the building's decor. The story of redemption is played out for the viewer here with extraordinary power, from the fall from grace to the Passion and Resurrection of Christ.

It was Sert's aim in life to see Classical-style murals reborn in Catalonia. In Vic he created his best work. He designed one version, and then a second that was destroyed between 1926–30 in the Spanish Civil War; he started the final version in 1940, which was finished by his pupils following his death in 1945. The tomb of the artist is in the cloisters. In comparison with the monumental fresco, other furnishings appear almost insubstantial. These include the alabaster retable with scenes of Christ and Mary, which Pere Oller created for the main altar in 1420–27 – today found in the choir. The tomb memorial of Canon Despujol of 1434 is by the same master.

After leaving the cathedral one can descend through the Porta del Queralt to the Riu Mèder, and then view the Romanesque bridge, or proceed on in the direction of the Plaça de la Pietat where the church of the same name is mainly based on the heavily restored 2nd-century remains of a Roman temple raised up on a podium (illus. p. 295, top). From the 11th century, the remains were incorporated within the fortifications of the noble Montcada family, and were first uncovered in 1882. Unfortunately only the outline of the walls remain of what had once been an obviously exquisite residence. The complex later became the seat of the city fathers as the Cúria Reial, and a grain store for the community. Next to the castle one finds more important homes of the nobility such as Casa Bojons (17th to 18th centuries), Casa Clariana (started in 1509), and the Casa Parrella (18th century). The Plaça de Don Miquel Clariana forms a

ABOVE:
Vic
*Detail from The expulsion from paradise*
*Retable of Guimerà, painted in the 15th century by Ramón Mur.*
*Museu Diocesà,*

OPPOSITE:
Vic
*Plaça Major (El Mercadal)*

Vic
*Cycle of frescoes created 1926–45
by Josep Maria Sert.
Cathedral*

particularly atmospheric corner with its Modernisme Casa Masferrer and the characteristic *esgraiats* (sgraffito) on its front façade (illus. opposite, bottom). Passing other churches and private houses along the way one returns to the Mercadal, to relax happily in one of its bars after a wander through 2,000 years of history. For those with a little more energy, the leather museum (Museu de l'Art de la Pell), brings together over a thousand artistic objects from every era.

Three delightful and venerable monasteries – poised around Vic like a wreath – take one on a journey of discovery into Catalan Romanesque architecture. The former Augustinian monastery of St. Maria de l'Estany, about 25 km (c. 16 miles) southwest of Vic, founded in 1080, owes its name to a pool drained in the 16th century. Its single nave church (dedicated in 1133) is not the object of our visit; much more can be seen in the cloisters themselves with four sets of ten twin columns topped with capitals displaying fantastic and exceptional scenes (illus. p. 296, top).

Dating the columns in the cloister is problematical, as this wing of the building dates from between the 12th and 14th centuries, was damaged by an earthquake in 1428, and afterward restored.

One should concentrate on absorbing the effect of both the whole and individual sculptures. Among the representations in the south and north wing in particular, are many that are extraordinary both in the worldly style and the craftsmanship of the sculpture on the capitals. One can recognize earthy scenes, such as the slaughter of a pig, entertainers, hunting, and family celebrations. More courtly scenes depict musicians and dancers, and a woman combing her hair. Elsewhere in the banded ornamentation is humor: an ox plays a fiddle with its hooves. Other capitals show mythological harpies and diverse leaf and plait motifs. Scenes from the New Testament are restricted to the older north wing of the cloister.

The manner in which four columns are mounted beneath a single supporting capital to form the corner pillars is of unusual architectural interest. A small museum enables one to delve into the monastery's history.

Much smaller, but equally exquisite, is the monastery of St. Maria de Lluçà, which can be reached from Vic along the delightful scenery of the C154 (illus. p. 296, middle). The fine working of the molding of the 12th-century capitals is similar in style to the earlier work at Ripoll, though Lluçà has other treasures to offer visitors.

Remarkable 14th-century wall paintings were discovered in 1954 beneath a thick layer of plaster. The cycle of frescoes, containing scenes of the lives of both Christ and Mary, a Pantocrator, and the deeds of St. Augustine, are today preserved for the admiration of visitors in a small museum. A 13th-century altar-cloth produced for the monastery by the "*mestre del Lluçanes*" can be seen today preserved in Vic's museum.

Close to the monastery of St. Maria de Lluçà, the remains of the castle of Lluça rise up, as does the Romanesque chapel of St. Vinzenz built in the form of a rotunda, a style rarely seen in Catalonia.

Although there are not sculptures at the Benedictine monastery of St. Pere de Casseres to the northeast of Vic (6 km/c. 4 miles by a stony road from the parador), the location in itself makes the place captivating and a worthwhile stop. Situated on a steep rock face high above the Sau reservoir, the restored gray-brown Romanesque

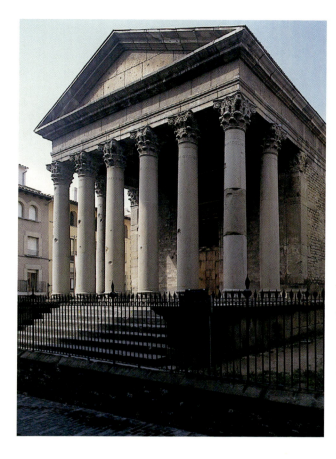

LEFT:
Vic
*The 2nd-century Roman temple*

BELOW:
Vic
*Plaça Don Miquel Clariana*

monastery radiates its austere beauty. The triple nave church with apses was dedicated in 1052. The cloisters were also built in the 11th century, though its sculpture is now in the museum at Vic.

After seeing these Romanesque cloisters, it is worth visiting Les Masies de Roda, which gently reintroduces us to the modern era. Estates here became independent of the community of Roda de Ter in 1806.

Some of the finest *masies* – self-supporting country seats from which medieval agriculture and forestry was controlled – have been preserved (illus. opposite top). The main house of the *masie* comprises the living quarters on the second floor, to which the warehouse and cellar space, stables, oil-mill, and winery all belong. Many of these *masies* have today been converted into stylish restaurants and bed and breakfasts. In Les Masies de Roda one could find among others, the historically rich Masia Bac de Roda (now a restaurant), Mas de Roda, Fontanelles, and El Viçenc.

On the way back to Barcelona one passes the small town of La Garriga, which derives its name from the heathland that surrounds it. The town became a place of summer retreat at the turn of the 19th century for the well-to-do people of Barcelona, thanks to its superb location at the edge of the Serra de Montseny and thermal springs. Countless villas built in imaginative Modernist, and Catalan Jugendstil design still stand witness to the use of this favored site (illus. opposite top). Among these villas,

TOP AND RIGHT:
St. Maria de l'Estany
The 12th- to 14th-century cloisters
founded 1133
Capital in the cloisters (right)

ABOVE:
St. Maria de Lluça
The 12th-century cloisters

the best known is the Mançana Raspall, a collection of
buildings by the architect Manual Raspall i Mayol, which
were built between 1910 and 1912.

Nature lovers should take a side-trip from La Garriga to
the waterfall of El Fai, reached by the breathtaking road
from St. Feliu de Codines. The beauty of the landscape
also appealed to the Benedictines who founded a
monastery here in 997. In the manner of troglodyte
homes, the church is built into the rock. Before today's
tourists arrived, the joint harmony of nature and the work
of man was admired by famous earlier visitors: Lord
Byron, Frederic Chopin, and George Sand. Contributing
to the agreeable aspect is the Serra de Montseny, which
lies to the north of La Garriga.

The picturesque landscape – famous for its rich variety
of flora and fauna – is pleasingly enriched by the gray-
brown walls of Romanesque churches and monasteries.
There are 65 such historic buildings in all and many serve
as an unusual weekend objective for many walkers in the
region. The nature reserve of the same name encompasses
310 sq km (c. 120 sq. miles), and reaches a height of 1712
m (c. 5,620 ft.) at the Turo de l'Home .

At Granollers, our last stopping point on the return
journey to the Catalan metropolis, there is a monumental,
open market-hall from 1587. The building supported by 15
massive columns was extensively reconstructed after
suffering heavy damage in the Spanish Civil War. More
than 200 people were killed in an attack because it
happened on market day.

ABOVE:
*Mas at La Garriga*

LEFT:
*La Garriga*
*Sculpture by the entrance to a villa*

# The Costa Daurada
# between Barcelona
# and Tarragona

# Modernisme, Sand, and Sparkling Wine

The Costa Daurada, the "gold coast" – the stretch of landscape between Barcelona and the Ebro Delta – takes its name from its golden yellow sands. The seemingly endless beaches, broken up by cliffs as far as Sitges, stretch westwards with their popular seaside resorts. They have a character quite different from that of the resorts of the Costa Brava.

Although modern mass tourism has not entirely ignored this region, the coast has to a large extent remained free of huge high-rise dormitory blocks. Happily, in many cases, attractive traditional places have survived, places that back in the 19th century already appealed both to the bohemian element and to art lovers from the upper bourgeoisie. Lively Sitges, busy El Vendrell, or the more sophisticated fishing villages of

Salou and Cambrils are examples. All these places take their character from their seaside location, and owe the greater part of both their wealth and their charm to their picturesque harbors. At the center of this chain sits Tarragona, an ancient Roman city imbued with history, which once gave its name to the entire province. (Separate chapters are devoted to the city and its hinterland.)

The region has a second asset: the fertile soil and mild climate of the inland area (which stretches to the foot of the Serralada Prelitoral), produce excellent grapes. The famous *cava*, the Catalan champagne from Sant Sadurní d'Anoia, and the fine wines of the Penedès are now, literally, "on everyone's lips." Discovering them is more than a gastronomic experience, for the "caves" – the wine cellars – are unique products of Modernista architecture.

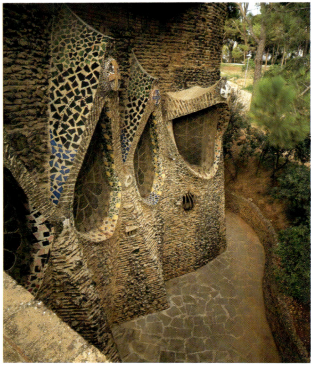

**A**BOVE AND BELOW:
*Santa Coloma de Cervelló*
*Colònia Güell, built 1908–14*
*by Antoni Gaudí and Francesc*
*Berenguer: the Güell crypt,*
*exterior view and detail*

**O**PPOSITE:
*Güell crypt, interior views*

## The Colònia Güell

Our tour begins – with delights for all the senses – at the Colònia Güell, a unique document of recent history and a milestone in the architecture which we will see on the western edge of Barcelona in the parish of Santa Coloma de Cervelló. Where today the upper classes of Barcelona may celebrate their weddings, a Modernista colony – the Colònia Güell (illus. p. 301, top) – came into existence toward the end of the 19th century. Its founder was the socially committed avant-garde textile manufacturer Eusebi Güell, an enthusiastic supporter of the artist Antoni Gaudí. In 1891 Güell transferred his workshops to Santa Coloma, and at the same time planned to create a workers' colony in accordance with ultra-modern standards of welfare.

In 1898 Gaudí and his colleague Francesc Berenguer began work on the extensive project, which was built between 1908 and 1914. However, it was not possible to implement all aspects of the colony as planned. Even the church, the colony's main tourist attraction, remained basically unfinished, being merely the crypt (illus. pp. 302–303) of a proposed larger religious building, of

OPPOSITE TOP:
Sant Joan Despí
*Casa Negre*
*Built by Josep Maria Jujol*
*in 1915*

OPPOSITE BOTTOM:
Garraf
*Bodeges Güell*
*Built by Antoni Gaudí and*
*Francesc Berenguer 1895–1901*

which only rough sketches are extant. Even in this incomplete form the building is a masterpiece of Modernisme. Antoni Gaudí's crypt is a "total work of art," such as could be created only in the Baroque era or the *fin de siècle*.

From the stoup (basin for holy water) and the pews to the windows in the shape of dragonflies, the architect himself designed every feature, large and small, within the building as well as its interior decoration, and also supervised the precise implementation of his plans with an eagle eye. Externally, Gaudí created a structure which, while perfectly blending with its surroundings, also encompasses the utmost perfection and artistry.

Gaudí's revolutionary constructional forms reveal a genius that is unsurpassed to this day, and show him to have been a supremely gifted empiricist – guided by experience. What in the ground plan looks like the imprint of a tortoise, turns out to be a sophisticated static system – the branch of mechanics dealing with fixed structures and equilibrium. Starting from the fact that the pressure of the vaulting corresponds to the pull exerted by a sandbag suspended by chains, Gaudí devised the "chain model," an upside-down simulation of his buildings (illus. p. 304). The architect derived the parabolic shape of the arches from the "hang" of the chains. This was later adopted as the constructional principle of the Sagrada Familia, and also used on a small scale in the Güell crypt.

But Gaudí was also very much a child of his time. In the interior, for the fan vaulting of the choir, he adopted brickwork techniques from Catalan Gothic, as also did his fellow artists Lluís Domènech i Montaner and Josep Puig i Cadalfalch (illus. p. 303, top). However, the difference between Gaudí and these two artists lies in the organic conception of his constructions. Gaudí's architecture creates an impression of natural growth, and it is this that produces its unique visual appeal.

For anyone interested in other aspects of Modernista architecture, a detour to Sant Joan Despí is highly recommended. Gaudí's colleague Josep Maria Jujol (1879–1949), whose ideas were undoubtedly closest to Gaudí's, built a number of villas in the one-time summer holiday resort near Cornellá de Llobregat.

Although he had a close affinity with the master, Jujol's buildings reveal his own individual stamp. For example, the Torre de la Creu of 1913 – also known because of its egg-shaped dome as the Torre dels Ous (Egg Tower) – is a hybrid of a villa and a castle, built to an idiosyncratic ground plan comprising five cylinders. Jujol's Casa Negre, begun in 1915 for a coach manufacturer, was given baroque ornamentation, but the most distinctive feature is the balcony in the shape of a barouche (illus. above).

Finally, via Castelldefels, we reach the picturesque coastal road. After a few miles of sharp bends, on the left we pass the cellars of Garraf, built by Antoni Gaudí and his colleague Francesc Berenguer (illus. right). Once again it was Count Güell who commissioned this unusual industrial structure. The building, of stone and brick, with its steep roof and elegant little towers, is almost like a medieval church. The entrance and the interior structure are supported by sweeping parabolic arches.

RIGHT:
*In the narrow streets of Sitges*

OPPOSITE TOP:
Sitges
*Evening atmosphere*
*On the left is the Esglesia*
*Sant Bartomeu*

OPPOSITE BOTTOM:
Sitges
*View of the Museu Maricel*

## Sitges

The spirit of the turn of the 19th century can be felt even more strongly in the legendary seaside resort of Sitges, which grew out of the Iberian settlement of Subur (illus. opposite, right and above). The picturesque resort with its long sandy beaches and cosy bars is the local holiday resort for Barcelona, from which it can be comfortably reached by fast train in half an hour.

Even in earlier times the attractive Old Town with its splendid view of the sea appealed to visitors escaping from the commotion and the social constraints of Barcelona. The first of them was the "Luminists," including the landscape painters Arcadi Mas i Fontdevila, Joan Roig i Soler, and Joaquim Miro i Argenter, who here discovered light and the beauty of nature. Around the turn of the century the avant-garde gave glittering parties in Sitges.

Santiago Rusiñol bought up dilapidated buildings which, with his friends, he rebuilt and refurbished. One of these is the Cau Ferrat, the "Iron Cave," which at first sight seems like a bizarre hotchpotch (illus. p. 308). But it was not so-named by chance: the building contained Rusiñol's collection of Catalan ironwork, along with notable paintings by his friends, especially Picasso, Ramón Casas, and Isidre Nonell. Two works by El Greco are important in the reception of this artist's work; they were acquired, and greatly admired, by Rusiñol at a time

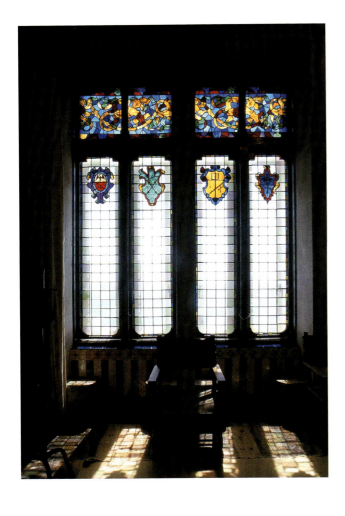

TOP AND BOTTOM LEFT:
Sitges
In the Museu Cau Ferrat

ABOVE:
Ramon Casas
Rusiñol sitting in an iron chandelier
Oil on canvas, 200 × 100 cm
Sitges, Museu Cau Ferrat

Sitges
*Carnival impressions
Down to the present day
the town has succeeded in
preserving a special avant-garde
aura, expressed in its extensive
carnival festivities*

when El Greco was completely unknown. The attraction of the little town remained undiminished during the early decades of the last century, most notably because it was the birthplace of Joaquim Sunyer, one of the leading painters of Noucentisme, who opened his workshop in Sitges in 1911.

The town has succeeded in preserving a special avant-garde aura, which can be seen and enjoyed today, especially at the annual Festival of Fantastic Film or during the riotous carnival festivities (illus. p. 309).

OPPOSITE:
Sitges
*In the Museu Romàntic*

OPPOSITE AND LEFT:
Sitges
*Interior view of the Museu Maricel*

Various collections provide a record of this lively artistic past. Cau Ferrat, mentioned above, is certainly the most original collection of its time. The Museu Maricel, formerly a late Gothic hospice, houses the impressive collection of the American Charles Deering, a great lover of Catalan art (illus. above). The works in the museum range from medieval sculpture and painting – a chapel with frescoes depicting episodes from the life and martyrdom of St. Bartholomew – to modern arts and crafts and also to the murals by Josep Maria Sert, which were commissioned by Deering himself; the subject of these murals is World War I.

The Museu Romàntic is housed in the late 18th-century Casa Llopis, containing, among other things, a collection of automata and music boxes (illus. p. 310, left). The heart of Sitges, situated on a promontory, in addition to its little Baroque church, has more buildings worth seeing from around the turn of the century. They include the neo-Gothic Town Hall (1889), the Casa del Rellotje, the clock house (1915), as well as the hospice of Sant Joan (1912),

Sant Sadurní d'Anoia
Cava production in the cellars of the firm of Cordoniú

## Cava

Since the second half of the 19th century Penedès, the region around Vilafranca and Sant Sadurní d'Anoia, has been one of the most outstanding wine-growing regions of Europe. Along with velvety red wines matured in oak casks, it is cava above all which has made the region famous. The term "cava" literally means "cellar," and denotes the sparkling wine produced by the champagne method of double fermentation, the second fermentation taking place in the bottle.

Catalan cava is in no way inferior to its distant ancestor developed by Dom Pérignon, and although the term "champagne" is protected by copyright, people in Catalonia generally simply order xampany. In its brut, sec, or semisec varieties, it may be drunk as an accompaniment to the main course of a hearty meal. The sweet variety, dulç, goes well with a rich dessert. The Raventós family in Sant Sadurní d'Anoia first became favorably disposed to the idea of the second fermentation, which takes about nine months, in 1872. The invigorating drink became very popular from 1879 on, and Raventós was appointed supplier to the court in Madrid. Today, in addition to the large-scale producers Codorniú and Freixenet, there are some 80 sparkling wine firms in Sant Sadurní alone, and almost as many in Vilafranca. The larger firms allow visits, which are also most interesting and worthwhile for the architectural historian: in many cases the cellars are housed in Modernist tiled halls designed with great artistry by the most important architects of the period c. 1900.

## Sant Sadurní d'Anoia and Vilafranca

Sant Sadurní is the capital of *cava* (see panel box opposite), the Catalan sparkling wine produced by the champagne method. There are about 80 firms engaged in this skilled and laudable activity, and many of them offer visits and tastings.

In addition to its high-quality products, Cordoníu – one of the largest producers – also has outstanding Modernist architecture, which is of great interest to visitors. Josep Puig i Cadafalch, Catalonia's famous architect and politician, restored the old country estate in the neo-medieval taste of the time, designing the venerable cellars between 1896 and 1906 (illus. opposite and below). Brick, stone, and gleaming green glass are the main materials used in this unique industrial monument. Parabolic arches, a typical feature of Modernist architecture, span the great halls in which the precious drink is stored.

A road through the vineyards brings us to Vilafranca del Penedès, the capital of Alt Penedès and the center of wine production. Before partaking of the sparkling wine, let us take a brief look at the history of the town. Even in the Middle Ages Vilafranca was renowned as a market where busy trade routes crossed. The kings of Aragon built two palaces here, in the 13th and 14th centuries respectively, and often lodged in them. Pere el Gran is said to have died in Vilafranca in 1289.

Today the rooms of the Royal Palace house the municipal museum, with its main attraction, the Museu del Vi. Here a visitor can learn, in graphic form, about wine cultivation in the region. In complete contrast, another department is devoted to ornithology. The church of the monastery of Sant Francesc, with a retable by the Catalan painter Llúis Borrassà (1392), is also worth a visit, as are the small Hospitaler chapel of Sant Joan (1307) and the late Gothic main church of Santa Maria, although the figured portal of the latter dates back no further than the early 20th century; in the crypt is a splendid entombment group by the Modernist sculptor Josep Llimona.

Even more than the Middle Ages, it is of course the turn-of-the-19th-century architecture that gives Vilafranca its particular character. Strolling through the town in a contemplative frame of mind, the visitor first passes the Town Hall built in 1912; then a visitor discovers a number of the sumptuous urban villas which the upper bourgeoisie commissioned to be built in the imaginative style of Modernisme. Among them are Can Soler (1904), Can Jané (c. 1910), Can Claramunt (1905), and the Güell Farmacia of 1905, all of which deserve a mention. Then there is the Calle of Santa Maria, a building retaining its original art-nouveau lanterns. Most of these buildings were the work of Eugeni Campllonch i Parès, the town's master builder from 1904 to 1910.

There are also, of course, festivities in Vilafranca. In late August the town's saint, Sant Feliu, is honored. Homage is paid in the form of human towers, *sardanas*, and colorful processions. Incidentally, Josep Canyas created a monument to the *castellers* – who create the human towers – which can be seen in front of the Palau del Fraret.

## Sant Martí de Sarroca, Vilanova i la Geltrú, and El Vendrell

A few miles north-west of Vilafranca, the road to Santes Creus or Santa Coloma de Queralt passes Sant Martí de Sarroca, a village grouped around the ruins of the former castle of Sant Martí. During more than a thousand years, the castle has absorbed the vicissitudes of history, which can be sensed by the visitor. The castle was finally destroyed in the first Carlist War (1833–40), but since 1963 efforts have been under way to preserve its medieval parts.

The present-day parish church of Santa Maria which served as the castle chapel, is considered to be one of the most outstanding works of Romanesque architecture in Catalonia (illus. left). The single-nave building, consecrated in 1204, owes its fame to the unusually rich and delicate sculpture adorning the apse. Its inner wall is faced with one elegant colonnade, while another colonnade, on a smaller scale, frames the windows and niches. The capitals are embellished with plant and animal motifs. The retable by Jaume Cabreras, depicting the Passion and Our Lady, dates from the late Gothic period. Further important items can be seen today in the MNAC in Barcelona.

From Sant Martí de Sarroca one can carry on to tour the Cistercian monasteries (see pp. 362–81). However, at this point we recommend returning to the sea. Here are two little towns, Vilanova i la Geltrú and El Vendrell, each full of variety, each worth a visit, particularly for the appeal of their museums.

Vilanova i la Geltrú, as its name suggests, consists of two main areas: the old fishing village of la Geltrú with its narrow streets, and the new town of Vilanova with its neo-classical character. The latter owes its origin to the *indianos*, as the merchants who had made their fortunes in Caribbean trade were called. Quite large numbers of these merchants settled in Vilanova in the 18th century, where they set up cotton and textile mills. The town's prosperity has continued down to the present, visible not least in important artistic collections which can be seen in wonderfully appropriate settings. Since 1882 the important oriental collection and the library of the statesman, poet, and historian Victor Balaguer (1824–1901) have been housed in the palace built in the Egyptian style by Jeroni Granell (illus. p. 315). These collections are complemented by paintings from the turn of the 19th century, including works by significant painters such as Ramon Casas, Isidre Nonell, and Santiago Rusiñol. Catalan painting and ceramics can also be seen in the museum of the castle at La Geltrú, on a site dating back to the 13th century.

The Museu Romàntic in the Casa Papiol of 1801 comes a close second to the Museu Balaguer. Furnishings, objects of daily use, jewelery, and clothing give a vivid picture of early 19th-century culture. A third museum houses the works and the collection of tiles of the Catalan landscape painter Joaquin Mir (1873–1940), who lived and worked in Vilanova i la Geltrú from 1921.

But there is also no lack of the grotesque in the harbor town. In the Museu de Curiositats, which was created by Francesc Roig i Toques in 1948, the visitor is confronted with the most outlandish entities brought up from the seas. A short way outside the town is the Masia Cabanyes, a country residence in the neoclassical style which is one of the finest of its kind (illus. p. 316, top).

Since we are visiting museums, we could take a detour to El Vendrell. The famous Catalan cellist and composer Pau (Pablo) Casals was born here in 1876 (see panel box). He grew up in Sant Salvador, one of the areas located directly by the sea, which had prospered mainly by exporting brandy, before being discovered as a summer holiday resort around the turn of the century.

The Casals family house, situated directly on the sea, has been rebuilt as an attractive, and very personal museum to the musician. In its immediate vicinity, in the Auditori (illus. p. 316, bottom left) concerts including works by the master take place. Anyone who wants to retrace Casals's steps further should proceed to the church of Sant Salvador; where the young artist may have played on its Baroque organ, for his father was organist here. On leaving the building look upward: the late Baroque belfry bears the most prominent landmark of El Vendrell, the angel made by the silversmith Josep Romeu and fitted as a weather vane in 1784.

El Vendrell can also point with pride to another of its sons: the poet and theater director Angel Guimerà also spent his youth here, and left numerous examples of his work. They are on show in the stately 18th-century villa of Can Guimerà in close proximity to the town wall.

From El Vendrell we now follow the N340 – the time-honored Via Augusta – which in classical antiquity led from Rome to Cadix and was one of the most important axes of the Roman Empire. To this day the road is still flanked by monuments bearing witness to its historical significance. We begin by passing the Arc de Barà, a

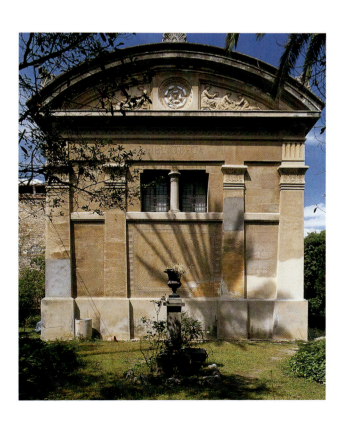

simple but impressive triumphal arch with a single opening framed by pairs of Corinthian pilasters (illus. p. 317, bottom). The arch was built, as an inscription records, in honor of the Consul Lucius Licinius Sura.

Not far away, near Tamarit, were the Roman stone quarries. These were of outstanding importance for the culture of the time. The largest of them, the Pedrera de Mèdol, can be visited. The excavation of the terrain can still be seen, and one stone column seems to have survived in the middle of the crater as evidence of the original level.

In contrast, Els Munts in the village of Altafulla illustrates the affluent lifestyle of a well-off Roman citizen. The villa, in what once would have been a splendid location, comprises a large number of rooms, all with mosaic flooring, an extensive portico, gardens, and – of course – thermal baths and a swimming-pool.

Close by the sea the castle of Tamarit rises up, no less full of history. It is of the starting points for the *Reconquista* on the Costa Daurada. Substantially restored and turned into a museum, the castle is a popular place to visit.

Finally, a few miles outside Tarragona, stands the Torre dels Escipions (Tower of the Scipioni from the 1st century), which actually owes its name to a misinterpretation of its images (illus. p. 317, top right). Torre dels Escipions is a burial monument of a kind that was often erected for important Roman citizens. It is comprised of three storys above a square ground plan, the second of which is adorned with symmetrical figures in high relief, one of which can be identified today as the Phrygian god Attis. Above it, suggestions of two people in low relief can just be faintly discerned, perhaps portraits of the deceased who were buried inside the tower. From here it is not much farther to the gates of Tarragona, the "city of the Scipioni."

ABOVE:
Vilanova i la Geltrú
*Biblioteca-Museu Balaguer, built by Jeroni Granell; opened in 1882*

OPPOSITE:
Sant Martí de Sarroc
*Santa Maria, consecrated 1204*

BOTTOM LEFT:
Vilanova i la Geltrú
*Biblioteca, Museu Balaguer*

### Pau Casals

Catalonia is a land of music. From the Middle Ages to the Nova Cançó (see panel box p. 112), from the "sardana" to "techno events," the country continues to live in harmony with sound and rhythm. It has produced numerous composers and performers. From among them Montserrat Caballé, Jordi Savall, and Josep Carreras may be mentioned.

But the best-known Catalan musician is Pau (Pablo) Casals, who was born in El Vendrell in 1876. He studied with Isaac Albéniz, and then began his career in Paris in 1899. From 1920 to 1939 he directed the Orquesta Pau Casals which he had founded, and the Working Men's Concert Association in Barcelona (illus. bottom right.)

As a groundbreaking cellist and an internationally known composer, the concert halls of the world were open to him. However, under the yoke of the Franco dictatorship he went into both spiritual and physical exile – residing in France, and appearing only rarely in public, for example during the Prades Festival (Prada de Conflent). In 1960 he composed the Oratorio El Pessebre ("The Manger") and in 1971 the Hymn to the United Nations. Casals spent the last years of his life in Puerto Rico, where he died in 1973. Six years later his remains were transferred to El Vendrell.

Today his parental home has been made into a museum, while concerts in the recently built auditorium (illus. bottom left) commemorate the great Catalan musician: Pau (Pablo) Casals.

OPPOSITE TOP:
Vilanova i la Geltrú
*Masia Cabanyes, 19th century*

OPPOSITE BOTTOM LEFT:
El Vendrell
*Auditorium in the Museu Pau Casals*

OPPOSITE BOTTOM RIGHT:
*Pau (Pablo) Casals in the Palau de la Música Catalana in Barcelona*

RIGHT:
*The Roman quarry at El Mèdol*

FAR RIGHT:
*The so-called Tower of the Scipioni, 1st century*

BELOW:
*The Arc de Barà, 1st century*

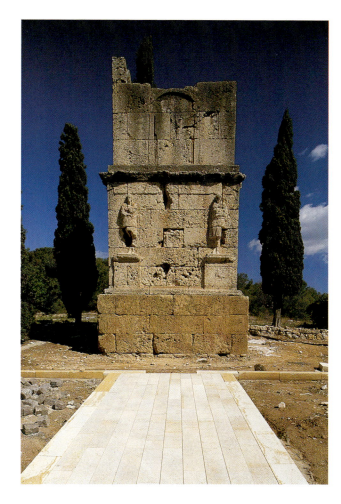

Tarragona

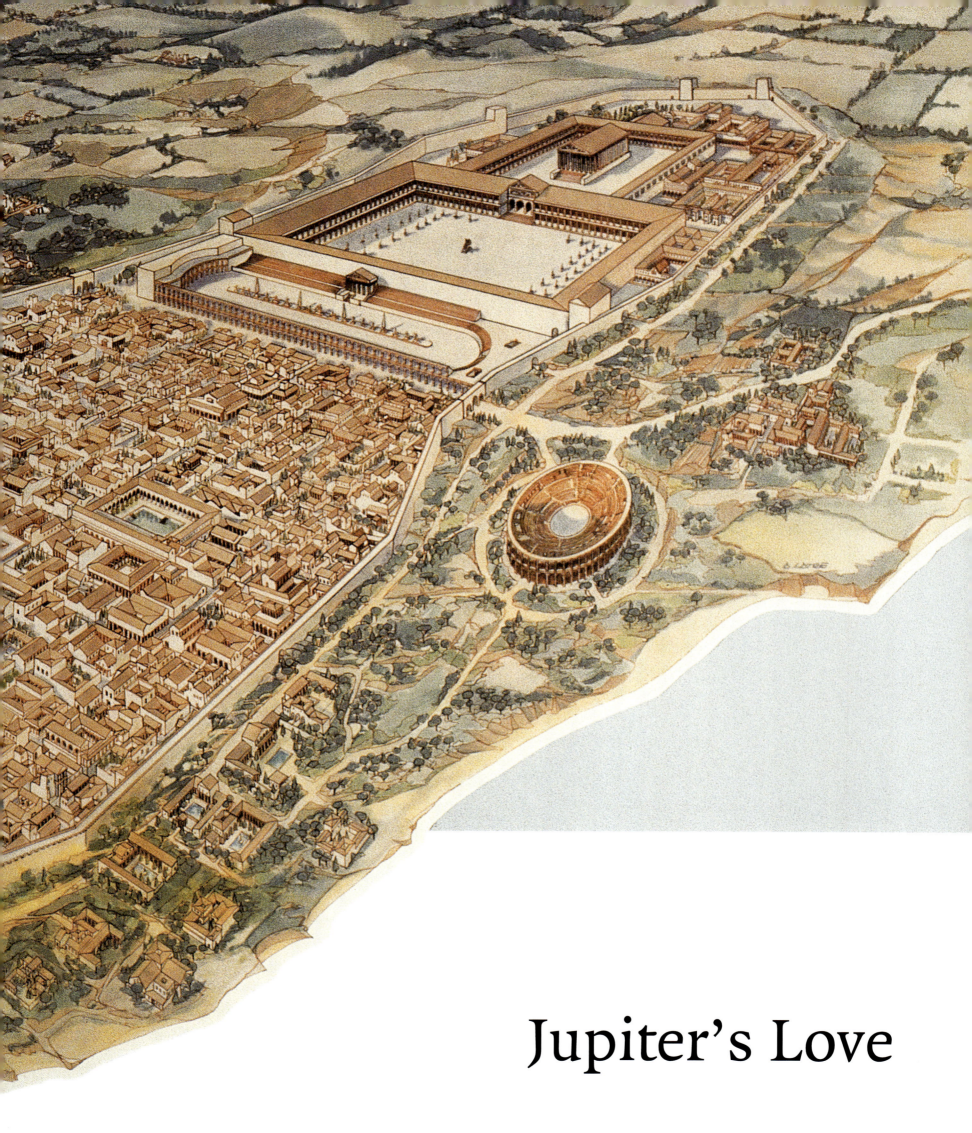

Jupiter's Love

The beauty of Tarragona, its magnificent situation on a rocky promontory above the sea, and its gentle climate have long excited praise. It is said that Jupiter left Tiria, his chosen one, because he had fallen undyingly in love with Tarragona. The Roman writer Pliny, describing the founding of the city during the second Punic War, took a more sober view: "Tarraco Scipionum opus" (Tarraco, the work of the Scipioni).

Although it is believed that there was an older Celtic settlement with the name of Kissis in the area, Pliny's statement seems to fit the facts. We have proof that in 210 B.C. Publius Cornelius Scipio the Elder chose Tarraco as a base from which to launch the conquest of New Carthage (Cartagena). The encampment was soon established in the strategically advantageous bay, and thanks not least to the fertile hinterland, it rapidly developed into an important city. From this first period the gigantic city wall has been preserved, and to this day impressively surrounds the "Acropolis" of Tarragona (illus. below, and opposite). It can be explored on the attractive *passeig arqueològic*, on which one may take a walk through the past. The building techniques used for the bulwarks were for many years a mystery because the irregular base area,

with its "cyclopic" masonry of huge rough blocks, had initially been dated as pre-Roman. Recent excavations confirm that this part of the wall, along with the six "cyclopic" city gates and three of the towers, were built toward the end of the 3rd century B.C. The site was extended around the middle of the 2nd century B.C., this time using regular blocks of stone, on which the builder's marks made by Iberian artisans can sometimes be discerned. The fortified ring once extended for 4 km (c. 2.5 miles) but underwent numerous alterations. The Middle Ages and the Baroque era also left their mark on it. The Torre del Arzobispo (the Archbishop's Tower), for example, dates from the 14th century, and the Torre di Minerva took its name from the relief fragment in its walls. The replica of Prima Porta's Augustus dates from a more recent period: it was bequeathed to Tarragona by the Italian state during the Mussolini era.

In 45 B.C. Julius Caesar bestowed the title *Colonia Julia urbs triumphalis Tarraco* on the city, which from 27 B.C. was entitled to call itself the sole capital of the whole of Hispania Citerior. With this, an unparalleled golden age began for Tarragona. Adorned with stately buildings, it ruled over the Ebro valley and the Spanish Mediterranean

PP. 318–19:
*Reconstruction of ancient Tarraco*

OPPOSITE TOP:
*View of the city and the harbor*

OPPOSITE BOTTOM, ABOVE, AND RIGHT:
*On the passeig arqueològic along the city walls*

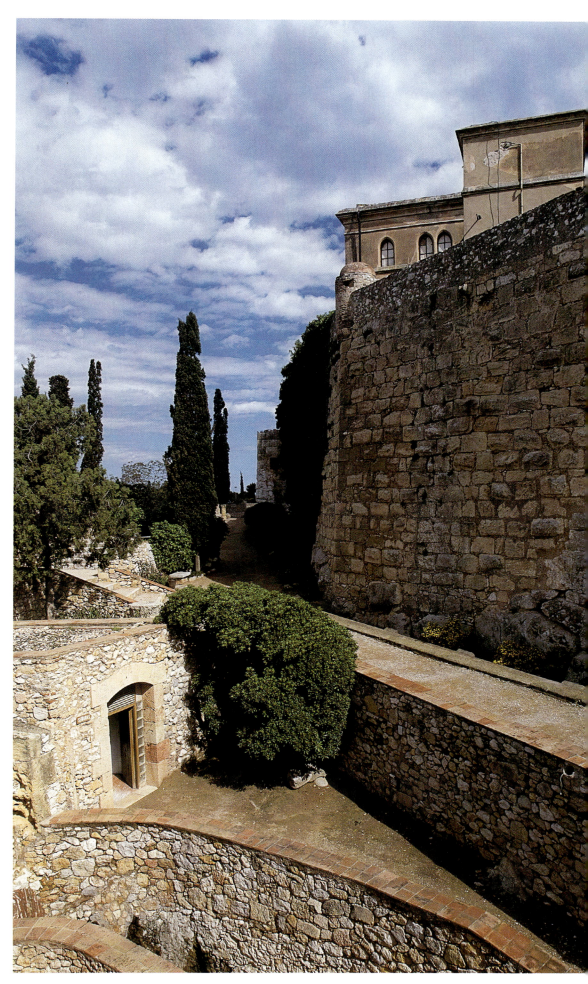

RIGHT:
*Remains of the circus, the Roman racing track*, A.D. 81–98

BOTTOM AND
OPPOSITE BOTTOM LEFT:
*The substructures of the circus*

coast until the beginning of the great migration of peoples. The metropolis of some 30,000 inhabitants provided accommodation for high-ranking officials, and even often for the emperor. As a cultural center, it played a decisive part in the Romanization of Spain. Tarragona seems to have been important to the early Christians; the apostle Paul is said to have preached here, and converted the citizens. Tarragona has succeeded in preserving an aura of its former greatness, and a tour of the museums brings the ancient capital of Eastern Spain to life.

Following the ideas of classical antiquity regarding town planning, and designed to suit the existing terrain, the city extended over a number of terraces, which fulfilled various functions. Almost the entire area of what is today the Old City was taken up by the Provincial Forum, of which, only a few remains have survived: at the Plaça del Pallol and in the so-called Praetorium (Pretori). Reconstructions show far more vividly what a magnificent site this once was (illus. above). About where the cathedral stands, a spacious square measuring 153 × 136 m (500 × 450 ft.) opened up, with porticos surrounding a temple dedicated to the cult of the Emperor and to Rome. This was adjoined by an even larger open space framed by two-story wings, leading to the circus, which today joins with the Praetorium to form a splendid archaeological complex. Here, in addition to the models mentioned above, one can also see the remains of the racing track used for races with two- and four-horse chariots during the rule of Emperor Domitian (A.D. 81–96). One walks

**TOP:**
Praetorium, 1st century B.C.
Rebuilt several times during the Middle Ages,
today it is the Museu Circ-Pretori.
In the background the Museu Arqueològic

**ABOVE RIGHT:**
Museu Circ-Pretori
Sarcophagus of Hippolytus, 3rd century

RIGHT:
*Museu Arqueològic
Head of Medusa (mosaic);
2nd century*

BELOW:
*The modern access to the
Museu Circ-Pretori*

through the impressive substructures on the way to the Praetorium, which once served as a corner tower of the Provincial Forum, and which in the Middle Ages was extended to become a noble residence (illus. p. 323, top). Its other name, Castell del Rei, tells us that the Aragonese kings also lodged here from time to time. The tall, block-like building, lit only by a small number of double and triple windows, has been completely restored in recent years. Today, in its splendid rooms, it houses archaeological treasures, including the sarcophagus of Hippolytus, an outstanding piece of work from the 3rd century (illus. p. 323, bottom right). In its immediate vicinity is the modern building of the Archaeological Museum, where a large number of ancient and early medieval artifacts documenting the history of Tarragona are to be seen. The mosaics deserve special attention: for example, the very graphic head of Medusa dating from the late 2nd century (illus. top), or the unique Roman jointed doll made of ivory which was found in a child's grave.

From an architectural point of view, the most exciting monument of ancient Tarraco is of course the Roman amphitheater at the foot of the acropolis (illus. page 325, top, and bottom left). It was designed to fit into the hillside, in the Greek manner, and was probably built in the first half of the 2nd century. It still clearly shows the typical features of this kind of building: the arena, the *cavea*, the auditorium with its curved rows of seats, the *orchestra*, the stage, and the *vomitoria* (exits). About 15,000 spectators could attend the gladiatorial contests and the battles between men and wild animals that were popular at the time. They presumably also witnessed the persecution of Christians which here as elsewhere claimed numerous victims. In 259 Bishop Fructuosus of Tarraco and his deacons Augurius and Eulogius suffered the savage martyrdom of being burned alive in the catacombs. The martyrdom of Christians was commemorated in the 6th century by building a basilica from the stones of the amphitheater. In the 12th century the basilica in its turn provided the foundations for the Romanesque church of Santa Maria del Miracle, some of the walls of which are still standing.

Outside the ancient city center, more monuments which exerted a decisive influence on Tarragona are found in the Calle Lleida, another spacious site where stumps of columns and colonnades have survived, along with another theater. A far more vivid impression is made by the early Christian necropolis at Sant Fruitós, discovered on the western edge of the town in 1923 when a factory was being built, and now considered to be the major site of its kind on the Iberian peninsula (illus. p. 325, bottom right). The necropolis owes its name to the martyred bishop mentioned above, whose bones were buried there. In addition to the remains of a 4th-century church, the site has yielded an immense wealth of artistically significant sarcophogi, mosaics, inscriptions, and cult objects. Preserved *in situ*, they convey a unique impression of the "world of the hereafter" during the transition from the ancient world to Christianity.

TOP AND LEFT:
*Roman amphitheater*
*1st half of the 2nd century*

ABOVE:
*View of the Sant Fruitós*
*necropolis*

In Tarragona, the golden age came to an end with the great migration of peoples. Franconians, Germanic tribes, Visigoths and Arabs all invaded the city in turn, razing large parts of it. Not until 1117, when the *Reconquista* of the Catalan coast was well under way, did the bishop and the counts of Barcelona begin to reconstruct and repopulate the city. Their prime concern was to build a new cathedral to mark the victory of Christianity and the continuity of the archbishopric. The site chosen was that part of the Roman city that had enjoyed the highest standing, namely the Provincial Forum. It may even have been the precise spot where the imperial temple had stood (illus. pp. 326–9). The fortified building was probably begun in 1174, and by around the end of the 12th century the three apses were in place up to the level of the capitals. By the mid-13th century work on the broad transept and the *cimbori*, that is the center tower (illus. opposite), was in progress. The building of the nave, with its mighty double-columned piers, lasted until the end of the 13th century. Only when this was done could the massive rib vaults be completed

and the great rose window incorporated into the façade; the pediment above it was never completed. It was consecrated by Bishop Juan de Aragón in 1351.

Because of the long period of construction, the cathedral combines Romanesque and Gothic features from various periods, including classical antiquity in the form of *spolia* incorporated into the columns and capitals. The chapels by the side of the nave with its three aisles were added in the Baroque and Classical eras.

This imposing building towers like a crown over the Old City. It is approached by a broad open flight of steps leading to the prominent Gothic main portal. Its walls are adorned with the apostles, its trumeau with Our Lady (illus. p. 327, top). The tympanum, topped by tall, unadorned archivolts or band of moldings, depicts the Day of Judgment. These inner parts of the portal were for a long time thought to be the work of Master Bartomeu under the inspiration of French models. Today, they are attributed to an anonymous French artist of c. 1330.

The sculptor Jaume Cascalls, who was much in demand at the time, was entrusted in 1375 with the sculptural work on the buttresses, but the execution of the somewhat crude figures would suggest that a workshop was involved. An echo of late antiquity can be seen above the right-hand side entrance, where a 4th-century sarcophagus was incorporated into the wall.

Only the most important of the cathedral's artistic treasures can be mentioned here. The Santa Tecla retable in the chancel apse is a masterpiece in the art of alabaster carving; it was commissioned by Bishop Dalmau de Mur and created by the Catalan sculptor Pere Joan between 1426 and 1436.

To depict the terrible martyrdom undergone by the patron saint of Tarraco, Pere Joan employed an extraordinarily elegant and supple formal language which reveals the influence of the art of the Flemish-Burgundian court. Even such gruesome scenes as the sufferings of the saint while being burned, or the bath in the pond of snakes (both at the predella) become, in his hands, a revelation of ethereal beauty (illus. p. 327, bottom).

The grave of Jaume de Aragó to the right of the high altar is also one of the supreme achievements of Catalan sculpture. The son of King Jaume II, who was appointed archbishop of Toledo at the age of 17 and archbishop of Tarragona at 28, died here in 1334, only five years after taking office. Whoever created the monument – the master's name is not known – succeeded in portraying the man of the church, who died at such a young age, in a manner both lifelike and timeless.

A third noteworthy work of sculpture can be seen in the Capella dels Sastres, the Tailors' Chapel, which was built toward the middle of the 14th century in place of the left-hand apse, which was not completed. Its sumptuous late Gothic architecture and stained glass windows reveal the refined taste (and of course the wealth) of the *confraria* (brotherhood) de Preveres, who commissioned the work. The tailors' guild that gave the chapel its name subsequently moved in here.

Beneath the spacious stellar vault, amid the filigree ornamentation of the walls and windows, Master Aloy's retable seems somewhat forlorn – yet it too is a milestone in Spanish art. The retable, completed in 1368 with scenes from the life of Our Lady, is valuable evidence of how the altars, in most cases painted, that were set up in the refectory, developed into the monumental, architecturally structured wall retables. In subsequent centuries these wall retables became typical throughout all of Spain. The cloister was probably begun at about the same time as the church, that is in the late 12th century, and completed in the first quarter of the 13th century (illus. p. 326, top, and opposite). Here also, late Romanesque features such as the vivid figures and floral motifs seen in the sculpture of the capitals (even rats and cats are immortalized here) combine with Gothic structures and the decoration in the Arabian manner that was popular at the time.

The noble Romanesque marble portal (late 12th century) linking the cloister and the church is particularly impressive. It divides a column which has the epiphany

depicted on its capital; in the tympanum above it the Pantocrator appears with the Evangelists' symbols.

Incidentally, the Arabian Mirhab of 960 was entombed in one of the cloister walls. Today his remains can be seen in the Diocesan Museum (in the adjoining cloister rooms). A visit here is also worthwhile because of the numerous astonishing Christian works of art.

At the foot of the cathedral lies the medieval and early modern city. In spite of numerous disasters it has preserved its wonderful picturesque quality. Still bounded on three sides by the city walls, it is threaded with narrow streets, some of them of astonishing regularity, with rows of houses and business premises dating from the 14th to the 18th centuries. Their imposing stone façades often conceal an elegant courtyard, the *pati*, with outside stairs that used to lead to the main story of the building.

The most sought-after address for the nobility was the Calle dels Cavallers, where many palaces from the period may still be admired. The grandest, the Palau Castellarnau, in which even Charles V is said to have spent a night, is now a museum. Not only its furnishings but even its architecture combines four centuries of living history. A glimpse of a different world is given by the narrow streets of the Jewish quarter (Plaça des Angels, Calle Santa Anna), situated close to the Museum of Modern Art. Medieval Tarragona had, of course, an important market, with massive porticos that still flank the Calle de la Merceria (illus. below). Close to the cathedral is the Hospital de Santa Tecla, its façade displaying a rare blend of Romanesque and Renaissance features.

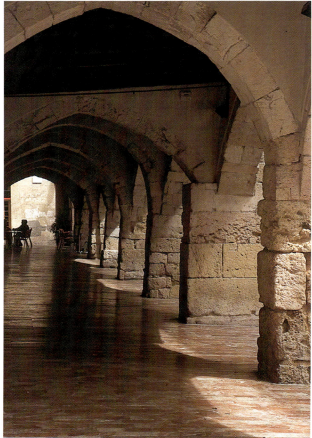

The Plaça del Pallol, with the medieval *Audiència* (courtroom) and the Church of Sant Domènec, also shows us a cross-section through the centuries.

Like Barcelona, Tarragona also broke free of its constricting walls in the mid-19th century. By demolishing their southern part, an attempt was made at the same time to link the city with its harbor, and to open up the sloping terrain below the historic city center to urban planning.

Where the old and the new met, the Rambla Vella and the Rambla Nova were laid out. They lead to the Passeig de les Palmeres, the palm-lined "Mediterranean balcony," which is situated 36 m (c. 120 ft.) above sea level and gives a unique view of the sea and the Roman theater. The broad Rambla Nova, lined with green areas, is the vital nerve of modern Tarragona, a street for strollers and shoppers leading past the stately buildings dating from the late 19th and the 20th centuries, such as the modernistic Casa de la Punxa or the rationalistic Cinema Modern.

Further interesting monuments from this era are the market at the Plaça Corsini (Josep Maria Pujol de Barberá, 1915), and the chapel of the Collegi de Jesús i Maria (in the design of which Antoni Gaudí was involved). This walk through 2,000 years of history can come to a relaxing end in the seamen's quarter of El Serallo. The best fish restaurants are still found in this 19th-century district.

On the outskirts of Tarragona one also encounters the lengthy history of the Hispanic capital at every step. In the immediate proximity of the motorway is the imposing Pont de les Ferreres, the two-level aquaduct which used to supply Tarragona with water (illus. p. 332). It is 27 m

OPPOSITE LEFT:
*In the Old City*

OPPOSITE RIGHT:
*The porticos at the Calle de la Merceria*

LEFT:
*Rambla Nova with casteller monument*

BELOW:
*Plaça de la Font with Town Hall (Ajuntament)*

LEFT:
Centcelles near Constantí
Mausoleum
Cupola mosaics with hunting
scenes (detail), c. 350

(c. 90 ft.) high, 217 m (c. 700 ft.) long, and built of ashlar blocks. It was contructed under Augustus in the 1st century, and is thought to be one of the oldest of its kind in Spain. Like many bridges across valleys, the Pont de les Ferreres was popularly believed to be the work of the Devil (Pont del Diable).

Also not far north of Tarragona is another monument from late antiquity which is utterly unique in its own way: the mausoleum at Centcelles near Constantí. It was not until 1877 that its true significance was realized, when mosaics were discovered in the villa complex, which was by then in private hands.

The work of excavation and research began in 1950, and these excavations brought an archaeological sensation to light: the main room of the site had obviously served as an imperial mausoleum, either as a grave monument to Constans (d. 350), the son of Constantine the Great, or as a memorial to the usurper Magnentius (d. 353). The exterior shape of the mausoleum is cubic, and is crowned by an eight-cornered tambour, or drum, while the interior

of the building is circular and extended by semicircular apses. Above the walls, that were probably once faced with marble, and an area devoted to murals, is the cupola, which was originally completely covered with decorative mosaics (illus. above). Thanks to restoration during the last few decades, many of the scenes can be identified.

At the lower level detailed hunting scenes may be discerned, probably depicting the owner and his family engaged in their favorite activity. Higher up there are the scenes of deliverance typical of sepulchral art – Daniel in the lions' den, Noah's Ark, the men in the burning fiery furnace, Lazarus, and so on.

At the top four groups of figures can be seen, separated by depictions of the seasons. Their significance – which would probably provide the key to our understanding of the entire villa – is controversial. The reference may be to the tetrarchs, the four rulers of the Roman Empire as it was at the time. Although the mosaics have been lost to a large extent, Centcelles is a unique and incomparable monument to the art of late antiquity.

# The Western Costa Daurada and the Ebro Delta

By the Riverside

PREVIOUS PAGES:
*The Ebro Delta has been
cultivated by human hands
for thousands of years*

336    The Western Costa Daurada and the Ebro Delta

Tortosa
*View of the city*

## Tortosa

After Tarragona, we continue our tour of the "Gold Coast." At Salou and Cambrils there are more of the splendid long beaches which gave the area its name. After passing the camping sites at Miami Plage, we come to the pretty fishing village of Ametlla del Mar. Then we go inland where history awaits us at Tortosa.

Tortosa – *la sopresa*, the surprise: the harbor town on the lower course of the River Ebro, which was esteemed in Roman times, is not often included in tours of Catalonia. The blame for this lies partly with the damage inflicted by the Civil War in 1938. More than 150,000 people died in the battle of the Ebre, and a large part of the Old City was destroyed by shellfire during the siege, which lasted for several months.

Tortosa nevertheless still contains a number of features that bear witness to its heroic past, in particular the magnificent Gothic cathedral, one of the most impressive ecclesiastical buildings in Spain. The Moorish castle of La Suda – now a four-star parador – gives a wonderful panoramic view of the town, the Ebro estuary, and the nearby mountain ranges of the Massís dels Ports and Montanyes de Cardó (illus. p. 338). As for palaces, monasteries, and museums, the city – once the seat of a bishopric – can hold its own. Finally, there are also tempting delicacies in the shape of *pastissets*, of Arab origin, and *Garrofetes del Papa*, a sponge cake which delighted the Antipope Benedict XIII throughout his later years, which he spent in Peñíscola on the coast.

Tortosa owes its historical importance, however, to the Ebro and to the fact that it is situated at the crossing point of the trade routes to Valencia, Aragon, and Barcelona. After the Romans, who gave the colony the name of Julia Augusta Dertosa, the Arabs also set store by its strategically important location. Caliph Abd al-Rahman III had the castle of La Suda (also known as the Castle of Sant Joan) built in 944. From it there is a breathtaking view of the town and the cathedral.

In 1018 Tortosa became the capital of a *taifa*, an independent partial kingdom, where trade and the sciences flourished. A number of attempts by Christian rulers to conquer the city failed, until Count Ramon Berenguer IV of Barcelona hoisted his Catalan-Aragonese banner here in 1148. A decisive part in the victory was played by the military orders, who hastened to his aid along with a host of Genoese knights. Immediately afterward the count restored the bishopric that had been founded as early as 516, and issued the *Carta del Poblament*, a municipal charter that was vital for the formation of the Christian community. It was also granted, in a similar form, to the city's numerous Jews.

The following centuries brought great prosperity to the city, which lasted until 1492, thanks to the peaceful coexistence of Arabs, Jews, and Christians. As early as 1279 the famous *Costums de Tortosa* regulated the legal affairs of the citizens. The economy boomed due to several factors: the control of the trade in salt and wheat; the assemblies of the various estates, and the Catalan parliament met several times a day in the city walls. This

*View of Tortosa and
its cathedral from the
castle of La Suda*

golden age came to a sad end first with the expulsion of the Jews, after 1492, then of the Moors during the 16th and early 17th centuries, leading to the disappearance of social groups that had helped found the community.

Today numerous buildings still bear witness to the glorious area of the late Middle Ages, above all the present-day cathedral, a sublime Gothic building that was erected over the one-time mosque and the remains of an earlier Romanesque building dating from 1158 (illus. above). Thanks to an extraordinary wealth of documentation, we know that the plans for the Gothic building dated from 1345, and that work was begun in 1347, but was delayed, and was finally completed only in the 18th century. This was when the majestic Baroque façade, designed by Martí D'Abaria, was added but the structure still remained incomplete.

Let us return to the Gothic building concealed behind the very prominent façade. Its first master builder, Bernat Dalguaire, was sent to Avignon at the chapter's expense to study "modern" South French Gothic. However, there were evidently other plans too, including those of one Antoni Guarc, that played an important part in the construction of the cathedral. As occurs so often in 14th-century Catalan religious architecture, the aisles are particularly high and broad, and seem to be striving to join the nave to form a spacious, unified area (illus. opposite). Massive clusters of pillars, with only tiny capitals to give them a vertical appearance, support the spacious arcades and the rib vaulting. As with Santa Maria del Mar in Barcelona, the flying buttresses in the lower part of the building do not extend beyond the chapel walls. A special feature is the double ambulatory, with nine radial chapels separated, or rather connected, by filigree tracery instead of walls on the north side. The arcades leading to the inner chancel have the most delicate flamboyant tracery.

The high altar, of 1351, deserves special mention. Its 24 scenes, carved on the inside and painted on the wings, illustrate the lives of Our Lady and of Christ. Another retable, depicting the Transfiguration, is attributed to the workshop of Jaume Huguet (2nd half of the 15th century).

There is an outstanding example of medieval textile work to be admired in the Aula Major: the Tapis de la Santa Cena (the carpet of the Last Supper). The Baroque Capella de la Verge (1642–1725) to the right of the nave contains the cathedral's most important relic. This is the girdle of Our Lady. In keeping with the importance of this revered relic, the chapel is faced with precious jasper and with marble.

An extensive series of frescoes (Dionís Vidal and Josep Medina, 1715–21) tells the wondrous story of how, in 1178, Our Lady, accompanied by Peter and Paul, appeared in the chancel of the old cathedral and gave her handwoven girdle to a priest. Adjoining the Capella de la Verge is the little trapezoid cloister, which dates from the 14th century, but in which a few Romanesque capitals can still be seen.

Here, in 1710 the Porta de l'Oliviera was added in order to provide a new access to the cathedral.

The treasury and the archives give the visitor further insight into the history of the bishopric and into the wealth of interest of its episcopal cathedral.

Tortosa
*Cathedral (present building begun in 1347)*
*Interior views*

TOP:
Tortosa
Bishop's Palace (Palau Episcopal)
Inner courtyard; 14th century

BOTTOM:
Tortosa
Col·legi de St. Luis
Courtyard and arcade;
16th century

Tortosa
*View from the river with the
monument to the Battle of the Ebre*

Opposite the cathedral stands the Gothic Bishop's Palace with its stylish 14th-century inner courtyard (illus. p. 340, top). The outside steps lead up to the three galleries of the upper story, behind which are the reception rooms and the chapel. Behind the fine portal, adorned with sculptures, is the rectangular devotional chapel roofed with an octagonal stellar vault.

The nobility, for example the Oriol and Despuig families and Oliver del Boteller, also built their city residences not far from the Bishop's Palace. However, the double-aisled hall of the Llotja, the Exchange (1373–9), was moved to the municipal park farther out. To the north, the cathedral is adjoined by the Jewish quarter, the Barri de Remolins, probably one of the oldest in Catalonia.

In another part of the city, below the castle, are the Col·legis reials: colleges which the Emperor Charles V had built in 1564 for the education of converted Moors. Visitors enter the Col·legi de St. Lluís (originally dedicated to Sant Jaume and Sant Maties) by a portal that is richly adorned in Renaissance style and crowned with the imperial coat of arms. Behind it the three-story courtyard flanked with arcades is likewise one of the few distinctly Renaissance works to be created in Catalonia (illus. p. 340, bottom). The balustrade of the main story is particularly attractive: it is formed from a sculpted frieze showing the likenesses and the coats of arms of the Catalan-Aragonese kings. The

Col·legi St. Domènec, of which only the façade dating from 1578 remains, was elevated to the status of a university. The Church of Sant Domènec, now a municipal museum and archive, also boasts a portal in the manner of a triumphal arch, lavishly adorned with statues, medallions, and grotesque ornamentation. As early as the 13th century the Poor Clares had established themselves somewhat to the south of this complex. As for their convent, with its attractive late Gothic cloister, little is left of the original building. It was destroyed during the Civil War, and has been only partially rebuilt.

The *eixample* – 19th-century urban extension – suffered irreparable damage during the raids. Most of the imaginative buildings from the period around the turn of the century have been lost, so that only a very few buildings are left to remind us of this period, which was also important for Tortosa. The most significant are two buildings which served practical purposes: the indoor market of Joan Abril i Guanyabens (1884–9) and the abattoir of Pau Montaguió i Segura (1908). Of the residential houses, the Casa Pallarès (1907), the Casa Grego (1908), and the Casa Brunet are worthy of mention. The Església del Roser (1914) is a somewhat ultamodern example of church architecture. The highly unconventional memorial standing in the waters of the Ebro (illus. above) is a reminder of the tragic events of 1938.

## From Tortosa to the Ebro Delta.

Tortosa's one-time historical importance can only be properly appreciated by visiting the surrounding area of the city and the Ebro Delta. Here, in fertile marshland, Spain's largest river, 927 km (c. 576 miles) in length from its source in Cantabria flows into the Mediterranean. In 1983 these wetlands – still subject to constant change even today – were declared a nature reserve. At present this area comprises some 320 sq km (c. 124 sq. miles), and gives a panorama of unspoiled nature and of both use and cultivation going back thousands of years (illus. pp. 342–3). Since time immemorial men have been drawn to the area, with its lagoons, dunes, and saltflats, to practice salt manufacture, hunting, and fishing.

It was, however, not until the 18th century, after various scourges such as pirate raids, floods, and malaria had been somewhat brought under control, that rice began to be grown; today the area supplies the whole of Catalonia. The work of laying out canals to control the irrigation and drainage of the area began a little later. The mosquitos and leeches were wiped out during the period of the Catalan *Mancomunitat* (1913–25); in their place rare insects and reptiles can be found on the shining surfaces of the water, in the reeds, and in the woods of willow and eucalyptus.

An immense variety of birds can be seen: short-eared owls, night herons, avocets, flamingoes, and wigeons are merely the most unusual of some 300 species that live permanently or temporarily in the Ebro Delta.

Dusk is particularly atmospheric, when the light over the alluvial terrain becomes gentler and the waters of the Ebro meander sluggishly toward the sea. Crickets and frogs accompany the spectacle with their indefatigable commentary. In spring an almost intoxicating green meets the eye when the new rice plants seem to form floating islands.

Although the Ebro Delta is crossed by a few highways, the recommended way to explore it is, of course, by boat. The trip begins in Amposta or Deltebre – where the tourist information centers will provide further details – and takes us through the alluvial terrain past thatched cottages to the Illa de Buda, the Illa de Sant Antoni, and the Garzal – tongues of land that jut out farthest into the sea. On the other hand, the most recent alluvial growth of land has been taking place at El Fangar since the 17th century.

Given the circumstances, it is not surprising that the inhabited areas in the Ebro Delta area exhibit some very unusual features. The oldest of them is Amposta, which is now connected with the facing river bank by means of an impressive suspension bridge dating from 1919 (illus. opposite bottom). The town itself owes its existence to the Hospitaler Knights, who founded a benefice here.

It was, however, only when the town that had been planned by Sant Carles de la Ràpita was laid out that the Ebro Delta began to be opened up systematically. On the orders of Charles III, La Ràpita came into being in 1780 around the natural harbor of Els Alfacs, which the monarch wished to expand to be used for trade with America. There had been a monastery on this spot

centuries earlier, but it had been abandoned in 1579 due to frequent attacks by pirates. Fate was kinder to the new town, which was built in the neoclassical style. Although the king's wishes were not entirely fulfilled, La Ràpita has remained a busy port living off fishing and tourism, and offering picturesque views (illus. top left). The town is famous for its outstanding *llagostins* (shrimp).

A walk through the town (illus. top right) shows the regular structure of the planned town, organized around the oval Plaça de Carles III. Its main axis forms the spine of the grid system, running from the mountains of the Serre de Montsià to the sea. Not all buildings were completed, however, as work came to a halt following the

death of the king. Thus the central part of the Església Nova, also known as *La Glorieta*, did not progress beyond the first story, but what remains is an imposing ruin (illus. bottom).

An excursion to Ulldecona takes us into other worlds, first the Middle Ages – picturesque evidence of which remains in the shape of the Hospitaler Castle dating from 1227 and the parish church of Sant Lluc (1373–1421) – and then into prehistory, which comes alive in the vicinity of the Santuari de la Pietat, a place of pilgrimage. At 11 *abrics* (overhangs) hundreds of astonishingly lifelike cliff paintings have been preserved, depicting hunting scenes, archers, and game in lively movement (illus. opposite).

TOP AND BOTTOM:
Ulldecona
*Cliff paintings with hunting scenes*

TOP:
*The mountainous landscape*
*of the Ports de Beseit outside*
*Horta de Sant Joan*

BOTTOM:
Horta de Sant Joan
*Village square*

If, starting from Tortosa, one follows the River Ebro inland, one comes first to Xerta, where the Arabs had built a dam 310 m (c. 340 yds.) in length to channel the river water. Farther north, where the landscape becomes more appealing, a narrow side valley branches off to the west leading to Horta de Sant Joan at the border with Aragon (illus. opposite top). The pretty village in front of the imposing cliff formations of the Ports de Beseit attracted Pablo Picasso, who on several occasions spent his vacation here with his friend Manuel Pallarès and the latter's wife Fernande Olivier (illus. opposite bottom). He painted his impressions in Cubist panel paintings, such as *Horta d'Ebre* or *Brick Factory* (both 1909, illus. above). The visitor is fascinated by the splendid location of this medieval town amid bizarre limestone cliffs. The Franciscan monastery

of Mare de Déu dels Angels below the Puig Sant Salvador is also worth a visit. Steep footpaths enable the visitor to explore the majestic slopes of the mountain massif.

Gandesa, the capital of the Terra Alta, in contrast, is situated on a plateau surrounded by mountain ranges. The principal attractions are two magnificent wine cellars built by César Martinell. They are veritable "wine cathedrals," Modernist brick buildings with spacious halls topped with parabolic arches (illus. p. 348). The Celler de la Co-operativa Agrícola in Gandesa was completed in 1919, two years after the even more impressive building in Pinell de Brai (illus. p. 349, top), situated c. 9 km (c. 5.5 miles) east of the town. The ceramic frieze with its motifs from the world of winegrowing and grape harvesting (illus. p. 349, bottom) was created by Xavier Nogués.

*Pablo Picasso*
Brick factory
*Painted in Horta de Sant Joan*
*in 1909.*
*St Petersburg, Hermitage*

## Cèsar Martinell

Cèsar Martinell i Brunet, born 1888 in Vals, is not one of the great, internationally renowned Catalan architects from the beginning of the 20th century. Nevertheless, he deserves to be set beside his teacher Antoni Gaudí, as well as Josep Puig i Cadafalch, Lluís Domènec i Montaner, and Josep Maria Jujol. Martinell's achievement was to raise Catalan industrial architecture to an extraordinarily high artistic standard, especially by building wine cellars and oil factories. Inventories of his works alone include 37 agricultural (in the broadest sense of the word) buildings in the Tarragona area (and in some cases farther afield) which he built to order for the cooperatives. The wine cellars in particular are veritable "wine cathedrals": spacious brick halls similar to the nave of a church, topped with breathtakingly thin layers of tiles forming the – in most cases parabolic – supporting arches. To give them extra strength they are supported, as in Gothic architecture, by perforated, and hence flexible, buttresses. A light roof protects the halls from the effects of the weather. The exterior of the building, dating from 1910–1920, draws once more on all the historical architectural styles: Gothic, Moorish, and even individual Renaissance elements adorn the storage vaults, that are both practical and beautiful. As everywhere in Catalonia, decorative tiles are very popular. For example the façade of the Celler Cooperatiu at Pinell de Brai is decorated with cheerful scenes from the life of the wine-growers, which in reality was often by no means so untroubled.

Martinell was not only a master builder, but also a scholar who took an intense interest in Catalan architecture, especially the work of his master Antoni Gaudí. He died in Barcelona in 1973.

Cèsar Martinell's most important wine cellars are to be found in El Pinell de Brai, Gandesa, Falset, Cornudella, Barberà de la Conca, Rocafort de Queralt, Espluga de Francolí, Montblanc, Vila-rodona, Nulles, Santes Creus, and Llorenç del Penedès. They were built for the most part between 1918 and 1922.

Gandesa
*Celler (wine cellar),*
*built by Cèsar Martinell in 1919*
*Exterior (top) and interior (bottom)*
*views*

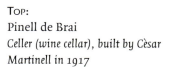

TOP:
Pinell de Brai
*Celler (wine cellar), built by Cèsar*
*Martinell in 1917*

BOTTOM:
Pinell de Brai
*Celler (wine cellar)*
*Ceramic tiles with scenes from the*
*life of the winegrowers, using*
*motifs by Xavier Nogués*

# The Hinterland of Tarragona

# Wine Cellars and Royal Monasteries

The Hinterland of Tarragona

PREVIOUS PAGES:
Poblet
Porta Reial, 14th century

TOP:
Vineyards in Priorat

BOTTOM:
Landscape near Siurana

Tear yourself away from the strip of coast around Tarragona, attractive and replete with history as it is. For other experiences, no less fascinating, await in the hinterland of this Roman city. The Camp de Tarragona plain, the course of the River Francolí, the hollow of Conca de Barberà – also full of history – and finally the picturesque cliff ridges of Priorat, leave the visitor with a wide variety of indelible impressions.

In the largely unchanged villages – much less affected by tourism than the coast – traditions have been preserved which make a visit a cultural and a gastronomic treat. The most spectacular custom is undoubtedly the creation of human towers, *castells*, which are the main attraction at all public festivals. The famed wine cellars of the province, offer fewer thrills but even greater delights for the palate. They are frequently housed in picturesque buildings dating from the turn of the century. A signposted tour, the *Ruta dels Cellers*, leads through vineyards on either side of the river, and includes the finest examples of buildings of their kind.

In addition to winegrowing, the moderate Mediterranean climate also makes it possible to grow almonds, hazelnuts (filberts), and olives on a large scale. They are part of the wealth of the country, and set their stamp on its character. The sunshine, which is plentiful even during the winter months, transforms the green of the trees and bushes, the yellow of the fields and the brown of the arable land into a carpet of gentle colors. The Arabs undoubtedly also appreciated these advantages, for it was not until the first half of the 12th century that they were driven out of the region of New Catalonia, as the territory between the Rivers Llobregat and Ebro is often called. The region was thus under Islamic rule for 300 years longer than the province of Barcelona, Old Catalonia. In spite of this great length of time, it remained relatively free from the influence of Arab culture.

All the greater was the impression made by the Orders which re-Christianized and cultivated the region in the wake of the *Reconquista*. The locations of the three Cistercian monasteries of Poblet, Santes Creus, and Vallbona form an imaginary triangle the sides of which measure some 30 km (c. 19 miles). Thanks to their architecture and their unique Aragonese royal tombs, they are among the highlights of any visit to Catalonia. Other places such as Montblanc, Santa Coloma de Queralt, Prades, and Siurana have a strategic position or the wealth of their nobles to thank for their picturesque medieval appearance. But Modernisme, the Catalan variant of art nouveau, also set its stamp on the region. Between Tarragona, Barberà de la Conca, and Falset the wine producers built imaginative villas and wine cellars that were both practical and beautiful. Reus, the main trading center for wine in the 19th century, likewise decked itself out with numerous Modernist buildings. In this creative ambience there grew up a young master builder who was to revolutionize architecture: Antoni Gaudí.

*View of the Cistercian monastery of Santes Creus, founded in 1158*

## Winegrowing and Architecture

Let us first visit the prosperous commercial town of Reus, which has been competing with Tarragona since the 18th century. "Reus, Paris, London" was the slogan at the time. The cloth trade, and, later, distilleries and wine vaults, did indeed make the town, after Paris and London, the third largest European marketplace for alcohol. Since then the hazelnut, and the sweet forms in which it is processed, have ousted spirits, at least. Over and above this, the town offers the shopper a wide variety of other goods. The Plaça del Mercadal and the busy Calle Monterols are lined with elegant shops.

Here in the middle of the historical center of Reus, remains of the Jewish quarter have been preserved in the Calle Jesús. Not far away is the church of Sant Pere, redesigned in the 16th century but still basically Gothic with its broad nave and slender, hexagonal belfry. The Centre de Lecture opposite, originally a 19th-century building, was given a *Noucentisme*-style façade in 1916–21.

In the other direction, the Calle Monterols passes the Plaça de Prim where a monument to the revolutionary General Prim i Prats was erected in 1887. Another important scion of the town, the Symbolist painter Marià Fortuny (1838–74), gave the Teatre Fortuny opera house its name (1881–2). The artist's works can be studied in the Museu Comarcal Salvador Vilaseca at the Plaça de la Llibertat. The archaeological department of this museum is housed in the Raval de Santa Anna 59. The house where Fortuny was born, in the Raval Robuster, is open to visitors. Finally, in the old town center, the Palau Bofarull dating from 1760 is worth a mention; its exterior is Baroque, but its interior is neoclassical. In the Great Hall a lavish series of frescoes pay homage to the Spanish kings Charles III and Charles IV.

Reus owes its appeal, however, to its turn-of-the-century buildings, which are almost exclusively the work of Lluís Domènech i Montaner, the eldest of the three architects of Catalan Modernisme. The Casa Navàs, with its "late Gothic" windows and bays reminiscent of Venice (illus.

*Reus*
*Casa Navàs, built by Lluís*
*Domènech i Montaner in 1901*
*Overall view (on the right) and*
*window detail (bottom)*

pp. 354–355, dates from 1901. Inside this town palace, all the furniture, designed by the equally famous sculptor and craftsman Gaspard Homar, has been preserved. Gaudí himself, or one of his cousins, is reported to have contributed to the sculpture adorning the façade. The whole building seems like a prelude to the Casa Lleó Morera in Barcelona, the corner house of the famous "Mançana de la Discòrdia."

A few yards farther on are the Casa Rull, with winged lions standing guard over its façade (1900), and the Casa Gasull (1911), with mosaics and sgraffito decoration.

However, the highspot is without a doubt the Pere Mata Institute, a psychiatric sanatorium situated some way outside (illus. above, and opposite, top). In its brick buildings this town displays, on a small scale, the entire spectrum of Modernist decorative forms. On this site, begun by Lluís Domènech i Montaner in 1897, and completed by his son Pere Domènech i Roura in 1919, East and West meet. A cheerful, almost idyllic atmosphere is created by the Moorish arches and ornamental forms, glass windows in Gothic style, little pediments and tracery, and tile mosaics with an enormous variety of plant motifs (illus. p. 357, bottom). Even so, practical and therapeutic considerations are pre-eminent here, as

they are in the Hospital de la Santa Creu i de Sant Pau in Barcelona, which was built a little later. The hospital wards and the catering arrangements are organized by way of a highly efficient system of pavilions.

From the Pere Mata Institute we plunge into a different world when we visit the Barri Gaudí, the work of the eminent Catalan architect Ricardo Bofill, not far away. Here too history is evoked, although not exactly subtly. With his oversize chimneys – that owe a debt to the Casa Milà – Bofill wanted to pay his respects to his forbear, the genius Antoni Gaudí i Cornet, born in Reus in 1852. But of Gaudí himself there are only a few traces. The later master of Modernist architecture soon left his native town to study at the architectural college in Barcelona.

After visiting the busy town of Reus, the westward journey offers attractive landscapes and ample opportunity for quiet reflection. From the cloister of the onetime Augustinian monastery Escornalbau (illus. p. 358, bottom) the visitor can enjoy the view over the Camp de Tarragona; in fine weather one can even see as far as the island of Mallorca. Falset, the capital of Priorat, attracts us in its turn by virtue of its Modernist architecture and fine wines. The Celler Cooperatiu provides both, a rewarding glass of wine and an atmospheric view of Cèsar Martinell's

TOP:
Reus
*Pere Mata Institute*
*Exterior views*

BOTTOM:
Reus
*Interior view of one of the*
*pavilions*

357

brick halls (1919) resembling a religious building. Afterwards one can rest and recover while traveling into the reddish, gleaming mountains of the Serra de Montsant, to which the Carthusian monks also once withdrew to found the monastery of Escaladei. The picturesque village and the ruins of the Arabian castle at Siurana cling to a limestone cliff 737 m (c. 2,400 ft.) high (illus. top).

After Espluga de Francolí, which likewise has note-worthy treasures to offer in food, wine, and Modernist architecture, we come either to the Cistercian monastery of Poblet (illus. pp. 362–71) or to the picturesque little town of Montblanc, a large part of which is still surrounded by an imposing ring wall (illus. opposite top). Within the walls, the varying levels are linked by narrow streets and flights of steps. Montblanc can look back on a proud past. Founded by Alfons I in 1163, it was elevated to a *Vila Ducal* by decree in 1387, as all the first-born sons of the Catalan-Aragonese kings bore the title of Duc de Montblanc (and continued to do so until 1700). Markets of its own, its self-confident citizens, and an important Jewish community all contributed to its renown and

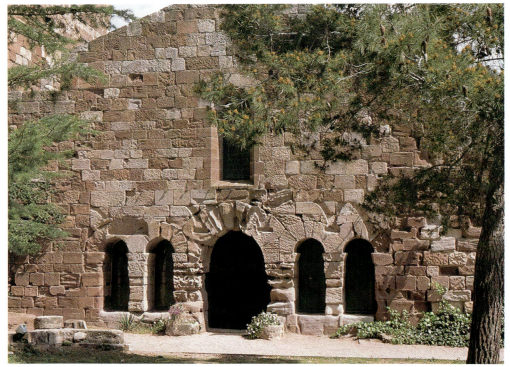

growth in the late Middle Ages. Its wealth is reflected in imposing public buildings, such as Sant Miquel dating from the period of transition from Romanesque to Gothic, within the walls of which the Catalan *Generalitat* often met, or the magnificent single-nave late Gothic church of Santa Maria which dominates the town. It was given a Baroque façade in 1673, its ornate portal having been destroyed in the War of Independence. In its interior, edged with 11 chapels, the furniture includes the colored Gothic stone retable by Reinard Desfonoll and the 1607 organ, one of the finest in Catalonia.

Grand residences cluster around the Plaça Major and the Calle Major, along with the Palau Reial, where the royal family lived when they stayed at Montblanc. Adjacent to the town wall is the church of Sant Marçal – today the Museu Frederic Marès.

Outside the fortifications, built under the direction of Brother Guillem de Guimerá in 1366–77, are more churches and monasteries worth seeing, along with the Santa Magdalena Hospital – now the municipal archives (illus. p. 359, bottom). Close by, the Romanesque-Gothic Pont Vell leads to the other bank of the Riu Francolí.

On the return journey to Tarragona we pass Valls, famous for its culinary specialities and customs. In winter the famed *calçots* are eaten here: barbecued young onions served with a piquant almond and garlic sauce. In combination with other delicacies, they form part of the *calçotada*, a rich, almost ritual regional meal.

But what is even more amazing are the *castells*, the human towers here created to perfection. On every major public holiday, acrobatic young men climb on each other's shoulders, to the accompaniment of shawms – an early woodwind instrument – to form living pyramids. The current record is nine tiers. There are various formations depending on the number and arrangement of those involved. The basis is the *pinya*, sometimes comprising several dozen strong men. Acrobatic youths clamber up to the upper tiers, and the one at the top, the *anxeneta*, must wave for a few seconds with a free hand for the *castell* to be considered complete. Though imitation is not recommended, the human towers are a unique sight, and should not be missed.

Before returning to Tarragona, a detour to Montferri and Vistabella is recommended, where the two most important buildings by Josep Maria Pujol (see panel box opposite) are found: Santuari de Montserrat and Sagrat Cor. Jujol – Gaudí's most gifted pupil – is in many respects indebted to his master's organic architecture. But in these two churches in particular, Modernist features are combined with an Expressionist Gothic revival. In it, Jujol creatively transformed motifs from the Sagrada Familia. Work on the Santuari de Montserrat in Montferr, begun in 1926, was discontinued for financial reasons in 1930. However, an association was founded which – with architects from all over the world – urged the continuation of this unique project. It was successfully finished on May 31, 1999 (illus. left). A total of 42 brick pillars support 33 small cupolas at various heights resting on overlapping parabolic ribs. The whole is crowned with two delicate pyramidal tower roofs, its outline resembling the needle-shaped cliffs of Montserrat. In Vistabella, brickwork and stones give the Sagrat Cor church (1918–23) the appearance of being part of the surrounding landscape. But it towers above the latter by virtue of a hexagonal brick pyramid reminiscent of late Gothic pyramidal tower roofs. The interior is dominated by a cupola above parabolic arches (illus. opposite).

LEFT:
Montferri
*Santuari de Montserrat,*
*begun by Josep Maria Jujol in 1926,*
*completed in 1999*

OPPPOSITE:
Vistabella
*Sagrat Cor, built by Josep Maria Jujol 1918–23*

**Josep Maria Jujol i Gibert**
Architect and artist in ironwork, Antoni Gaudí's most important pupil and colleague. Jujol developed his teacher's Modernist architecture by reinforcing its calligraphic features. In his late works classical Modernism blends with surrealistic motifs.

**Life and Work**
1879 born in Tarragona
1906 completed study of architecture
1919 professor at the Escola d'Arquitectura in Barcelona
1905–07 collaborated with Antonio Gaudí on the Casa Batlló, and 1905–11 on the Casa Mià; in both projects worked especially on the balcony parapets
1904–14 in the Parc Güell, among other things worked on the decoration of the "Hall of a Hundred Columns" and the "snake bench"

**Independent works**
1908 Tarragona, new interior décor of the Teatre Metropol
1913 Barcelona, elevator in the Casa Farreras (Calle Mallorca 284)
1913–19 Sant Joan Despí near Barcelona, Torre de la Creu ("Torre dels Ous," "Egg Tower")
1914–30 Sant Joan Despí near Barcelona, Can Negre
1914–31 Els Pallaresos near Tarragona, Casa Bofarull
1916–22 Barcelona, Tallers Mañach
1918–23 Barcelona, Casa Planells (Av. Diagonal 332)
1926 Designed the Santuari de Montferri near Tarragona, 1999 posthumously completed
1928–29 Barcelona, architecture of the fountain on the Plaça d'Espanya on the occasion of the 1929 International Exhibition
1949 died in Barcelona

*The Cistercian monastery of Santa Maria de Poblet*

### The Cistercian Monasteries

Not even in Burgundy, the home of the Cistercians, nor in its French daughter foundations, is the importance of the Order and the beauty of its architectural monuments more tangibly evident than in the area inland from Tarragona. In Poblet, Santes Creus, and Vallbona, three monasteries have been perserved, all within a very small area. They are unique in Europe, not only for their exemplary layout and architectural quality, but also for their political significance. One should set aside at least a day – two days would be even better – to appreciate these three most impressive monasteries.

The history of the Cistercians, in brief, is as follows. In 1098 a small number of Benedictine monks led by Robert de Molesme, discontented with the secularization of their Order, resolved to establish a new community with the aim of reviving the ideals of austerity and seclusion. They found a home in Citeaux, and their first constitution in Stephan Harding's *"Charta caritatis."* Their white, undyed habits became their outwardly visible identifying feature. Within a short time, four more monasteries were added, at Clairvaux, La Ferté, Morimond, and Pontigny. The meteoric rise of the young Cistercian Order, now named after the place where it was first established, began with Bernhard of Clairvaux. By 1153, the year of Bernhard's death, it comprised 343 abbeys scattered all over Europe. The community owed the rapid and altogether successful spread of its principles to its rigid, hierarchic rules. Groups of 12 monks each, led by an abbot from among their ranks, left their mother monastery to establish, in isolated but fertile surroundings, a new monastery, which served in its turn as a center for further missionary work. These "subsidiary" daughter monasteries, as a rule reflect the structure and ground plan of their mother house. The

church buildings usually have three naves with a protruding transept adjoined either by rectangular chapels or by a chancel with a ring of chapels which could be polygonal or rectangular.

The monastery site as a whole follows a clever and eminently practical system (illus. p. 364,). It was always selected to be close to a watercourse, for the necessary provision of daily needs and waste disposal.

Around the cloister, situated in most cases to the south of the church, were grouped the chapterhouse, the refectory with the dormitories above it, the scriptorium, the library, the parlor, kitchen, calefactories, and latrines. Gardens and sick wards, storehouses, and wine cellars completed the monastery complex.

Bernhard originally demanded simplicity even in formal architectural language – which, be it noted, did not mean carelessness, but rather unpretentious, refined building techniques. He was always opposed to pictorial decoration and the use of stained glass. Even a steeple was regarded by the Order as an impermissible luxury. These inflexible demands rapidly proved untenable. Indeed, in all Cistercian churches the high quality of the stonemasons' work is still plain to see.

The piety of the monks and their prayers for spiritual salvation attracted the nobility and the monarchy, who had themselves buried in Cistercian churches. In New Catalonia a further factor was involved. In the 12th century, when the order spread like wildfire, the country had come to the end of the *Reconquista*. In the re-conquered territories there was therefore a high demand for pastoral care and agricultural instruction. It is thus hardly surprising that the three most important Catalan Cistercian daughter houses were established within only a few years, between 1150 and 1158.

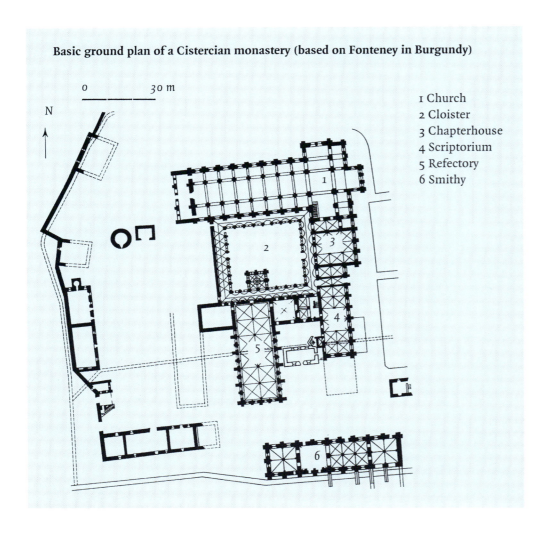

**Basic ground plan of a Cistercian monastery (based on Fonteney in Burgundy)**

0   30 m

N

1 Church
2 Cloister
3 Chapterhouse
4 Scriptorium
5 Refectory
6 Smithy

Poblet, in the watery Conca de Barberà, is the oldest and historically most important of the three monasteries (illus. pp. 362–71). The founder was Count Ramon Berenguer IV, who by marrying Petronella of Aragón linked the Catalan dynasty to the royal title. In 1151 he donated the site to the monks from French Fontfroide, who named their new domicile after a grove of poplars, *populetum*. Due to wide-ranging privileges, the monastery, on the border of New Catalonia, quickly acquired economic and political influence. By the 14th century its abbots ruled over more than 60 villages, and exercised great influence in the *Generalitat*, the body representing the various classes or estates. Members of the royal family regularly sought refuge behind the monastery walls. Finally, in 1340, Pere III el Ceremoniós declared Poblet to be the pantheon of the Catalan-Aragonese dynasty.

Centuries of prosperity were followed, in the Baroque era, by periods of decline, until the monastery was dissolved in 1835. The site was not demolished, but left to its fate: left to be vandalized. In the late 19th century a beginning was made on securing and restoring what remained of the buildings, but it was not until 1921 that Poblet was put under a preservation order. In 1940 the monastery was reoccupied by Cistercian monks.

The architecture and furnishings were entirely in keeping with Poblet's eminence. Three ring walls fortified with towers encircle one of the largest monastic residences of its time, an entire monastic town which, from its enclosure, opens up a little at a time to the outside world. All its institutions are organized in a practical fashion and in accordance with the rule of the order. The church and the cloister (in this case situated to the north

due to the nature of the terrain) are adjoined by the chapterhouse, the library, the kitchen, the refectory, dormitories, calefactories, and parlors. The royal apartments were initially located in an area to the east of the enclosure, until in 1392 King Martí had a new late Gothic palace built to the side of the entrance.

Let us approach the ensemble in a contemplative frame of mind. The visitor must pass through three portals. The first is the Porta de Prades; on the left is the porter's lodge of 1531. Turning right, one comes to the small but attractive Capella de Sant Jordi in the late Gothic style. It was built by Alfons el Magnànim as an act of thanksgiving for the conquest of Naples in 1442. The king's coat of arms, crowned with a dragon, appears everywhere. A play on words is involved here: in the Catalan language *dragó* sounds almost identical to *d'Aragó* (= of Aragón). The

OPPOSITE, BOTTOM:
*Cistercian monastery of Santa Maria de Poblet*
*Porta Daurada, 15th century*

ABOVE:
*Cistercian monastery of Santa Maria de Poblet*
*View of the church façade from the Plaça Major*

Cistercian monastery of Santa
Maria de Poblet
Monastery church, royal tombs
Sculpture by Aloi de Montbrait,
Jaume Cascalls and Jordi Johan;
2nd half of the 14th century

remaining buildings inside this outer ring served as storehouses and workshops and as accommodation for day laborers.

The Porta Daurada, the golden doorway, now leads into the second area (illus. p. 364, bottom). It comprises the Plaça Major, with the 12th-century St. Catherine's Chapel, the Abbot's palace, and the monumental stone cross dating from the 16th century, along with hospices, shops, and the joiner's workshop. Somewhat to the side, in the gardens, a more recent Abbot's house was built in the 16th–17th centuries. The portal itself, adorned with a coat of arms, dates from the late 15th century, but was not given its name until 1564 when Philipp II had the wings of its door gilded during a visit.

From the Plaça Major one first sees the actual monastery, which is still concealed behind massive walls 11 m (c. 36 ft.) high and 2 m (c. 6.5 ft.) thick (illus. pp. 364–5). Pere III had the fortification built, 608 m (c. 2,000 ft.) long and with 13 towers, from 1336. The Porta Reial, with its massive hexagonal bastions, is a simple but unusually impressive sight. A few steps away from it a Baroque portal, delicate in comparison, opens up. It was incorporated into the formidable wall in the 17th century

at the request of the Count of Cardona. It leads to the monastery church built under Alfons I (1162–96) and to King Martí's unfinished late Gothic palace.

The interior of the church is of sublime simplicity (illus. p. 366). Behind the broad transept its three naves lead to an ambulatory with a ring of chapels, evidence that Poblet was based on its original model in Clairvaux (probably via the Moreruela monastery in the province of Saragossa). Again, the stonemason's technical artistry gives the building, located at the transition from Romanesque to Gothic, its particular dignity. There is no ornamentation at all, not even plant motifs. It is the arrangement of the support system alone that lends nobility to the architecture. Sturdy cruciform pillars with half-columns bear the weight of the aisle arcades, and slender members support the transverse arches of the pointed barrel. The aisles, incidentally, have cross rib vaulting, but the right-hand aisle was altered in the 14th century by the incorporation of chapels. The filigree octagonal center tower also dates from this period, but is today largely the product of 19th- and 20th-century restoration.

What catches the eye in the interior is the huge retable carved by Damià Forment *a lo romano*, that is to say, in

Renaissance forms, c. 1527 (illus. p. 367). Scenes from the life of Our Lady and statues of the apostles and saints are spread over six levels, and framed by grotesque ornamentation.

This monumental altarpiece is crowned by a Mount Calvary. The renowned and much sought-after artist seems, however, to have approached his task somewhat negligently. A commission criticized both the materials and the workmanship, with the result that Forment was paid only part of his fee, plus a mule.

For the pantheon, Jordi de Deu came up with an unusual design in 1380: the sarcophagi, with the recumbent figures of the royal family, rest on shallow basket-handle arches between the center pillars, evidently so as not to impede the celebration of Mass (illus. opposite). On the north side Jaume el Conqueridor (d. 1276) lies at rest, along with Pere el Ceremoniós (d. 1387) and his three wives: Maria of Navarre, Eleonor of Portugal, and Eleonor of Sicily (sculpture by Aloi de Montbrai, Jaume Cascalls and Jordi Johan, 2nd half of the 14th century). On the south side Alfons el Cast and members of the Trastámara dynasty are buried: Juan I with his two wives, and Juan II and Juana Enriquez, the parents of Ferran the Catholic.

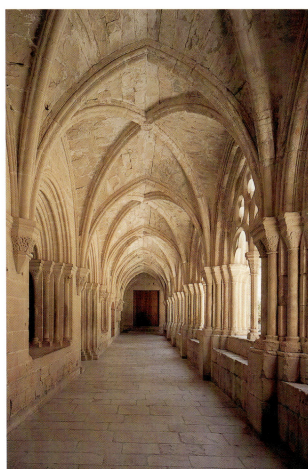

TOP AND BOTTOM:
*Cistercian monastery of Santa Maria de Poblet*
*Views of the cloister, completed in the 13th century*

369

RIGHT:
*Cistercian monastery of Santa
Maria de Poblet
Pump-room, 12th century*

OPPOSITE:
*Cistercian monastery of Santa
Maria de Poblet
Chapterhouse, 14th century*

Martí l'Humá and Alfons Magnànim were buried later in different parts of the church. After the monastery was disestablished in 1835, the royal tombs of Poblet suffered irreparable damage. In 1940 the collector and sculptor Fréderic Marés turned his attention to what little was left, and recreated the ensemble as far as was possible.

Probably because of the nature of the terrain, the great cloister lies to the north of the church. It took more than a century to build, the work only being completed c. 1300. The transition from Romanesque to Gothic can be clearly seen, for the wings adjoining the church still rest on a Romanesque structure, but already have cross-rib vaulting (illus. p. 369, top). The other wings (illus. p. 369, bottom) open up with noble tracery. Here too one is struck by the quality of the capital sculpture, in which ornaments and leaf motifs are interwoven with great artistry. The Romanesque parts also include the hexagonal pump-room, a visit to which is an indispensable part of the Cistercians' daily routine (illus. above). The square chapterhouse rests on four elegant pillars which support the delicate 13th-century fan vaulting (illus. opposite). The memorial slabs of a number of abbots of the monastery are set into the floor. Other things worth seeing in the monastery complex include the refectory, the scriptorium, and the library with the dormitory above, the latter measuring 87 × 10 m (c. 285 × 33 ft.), making it one of the largest sleeping rooms of its time. As is frequently the case in Catalonia, the long room is topped by a series of flying buttresses on which the wooden roof rests. The kitchen, the wine cellar, the calefactory, the locutorium, and other humanitarian features ensured such physical welfare as was appropriate within the rule of the Order.

Santes Creus can also look back on a similar historical development. It is situated only about 30 km (c. 19 miles)

TOP AND BOTTOM:
*Cistercian monastery of Santes
Creus, founded in 1158*

away from Poblet, likewise in a harmonious setting with a plentiful supply of water (illus. p.372). The monastery was founded in 1158, and owes its name to a number of crosses which miraculously appeared in the sky; after this, the monks from the Languedoc gave up lands in the neighboring Valldaura, which had been donated to them by the Montcada family, and chose this site instead.

Santes Creus was at the height of its power in the 13th and 14th centuries, thanks to outstanding personalities among the abbots and excellent connections with the royal house. It served at times as the Pantheon for the kings of Aragon, and enjoyed the privilege of being subject only to the Pope. The monastery frequently played an active part in Catalonia's political fortunes, including decisive support for the founding of the military order of Montesa. In the 16th century it was still a center of humanistic studies, but it later suffered the same fate as Poblet, and was not revived until the 1930s.

Notwithstanding the similarities regarding these circumstances, these two Catalan Cistercian monasteries make quite different impressions on the visitor. Poblet is stern and majestic, never entirely denying its character as a fortress of the faith. Santes Creus is of more modest proportions and far less monumental. Stepping into the cloister one feels light-years removed from Cistercian austerity (illus. opposite). The delicate cluster pillars of the exterior walls are interspersed with elegant tracery windows. Master Reginald Fonoll, who was probably an Englishman, gave each wing different flamboyant ornamentation. However, what is quite astonishing in a monastery of this Order are the capitals, on which – in spite of St. Bernhard's prohibition – the most colorful

TOP AND BOTTOM:
*Cistercian monastery of Santes Creus*
*Cloister, built by Reginald Fonoll*
*1330–50*

  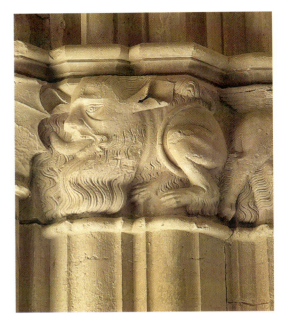

 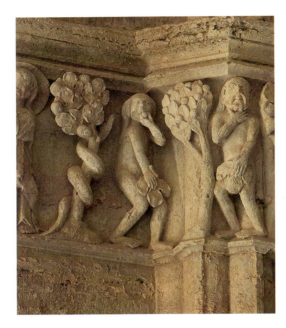 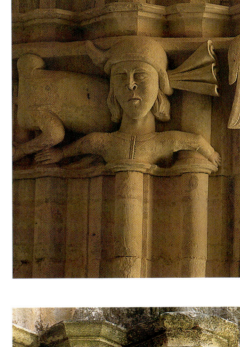

 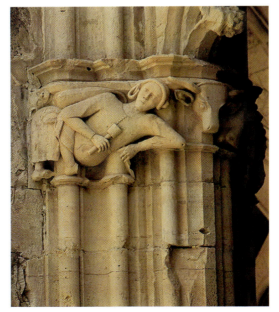 

OPPOSITE:
*Cistercian monastery of Santes Creus*
*Consoles and capitals in the cloister, 14th century*

scenes are depicted. The artist did not even restrict himself to biblical scenes, but treated everyday, mythological, and even satirical subjects with evident delight. There is a musician reaching for his bagpipes, a monkey riding on a dromedary, an artisan lounging casually across several capitals. Finally, the master has even immortalized himself, with chisel in hand. Work on the cloister began in 1313, and older parts were incorporated, such as the rib-vaulted pump-room, which is still entirely in Romanesque fashion, and hence out of keeping with the Gothic transoms of the cloister wing (illus. right, top).

The chapterhouse is another architectural gem, opening onto the cloister with a magnificent façade of windows (illus. right, bottom). Its nine vault transoms rest on four slender columns which are as delicately worked as the arches that they support.

The other rooms of the enclosure are no less carefully – though not so ambitiously – designed, in particular the spacious dormitory (illus. pp. 376–7) which is almost 50 m (c. 164 ft.) in length, and which used to be connected with the church by way of a staircase.

From the dormitory one proceeds via the locutorium (room for speaking) to the rear of the cloister (16th century, rearranged in the 17th century) around which are grouped the kitchen, the refectory, the wine cellar, and the dungeon. Here too is the adjoining royal palace wing, which was built from the 13th to the 16th centuries. The elegant interior courtyard, incorporating a porphyry column, dates from 1341. Weird hunting scenes are depicted on the balustrade of the outside stairway: a lion digging its claws into a gazelle and a wild boar – probably references to the king's strength.

After these excesses, we now turn to the church, which is one of the supreme achievements of late Romanesque architecture in Catalonia. Here, St. Bernhard's architectural demands are truly met, for the building, begun in 1174 and consecrated in 1211, is a prime example of Cistercian austerity and clarity (illus. p. 378). Free of any ornamentation but fashioned down to the smallest constructional detail with the utmost precision, it illustrates the harmony of pure architecture.

The interior appears monumental, though it is in fact a third shorter than that of Poblet. It contains three naves adjoining a narrow transept which opens to the east in five rectangular chapels.

The central chapel is clearly broader and deeper than those at the sides. This arrangement is very close to that of the original Cistercian monastery in Citeaux. Massive cruciform pillars support the broad ribs of the vaults, their wall members leveled off toward the nave in several places – a most subtle motif and one which is typical of Cistercian architecture.

One should look carefully at the perfection of the cutting and the setting of the stone to be truly convinced of the exceptional ability of these master builders.

The only additional interior adornment is the large rose window in the rear wall of the apse – an unusual motif, not only for the Cistercians but for Romanesque architecture in general.

RIGHT, TOP:
*Cistercian monastery of Santes Creus*
*Pump-room, 12th century*

RIGHT, BOTTOM:
*Cistercian monastery of Santes Creus*
*Chapterhouse, 14th century*

FOLLOWING PAGES:
*Cistercian monastery of Santes Creus*
*Dormitory, 14th century*

An eloquent contrast to the purism of the architecture is provided by the two temple-like tombs built in honor of Pere el Gran (d. 1285) and his wife Constance, as well as their son Jaume II (d. 1327), and Blanche of Anjou (illus. above right). Beneath filigree Gothic baldachins the sarcophagi of the deceased, in the form of shrines, exhibit strikingly different concepts.

Pere's colored shrine, adorned with the figures of saints, rests on an ancient porphyry vessel, a motif echoing the Hohenstaufen tombs in Palermo. The Aragon king was indeed married to a grand-daughter of Frederick II, and even put forward a claim to the crown of Sicily.

In contrast, the tomb of Jaume and Blanche of Anjou catches the eye by virtue of the two prominent recumbent figures which – unusually for Catalonia – adorn the cover of the sarcophagus. The couple are portrayed in a lifelike manner, wearing both Cistercian habits and crowns at the same time. In the former case, the sources identify the artist as the very well-known Master Barthomeu, and give the date as 1291–1300. But in the case of the second tomb two different names are given: Master Bonull and Francesc Montflorit, who also created the figure of Our Lady above the tomb. Other important nobles are also buried in Santes Creus, incidentally, including the relatives of the founders, the Montcada family, and Roger de Lluria, who led the Catalan expedition to southern Italy.

On leaving the church, take another, closer, look at the attractive entrance to the monastery. Like Poblet, Santes Creus also had three ring walls, but only the section with the church façade has survived. The area in front of it with the abbot's apartments, the administrative buildings, and the pretty fountain are of Baroque appearance. Access is via the Rococo Porta Reial (illus. above left) with Our Lady ascending to heaven, and the delicate *esgrafiats*, the sgraffito ornamentation. The outer courtyard was once situated in front of it, but of this only a modest gateway and the chapel of Santa Llúcia, built on top of an earlier Romanesque building, have survived the passage of time.

The third important Cistercian settlement, the abbey for Cistercian nuns at Vallbona de les Monges, is situated today in the Lleida region, but is included here on thematic grounds, particularly since the convent (illus. left bottom) was part of the archbishopric of Tarragona. Vallbona was the most important nunnery in Catalonia. It was founded as a hermitage in 1157, and in 1175 Berenguera of Cervera arranged to have the community – by then consisting exclusively of women – admitted to the Cistercian order. As with Poblet and Santes Creus, the kings gave the convent their support through numerous privileges. From 1201 it was an *abatia nullius*, subject only to the Pope. The daughters of the wealthiest families in Catalonia sought to be admitted, their endowments adding to the wealth of the convent. They cultivated the land, drained marshes, and organized provisions for the surrounding villages.

At the same time Vallbona established itself as an outstanding center for study, its library and scriptorium well-known far beyond the boundaries of Catalonia.

In 1573 the provisions of the Council of Trent prohibited nuns from living in remote areas. As a result, the nearby village of Montesquiu was moved to bring it within and around the site of the convent in order to comply with the decree. The community was the only one of the three Cistercian foundations to survive the anticlerical excesses of the 19th century, and has been continuously active to the present day.

The building of the convent church lasted from the 13th century until well into the 14th century. It is simpler than the men's monasteries. There is a single nave, with accordingly only three rectangular chapels adjoining the transept. The elevation is in keeping with the architectural transition from Romanesque to Gothic, but the elegant octagonal center tower was not completed until the 14th century. This convent was also chosen as a burial place by the pious and class-conscious nobility, including Violant of Hungary (d. 1251), wife of Jaume I.

The trapezoid cloister is an object lesson in style, each of its wings revealing a different date of origin (illus. top). The oldest section, to the south, is Romanesque. It is adjoined by the eastern section with its quasi-Arabian forms; 14th-century Gothic can be seen in the north wing with its delicate leaf capitals, while the west wing takes us into the 15th century.

The chapterhouse, in its turn, is both simple and memorable, and it houses a terracotta Madonna by Pere Johan (15th century).

After this excursion into the world of the Cistercians, each individual must decide whether to return to Tarragona and the Costa Daurada – with their sensory delights, or to continue the journey into the province – so rich in history – of Lleida.

# Lleida

# The "Distant City"

*View of the city with the Seu Vella (the Old Cathedral) enthroned above it*

ABOVE:
*In the Calle Millar*

OPPOSITE:
*The south flank of the Seu Vella, consecrated in 1278*

If the legends are to be believed, the proud city beside the Segre was founded by the Trojan hero Aeneas. It is at least a historical fact that, as Iltirda, it was the capital of the Iberian Ilergeti in the 4th and 3rd centuries B.C. and offered considerable resistance to the Roman conquerors during the Second Punic War, although ultimately in vain. In the 1st century A.D. it became involved in the civil war between Caesar and Pompey, as reported by Caesar in his *Commentarium belli civilis* and Lucan in the *Pharsalia*.

A little later, renamed Ilerda, it rose to the rank of a Roman *municipium*. The city was also subject to continual siege during the period of the great migrations. It was, after all, situated at an intersection of the Iberian peninsula and what is today the south of France, hence of outstanding strategic importance. Lleida has been a bishopric since 417, and in 546 was able to organize an important Council, the records of which have been preserved to this day.

Lleida was called Lareda – or simply "the distant city" – by the Arabs, because it was situated at the farthermost boundary of the Caliphate of Córdoba; they ruled over it for more than four centuries, a period that was a golden age. Protected by its fortifications, there were orchards and cornfields, all irrigated by a cleverly devised connected series of canals that is still in existence. In the *Mesquita*, where today the cathedral stands, Allah was praised, although Louis the Pious destroyed the city at the beginning of the 9th century. A few decades later, to defend themselves from the Christians, the Arabs built the

castle of La Suda – extended by the Almoravids in the 12th century – as well as the fortified walls that protected the city. The centuries of Arab rule were marked by the peaceful coexistence of Muslims, Christians, and Jews, each religious community contributing to the city's economic prosperity. The irrigation system created the necessary conditions for agriculture and fruit growing that are still Lleida's main economic activity.

In 1149, when the power of the Almoravids was in decline, Counts Ramon Berenguer IV of Barcelona and Ermengol VI of Urgell divided the city between them, with a further part being given, along with the castle at Gardeny, to the Templars. Bishop Guillem Pere de Ravidats moved into the *Mesquita* below the Arabian castle, and established once again a mighty bishopric extending far out toward Aragon. In 1150 the city was given its first statute, and in 1197 the *Consolat* – the Town Council – was created; it later became the *Consell General de la Paeria*. From 1238, however, the crown assumed power when Jaume I placed Lleida under royal jurisdiction.

By then the building of a new cathedral close to the *Mesquita* was well under way, the foundation stone having been laid in 1203. The work was carried out under the direction of Pere Sa Coma and Pere de Prenafeta, and in 1278 the Seu Vella was consecrated to Our Lady. Its magnificent outline still dominates the city (illus. above, and opposite). In 1300 Jaume II founded the "Estudi General" in Lleida, for a long time the only university in the kingdom of Catalonia-Aragon. Important personalities taught and studied there, including Alfonso de Borja, later Pope Calixtus III. The city by the Segre enjoyed a period of cultural and economic prosperity that lasted until the end of the 14th century. But in the following centuries Lleida also was sucked into the general recession and the upheavals of civil war.

When King Juan II laid siege to the Catalan city in 1464, more than 400 houses and the precious garden sites were ravaged. When the Jews – who had made an important contribution to the welfare of the community – were expelled in 1492, Lleida lost more than half its former population. But worse was to come: in the clashes of the *Guerra dels Segadors*, the War of the Reapers, large parts of the residential area were reduced to rubble. In the War of the Spanish Succession, in 1707, the old city around the castle and the cathedral suffered the same fate. It was even forced to undergo a transformation into a gigantic stronghold, with the cathedral being used as a barracks. But an even harsher blow to the city was the loss of its hereditary institutions: the Estudi General was moved to Cervera and the *Paeria* abolished.

Under Bourbon administration the appearance of the entire city was transformed. At the foot of the old city, now a fortress, municipal districts were planned and built. In 1761–92 Francisco Sabatini, using designs by Pedro Cermeños, built a new cathedral in the neoclassical style.

At the beginning of the 19th century it was Napoleon's troops at whose hands Lleida suffered. Large parts of the castle and parts of the old city were destroyed when a gunpowder factory exploded. Lleida sank into lethargy.

Not until after 1861, when it became possible for the constricting fortress walls to be demolished, did the citizens once again develop an urban civil life.

As in Barcelona, the *Renaixença* movement took root here. It led to an increased awareness of Catalan culture and encouraged the emergence of a varied cultural life. Among the artists from Lleida during this period, the composer Enric Granados deserves special mention.

Lleida suffered what will hopefully be the last degradation in its changing fortunes during the Civil War. In 1940 the inhabitants, of whom only some 40,000 remained, had to rebuild their city once again.

Today Lleida, thanks not least to its university, is once again a youthful center, with the advantages of centuries of tradition. A particularly lively festival is that of the city's patron saint, St. Anastasi, in May. In his honor the peaceful dragon Marraco and a total of 43 "giants" – representing various associations, institutions, and so on – dance through the streets. Ritual battles between Christians and Moors are of course included; here they are fought out principally in the form of verbal disputes. At the beginning of February the city celebrates the *Aplec del Caragol*, during which around 12 tons of snails find their way, in three days, into the visitors' stomachs.

In keeping with its history, a visit to Lleida should start at its highest point. However, few recognizable traces of the Arabian fortifications – the Suda – have survived. The medieval fortifications laid out on the orders of Jaume I and Pere III are limited, as a result of the explosion of

gunpowder during the Napoleonic period, to one single authentic wing. Even so, one can sense the dominance once exerted by the fortress, along with the 13th-century cathedral. Today the park, dedicated to Enric Granados and located around the so-called Roca Mitjana, invites the visitor to take a contemplative walk. It requires a certain amount of imagination to form a mental picture of the change from the early medieval buildings to the Arabian period, followed by the re-Christianization of the castle in the 12th century.

After all, the palace that was once built to a commission by Caid Isma'il ben Musa al-Quasit saw the wedding of Ramon Berenguer IV, Count of Barcelona, and Princess Petronella of Aragon; this event laid the basis for the unification of Catalan and Aragon lands, and elevated Catalonia to the status of a kingdom. Regrettably, the ruins no longer reflect this. What the visitor will be able to imagine most vividly is probably the Bourbon and Napoleonic period, when the castle on the hill controlled the entire life of the city.

It would seem impossible to do justice, in a few lines, to the complex architectural history of the Seu Vella, and to its outstanding importance in the history of art. Suffice to say that this compact building – with its three naves, its prominent transept, and the center cupola – originally had five apses, increasing in depth toward the center, of which the two southern ones were renovated in the Gothic style in the 15th century. Nor has the northern apse been preserved. The location of the cloister to the west – in front of the cathedral entrance – is most unusual. The explanation probably is that the forecourt of the Arabic *Mesquita* had obviously been located in this place, and its structures were re-used.

The early medieval cathedral, on the other hand, had been situated at the north wing of the cloister. As mentioned earlier, the names of the master builders are preserved in an inscription, and the Seu was consecrated in 1278, although still incomplete. Work on the cloister and the octagonal central tower continued well into the 14th century. Work on the belfry, for which Jaume Cascalls was initially responsible, finally began in 1364, and the crown was completed by Master Carlí in 1426.

In keeping with when it was built, Lleida cathedral belongs to the transition from Romanesque to Gothic. At the same time, its weighty interior walls, the sturdy pillars with their double columns, and the massive transverse and arcade arches supporting the cross-vaulting indicate a wish to cling to regional traditions (illus. opposite). The progress of the building work can also be followed in the sumptuous sculpture – which has much more to offer than clues to the dates. The extraordinarily delicate and varied capitals with their decoration combining figurative, plant, and quasi-Arabic elements, and the sculptures of the Porta de l'Anunciata and the Porta dels Fillols (Portal of the Annunciation and Portal of the Children) are regarded as supreme achievements of medieval Catalan sculpture (illus. right). The unique blend of Toulousan, Provençal, and Arabic motifs – which first appeared here and of which there is evidence as far afield as Valencia – is known

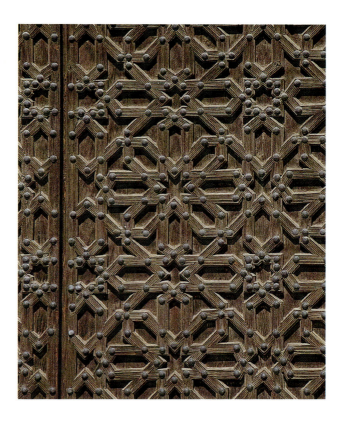

OPPOSITE:
*Seu Vella,*
*interior, 1213–78*

*Details of the sculpture of the*
*Portal of the Annunciation,*
*13th century*

as the *Escola romànica de Lleida*, the Leidatan school. It is difficult to single out individual items from the *embarras de richesse*. Let your gaze roam over the capitals of the apse and the center tower, or take pleasure in the oriental effect of the battle of lions in the Porta dels Fillols. The thematic arrangement follows a well thought-out system, for the scenes from the Old Testament are restricted to the apse and the transept, while the New Testament is predominantly illustrated in the nave. The late Gothic keystones of the Capella Requesens, to the right in front of the transept, from around the end of the 15th century, also deserve admiration.

The cloister (illus. above, and opposite, top), completed during the 14th century, is a gem of Gothic art. A Berenguer de Prenafeta was the master builder, and he succeeded in creating a wonderful piece of work. Delicate and complex tracery fills the spacious arches of the somewhat irregular wings. An amazing variety of elegant chisled capitals, along with filigree strips and friezes, create an utterly delightful ambience: one might almost imagine oneself in the courtyard of a royal palace. Some visitors are even reminded of the splendour of Arabian castles. It is scarcely credible that for more than 200 years this unique ensemble was diverted from its proper purpose to be used as a military barracks. Only in 1947 did the city reacquire this architectural monument, and restoration work remains unfinished.

After visiting the Seu Vella we take a great leap into the modern era, for the Seu Nova, the New Cathedral, from the 18th century. This clearly structured building, dominated by its double-tower façade (illus. opposite, bottom) was begun in 1761 under Carlos III, using plans

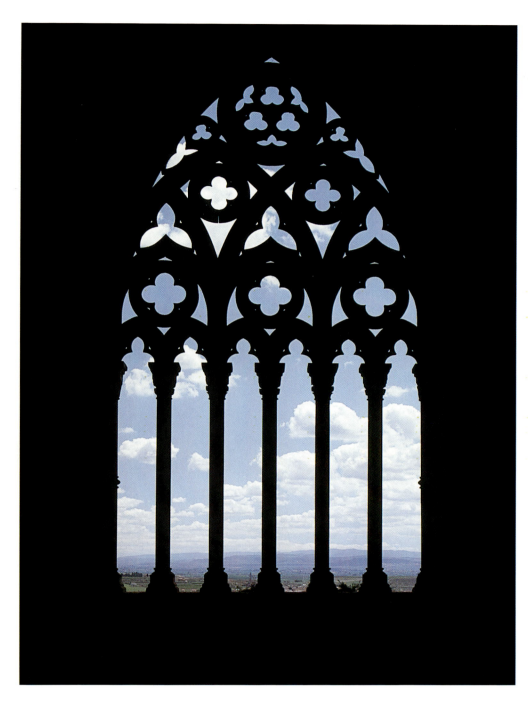

drawn up by Pedro Martín Cermeño. The Seu Nova is a pioneering neo-classical work. Corinthian pillars divide the three naves of equal height leading to chapels at the sides. The transept and ambulatory are adjoined by the sacristy, the communion chapel, and the museum, where there is a substantial collection of Baroque paintings – like Alonso Cano's picture of the crucifixion – and a series of Flemish Gobelin tapestries. The church furniture, including unique choirstalls by Luis Bonifás Massó, was lost in the Civil War.

Fortunately the interior decoration of the nearby parish church of Sant Llorenç was not destroyed, for this essentially late Romantic building contains wonderful Gothic tombstones and stone retables. Very fine examples of these altarpieces – especially widespread in Catalonia – can be seen in the Laurentius retable in the main apse and the Ursula retable in the aisle, both from the 14th century. Jaume Cascall created a vivid picture of the princess's life and her journey to Rome accompanied by 11,000 virgins. The statue of Our Lady, Mare de Déu dels Fillols, from the cathedral, was also housed here. Stone sculpture is kept in the little Romanesque church of Sant Martí, now the Museu Diocesà.

There are also important secular buildings that escaped destruction. The Santa Maria Hospital (illus. p. 390, top), in front of the New Cathedral, is an archaeological museum as well as the municipal archives; it was built between 1454 and 1522 to amalgamate seven different municipal hospitals. As is customary, it has a stylish square inner courtyard, from which an open stairway leads to the upper story with a gallery. The façades are almost devoid of ornamentation; only a figure of Our Lady as well as the municipal coat of arms adorn the entrance.

From here, taking the Carrer Major – the main axis – we come to the *Paeria* (illus. p. 391, top) on the right. Built in the 13th century as a town palace with its splendid triple windows for the Sanahuya family, only a hundred years later it became the seat of the municipal council; it was extended in neoclassical style in 1868.

Traces of Roman buildings were recently discovered during excavations, leading to the establishment of a

TOP:
*Seu Vella,*
*Cloister, detail*

RIGHT:
*One of the two towers of the Seu*
*Nova (New Cathedral), built by*
*Pedro Martín Cermeño from 176,*
*with its storks' nests*

*Santa Maria Hospital, 1454–1522, today the archaeological museum and municipal archives. View of the inner courtyard (top) and statue of Our Lady on the façade (right)*

small archaeological museum in the basement of the palace. The treasures found in the archives include the *Llibre Verd de Lleida* and the *Llibre del Usatges*, a kind of Catalan constitution dating from the 14th century. A little farther on we pass the neoclassical Porta de L'Arc de Pont with the monument erected in 1882 to Indibil and Mandoni, the leaders of the Ilergeti who put up resistance to the Roman invasion.

The Pilar del General, between the *Paeria* and the arcades of the Porxos de Dalt and Porxos de Baix, was once used to display the decisions of the provincial government or the royal house as a way of informing the general public. The redesigning of the Plaça Sant Joan, recently carried out by the Basque Peña Ganchegui (illus. opposite bottom), did not meet with overwhelming enthusiasm.

Lleida's modern artery, the spacious Rambla de Ferran, leads, somewhat askew, into the Carrer Major. Here a row of stately administrative buidings from more recent times can be seen by visitors.

If we first cross the Segre by way of the Pont Vell, we come to the Camps Elisis park with its aquarium, the Xalet Café, and the "music temple," all designed by Francesc Morera between 1916 and 1926.

Finally, having crossed back to the city side, Gardeny castle must be mentioned. This castle is situated somewhat outside the city, and it was handed over to the Templars in 1149. This impressive building owes its survival to a decree issued by Philipp V, who ordered Lleida to restore it after he visited it.

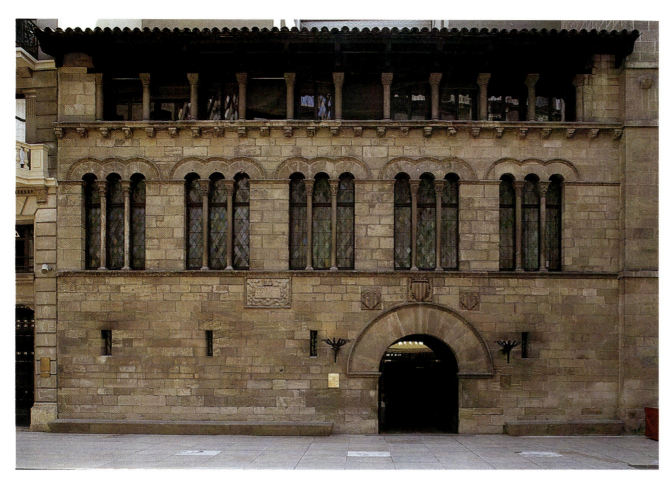

TOP:
Paeria municipal council,
13th–19th centuries

BOTTOM:
Plaça Sant Joan

## Lleida's Immediate and More Distant Surroundings

The province of Lleida offers a wide variety of cultural experiences, even going back into prehistory. It is, however, difficult to suggest a precise itinerary here, as the monuments are so widely scattered. This means that, in the north, we must leave the plain around Lleida, and proceed to the foothills of the Pyrenees.

El Cogul, about 20 km (c. 12 miles) south of Lleida, is well known, and not only on account of ducal palaces. On the contrary, it is the prehistoric wall-paintings of the Cova dels Moros that attract visitors from all over the world. There are 45 figures drawn or scratched in vivid red and black, depicting with astonishing precision and elegance hunting scenes and scenes from everyday life. Bulls, goats, and stags are sketched, in a few strokes, but with amazing fidelity to nature. The best known picture, however, is the *Dance of the Ten Women*, in which the women are dressed in a kind of flared skirt and dance around a naked man. They probably date from the Mesolithic period, making them up to 7,000 years old.

One can take the road to Vallbona de les Monges via Les Borges Blanques and Maldà – situated on a hill – for the tour of the magnificent Catalan Cistercian monasteries (described in another chapter).

Our route, however, takes us farther on to Bellpuig d'Urgell, the seat of the barons of Bellpuig, though they were absorbed into the Count of Cardona's family in 1386. Little survives of their castle, but this is compensated for by the Sant Nicolau church which contains an unusually fine Renaissance tombstone (illus. left) – perhaps the most important work from this period found in Catalonia. (Originally, however, it was kept in the Franciscan monastery and was not transferred to Sant Nicolau until 1841.) The Italian Giovanni Merliano da Nola made the monument of Carrara marble in 1522–5 in the form of a Roman triumphal arch. In the archway the deceased rests on a sumptuous sarcophagus; above him there is a Pietà who, as it were, mourns equally for the man buried there. Allegorical figures of evil, half dragon, half full-breasted woman, writhe beneath the burden of the coffin. In the lavish architectural ornamentation further figures and reliefs give an account of the deeds of the deceased. Who was this man, who commissioned such a resplendent and unusual tombstone to be erected in Bellpuig, immortalizing himself in such a supremely self-confident

LEFT:
Bellpuig d'Urgell
*Sant Nicolau*
*Tombstone of Ramon Folc de Cardona-Anglesola,*
*created by Giovanni Merliano da Nola 1522–5*

OPPOSITE:
Agramunt
*Santa Maria*
*Main portal, 13th century*

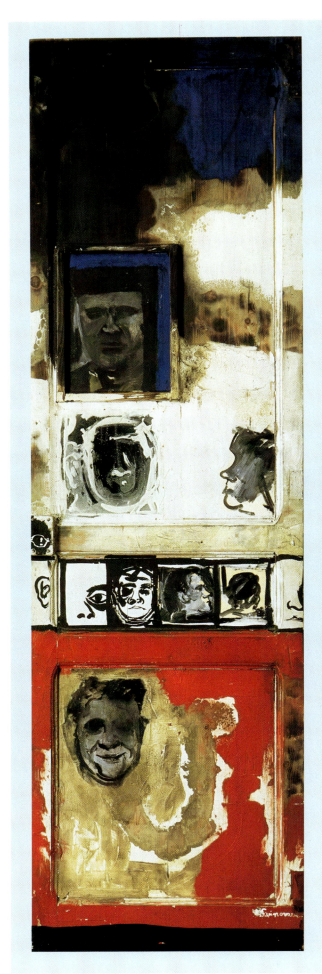

### Josep Guinovart

*Josep Guinovart is regarded as one of the great Catalan artists of the postwar period. After initial experiments in representational painting he turned, in the early 1960s, to informel, an abstract pictorial language, which he broke up by interspersing various materials and forms. Again and again, the reality of nature and the outside world finds its way into his poetic collages. Cement, earth, and chaff complement the large-scale paintings that are often executed in dull grays and browns.*

*Since the 1970s he has caused a stir with his unusual installations, for example the profoundly disturbing* Tapís de la mort *(Carpet of Death, 1972) made of hemp rope and hangman's nooses.*

### Life and Work

*1927 born in Barcelona*
*1941 worked as a house-painter, attended several art schools and colleges of art and design*
*1952 scholarship to study in Paris, first public commissions*
*1955 founded the Taull Group; throughout the 1960s involved in numerous stage and theatrical décor projects*
*1969 studio in Castelldefels*
*1980 large exhibition in Madrid*
*1982 Spanish representative at the Venice Biennale; numerous one-man exhibitions in Spain and the USA into the 1990s; 1990 one-man exhibitions inter alia in Bochum, Hamburg, and Esslingen*

### Main works (selection)

Escena de pobres, 1946
Els braus, 1950
La finestra, 1964
*Wall relief in the Col·legi d'Arquitectes in Barcelona, 1971*
Tapís de la Mort, 1972
Homenatge a Picasso, 1973
Agramunt IV. 1976
Contorn-Entorn, 1976
Terra, 1980
La Pava, 1989

manner for all time. It was Ramon Folc de Cardona-Anglesola (1467–1522) who was indeed an influential man. He was viceroy of Naples and Sicily from 1506. In part, thanks to his policies, the Inquisition which wreaked havoc in Castille and Aragon, was not introduced in the Mediterranean empire.

The former Franciscan monastery of St. Bartomeu, founded by Ramon Folc in 1507, stands outside the city gates. A very fine example of the transition from late Gothic to Renaissance can be seen here, especially in the great cloister. Whereas the ground-floor arcades still have pointed arches, the next story has a surrounding gallery with small, convoluted, late Gothic columns. Then, in the second upper story, with its classical shape, the Renaissance style is fully established.

Agramunt is another gem of the region around Lleida. Although this market town, which once belonged to the Count of Urgell, has forfeited its walls, it has managed to preserve its medieval character. A particularly attractive impression is made by the church of Santa Maria, built between the 12th and 13th centuries, the main portal of which has unusually lavish ornamentation (illus. p. 393). The eight layers of its wall provides abundant space for sculpture. The capitals are adorned with filigree plant-and-animal motifs, the archivolts with geometric ornamentation. Strangely enough, no tympanum was included, instead there are small, fully-rounded figures at the summit of the arch. From the vantage point of the observer, they show Our Lady with the Adoration of the Magi to her left and the Annunciation to her right. The style of the sculpture is very close to that of the Porta dels Fillos at the Seu in Lleida; master craftsmen from Lleida were probably involved here also. An inscription states that the group of Our Lady was paid for by the city's weavers in 1283. Incidentally, the sculptor's art is also celebrated in the form of confectionery, *xocolat a la pedra* (stone chocolate) and *turró d'Agramunt* (nougat) being very popular here.

The Baroque town hall is also worth seeing. It was built in 1734 at the Plaça Major over the foundation walls of the medieval *Paeria*. Contrast is provided by the *Espai Guinovart* housed in the old market hall. This is an exhibition hall dedicated to the work of the pioneering postwar Catalan avant-garde artist Josep Guinovart (see panel box, left).

The two final destinations of our journey of discovery take us to the wild, romantic landscape surrounding the River Noguera Palleresa to the north of Balaguer (illus. opposite top). Baronia de Sant Oïsme has only a few inhabitants, but boasts a noteworthy Romanesque church and the remains of a picturesque castle, both set high above the Camarassa reservoir. The castle and the monastery of Santa Maria del Mur (illus. opposite, bottom) are in an even more idyllic setting, but can only be reached via a gravel road. The frescoes have now been moved to the museums of Boston and Barcelona, but this loss of interior decoration is compensated for by the romantic ruins of the once important monastery and the splendid view of the Pyrenees.

OPPOSITE:
*Self portrait 1966*
*Mixed technique, 225 × 65 cm*
*Josep Guinovart*
*Privately owned*

TOP:
*Landscape in the valley of the*
*Noguera Pallaresa*

LEFT:
*Castle and monastery*
*Santa Maria de Mur*

# The French Part of Catalonia

# From the "Center of the Universe" to the Edge of the Pyrenees

PREVIOUS PAGES:
*Château at Salses, 1497–1505*

ABOVE:
*Mont Canigou seen from
Ille-sur-Têt*

The linguistic and cultural region of Catalonia, which had existed for almost 900 years, was torn apart and shared out between the Spanish and the French crowns by the Treaty of the Pyrenees in 1659. The agreement established the political boundary that remains valid today.

The division came after many years of conflict, the object of which – the unity and independence of Catalonia – was the precise opposite of what came into force. During the course of the 17th century the partial empires situated at the extremities of the Iberian peninsula – Portugal and Catalonia/Aragon – had repeatedly demanded to be released from Castilian dominance, and had allied themselves with the enemies of the Habsburgs.

Portugal regained its independence in 1640, but Catalonia was drawn into Philipp IV's war with France, and used as a deployment area for Castilian troops. Acts of aggression against the soldiers of central Spain, perceived as an occupying force, increased, and there were also tensions in the sphere of social policy arising from the loyalty of the aristocracy to Castile. The lesser nobility, in contrast, sought a rapprochement with France.

The Guerra dels Segadors (the "War of the Reapers") broke out. In 1640 Catalans and Frenchmen formed a military alliance in Céret, and in 1641 their combined forces defeated the Castilians at Montjuïc in Barcelona. It

seemed that the way was clear for a Catalonian free state under French protection. But French administration also restricted the Catalans' constitutional rights, causing resentment to grow once again.

When the civil war of the Frondes weakened France during the years around 1650, French troops withdrew from Catalonia, leaving Castile with a clear field. Barcelona fell in 1652, after a siege lasting a year.

For the next seven years resistance continued to flare up, especially in the mountains, until in 1659 Louis XIV and Philipp IV finally decided to divide the country in the Peace of the Pyrenees mentioned above. Castile ceded the northern parts of Catalonia – the provinces of Rosselló, Vallespir, Conflent, and Capcir, for which it had no great love – and consented to the division of the mountain region of Cerdanya. This severe blow to Catalonia was somewhat mitigated by the fact that Philipp IV's son, Carlos II, was scarcely in control of his empire, enabling Catalonia to achieve some freedom of action.

As a cultural entity Catalonia remained divided. Today, the regions that were split off are, along with Fenouillèdes, part of the Département of Pyrénées Orientales. Its northern boundary is marked impressively, by the Château at Salses in the immediate vicinity of the A9 motorway (illus. pp. 396–7).

Geographically speaking, the Catalonian area of southern France comprises the "Garden of Roussillon," the fertile basin on the Mediterranean shore through which the Rivers Têt and Tech flow, and the steeply rising northern part of the Pyrénées Méditerranéennes.

The sandy beaches of Rousillon stretching between the lagoons of Salses and St. Nazaire (Sant Nazarí), or the Costa Vermella – the "Red Coast" around Cerbère (Cervera) – are only a bare 50 km (c. 30 miles) as the crow flies from 2784-m (c. 9,100-ft.) high Mont Canigou. Myths cluster around this lofty mountain of southern France (illus. opposite and above). The terraces of the Aspres and the high erosion zones of Capcir and Cerdanya (1200- and 1600-m/c. 4,000- and 5,300-ft. high respectively) make their own distinctive contribution to the varied landscape.

Millions of years ago the sea still flowed here, until the land masses of the European base and the Iberian peninsula collided, throwing up the Pyrenees. Granite and limestone formations rose above the crystalline core of the mountain massif, forming narrow valleys and steep ravines, into which rivers made deep cuts. Today, thermal baths use the plenitude of water and mineral springs. The process of erosion, which has been in progress for thousands of years, on a number of occasions created bizarre stone formations such as the "organs" at Ille-sur-Têt (illus. p. 423). Extensive systems of caves invite the visitor to explore the subterranean world, which should only be done with an experienced guide. Here, stalactites and stalagmites form fairytale landscapes. One imagines one can discern the work of human hands, and sometimes even animals and plants, but this fairytale world has in fact been produced by calcareous deposits from the water, which accumulate extremely slowly.

Like the landscape, the plant life is also varied. In the flat zones close to the sea there exists the entire spectrum of cultivated plants, such as olives, almonds, figs, citrus and other fruit trees, and of course grapes. Outstanding local vines – the red Mourvèdre and the white Macabeu – have been developed in keeping with the terrain. Nor should the sweet wines of Rivesaltes, Banyuls, and Maury be forgotten. The slopes of the Pyrenees are clothed with forests of oak, beech, and coniferous trees, up to about 2300 m (c. 7,550 ft.), where plant life adapts to both sub-alpine and alpine conditions.

As in the Spanish part of the Pyrenees, chamois (mountain goats) and genets roam the forests. Wild boar, red deer, and roedeer can be seen – not only on restaurant menus. Vultures and eagles circle, and sometimes the capercaillie performs its mating display. Rarely, one of the few remaining wild brown bears will be spotted.

*The Côte Vermeille*

## Perpignan (Perpinyà)

Pulsating life, Mediterranean atmosphere, and multi-cultural variety: the Roman settlement of Villa Perpiniani is today one of the liveliest and most attractive towns in the South of France.

Its golden age was in the late Middle Ages when, located at the center of the "Rosselló," it was elevated to the seat of the Majorcan kings. This event – puzzling at first sight – came about as follows. Jaume I of Aragón (the conqueror) had divided his empire, which comprised half of the Mediterranean, between his two sons. The younger son, also baptized Jaume, was given the newly established kingdom of Majorca, to which, in addition to the Balearic Islands, were affiliated Montpelier and the provinces of the Rousillon.

As Jaume I of Majorca, the young ruler decided to have both Perpinyà and Palma extended as residences on a equal footing with each other. As a result, the city on the banks of the Têt was given its imposing palace, its new city wall, and its Gothic cathedral.

The Majorcan empire was not destined to last for long. As early as 1344, under Pere IV of Aragón, it was once again united with the Catalan-Aragonese crown. This did not, however, mean the loss of Perpinyà's importance. In 1349 the city received – even before Barcelona – a university, and building continued apace. The Castillet (Castellet), the impressive entrance that still provides a formidable gateway for the Old Town (illus. opposite) was built in 1368. The Llotja de Mar, the maritime exchange and commercial court, was inaugurated in 1397.

During the 15th and 16th centuries the metropolis continued to suffer from the wearying struggles between French and Catalan/Aragonese rulers. The great distress, which its inhabitants endured during this period – but also their resistance to it – earned for Perpignan epithets that were not always flattering: the French vilified it as a city of "rat eaters," while the Aragonese king honored it as *Fidelissima*, the most loyal.

The worst chapter in Perpinyà's history was yet to come, in the siege by Louis XIII, between 1640 and 1642, in which the city was systematically starved into submission before the eyes of the French king. Only the Treaty of the Pyrenees finally ended the lengthy and damaging power-struggle between the two rival empires.

Today only the massive buildings of the Old City bear witness to its warring past. The encircling fortifications that were laid out under Vauban in the late 17th century, have long since been replaced by the suburbs of modern Perpignan. Elegant shops nestle beneath the arcade galleries, the narrow streets are bordered with pavement cafés; here and there are smart squares where homage is paid to famous scions of the city, or to the *Sardana*, the Catalan national dance. The fortified exterior of the historical monuments contrasts pleasingly with the busy life in the medieval heart of the city.

A magnificent opening flourish is provided by the above-mentioned bulwark of the Castillet, which has become Perpignan's best-known landmark. The massive double tower with its battlements, its bays for pouring down pitch, and its belfry is made entirely of bricks. It was built in 1368, almost at the same time as the Bastille in Paris and the Fort St. André in Villeneuve-lès-Avignon. In 1483 a portal of Our Lady was added to make a city gate, and in 1542 the building was adapted to meet the requirements of modern fortifications.

In later ages the Castillet served as a prison, which was feared by all far and wide. But today its massive walls surround the Casa Païral: the museum of Catalan folk art. Costumes, furniture, and articles of daily use give a vivid overall picture of the traditions of Rousillon. A visit to the museum culminates in more than 142 steps that lead up the tower, from the top of which there is a fine view to be enjoyed of the immediate and more distant surroundings of Perpignan.

Directly below the Castillet the River Basse meanders between banks adorned with floral borders along its promenades. On the side facing inward toward the town the rue Louis Blanc, leading to the Place de la Loge, the heart of the city, comes into view. To the north is the idyllic Promenade des Platanes, its green areas adorned with fountains, mimosa bushes, and palms.

In fine weather the mountains of the Pyrenees beckon with all they have to offer: their foothills, the majestic Canigou (Canigó), the Albères to the south, and the Corbières to the north.

Let us begin our visit to Perpignan at the spot where the history of the Majorcan empire was written. The palace of the kings of Mallorca is at the southern edge of the city, forming part of the Baroque fortifications which were laid out by, among others, Vauban, the famous master builder of fortifications (illus. p. 402).

We start by passing through the massive citadel walls before approaching the regular medieval residence. In

Perpignan
*In the Old City*

contrast to the elaborate fortifications, the palace makes an almost intimate impression, but – together with the Almudaina and the Castell de Bellve in Palma de Majorca – it is the grandest public building of the short-lived Majorcan empire. The almost square, four-winged layout of the structure, with towers at the corners and sides, receives visitors (or repels attackers) from behind a moat and drawbridge with a tower-capped portal that alone gives access to the elegant inner courtyard. There, one ascends to the main floor via the two monumental flights of steps.

Opposite the entrance, the two-story palace chapel divides the wings; on the left are the king's apartments, on the right those of the queen. In the chapel, however, the division is different. The lower part, dedicated to Mary Magdalen, was reserved for the queen; the upper part, beneath the patriarchate of the Holy Cross, served as a oratory for the king. Both have cross-rib vaulting and figured keystones; frescoes and stained glass windows further contribute to the adornment of the rooms. However, the greater importance of the upper chapel is unmistakable: the ornate marble portal with its delicate Roussillonesque sculpture makes it quite clear to all.

The wings, which open onto the courtyard with broad arcades and galleries with pointed arches in the upper story, are also in places faced with marble. Behind them, in the southern part, is the great banqueting hall: the Sala de Mallorca. In the tradition of Catalan halls and dormitories, it is topped with wide transverse arches that support the tiled roof. The interior decor of the palace has been entirely lost. The retable in the upper chapel, dating from the 16th century, comes from a hamlet near Valcebollère. The palace was begun back in 1276, that is, at the same time that the Majorcan empire was established. For the chapel, the documents give the building date as 1295–1309. The site was fortified in 1344.

After the end of Majorca's independence the palace served as a secondary Aragonese residence, and in 1408 it housed the anti-pope Benedict XIII. What is remarkable is the unusually systematic distribution of space within the palace complex, which has no equal. The building may have served as a model as far afield as Avignon and perhaps even the Vatican.

To this day, it has not been possible to determine the place of the Palau dels Reis de Mallorca – or of the other Majorcan palaces – within the history of architecture.

Perpignan
*Le Castillet, 1368*

Returning to the hustle and bustle of the Old City, let us follow the rue Louis Blanc to the Place de la Loge (Plaça de la Llotja), taking its name from the market exchange of 1397. A fast food chain has a foothold here, in a place where fabrics were once traded before traveling the whole of the Mediterranean. By the end of the 14th century, the building was even more modest, comprising a hall, open on the ground floor, supported by arcades with pointed arches. The maritime court was situated above, along with the chapel. In 1540 the site was doubled in size in the style of the original building, which is on the corner of the rue des Marchands. The 16th-century weather-vane shaped like a ship is a reminder of the source of Catalan wealth.

The retable from the market exchange chapel is preserved in the Musée Hyacinthe Rigaud (Museu Jacint Rigau); this piece from the end of the 15th century has an iconographically noteworthy representation of the "seat of mercy": an image of the Trinity in which God the Father carries in his hands the crucifix crowned with the dove of the Holy Spirit (illus. p. 404, top right). The scene is

framed by the Old Testament prophets and the insignia of the evangelists, complete with banderoles. In the lower part of the painting, on the right, is the original Llotja of Perpignan, and behind it the skyline of Collioure, the harbor, with its many towers. Citizens and carriers go about their business, and St. Elmo rescues a sailing ship.

Although the master who created this altarpiece is unknown, he carried out the instructions of his employers – the two consuls François Pinya and Jean Garau – in a manner both poetic and faithful to history: Perpignan, the maritime trading metropolis, bows to heavenly and earthly justice. The museum also contains outstanding works by the artist from whom it takes its name, for example the wonderful self-portrait with turban which shows the painter, born in Perpignan, at the age of 39 (illus. p. 404, top left).

The town hall adjoining the exchange dates originally from the 13th century, but was substantially rebuilt, apart from one portico, in the 17th century (illus. p. 405, top). Three strange bronze arms jutting out from the façade

catch the eye. They are said to refer to the three classes from whose ranks the five consuls of the town council were elected; they probably solely served as torch brackets. Inside, only the Salle des Mariages has survived from the late Middle Ages, and a fine 15th-century wooden ceiling is preserved. In the inner courtyard of 1679, Aristide Maillol's famous bronze *La Méditerranée*, a reflective female nude in the neoclassical manner, is on display. Another work, the *Venus* of 1928, by this artist, who came from Banyuls, also adorns the square in front of the town hall.

The third great historical building flanking the Place de la Loge, is the Palais de la Députation (Palau de la Diputació or Generalitat), the former seat of the Catalan government. Built in 1448, it clearly shows, with its lavish portal frame and elegant triforium windows, the influence of the style of Catalan-Aragonese secular architecture. To build it, valuable materials were obtained from the best quarries in the empire: Montjuïc near Barcelona and Girona. A short detour via the rue des Fabriques leads to one of Perpignan's few preserved grand town houses, the

Perpignan
*Market exchange, begun 1397, extended 1450*

**TOP LEFT:**

*Hyacinthe Rigaud*
*Self-portrait with turban*
*c. 1698*
*Perpignan*
*Musée Hyacinthe Rigaud*

**TOP RIGHT:**

*Hyacinthe Rigaud*
*Picture of the Trinity*
*End of the 15th century*
*Perpignan*
*Musée Hyacinthe Rigaud*
*Beneath the group of figures the*
*original market exchange of*
*Perpignan is seen, and behind it*
*the skyline of Collioure, the city's*
*harbor. On the left, St. Elmo*
*rescues a sailing ship in distress.*

**BOTTOM:**

*Perpignan*
*Musée Hyacinthe Rigaud*
*View of the exhibition room*

Maison Julia with its innner courtyard and galleries dating from the 14th century.

Just a short way to the northeast of the Place de la Loge is the church of St. Jean (Sant Joan), which was elevated to a cathedral in 1601 (illus. p. 406). The foundation stone of the building, originally designed with three naves, was laid jointly by King Sanç I of Majorca and the bishop of Elne in 1324. Continuation of work on the building was, however, prevented by turbulent power struggles and the eventual collapse of the Majorcan empire. It was not until 1433 that a decision was taken to proceed with the building of a spacious, single-nave vaulted church with side chapels. Only the chancel with the main apse and two smaller additional apses were completed according to the original design. It was consecrated on 16 May 1509.

Notwithstanding the lengthy period during which it was built, the spatial impression made by the interior is one of splendor and unity. Among the items of furniture two stand out: the marble retable by the Burgundian sculptor Claude Perret (begun in 1618) and the retable of the Vierge de Magrana in the right-hand transept, dating from the late 15th century. Unfortunately the central figure of the latter, the virgin with the pomegranate, who gave her name to the altar, has been replaced by a modern statue. The organ casing of 1504, with scenes of the Baptism of Christ and Herod's feast, is worth a closer look. The deepest reverence is reserved for the figure in wood, captivating in its realism, of the *Devot Crist*, the humble Christ, from the beginning of the 14th century, which in the literature is attributed to a Rhenish artist. This moving piece of sculpture accompanies the faithful on their processions through the streets of Perpignan.

The passageway beneath the organ leads to the Romanesque chapel of Notre-Dame-dels-Correchs (Mare de Déu del Còrrecs), which was part of the earlier building on this site, St. Jean-le-Vieux (Sant Joan el Vell), to the north of the cathedral, which was consecrated in 1025. Thanks to the initiative of the collector Fréderic Marés and to the generosity of the municipality of Palma de Majorca, the sarcophagus of the Majorcan King Sanç I was located here in 1971, confirming Perpignan to be the last resting place for the dynasty that was of such significance for Roussillon (illus. p. 406, top left). The fine portal of the old St. John's church, in the middle of which a delicately chiseled representation of Christ enthroned with angelic figures can be seen, dates from c. 1220 (illus. p. 406, bottom left). It was evidently part of a larger ensemble, of which only a few figures of apostles and evangelists of varying quality have survived. The Maestá is attributed to the workshop of Raimond de Bianya, of which there is evidence in many locations in Roussillon. Among the cloister buildings the chapterhouse stands out, an irregular room built above a single pillar. Guillem Sagrera, probably the most resourceful master builder of Catalan Gothic, is said to have been involved in its construction.

The *Campo Santo* to the south of the cathedral is one of the most important medieval cemeteries in France. The early 14th-century four-winged site contains a number of lavishly sculpted wall graves, where clerics, noblemen, and wealthy citizens set up monuments to themselves. The common people, in contrast, were buried directly in the ground. The cemetery chapel was built between 1382 and 1389, and later served as the university banqueting hall. The *Campo Santo* was taken out of use during the Revolution, and its western flank was destroyed in 1826. Painstaking restoration of the site was completed in 1990.

Our route now leads through the lively Arab quarter to the eastern outskirts of the city, where the single-nave church of St. Jacques (Sant Jaume) stands enthroned on the slope of the city's Puig (hill). It was begun in the second half of the 13th century, and is thus, after St. Jean, the second-oldest church in Perpignan. It is the one with the greatest wealth of tradition. Its history is inseparably bound up with the guilds of the gardeners and cloth weavers who settled here, close to the city wall. They had not inconsiderable financial resources at their disposal, and in order to safeguard the pastoral care of their members they established lay brotherhoods, who founded chapels in St. Jacques and devoted themselves to charity work. The most famous of them is the "Confrèrie de la Sanch" (Brotherhood of Blood), registered in 1416, which was dedicated to the spiritual care and burial of prisoners

Top:
Perpignan
Town hall, 13th–17th centuries
*Bronze sculptures on the façade*

Bottom:
*Good Friday procession by the "Confrérie de la Sanch"*

TOP LEFT:
Perpignan
St. Jean
Chapel of Notre-Dame-dels-
Correchs, sarcophagus of the
Majorcan King Sanç I (d. 1324).
Detail, 14th century

TOP RIGHT:
Perpignan
St. Jean
Console with the head of a
Moorish king (beneath the organ),
end of 15th century

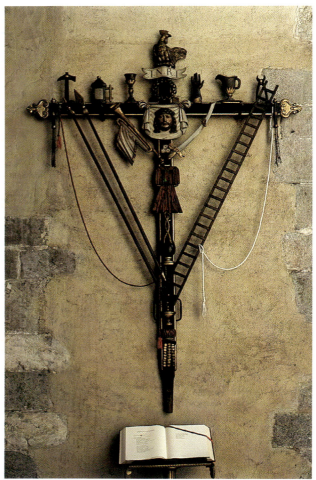

BOTTOM LEFT:
Perpignan
St. Jean
Portal of St. Jean-le-Vieux, 1220

BOTTOM RIGHT:
Perpignan
St. Jean
The Cross of the "Improperis" with
the instruments of the Passion of
Christ heads the annual procession
of the "Sanch"

who had been condemned to death. Its members gathered on the night of Maundy Thursday, on the eve of Good Friday, and set out on an emotionally charged procession reenacting the Passion of Our Lord. Groups of flagellants and citizens, incognito beneath their black cloaks with hoods, the *caperutxa*, followed the *misteris*, heavy wooden Passion groups, which required the greatest effort by the participants to carry them through the narrow streets (illus. p. 405, bottom), accompanied by the sound of drums and an iron bell, and led by the *regidor* carrying the huge cross of the brotherhood, donated in 1536. *Goigs*, ritual Catalan songs, were performed at intervals. For centuries this macabre spectacle cast its spell over penitents from the entire region. Excesses during the nocturnal procession were not uncommon. The procession was moved to Good Friday in 1770, and had to finish by four o'clock in the afternoon.

After this sober performance by the "Sanch," a change of scene is welcome. The La Miranda garden adjoining St. Jacques provides an enjoyable look at the plant life of the *garrigue*, a kind of heath. If we then turn again toward the inner city, the Science Museum awaits us at the Place de la Font Neuve. It is housed in the Sagarriga Palace (15th and 18th centuries), and contains, in addition to the natural history collections, an Egyptian sarcophagus. The historical Casa Pams (architect Petersen, rue Emile Zola) is also worth looking at. The municipal library is located there, with noteworthy manuscripts and incunabula.

For travelers or lovers of surrealism our walk ends at the "center of the universe." That was the title given by Salvador Dalí to Perpignan railway station after experiencing a "cosmogonic ecstasy" here on September 19, 1963: "It was at this precise point that Spain turned around its own axis when the continents drifted apart and formed the Bay of Biscay. If this phenomenon had not occurred we would have been pushed down to Australia and would now be living among kangaroos, which would be the most horrible thing in the world." Two years later Dali's dream was to give rise to a visionary painting (illus. above).

*Salvador Dalí*
*Perpignan railway station,*
*1963, oil on canvas,*
*295 × 406 cm*
*Cologne, Museum Ludwig*

## The Fenouillèdes, the Cathar Castles and Heresy in the South of France.

Until the Treaty of the Pyrenees, the Fenouillèdes (Fenolleda), the "fennel country," with its austerely beautiful landscape, was also a Catalan province. Its history goes back very much further than the Middle Ages. It was in Tautavel (Talteüll) that bones from one of the oldest human beings in Europe were found: the skull of "Tautavel Man," who died c. 450,000 years ago; a replica can be seen in the local museum of prehistory.

But the breathtaking gorges and craggy cliffs, which so characterize the countryside that lays to the west of Perpignan, are almost more thrilling and impressive than the prehistoric bones.

The most beautiful are the Gorges de Galamus (Galamús) to the north of St. Paul-de-Fenouillet (Sant Pau de Fenollet) (illus. top), where the waters of the Agly have cut a path through the stone for over 5 km (c. 3 miles). In places it is several hundred meters deep and completely inaccessible.

In view of the craggy cliff faces, it seems almost miraculous that men were able, in 1890, to build a road here. It must have been a similarly bold project to build a hermitage at the entrance to the ravine, which, as early as the 8th century, provided a retreat for hermits. It later became the property of the Benedictine monastery of St. Paul-de-Fenouillet, of which an 11th-century chapterhouse with a cupola (Le Chapitre, Lo Capitol) survives. Before leaving St. Paul (and neighboring Maury) be sure to sample the wine.

Montségur, Peyrepertuse, Quéribus, Puivert – the Cathar castles of the Midi – clinging like eagles' nests to the gray-brown cliffs – are relics of a period of grave crisis which the South of France underwent during the 12th and 13th centuries (illus. pp. 410–11). They are symbols of the harsh sufferings of a religious community caught between the millstones of world history.

What began as a naive reform movement tragically ended with the systematic extermination of the "heretics." Thousands of people were burned at the stake, and whole towns, such as Béziers in 1209, were pillaged and threatened with burning. It was by no means only Cathars who were put to death.

Crusades and the Inquisition – instigated with rare unanimity by both the Pope and the French crown – left scorched earth behind them, with the result that both the clergy and the common people were compelled to flee into hiding or into exile.

The formidable strongholds, which were enthroned almost inaccesibly on the rocky spurs of the foothills of the Pyrenees, often gave the outlaws natural protection that lasted for decades. In those unfeeling walls and cramped dungeons they eked out their meager lives, sustained by their faith.

Today, for all the romanticism of the setting, one cannot repress a slight shudder. Quéribus and Peyrepertuse (Peirapertusa) in particular still give a striking picture of the unforgiving existence in that period of the high Middle Ages (illus. p. 411, top).

TOP:
*The Gorges de Galamus*

BOTTOM:
*Prehistoric hunting scene in Tautavel museum*

It all began with entirely justified criticisms of the machinations of the Catholic clergy. In other cases, for example those of the itinerant preachers and the mendicant orders, the critics were successfully taken into the bosom of the Church, and used for propaganda purposes; the Cathar movement, however, drove its members into heresy, making them traitors to Christian dogma. The Cathars' faith was based on radical adherence to the principles revealed in the Gospels, a ban on killing (and a related refusal to eat food derived from animals), complete sexual abstinence, and the commandments to work and to fast.

Their philosophy took its bearings from dualism, the idea that the world, imperfect as it was, could not possibly be the work of a single Creator, and therefore combined two antagonistic principles within itself. "Good" existed, but the realm of the spirit, created by God, was confronted with "evil," the work of the Devil. The only solution, they believed, was to become "pure" and conquer evil through strict obedience to the rules of the New Testament.

The name "Cathar," derived from the Greek katharós (pure), indicated their striving for a simple, pure way of life (the epithet "Albigensian" came into use later; it referred to Albi, the community's main center.) The path to be taken by the Cathar believer in the quest for inner purity led via baptism, the *consolamentum*, to the status of a *parfait* (perfect one). The believers had to honor him as a kind of priest and to ask for his blessing, the *melioramentum* by bowing three times.

These ideas that sound harmless enough to us today were pure dynamite at the time. By acknowledging only one sacrament – baptism – the Cathars were violating the principles of Christian doctrine.

However, what proved to be even more explosive was a different train of thought: since the earthly world belonged to the Devil, techniques of intimidation used by the Church – otherwise extremely effective – lost their power. Faced with the daily "experience of Hell," the Cathars were not to be frightened by the "Day of Judgment." Accordingly, they were not prepared to go along with the usual ritual of indulgences, or to pay church taxes. This involved wholly secular strategies and hierarchies, which the Church could not possibly permit to be flouted.

But it had long since ceased to be a matter of questions of faith. The fertile lands at the foot of the Pyrenees, Languedoc and Aquitaine, had always been a thorn in the flesh of the French crown. The history and culture of the region linked it more closely to the Aragon empire than to the Île de France. Even so, it had initially adopted a wait-and-see attitude toward the deviants in southern France, leaving the resolution of the conflict to the Pope. When, in 1208, the papal legate Pierre de Castelnau lost his life under mysterious circumstances in the vicinity of St. Gilles, existing tensions escalated. A territorial war began, encouraged by Innocent III as a crusade against the heretics. The feudal barons of northern France were dubbed Knight Crusaders, and joined in this "Holy War," having been promised forgiveness of sins and the heretics'

*Vineyards with Roman acqueduct near Ansignan*

TOP:
Montségur
*Le Pog (rock) with fortress dating from 1204*

BOTTOM:
Fanjeaux
*Disc-shaped cross, 13th century*

property. By 1209 Béziers and Carcassonne had been brutally conquered, in 1210 the fortresses at Minerve, Terme, and Puivert fell. In Minerve 140 Cathars went to the stake, throwing themselves – allegedly of their own accord – into the flames.

Led by Simon de Montfort, the Crusaders continued to make their way through the country, murdering and burning as they went. In 1211 they took Lavaur, fought for Castelnaudary, and besieged Toulouse for the first time – without success. In 1213 at the castle of Muret the issue was momentarily decided when Pere II, the Aragon king, fell in hand-to-hand fighting, and his troops retreated. French supremacy in the Midi was thus established. Simon de Montfort died, however, in 1218 when Toulouse was again besieged, and his son fell foul of the Crusaders' pragmatic attitude. Since they had been granted indulgences in return for only 40 days of military service, they returned home to northern France immediately at the end of this period, the very moment when the provincial capital was under siege. For a short time the Cathars and their allies the Occitan princes gained a breathing space. But then Louis VIII came to the throne. He was a relentless fighter whose ambition was to extend his kingdom as far as the Mediterranean. In 1226 he invaded the south in a bloody campaign that ended in Meaux in 1229 with the surrender of Count Raymond VII of Toulouse.

The political situation in the south of France was thus clarified, the relative independence of the provinces broken once and for all. The conflict with the Cathars continued to smoulder, however, leading Gregor IX to set up the Inquisition, an institution which was to be a weighty embodiment of the power of the Church into the distant future. Its henchmen were the Dominicans, who were given responsibility for the persecution and burning of heretics. This now took place intermittently, but no less dramatically, since the Cathars, following the Treaty of Meaux, had withdrawn to inaccessible strongholds.

The names of the castles at Fenouillèdes, Puilaurens, Peyrepertuse, and Quéribus stand for the legendary struggle of the rebels to resist the power of the Church; the only opposition offered was the "spiritual purity" of the castles' occupants.

By 1244, after the conquest of Montségur, which had withstood the siege of the royal armies for over a year, the writing was on the wall. The supposedly impregnable fortress, to which 400 to 500 men, women, and children had retreated, was conquered due to treachery. The occupants had to either confess their "errors" or go to the stake. At least 200 Cathars chose death. According to tradition, only four *parfaits* managed to escape. They are said to have rescued the legendary treasure of the Cathars and to have hidden it in a hitherto unknown place.

TOP:
*The Cathar castle at Peyrepertuse, early 12th and second half of 13th century*

BOTTOM:
*The Cathar castle at Puivert, 14th century*

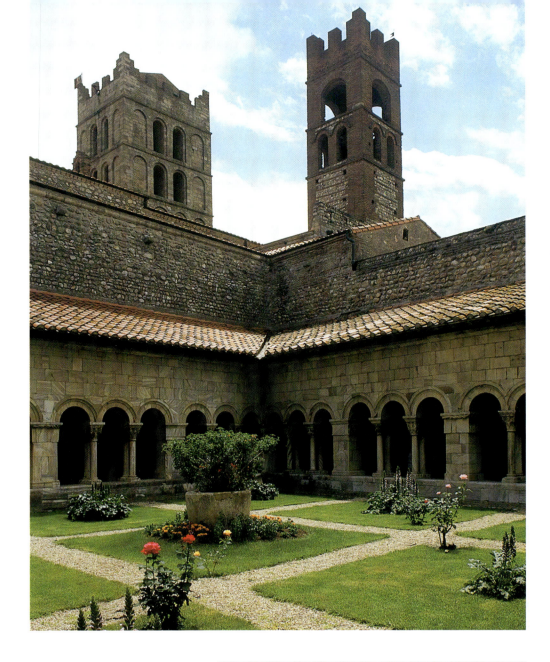

TOP:
Elne
*Cathedral*
*View of the cloister, after 1172*

BOTTOM:
St. Martin-de-Fenollar
*Frescoes with scenes from the*
*apocalypse and the life of Christ,*
*12th century*

## From Perpignan to the Albères

After these grisly tales, some may wish to visit the sandy beaches of Canet-Plage, St-Cyprien-Plage, or Argelès-Plage. Others may want to go on a tour of the beginnings of medieval architectural sculpture. In the region to the south of Perpignan, there is a wealth of venerable abbeys from the 9th, 10th and 11th centuries which are found in any work of art history because of their early stone sculptures.

Every scholar is familiar with Cabestany, on the outskirts of Perpignan, thanks to the famous "Master of Cabestany," who was active in north Catalonia in the second half of the 12th century and whose works are to be found in the great museums of the world (see panel box p. 84). Fortunately, one of his works is preserved *in situ*, namely the unique Tympanum of Our Lady, which today can be seen inside the church of Notre-Dame des Anges (illus. opposite top). It shows, from right to left: the Assumption of the Virgin Mary, Christ giving his blessing next to the Virgin, doubting Thomas with the donation of the girdle, and finally the Raising of the Virgin Mary. The scenes are depicted next to one another in a small space, and framed by angels. The characteristic style of the Master of Cabestany can be clearly seen in the faces: their bulging eyeballs, the extended fingers, and the two-dimensional treatment of the folds. Notwithstanding this occasional slight clumsiness in the figurative style, the tympanum is a masterpiece of Romanesque sculpture, and obviously modeled on works of sarcophagus sculpture. Cabestany has a second important artist to call its own, the Troubador Guillem de Cabestany (c. 1162–1212) who became a literary figure as a "martyr to love."

As "Illiberis" – Hannibal's military camp – Elne (Elna) has, since the 4th century A.D., borne the name of Helena, the mother of the Roman Emperor Constantine. This town at the heart of Roussillon was elevated to a bishopric in 571, a privilege which it was obliged to cede to Perpignan, along with the relics of St. Eulalia and St. Julia, in 1602.

The appeal of the Romanesque cathedral and its cloister, and the impact of its artistic treasures remain unaffected by this change. We approach the church, situated on a hill, via steep steps which give a view of its fortified façade. It is flanked on the right-hand side only by a tower dating from the 11th century, when the church was built. The brick tower on the left was added later. Behind the portico are three naves pointing east, but no transept. On the south side six chapels from the late Gothic period have been added. The high altar was consecrated in 1069, which means that by then work on the chancel with its three apses was at least well advanced. Regarding the interior, two items stand out: the grave of Bishop Ramom Costa (d. 1310) in the first chapel, and the St. Michael retable, the work of a Catalan master, end of the 14th century, in the third chapel.

However, the jewel of the former cathedral of Elne was, and still is, the cloister with its fascinating capitals (illus. top). Even though it took over 200 years to build it, a visible effort was made to achieve an aesthetic unity

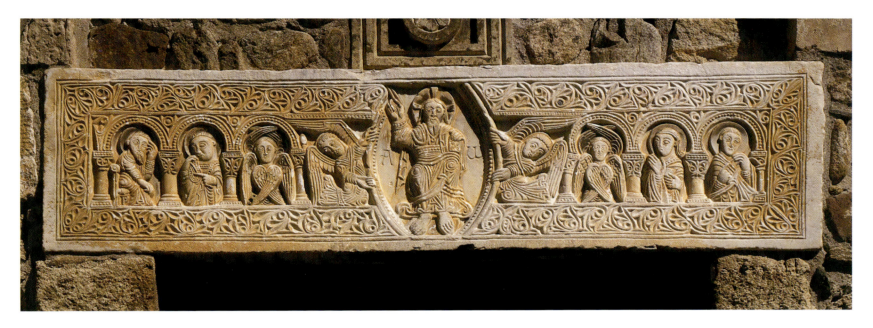

between its four wings. Thus, each side is open, with four three-fold arcades separated by three massive pillars. The almost unadorned arches rest on a wide variety of double columns which support delicately sculpted capitals and imposts.

The south wing, begun under Bishop Guillem Jordà (d. 1186), is the oldest. Here, in precious blue-veined marble from Céret, scenes from the Old Testament are depicted, along with the life of St. Peter, including the famous "Quo vadis" scene in which the apostle encounters the risen Christ. All manner of wild animals, sirens, griffins and lions, along with men's and women's heads, complete the repertoire.

The later wings took up these same images or else, in the case of the eastern part, translated them into Gothic formal language.

Three more "places of pilgrimage" for lovers of Romanesque sculpture are found in the immediate neighborhood of Elne: (Sant Genís de Fontanes), St.

André-de-Sorède (Sant Andreu de Sureda), and St. Martin-de-Fenollar (Sant Martí de Fenollar). The church of St. Michael at St. Genis-des-Fontaines can claim to possess what is perhaps the oldest surviving sculpted lintel in Christendom, and thus to stand at the beginning of the splendid development of the figured portal (illus. p. 413, bottom). This unique piece made of white marble is worked in a two-dimensional decorative style, reminiscent of ivory carving. Christ is depicted in his aureole, carried by angels, flanked by six apostles separated by delicate little columns. Thanks to its inscription, this piece, the significance of which in the history of art can hardly be exaggerated, can be dated 1019–20. What we do not know, however, is whether at that time the relief was already located in its present position or served as part of an altar.

Accordingly, the church and the cloister of the abbey, which was founded in 819, and rebuilt in 981 following onslaughts by the Arabs, also deserve a visit. It should be noted, however, that parts of the attractive cloister are copies of recent origin, for some of the arcades and the well went to the United States in 1924 when the monastery was closed down. Today they can be seen in the Cloisters Museum in New York and the museum in Philadelphia.

Hardly more than a stone's throw away is St. André-de-Sorède, which has a prominent lintel similar to that at St. Genis but which seems to be the work of a different hand (illus. p. 413, center). Here too one should look closely at the architecture, for the 12th century building has retained important parts of its Carolingian predecessor.

The third "place of pilgrimage" is the church of St. Martin-de-Fenollar, situated beyond Le Boulou, which is, however, more famous for its outstanding chancel frescoes rather than for its architecture. The frescoes, in gleaming red and yellow, depict the life of Christ with unusual freshness, and in the sphere of the apse show the 24 elders of the Apocalypse with the all-powerful Pantocrator above them (illus. p. 412, bottom).

OPPOSITE:
*Tour de Madeloc, 14th century*

ABOVE:
*Collioure*

*Port Vendres*

Leaving Elne and proceeding toward the sea, one reaches the legendary region of Argelès (Argelers), where the Greek hero Hercules is said to have dropped anchor with nine ships and founded the city. Soon after this seaside resort, with its long sandy beach, the landscape begins to change.

Here the foothills of the Pyrenees – more precisely the Albères – meet the sea, creating the picturesque landscape of the Côte Vermeille (Costa Vermella, the Red Coast). At the turn of the century its mild climate, and not least the excellent wine that grows on its slopes, once again attracted painters. The blazing sunlight and the bright blue sky are regarded as the impetus behind Fauvism, a movement which worked with the contrast of expressive colors and was significant for 20th-century art.

Collioure (Cotlliure), in particular, has to this day preserved an appealing atmosphere of both tradition and avant-garde. Today artists still mingle with tourists in this fishing village (illus. pp. 414–15), which was founded by the Phoenicians and which has been fought over many times during the course of history. One thing has lasted above everything else: anchovies. These salted sardines are considered by many to be the best found on the coast.

Some way inland, there is a unique view of the Côte Vermeille and Roussillon (illus. p. 414) from the Tour de Madeloc, an Aragonese defensive tower, which has also been called the "Devil's Tower." It can also be reached from Collioure via a footpath.

Those traveling by car should return to the harbor of Port Vendres (illus. above) or, better still, head for Banyuls-sur-Mer (Banyuls de la Marenda) where the wine, which grows on slate hills, was held in high regard – even by Louis XIV. Apart from the sea-water aquarium, it is above all the personality of Aristide Maillol that is associated with this last major stop before the present-day political boundary. This important Catalan sculptor was born here in 1861, and also died here in 1944 following a car accident. The house where he was born, a little way outside the village, is being extended to contain a museum. The memory of the great artist is kept alive in particular by the stone war memorial behind the town hall (illus. opposite bottom).

Near Cerbère we reach the border to Spain.

TOP:
Banyuls-sur-Mer
Aristide Maillol
*La Méditerranée*, 1905

BOTTOM:
Aristide Maillol
*War memorial in Banyuls-sur-Mer*

## The Vallespir

At the busy town of Le Boulou (El Voló) – seen from the highway – we begin the journey through the Vallespir, the valley of the Tech, which winds its way along the edge of the Pyrenees. Here there is a fairly rapid transition from the mild regions close to the sea, which provide ideal conditions for fruit growing, to the cooler high mountains with their alpine vegetation.

Our first stop is Céret, the home of cherries, which ripen there already in April (illus. above). Situated at the foot of the often snow-capped Canigou, molded by the bright light, and famous for its mild climate, this attractive town was regarded by artists back at the beginning of the 20th century as an ideal place to stay. The first to settle here, in 1909, was the Catalan sculptor Manolo Hugué (1872–1945), who was soon followed by Picasso, Georges Braque, Juan Gris, Raoul Dufy, the poet Max Jacob, and later Marc Chagall. What they were looking for was the clear light which produces sharply outlined forms, the sun that not only warms but also makes all colors gleam with unusual radiance. It is therefore not surprising that the Cubist movement, which draws on these effects, came to full fruition here.

To this day Céret has retained a breath of the avant-garde and the bohemian world, not only in the Museum of Modern Art, established in 1950, where, in addition to works by the above-named artists, postwar Catalan art is also on display. Pau Gargallo, Joan Miró and Antoni Tapies are represented there, as are the artists of the younger generation such as Joan Brossa and Perejaume.

But every kind of art and artist is also encountered in the attractive narrow streets of the Old Town and the boulevards lined with plane trees. The townspeople dedicated the memorial *Sardane de la Paix* to Picasso; Maillol created a war memorial for them.

Of the historical monuments, the church of St. Pierre stands out. It is basically Romanesque, but was so severely damaged by a blizzard in 1734 that it had to be substantially rebuilt.

Beside it, water bubbles up from the Gothic "Well of Nine Streams." But it is almost impossible to imagine that this town – like the entire Vallespir – was once completely cut off from the major traffic routes. That is the reason why Catalan customs such as the dance of the Sardana (see panel box p. 159) have retained such vigor here to this day (illus. p. 136).

Before leaving Céret there is a "work of the devil" to be seen: the Pont du Diable (illus. right, bottom), famous for its bold construction. It spans the Tech with a single arch measuring 45 m (c. 148 ft.) at a height of 22 m (c. 72 ft.). This magnificent edifice was built in the 14th century by order of the Majorcan king.

The seaside resort of Els Banys d'Arles was renamed Amélie-les-Bains in 1840, in honor of the French queen Amélie. Its sulfurous springs had already cured the ailments of the Romans, whose thermal baths have been restored with great care. The large vaulted hall with its swimming pool measuring 16 × 8.40 m (c. 52 × 28 ft.) is particularly impressive. The modern baths are popular with the older members of the community. A good walker can explore the nearby ravines of the Mondony and the attractive village of Palalda on the other side of the river which is also worth a visit. For the culture of everyday Catalan life, visit the Musée des Arts et Traditions.

A very different atmosphere awaits the visitor in Arles-sur-Tech (Arles). This historic town grew up around the Benedictine abbey founded in 778, which dominates it. In the 9th century Bishop Arnulfe procured for the monastery church the remains of St. Abdon and St. Senen, two Kurdish princes who had died in 250 as martyrs in battle with lions (illus. right, top). They were expected to provide protection from wild beasts and natural disasters. Their bare bones were transported to the Tech by donkey.

The church with three naves was founded in the 11th century, vaulted in the 12th century. The building of the Gothic cloister can be dated between 1261 and 1303. But the best item is the Romanesque tympanum with Christ enthroned in an aureole, which illustrates yet again the quality of early Catalan architectural sculpture.

A modest sarcophagus to the left of the entrance is of far greater interest. The so-called Santa Tomba, probably dating from the 4th century, each year fills up inexplicably with several hundred liters of fresh water believed to possess miraculous powers; the knight Guillem Gaucelm, for example, is said to have been cured of an affliction to his face, as depicted on his tombstone.

A natural miracle of a different kind awaits us only 2 km (c. 1 mile) away from Arles in the Gorges de la Fou. Here the tributary of the Tech has cut a breathtakingly narrow bed into the rock – said to be the narrowest ravine in the world. The path leads down over 250 m (820 ft.) to the raging torrent; one is grateful to be able cross the gloomy Klamm, with its overall length of 1739 m (c. 5,700 ft.), by a safe bridge. The waters of the Fou have created other effects: a labyrinth of subterranean caves with which the entire mountain massif is riddled.

Anyone continuing in the direction of the Spanish border and Camprodon, first passes the former smugglers' paradise of Prats-de-Mollo (Prats-de-Molló), where the inhabitants have always been famous for their rebellious pro-Catalan attitude. The town wall and Fort Lagarde, built by Vauban and sited menacingly above the valley, recalls those days.

We now stay in the French part of Catalonia, and turn our attention to Mont Canigou and its surroundings.

TOP:
Arles-sur-Tech
*Abbey church*
*Mural painting on the inside wall of the church façade (detail),*
*12th century*

BOTTOM:
Céret
*Pont du Diable, 14th century*

TOP:
Serrabone
*Former Augustinian "Canons'
Priory" of Notre-Dame, 2nd half
of the 11th century*

CENTER:
Serrabone
*Former Augustinian "Canons'
Priory" of Notre-Dame, capital in
the cloister*

BOTTOM:
Serrabone
*Former Augustinian "Canons'
Priory" of Notre-Dame
Choir loft (detail), after the
mid-12th century*

## Around Mont Canigou: Conflent, Aspres, and Fenouillèdes

The Canigou (Canigó) shares with Montserrat the description of "Holy Mountain of the Catalans." Unlike the "serrated mountain" in the hinterland of Barcelona, its fascination does not derive to the same extent from its craggy ridges. Its slopes are milder to begin with, ascending from soft green fields and extensive fruit plantations, which in the spring are like a sea of blossom.

Only above this gently contrasting lowland do the treeless flanks and the well-proportioned peaks of the Canigou – which remain covered in snow until well into spring – tower up (illus. p. 422). At 2785 m (c. 9,100 ft.), it not only dominates Roussillon, it also looks across the Pyrenees far into Old Catalonia. Every year, on the evening of Midsummer's Day, June 24, bright fires are lit on its slopes, giving it an air of mystery.

Jacint Verdaguer, the great 19th-century Catalan poet, dedicated his most important work, *Canigó* (published 1886), to Mont Canigou. It became the national tribute of the French Catalans to this majestic mountain.

The Canigou is a mountain with a history. Its fascination was so great that as long ago as 1285 the Aragonese King Pere II dared to climb it. At the beginning of the 18th century trigonometrical measurements were made from its summit, an achievement for which the geographer Francesc Aragó was made a member of the Académie Française. It is also alleged that its iron ore deposits interfere with aircraft instruments and that a number of fliers have lost their lives as a result.

Coming from Amélie-les-Bains, we begin our tour of the Canigou at Serrabone (Serrabona) – or alternatively, if one chooses to arrive from Perpignan or Prades, at Ille-sur-Têt (Illa). The landscape around Serrabone displays the austerely romantic character of the Aspres, the rocky foothills of the Pyrenees.

After a twisting journey through the ravines of the Boulès we arrive at the former Augustinian priory, secluded in a holm-oak coppice, which, with its slate walls, seems to be part of the mountain landscape (illus. opposite, top). The rustic exterior is deceptive. The almost unadorned walls conceal unique evidence of Romanesque architecture and sculpture.

The priory has a complex history. A church here, consecrated to the Virgin Mary, is first mentioned in 1069, but the development of the monastery did not begin until 1082 when at the instigation of the Viscount of Cerdagne and the Master of Corsavy 16 Augustinian canons settled in the inaccessible wilderness.

The community grew quickly, with the result that the north aisle, the transept, the apse, and the open south gallery were soon added to the 11th century nave. Consecration was in 1151, and the priory enjoyed high repute down to the 14th century. Then moral laxity appears to have set in, for numerous scandals are mentioned in the archives. In 1592 the monastery, which by then had been almost completely abandoned, was de-consecrated.

But let us return to the golden age of Serrabone and enter the abbey via the former scriptorium. From here we come to the south gallery, where the visitor is immediately captivated by the magnificent harmony of art and nature. Through the apertures of the Romanesque arcades one looks – as the canons once did – with fascination at the untouched landscape. However, one should also note the capitals, where all manner of imaginative animal forms disport themselves, and by no means peaceably (illus. opposite center). Lions devour their prey licking their paws, and griffins and eagles hurl themselves into the air. This animal world includes virtually no human beings, let alone biblical characters.

But Serrabone's major attraction is to be seen as soon as one enters the interior of the church, and is confronted with the three-arched choir loft which splits the nave (illus. opposite bottom, and below). Originally, however, it was in a different place and was moved here in the 17th or the 19th century.

We know little regarding its actual function, but even without this knowledge the high quality of this work of art is plain to see. Made of polished pink marble, the choir loft, in two sections, is most sumptuously adorned with sculpture; the façade is covered with reliefs – plant ornaments for the arcade arches, Christian motifs at the spandrels. The edifice is topped with an elegant toothed frieze. The capitals of the columns and pilasters, on which the struggle between Good and Evil, Christians and heathen, is fought out, are particularly fine and

Serrabone
*Former Augustinian "Canons' Priory" of Notre-Dame*
*Choir loft*

Mont Canigou

impressive. Once again animals and fabulous beings are used to illustrate ethical themes. The Christian faith, for example, may be represented by the stag which is under attack from a centaur, representing the heathen. The monkey symbolizes spiritual pride and the work of the Devil, held in check by an angel's smile alone. The only biblical scene that can be interpreted with certainty again shows a struggle: this time the archangel Michael attacking the dragon.

Whoever chiseled these scenes into the precious stone had a complex view of the world, along with the ability to illustrate his nightmares with great skill. To some scholars, the consummate artistry in the graphic depiction of animals has suggested the influence of Arabian art, which could have come, for instance, via Córdoba. Be that as it may, a close connection may be presumed to exist with the architectural capitals in the nearby monastery of St. Michel-de-Cuxa (St. Miquel de Cuixà), which show similar motifs and a related formal language.

At the exit from Ille-sur-Têt (Illa), where the mountain landscape yields to the plains, nature has once again

pulled out all the stops. The sandstone cliffs of the *orgues* tower up like gigantic organ pipes into the usually blue sky (illus. p. 223). They originated in the tertiary period, when the thrust of the Pyrenees met the basin of the Têt and layers of stone of varying degrees of hardness collided. Thousands of years of erosion produced these very strange sandstone formations. Of course, the common people have given each one a name as a way of bringing their enchanted world under control. They saw sibyls and fairies, but also such prosaic objects as chimneys. Ille has also, of course, culture to offer. No fewer than four museums await the visitor, including the Centre d'Art Sacré and the Fire Brigade Museum.

Like Ille, Prades (Prada) is also situated amid extensive fruit plantations. Apricots and peaches in particular thrive splendidly in the mild climate of the Têt valley. Apart from fruit, it is music that determines the character of this busy little town.

In 1939 the Catalan cellist Pau (Pablo) Casals settled in Prades to escape the repressive Franco dictatorship. In 1950 he founded a classical music festival, which to this day draws numerous music lovers to Prades and to the

nearby monastery of St. Michel-de-Cuxa. International film festivals and the Catalan summer university likewise attract thousands of visitors.

From here it is not far to the attractive mountain village of Eus, where the village houses nestle closely against the granite slopes. Turning in a southerly direction St. Michel-de-Cuxa awaits the visitor, its massive belfry welcoming him or her from afar (illus. p. 424). The abbey at the foot of the Canigou enjoyed great prestige during the Middle Ages. We know, for example, that the Venetian Doge Pietro Orseolo withdrew to this Pyrenean monastery in 978 to renounce worldly life. He was accompanied by five noblemen, including Romuald, who later founded the Camaldolite order, and was canonized.

The monastery owed its repute to the scholarly and widely traveled Abbot Garin, who led the Benedictine community from 961, and who in 974 was able to consecrate the present church, dedicated to St. Michael. The structure was preceded by several earlier buildings, which included a Mozarabic site, that we know was completed in 953.

When the mighty Oliba (c. 971–1046) assumed the office of abbot in Cuxa as well as Ripoll in 1008, the monastery enjoyed another golden age. In the years that followed, the church acquired a new square ambulatory, the belfry, and, to the west, two round chapels built one above the other, of which only one – the undergound Chapelle de la Crèche – has been preserved.

The Romanesque cloister with its important capital sculpture dates from the 12th century. However, much in St. Michel has been reconstructed or had to be reassembled following what can be considered a sculptural odyssey. The French Revolution abandoned the monastery to dereliction, and toward the end of the 19th century began a sell-off of its artistic treasures and even of its very architectural substance.

Only a few miles away from Prades, the road to Vernet branches off, taking us to Corneilla-de-Conflent (Cornellà de Conflent), the former residence of the Count of Cerdenya. The Romanesque church of St. Marie still bears witness to its former greatness, its sculptures being among the finest products of the stonemason's art to be found in Roussillon (illus. p. 426, top right). The west

Ille-sur-Têt
*The sandstone cliffs of the "organs"*

TOP:
*St. Michel-de-Cuxa, completed
c. 1040, monastery church,
overall view*

BOTTOM:
*St. Michel-de-Cuxa
Chapelle de la Crèche*

OPPOSITE
*St. Michel-de-Cuxa
Interior of the monastery church*

portal, adorned with archivolts and with its tympanum embellished by the Virgin Mary, dates from the 12th century. The exterior decoration of the apse is painstakingly executed and at least equally worthy of attention. The walls are structured by a delicately carved toothed frieze; each window aperture is framed by four small columns supporting figurative capitals and archivolts with lavish ornamentation.

The interior contains two valuable Madonna figures, the more important of which is the colored wooden figure of the Virgin Mary of Corneilla (late 12th century). The marble retable with scenes from the life of Our Lady, which formerly adorned the high altar (illus. p. 426, top left), was created by Jaume Cascalls from Berga in 1345.

Our route now leads via the thermal baths at Vernet-les-Bains (Vernet) to the third monastery in the shadow of the Canigou, at St. Martin-de-Canigou (Sant Martí del Canigó), which is in every respect the highlight of the tour. However, in order to enjoy the picturesque monastery and the unique view from its terraces, there is an uphill walk of some three-quarters of an hour, taking us up from the car park to a height of 1055 m (c. 3,460 ft.). The gray-brown abbey walls nestle against the rocks like an eagle's nest, supported by steep substructures (illus. p. 427).

This house of God owes its existence to a miscarriage of justice. Count Guifré had accused his nephew of treachery, and had him executed here – wrongly as it later transpired. Condemned by the Pope to do penance, the count founded a monastery in 1007 at the place of execution, and donated it to the Benedictines. As early as 1009 the church was to be consecrated.

It has two stories, with three barrel-vaulted naves on each floor, but with cross-beams of different lengths, and of different overall length. Monolithic columns without bases and with clumsily cut block capitals create an archaic impression. The lower church is, appropriately, dedicated to Notre-Dame-sous-Terre, while St. Martin is commemorated in the upper story. The relics of St. Gauderich, who acquired the abbey – not entirely legally – in 1012, are venerated in a chapel of the upper church. Of the trapezoid cloister, only three wings of the lower story are preserved. The fourth was formed in the 12th century by a gallery which gives a most magnificent view of the mountain landscape and the depths of the Cadí ravine (illus. p. 427).

It is difficult to tear oneself away from this rocky panorama and turn one's attention to the capitals in the south wing, chiseled in marble and showing wild beasts and hideous faces. As in Serrabone, here too the struggle between Good and Evil, virtue and vice, is depicted. Presumably the semi-nude figure of the so-called dancer represents lust and is intended to be seen in that light.

A tour of the monastery also takes the visitor past Count Guifré's tomb, which he is said to have cut into the rock with his own hands.

Anyone who has any energy left after the climb and the tour should go on the half-hour excursion to the neighboring rocky plateau. From here there is a unique view of the monastery and its majestic surroundings.

TOP LEFT:
Corneilla-de-Conflent
*St. Marie, marble retable by*
*Jaume Cascalls, 1345*

TOP RIGHT:
Corneilla-de-Conflent
*St. Marie, 11th–12th centuries*

BOTTOM LEFT:
St. Martin-du-Canigou,
*consecrated 1009, interior view*

FOTTOM RIGHT:
St. Martin-du-Canigou,
*capitals in the south wing*
*of the gallery, "Dancer,"*
*12th century*

OPPOSITE:
St. Martin-du-Canigou

Mont-Louis
*"Solar oven,"* 1949

## En route to the Cerdagne

After rounding the Canigou and visiting its monasteries, we now continue along the course of the Têt and again approach the border with Spain. Shortly after Prades the landscape of the Cerdagne (Cerdanya) begins, the impressive high-lying valley that, as noted above, was divided between France and Spain by the Treaty of the Pyrenees.

It has already been mentioned that Corneilla was once the winter residence of the Count of Cerdagne. Its fortifications suffered from the upheavals of numerous wars. The turbulent times that the valley has seen also come to life in Villefranche-de-Conflent, which despite everything, has retained its attractive medieval appearance, even though Vauban's Fort Liberia stands guard high above the town.

Mont-Louis (Montlluís) is regarded as the gateway to the Cerdagne, but it is a high gateway, for we have by now reached a height of 1600 m (c. 5,250 ft.). The place owes its name to one of Louis XIV's fortresses, built to provide protection from Spanish incursions. It too was based on plans drawn up by the military architect Vauban, and determines to this day the profile of the little town. The great attraction of Mont-Louis, however, is the "solar oven," a laboratory built in 1949 for research into solar energy (illus. above). It was the model for the solar power

station in Odeillo (Odelló), only a few miles away, which was brought into service in 1983, and is regarded as a pioneering achievement in this field.

Font Romeu is a booming center for winter sports. But only the Grand Hotel, bears witness to its feudal past. The hustle and bustle which gives the town its character is a mere foretaste of busy Llívia, the Spanish enclave on French territory. Here, thanks to differences in taxation in the two countries, it is – above all – the shops selling wines and spirits that attract queues of purchasers.

Our tour, and the book, comes to an end with a more contemplative excursion, a journey on the "petit train jaune" ("Tren Groc"), the "little yellow train" that rolls through the Cerdagne slowly, but over breathtaking bridges. There is a distance of 62 km (c. 39 miles) to cover, from Villefranche-de-Conflent to Latour-de-Carol (La Tor de Querol) – the roof open in summer. There are both steep climbs and descents at tremendous speed. The line, built between 1903 and 1911, crosses viaducts such as the two-story Pont Séjourné, and suspension bridges like the 222-km (c. 138-mile) long Pont Giscard (illus. above). The power for the electric motors of the "little yellow train" is provided by hydro-electric power stations, built at the same time as the railway line. Today a tourist attraction, the line once served to free the Cerdagne from its isolation, and to speed up the transport of iron ore.

The "little yellow train" (1903–11) making its way across the viaducts and suspension bridges (built 1903–11)

## Author's Postscript

Seldom does one have the good fortune to express, through a portrait in the form of a book, gratitude to a region to which one has so often traveled with great longing, and to a city such as Barcelona, which has left distinct traces in one's own biography. The publishers and the editor have given me this rare opportunity, and have granted me much valued freedom in carrying out this project.

My heartfelt thanks go to everyone who has contributed to the book's success, most especially to the photographers and the layout team, with whom personally it has been such a pleasure to work.

# Appendix

# Index of Place Names

# Index of Persons

# The History of Catalonia: Chronological Table

| | |
|---|---|
| Paleolithic period | Traces remain of cave drawings showing human habitation |
| Neolithic period c. 5000 B.C. | Farming |
| c. 3000 B.C. | Iberians from North Africa advance into the Iberian Peninsula; megalith tombs |
| 2000 B.C. | Bronze Age |
| c. 1100 B.C. | Phoenician merchants set up the first trading posts on the coast |
| c. 776 B.C. | The Greeks found Rhodes/Roses |
| c. 575 B.C. | Emporion/Empúries founded |
| 6th–5th centuries B.C. | Celts arrive |
| 6th century–206 B.C. | The Carthaginians conquer the Iberian Peninsula from the south |
| 264–41 B.C. | First Punic War |
| 227 B.C. | Cartagena (Carthago Nova) founded |
| 226 B.C. | Treaty of the Ebro: the River Ebro marks the boundary between the Carthaginian and the Roman Empire |
| 219 B.C. | Capture of Sagunt, which is allied to Rome; outbreak of the Second Punic War |
| 201 B.C. | The Romans finally defeat the Carthaginians, Romanization of the entire Iberian Peninsula |
| 27 B.C. | Tarraco (Tarragona) becomes the capital of the Province of Hispania Citerior |
| 1st century A.D. | Christianity takes root in the area that is now Catalonia |
| 4th century | Invasion of the Vandals |
| 5th century | Rule of the Visigoths, who make Toledo their capital |
| 476 | Conquest of Barcelona by the Visigoths |
| 771 | The Arabs invade the Iberian Peninsula via Gibraltar |
| 732 | Battle of Poitiers |
| 785 | Reconquest of Girona |
| 801 | The Franks capture Barcelona and establish the "Spanish March" |
| 9th century | Count Guifré el Pilós ("Wilfred the Hairy," 874–97) is given the right, by Karl the Bald, to make his titles and estates hereditary. Several Catalan counties unite and establish the House of Barcelona |
| 10th century | Under Count Borrell II the Catalan counties become independent of France |
| 985 | Almansor conquers Barcelona |
| 1010 | Catalan mercenaries pillage Córdoba |
| 11th–12th centuries | Consolidation of Barcelona's hegemony |
| 1112 | Ramon Berenguer III becomes heir to Provence by marriage |
| 1137 | Ramon Berenguer IV marries Petronilla of Aragón, and founds the Catalan/Aragonese Kingdom |
| Mid-12th century | Conquest of the *taifas* Lleida and Tortosa, reconquest of Tarragona |
| 1162 | Establishment of the *Corts Catalanes*, the Catalan parliament |
| 1229–38 | King Jaume the Conqueror captures the Balearic Islands and Valencia |
| 1272 | Ramon Llull writes the *Ars Magna* |
| 1282 | Pere II captures Sicily |
| 1303–24 | Campaign by Catalan mercenaries against the Ottomans, part of the Aegaen is under Catalan rule until 1390 |
| 1324 | Jaume II conquers Sardinia |
| 1343 | Pere IV annexes the Kingdom of Majorca, which extends as far as the South of France |
| mid-14th century | Publication of the *Llibre del Consolat de Mar*, the first maritime code of practice |
| 1359 | The *corts Catalanes* establish the *Generalitat* to assert its rights |
| 1410 | With Martí I, l'Humà (the Humane) the House of Barcelona dies out |
| 1412 | In the "Caspe Compromise" the Catalan-Aragonese crown passes to the House of Trastámara of Castile |

| | |
|---|---|
| 1442 | Alfons el Magnànim transfers his seat of government to Naples; restriction of special rights for Catalonia; introduction of the Castilian language |
| 1462–72 | Revolt of the Catalans against Juan II |
| 1469 | Marriage of Ferrans II of Aragon to Isabella the Catholic unites the Aragonese and Castilian kingdoms |
| 1478 | Establishment of the Inquisition |
| 1492 | With the surrender of Granada the Reconquista is complete; Columbus discovers America |
| 1516–1700 | Catalonia under the rule of the Spanish Habsburgs |
| 1640–52 | Revolt of the Catalans against Phillip IV: the "War of the Reapers/Harvesters" |
| 1659 | Peace of the Pyrenees; Spain forced to cede Roussillon and part of the Cerdagne to France |
| 1700–14 | War of the Spanish Succession. Catalonia sides with the Habsburgs; Barcelona beseiged by French troops |
| 1714 | Barcelona forced to surrender on September 11 |
| 1714 | Present-day Spain is ruled by the House of Bourbon |
| 1716 | Abolition of Catalan self-government |
| late 18th–19th centuries | Industrialization and trade with America bring economic prosperity to Catalonia |
| 1808–14 | Advance of Napoleon's armies; abdication of the Spanish king; war of liberation |
| 1814 | Restoration of absolutism in Spain |
| 1833 | Beginning of the *Renaixença*: the rebirth of Catalonia |
| 1833–9 | First Carlist War |
| 1835 | Secularization, the state expropriates church property |
| 1847–49 | Second Carlist War |
| 1859 | Ildefons Cerdà designs the Eixample, the urban extension of Barcelona |
| 1873–6 | Third Carlist War and first Spanish Republic |
| 1874 | Restoration of Alfonso XII |
| 1888 | International Exhibition in Barcelona |
| 1898 | Loss of the last Spanish colonies in America, severe economic crises |
| 1909 | "Setmana Tràgica" in Barcelona: strikes, anarchy, and violence dominate the city |
| 1914 | The *Mankommunitat Catalana* constitutes a preliminary form of autonomous Catalan government |
| 1923–30 | Dictatorship of Miguel Primo de Rivera |
| 1931 | On April 14 Francesc Macià proclaims the First Catalan Republic (before the proclamation of the First Spanish Republic) |
| 1936–9 | Civil War |
| 1939–75 | Dictatorship of General Francisco Bahamonde Franco; dissolution of the *Generalitat*; suppression of Catalan culture and language |
| 1940 | Catalan President Lluís Companys murdered |
| 1947 | Spain declared a monarchy |
| 1975 | Death of Franco; Juan Carlos I becomes King |
| 1977 | Free elections; the *Generalitat* is restored |
| 1979 | Catalonia given statute of autonomy |
| 1980 | First autonomous elections in Catalonia: victory for the CiU (*Convergència i Unió*); Jordi Pujol becomes President of the *Generalitat* |
| 1992 | Olympic Games in Barcelona |

# Bibliography

Numerous travel guides and books of photographs have been published relating to Catalonia, and to Barcelona in particular. Some guides on cultural history have been included here.

Andrews, Colman: *Catalan Food*, London 1989
Chaytor, Henry, J.: *History of Aragon and Catalonia* (Bcl Series: No 11), 1979
Cogarty, Paul: *Barcelona and Catalonia*, 1993
Fernandez, Juan Antonio: *Cataluña*, Madrid 1992 (Text in Spanish, English)
Hargreaves, John: *Freedom for Catalonia: Catalan Nationalism, Spanish Identity, and the Barcelona Olympic Games*, 2000.
Insight Guides: *Catalonia*, London, 1991, 1994
Julier: Guy: *Modern Spanish Design*, London 1991
Kamen, Henry Arthur Francis: *The Phoenix and the Flame: Catalonia and the Counter-Reformation*, 1993
Kuhn, Charles L.: *Romanesque Mural Painting of Catalonia*, Cambridge 1930
Lewis, Archibald, R.: *Medieval Society in Southern France and Catalonia*, 1984
Loyer, François: *Art Nouveau in Catalonia*, Cologne 1999
Medrano, Juan Diez: *Divided Nations: Class, Politics, and Nationalism in the Basque Country and Catalonia* (Wilder House Series in Politics, History, and Culture), 1995

Orwell, George: *Homage to Catalonia*, 1938, 1987
Porter, A. Kingsley: *Romanesque Sculpture of the Pilgrimage Roads* (Vol. V: 513–636, Catalonia & Aragon), Boston, 1923
Post, C.R.: *A History of Spanish Painting*, Vols VII and XII, Princeton 1938, 1958
Read, Jan: *Catalonia: Traditions, Places, Wine and Food*, 1990.
Sobrer, Josep Miquel: *Catalonia: A Self Portrait*, 1992
*This Is Catalonia: A Guide To The Architectural Heritage*, Barcelona 1988
Young, Alan: *Wine Routes of Penedès & Catalonia*, 2000
Zervos, Christian: *Catalan Art. Architecture, sculpture, painting from the ninth to the fifteenth centuries*, London 1937

**Barcelona**
*Architectura de Barcelona*, Barcelona 1990 (Text in Catalan, Spanish, English)
Baedecker Guides: *Barcelona*, 1992
Barril, J.: *Barcelona, Conquest of Space, Architecture*, 1993
Blue Guides: *Barcelona*, Michael Jacobs, London/New York, 1992
Bohigas, Oriol, et al.: *Barcelona, City and Architecture, 1980–92*, Barcelona 1991
Boyd, Alastair: *The Essence of Catalonia: Barcelona and Its Region*, London 1988

Cirici, Alexandre: *Barcelona pam a pam*, Barcelona 1971, 1990
Eyewitness Travel Guides: *Barcelona and Catalonia*, London/New York, 1999
Fernández-Armesto, Felipe: *Barcelona, a Thousand Years of the City's Past*, London 1991
Gili, Gustavo: *Barcelona Design Guide*, Barcelona, 1991 (Text in Spanish, English)
*Homage to Barcelona. The city and its art 1888–1936*, London 1986
Hughes, Robert: *Barcelona*. New York/London, 1992, 1999
Mackay, David: *Modern Architecture in Barcelona 1854–1939*, Rizzoli, New York, 1989
Mendoza, E. and C.: *Barcelona Modernista*, Barcelona 1989
Mendoza, Eduardo: *City of Marvels*, 1989
Rough Guides: *Barcelona*, London/New York 1997
Tóibín, Colm: *Homage to Barcelona*, London 1990
Turner, Christopher: *Barcelona Step by Step*, London 1991

**Books on individual artists**
A selection of the many that are available.

Barr, Alfred H.: *Picasso, Fifty Years of His Art*, New York, 1967
Becraft, Melvin E: *Picasso's Guernica, Images within Images*, 1987

Chipp, Herschel B.: *Picasso's Guernica, History, Transformations, Meanings*, 1988
Costa Clavell, Xavier: *Picasso. Museo Picasso de Barcelona*, Escudo de Oro, Barcelona 1991
Dali, Salvador: *Diary of a Genius*, London 1960
Dali, Salvador: *My Secret Life*, New York 1948
Descharnes, Robert, and Néret, Gilles: *Salvador Dalí 1904–1989*, Cologne 1998 (up-to-date bibliography and exhibition catalog)
Dollens, Dennis, *Josep Maria Jujol: Five Major Buildings, 1913–1923*, New York 1994
Franzke, Andreas: *Tàpies*, Munich 1992
Gimferrer, Pere: *Tàpies and the Catalan Spirit*, Poligrafa, Barcelona 1986
Güell, Xavier, *Antoni Gaudi: Works and Projects*, Barcelona, 1986, 1992 (Text in Spanish, English)
Llinàs, José: *Jujol*, Cologne 1994
Masini, Lara Vinca: *Antoni Gaudi*, London 1970
Mower, David: *Gaudi*, London 1977
Nonell, Juan Bassegoda: *Gaudí*, Barcelona 1986
Nonell, Juan Bassegoda: *Doménech i Montaner*, Barcelona 1986
Nonell, Juan Bassegoda: *Antonio Gaudi: Master Architect*, New York 2000

Ocana, Maria T.: *Picasso and Els 4 Gats, The Early Years in Turn-of-the Century Barcelona*, 1996
Palau I. Fabré, J.: *Picasso, Barcelona, Catalunya*, Barcelona 1981
Palau I. Fabré, J.: *Picasso, Cubism (1907–1917)*, 1990
Penrose, Roland: *Miró*, London 1970
Penrose, Roland: *Picasso*, London 1958
Perucho, Juan: *Miró and Catalonia*, London/ New York 1988 (Text in English, French, German, Spanish)
Richardon, John: *A Life of Picasso*, Vol. I: 1881–1906, London 1991
Secrest, M.: *Salvador Dalí*, Berne 1987
Sert, Josep Lluis, *Cripta De La Colonia Guell De A. Gaudi*, Barcelona 1972 (Text in Spanish, French, English, German)
Solà-Morales, Ignasi de: *Jujol*, New York 1991
Tàpies, Antoni: *Memoria Personal*, Barcelona 1977
Zerbst, Rainer: *Antoni Gaudí*, Cologne 1987

# Glossary of Catalan Terms

| | | | |
|---|---|---|---|
| *ajuntament* | town hall | *major* | biggest, main |
| *art* | art | *mar* | sea |
| *arxiu* | archive | *Mare de Déu* | Mother of God |
| *avinguda* | avenue | *mas / masia* | estate, country house |
| *barri* | suburb, quarter | *mercat* | market |
| *casa, can...* | house, house of... | *modernisme* | art of the period around 1900 |
| *cap* | cape | *monestir* | monastery |
| *carrer (c/)* | street | *mont, munt* | mountain |
| *capella* | chapel | *municipal* | urban, municipal |
| *casa de la ciutat* | town hall | *muntanya* | mountain, mountain range |
| *castell* | castle | *museu* | museum |
| *cava* | Catalan sparkling wine, | *nau* | ship |
| | fermented by the Champagne | *nou, nova* | new |
| | method | *palau* | palace |
| *celler* | wine cellar | *parc* | park |
| *ciutadella* | citadel | *passeig* | promenade |
| *ciutat* | city, town | *pati* | court |
| *claustre* | cloister | *pessebre* | crib, nativity scene |
| *cobla* | band of musicians to | *petit* | small |
| | accompany *Sardana* | *pic* | mountain peak |
| *col·legi* | college, chamber | *pla* | plan, map |
| *comte* | count, earl | *plaça* | square |
| *comtat* | county, earldom | *platja* | beach |
| *convent* | convent | *poble* | village |
| *costa* | coast | *pont* | bridge |
| *cova* | cave | *port* | port |
| *creu* | cross | *puig* | hill |
| *eixample* | urban extension | *rambla* | boulevard |
| *església* | church | *rei* | king |
| *estació* | station | *reial* | royal |
| *estany* | lake | *retaule* | retable |
| *font* | spring, well | *riu* | river |
| *fundació* | foundation | *Sant, Santa (St., Sta.)* | Saint |
| *funicular* | funicular, cable railway | *sardana* | Catalan folk |
| *Generalitat* | government of Catalonia or | | dance |
| | Valencia | *serra* | mountain range |
| *gran* | big | *seu* | cathedral |
| *guia* | guide | *torre* | tower |
| *horta* | horticultural/market | *tren* | train |
| | gardening region | *vall* | valley |
| *illa* | island | | old |
| *jardí* | garden | *verge* | virgin |
| *llotja* | stock exchange | *via* | way |

# Picture Acknowledgements

*The editor and the publishers have made intensive efforts to locate all copyright holders prior to publication. Persons and institutions not contacted, and who hold the copyright for any of the illustrations, should contact the publisher.*

© aisa Archivo Iconográfico, Barcelona: 10 bottom, 130.

© Institut Amatller d'Art Hispànic, Barcelona/Foto: Arxiu Fotogràfic: 308 right.

© Archiv für Kunst und Geschichte, Berlin: 131 bottom.

© Arxiu Històric de la Ciutat de Barcelona/Foto: Arxiu Fotogràfic: 207, 316 bottom right; Foto: AF/Dominguez: 131 top; Foto: AF/A. Esplugas: 41 bottom; Foto: AF/F. Serra: 168 bottom, 227 bottom, 228 bottom.

© Beerfoto, Barcelona/Foto: Günter Beer: 157 bottom, 167 right, 184, 185, 187 top right, 192, 220, 221 top, 221 bottom left, 255 left, 257 bottom, 258 bottom, 262 top, 263 bottom, 265 top, 266–7, 268 top, 312, 313; Foto: Mariano Herrera: 68, 69 bottom left, 115 bottom, 115 top left, 274, 275, 278 bottom, 281 bottom, 284, 285, 295, 296, 297, 300, 307, 308 left, 310, 311, 314, 315, 316 top, 316 bottom left, 317, 322 bottom, 323 bottom left, 323 top, 324 bottom, 326 bottom, 327 bottom, 328, 330 left, 332, 334–5, 343, 344, 345, 385, 387, 388, 389 top, 390, 391 top, 392, 393, 395.

© Barbara Borngässer, Dresden: 13, 55 bottom, 75 top right, 346 top, 349 bottom right, 358 bottom

© Catedra Gaudí, Barcelona: 212.

© Demart pro Arte B.V./ VG Bild-Kunst, Bonn 2000/Foto: Archiv für Kunst und Geschichte, Berlin: 407; Foto: Fundació Gala-Salvador Dalí: 107 bottom; Foto: Könemann Verlagsgesellschaft mbH, Cologne/Günter Beer: 90, 91, 103, 104, 105, 106 bottom.

© dpa, Frankfurt: 112 bottom.

© Bildarchiv Foto Marburg: 46.

© Klaus Frahm, Börnsen: 182.

© Fundació Antoni Tàpies Barcelona/VG Bild-Kunst, Bonn 2000: Foto: Archivo Fotográfico Oronoz, Madrid: 224 bottom; Foto: Könemann Verlagsgesellschaft mbH, Cologne/Achim Bednorz: 163 bottom.

© Fundació Gala-Salvador Dalí, Figueres: 15, 87, 89.

© Roland Halbe, Stuttgart: 223 top, 223 bottom right.

© Mariano Herrera, Barcelona/Günter Beer: 342.

© Markus Hilbich, Berlin: 6/7, 61 bottom, 69 top, 139, 140 top, 141 bottom, 143, 144 top, 145, 146, 147, 153 top, 158, 159, 160 bottom, 163 top, 164 top, 170, 171 bottom, 174, 180, 181, 183, 186, 187 (except top right), 188 top, 189, 190 bottom, 191, 205 left, 206 bottom, 213, 216, 222 left, 223 bottom left, 226, 227 top, 237, 254 right, 254 bottom, 257 bottom left, 264, 265 bottom, 270–71, 273, 276, 277 bottom, 278 top, 279, 280, 306.

© The Kobal Collection España, Barcelona: 53, 59 bottom, 115 top right; Foto: © Album/Ramon Manent: 338, 357 bottom.

© Könemann Verlagsgesellschaft mbH, Cologne/Foto: Markus Bassler: 72–3, 120, 128, 129, 133, 148–9, 150, 153 bottom, 156, 157 top, 176, 177, 178 top left, 178 bottom, 202, 204, 211, 214, 228 top, 230, 231, 232 top, 233, 234, 235, 238 top, 239, 245 bottom, 246 top, 247 left, 257 top, 257 bottom right, 258 top, 269 bottom, 301 top, 302, 303, 305 top; Foto: Achim Bednorz: 8, 23, 25, 28, 29, 36 left, 42–3, 44, 45, 47, 54 top, 60, 76–7, 80–81, 82, 83, 84, 85, 86, 144 bottom, 151, 152, 154, 155, 161, 162, 172–3, 175, 190 top, 193, 194, 195, 196, 197, 198, 199, 215 top, 217, 218–19, 224 top, 225, 259 top, 260, 261, 272, 277 top, 281 top, 282, 286 top, 287, 288 top, 289, 292, 320, 322 top, 325, 326 top, 327 top, 329, 330 right, 331, 336–7, 340 bottom, 348, 349 top, 349 middle, 349 bottom right, 350–51, 352, 353, 354, 356–7 top, 358 top, 360, 361, 362–3, 364 bottom, 365, 366, 367, 368, 369, 370, 371, 372, 373, 374, 375, 376–7, 378, 379, 380, 381, 382–3, 384, 386, 389 bottom, 391 bottom, 396–7, 398, 399, 400, 401, 402, 403, 404 bottom, 405 top, 406, 408, 409, 410, 411, 412, 413, 414, 415, 416, 417, 418, 419, 420, 421, 422, 423, 424, 425, 426, 427, 428, 429; Foto: Günter Beer: 2, 12, 14, 16–17, 18, 19, 20, 22, 24, 26–7, 30, 31, 32, 33, 34 bottom, 35, 36 right top, 36 right bottom, 37, 38, 39, 40, 41 top, 48, 50, 51, 52, 55 bottom, 56–7, 58, 62–3, 64, 69 bottom right, 70, 71, 74, 75 top left, 75 bottom, 78, 79, 88, 92–3, 94, 95, 96, 97, 98, 99, 100, 101, 102, 106 top, 107 top, 108, 109, 110, 111, 112, 113, 114, 116, 117, 118, 119 top, 121, 122, 123, 126–7, 132, 134 bottom, 137, 138, 140 bottom, 142, 160 top, 164 bottom, 166, 167 left, 178 top right, 179 top, 188 bottom, 205 right, 206 top, 208, 209, 210, 215 bottom, 222 left, 229, 236, 244, 245 top, 246 bottom, 247 right, 251 top, 256 top, 259 bottom, 263 top, 268 bottom, 269 top, 286 bottom, 288 botttom, 290, 291, 298–9, 301 bottom, 305 bottom, 309, 321, 339, 340 top, 341, 346 bottom, 355, 359, 430–31;

© lkt Studio für Landkartentechnik, Norderstedt: 9, 135.

© Museu d'Arqueologia de Catalunya, Barcelona: 254 top left.

© Museu d'Història de la Ciutat, Barcelona: 141 top, 203.

© Museu Nacional Arqueològic de Tarragona: 318–19, 323 bottom right, 324 top.

© Archivo Fotográfico Oronoz, Madrid: 10 top, 11, 21, 34 top, 49, 61 top, 65, 66–7, 171 top, 179 bottom, 221 bottom right, 241, 242, 243, 262 bottom, 283, 293, 294, 333.

© photodéco, Montpellier/Foto: Francis de Richemond: 404 top.

© Picture Press, Hamburg/Foto: Corbis/Stephanie Maze: 136.

© Winfried E. Rabanus, Munich: 255 right.

© Sipa Press, Paris: 134 top left, 134 top right.

© Succession Picasso/ VG Bild-Kunst, Bonn 2000/Foto: Archiv für Kunst und Geschichte, Berlin: 168 top left, 347; Foto: Archivo Fotográfico Oronoz, Madrid: 169; Foto: Scala, Antella-Firenze: 168 top right.

© Tavisa, Barcelona: 200–01.

© Temple Sagrada Familia, Barcelona: 304.

© Ullstein Bilderdienst, Berlin/Foto: Ullstein-MAS: 232 bottom.

© VG Bild-Kunst, Bonn 2000/Foto: Beerfoto, Barcelona/Günter Beer: 253 right; Foto: Könemann Verlagsgesellschaft mbH, Cologne/Achim Bednorz: 248–9, 251 bottom, 252; Könemann Verlagsgesellschaft mbH, Cologne/Günter Beer: 165, 250; Foto: Archivo Fotográfico Oronoz, Madrid: 253 left, 394.

From: Erlande-Brandenburg, A., and Mérel-Brandenburg, A.-B.: *Histoire de l'architecture française du moyen âge à la renaissance*, Paris 1995: 364 top.